WOMEN AND RELIGIOSITY IN
ORTHODOX CHRISTIANITY

ORTHODOX CHRISTIANITY AND CONTEMPORARY THOUGHT

SERIES EDITORS
Aristotle Papanikolaou and Ashley M. Purpura

This series consists of books that seek to bring Orthodox Christianity into an engagement with contemporary forms of thought. Its goal is to promote (1) historical studies in Orthodox Christianity that are interdisciplinary, employ a variety of methods, and speak to contemporary issues; and (2) constructive theological arguments in conversation with patristic sources and that focus on contemporary questions ranging from the traditional theological and philosophical themes of God and human identity to cultural, political, economic, and ethical concerns. The books in the series explore both the relevancy of Orthodox Christianity to contemporary challenges and the impact of contemporary modes of thought on Orthodox self-understandings.

WOMEN AND RELIGIOSITY IN ORTHODOX CHRISTIANITY

INA MERDJANOVA
EDITOR

FORDHAM UNIVERSITY PRESS
New York • 2021

Library of Congress Cataloging-in-Publication Data

Names: Merdjanova, Ina, (date)– editor.
Title: Women and religiosity in Orthodox Christianity / Ina Merdjanova, editor.
Description: First edition. | New York : Fordham University Pess, 2021. | Series: Orthodox Christianity and contemporary thought | Includes bibliographical references and index.
Identifiers: LCCN 2021017794 | ISBN 9780823298600 (hardback) | ISBN 9780823298617 (paperback) | ISBN 9780823298624 (epub)
Subjects: LCSH: Women in the Orthodox Eastern Church. | Christian women—Religious life.
Classification: LCC BX342.5 .W67 2021 | DDC 248.4/815—dc23
LC record available at https://lccn.loc.gov/2021017794

Printed in the United States of America

23 22 21   5 4 3 2 1

First edition

CONTENTS

WOMEN IN ORTHODOX CHRISTIANITY: A FOREWORD

Kristin Aune

As the smallest of the three branches of Christianity, there has been much less academic work on women in Orthodox Christianity than in Roman Catholic or Protestant Christianity, and this broad-ranging and fascinating volume fills a gap in scholarship and is very welcome. The book has many impressive elements: its wide geographical focus, its interdisciplinary approach, its rich case studies, and its conceptual contributions to the study of gender and religion.

In terms of the volume's wide geographical scope, the chapters focus on specific country contexts: Bulgaria, Finland, Georgia, Greece, Moldova, Romania, Russia, Serbia, and the United States. These chapters also discuss how the gendered dynamics of Orthodoxy in each context relate to Orthodoxy as a global and what Kupari and Tiaynen-Qadir call a "glocal" religion or movement, as both national and transnational. The scholars also form a global and "glocal" community, with some living and working in the countries they research and others working or studying elsewhere.

The volume's interdisciplinary nature is impressive. Many of the chapters use methods from different disciplines—history (including a large set of oral history interviews), theology, anthropology, sociology, religious studies, politics and international relations, media and communications. This reflects the wide disciplinary base of the authors, who also are at different career stages; this shows how vibrant the field of women and Orthodox Christianity is today. The volume exemplifies the "deep interdisciplinarity" that Vuola has recently called for and that is often lacking in gender and religion research.[1]

Key Conceptual Contributions

This book contributes to several key topics and debates in the field of religion and gender, tackling them with reference to the Orthodox Church: how changing social conditions shape women's religiosity, gendered power relations in the Church, negotiating and challenging gender relations in the Church, understanding women's agency, and how feminism intersects with religion.

How Changing Social Conditions Shape Women's Religiosity

Religion is shaped not only by religious doctrines, practices, and structures but also by the social and political conditions in which it operates. As Merdjanova remarks in her chapter, "Orthodoxy is not the sole factor determining female subjugation; it intersects with political, social, cultural, and economic forces, all of which need to be taken into consideration when explaining how women operate under specific historical conditions and how gender regimes are formed and transformed." This book provides detailed examples of how changing social and political conditions shape religiosity in general and Orthodox women's religiosity in particular. This includes a number of insights:

Women played a major role in Orthodox Christianity's survival despite the communist regimes' attempts to suppress it. Under communism, the state's determined enforcement of atheism, secularism, and secularization marginalized the institutional Orthodox Church and/or tried to use the Orthodox Church to support its nationalistic agenda. Ending the Church's institutional power was the state's priority; the state was less effective and less focused on policing informal religiosity, which was predominantly maintained by women. Their importance dismissed because of their gender, women were able to safeguard the traditions and practices of the Church and to feminize or "domesticate" them (Kapaló). The forms of Christianity practiced under state persecution were centered on the home, involving food, family rituals, rites of passage, and informal education of children. During the communist period, women kept Orthodox Christianity alive. Older women were the most involved in this, as Merdjanova shows in Bulgaria, and Gurchiani in Georgia. In Georgia, militant atheism in the 1920s led to convents being closed. Nuns became caretakers for former religious buildings, while women orchestrated Christenings and Easter and Christmas celebrations in their homes, revising the deaconess role they had lost around the eleventh century. Women celebrated saints' festivals at home and performed rituals for the dead. The Moldovan Orthodox Church, Kapaló shows, experienced "Russification" (with Russian priests brought in) in the nineteenth century and mid–twentieth century. This led to the stamping out of nonauthorized forms of religion, with many Orthodox churches and monasteries forced to close and aggressive promotion of atheism under Khrushchev in the 1950s and 1960s. That communism was seen by its ideologues as bringing gender equality while secretly Orthodox women were rebelling by practicing their faith in their homes is a reminder that secularism should not be automatically—as some Western feminists assume—equated with equality or empowerment for all women.[2]

The book shows that communism repressed public forms of Orthodox Christianity but indirectly enabled Orthodox women's (private) Christianity to flourish. As male priests lost their power and positions, women gained power as informal religious leaders, teachers, and ritualists.

Women's religious roles bear a certain resemblance to their social roles. After the fall of communism, as the locus of religious authority moved away from the home and back to the churches, which were again allowed to operate freely, women lost some of their (informal) religious authority. Nevertheless, democratization brought some advantages to women in terms of increased choice and freedom, alongside greater economic fragility and a resurgent backlash against women's reproductive rights. The Orthodox Church was part of the backlash and reasserted women's role in the family. The domestic realm has continued to be the site of activity for most women, especially religious women, and as Gurchiani explicates in the Georgian context, "the roles performed in the domestic arena and in the Church resemble each other. Women live out in the Church what they are in their domestic space, and vice versa." Thus despite profound economic changes, women's religious role has continued to be mostly family centered.

In Romania, too, where most people live in the countryside, women's domestic and religious roles have not changed much despite the fall of communism. In rural areas, Bucur explains, older women continued to pass the faith down to children and grandchildren irrespective of whether the

Orthodox Church was officially recognized or active. Women's informal role is crucial to understanding religiosity in Romania. Throughout its history, the institutional Church has been less important to religiosity than scholars or Orthodox theologians say. The hundred-plus women Bucur interviewed recalled being religious both during communism and today. They report continuing their religious practices even when they were not allowed to (for example, going to church at Easter), and Bucur notes that there was actually an increase in nuns and female monasteries during the communist period, attributing this to a nun being a more viable option for rural women who had lost their livelihoods as farms were collectivized.

Gendered Power Relations in the Orthodox Church

The book shows with vivid detail one of Orthodoxy's paradoxes—that femininity is on the one hand highly valued but on the other subject to restrictions. Women are the majority of church members, several authors point out (for instance, Merdjanova in Bulgaria, Tocheva in Russia, and Bucur in Romania). Mary the Mother of God is venerated, as are female saints, monastics, and nuns and martyrs (Gurchiani details this in Georgia). Bakić-Hayden gives the example of the famous Kassiani, a ninth-century Byzantine nun and composer who remains admired today. She was regarded as symbolizing heaven, where there would be no marriage and people would be like angels, and Bakić-Hayden points out that monastery life, though segregated by gender, was very similar for men and women. This older tradition of gender equality has been forgotten by many in the Orthodox Church, Bakić-Hayden argues, remarking, "it is . . . somewhat ironic that the tradition of the Church Fathers (many, if not all) turns out to be more inclusive of women than the traditions of national churches, embedded as they are in their cultures' stereotypes about women." Female monastics are still present, and those she interviewed in Serbia talk about having renounced worldly concerns in order to focus on their spiritual life. In the Orthodox Church worldwide, female monastics are few, but they are increasingly recognized by the Church, including Sister Vassa, an American of Russian background who teaches at the University of Vienna and produces a popular online catechetical video program.

Yet women are unable to be priests and often subject to spatial segregation in churches, being forbidden to enter the altar—the center of the Eucharistic liturgy. Even the deaconess role they held for the first millennium still has not been rejuvenated. Women do hold senior roles as managers and administrators, and Tocheva's chapter explains that these are good job opportunities in the Church for Russian women in a society where women's salaries are much lower than men's. In Georgia, women are employed as secretaries to priests in most churches, running the priest's household and accounts. This allows them considerable authority, and "by employing everyday tactics and skillfully performing their gendered role, women become matriarchs in a patriarchate" (Gurchiani); in one famous recent example, a priest tried to poison the secretary to the Georgian patriarch, reportedly to challenge her considerable authority.

Negotiating and Challenging Gender Relations in the Orthodox Church

Both migration and the survival or growth of the Orthodox Church in countries where gender equality and equal opportunities for men and women are enshrined in law or have a strong cultural value have led to an expanded role for women. Finland is a case in point. The Church has a complex migration history, with older women having migrated during World War II from the Russian part of southeastern Finland (Karelia), which had adopted Orthodoxy in the tenth century. After being ruled by Sweden from the Reformation and then by Russia in the nineteenth century, Finland achieved independence in 1917. Today, members of the Orthodox Church make up 1 percent of the Finnish population, with growing numbers of Eastern European migrants. "Glocalization," explain Kupari and Tiaynen-Qadir, is happening: "the merging of global and local elements resulting in the creation of *glocal* cultural forms." Finland's Orthodox Church is constantly changing, shaped by nationalization, transnationalization, and local contexts. In the Orthodox Church of Finland, women may not be priests, but they conduct the choir, are readers in services, paint icons, are equal members of church councils, and run the prominent Tuesday Club (community activities including raising funds for charities, hosting lectures, and hosting coffee mornings). In this way, the Church reflects the Finnish state and population's support for gender equality.

But the Church acts as a mediator of gender-related values, and this ensures that gendered traditions are maintained. Kupari and Tiaynen-Qadir explain that the women Vuola interviewed in a separate study praised the Orthodox Church for valuing motherhood more than the state Lutheran

Church does. Women often maintained home altars featuring textiles of icons painted by deceased family members, as their mothers and grandmothers did. Women's bodily practices during the liturgy were also important ways that women, many of whom had migrated or had family members who had done so, connected to family members in Russia. By repeating actions from childhood they recreated a feeling of home, despite that "the Liturgy as glocal homemaking is also a process that triggers tensions and necessarily involves the negotiation of such tensions." Praying for family members was also a way that they exercised agency—agency through submission to God.

Women's roles are expanding in some Orthodox contexts, and some women are challenging traditionally gendered restrictions. But in others, there is a backlash or resurgence of gender traditionalism. Sotiriou's chapter points to an increasing traditionalism in the Orthodox Church in Greece, relating this to Greece's recent economic crisis. The crisis produced unprecedented unemployment, and this was regarded as an emasculation of men and their breadwinner role (despite the fact that women suffered the worst economically and physically, due to domestic violence increasing). Men began involving themselves more in church work, many training to join the priesthood. National initiatives to reinstate the female diaconate were shelved, and male priests and leaders strengthened their roles while leading the country out of crisis. But while this arguably resembles a masculinization of the church, Sotiriou instead sees it as a "'feminization' of men," since men were taking on church service roles (such as providing food to people in poverty) previously associated with femininity and that women still performed. However, Sotiriou also discusses how "women under forty" often challenge conservative clergy and the institutional Church and notes that they did so particularly during the crisis. Digital media creates a space for women to express their views, including criticisms of authoritarian clerical attitudes, notwithstanding the fact that in the Greek case, as Sotiriou points out, the majority of Orthodox female bloggers "use their blogs more to support male religious authority than to oppose it."

Understanding Orthodox Women's Agency

Agency is an important theme for scholars of religion and gender, and this volume pinpoints the dilemma Orthodox women's agency presents to feminist scholars. Religious women often act in ways that do not fit with modern feminist ideas of agency as autonomy and resistance to gendered norms. As Kupari and Tiaynen-Qadir argue, referencing Vuola's work and recalling Mahmood's important work on agency realized through piety,[3] "our interlocutors' agency is realized through their virtuoso religiosity, that is to say, their endeavor to abide by the demands of the Orthodox faith—as they understand them." "Women's virtuoso religiosity can and should be seen as agentic action," they argue. Kupari and Tiaynen-Qadir's identification of several "modalities of agency" used by Orthodox women offers a helpful expansion of what agency involves for conservative religious women. It is not simply about finding agency in submission to the divine and in community with other religious people. It is also about "their experiential, interpretative, and inventive engagements with Orthodoxy"; "embodied and embedded practices of religion—including sensations, feelings, the unspoken, and the body as the matrix and medium of human experiences"; and "their contemplative practices of liturgy, sensorial and corporeal experiences of religion, as well as in their nurturing and care-taking acts." They continue:

> All of these modalities of agency are pertinent to our interlocutors' glocal making of religion, in that they are integral to the women's capacity to create and sustain home-like spaces. Such a multifaceted agency serves both social ends and the goals of inner spirituality. . . . Overall, many manifestations of the women's agency were characterized by relationality, altruism, and submission—their understanding of prayer being a case in point. However, the women did also exert active and project-oriented agency, for example through their voluntary work in parishes.

Avishai's discussion of agency in conservative religion—her example is Orthodox Jewish women in Israel—also, I think, offers an important insight not explicitly made in this volume: that "religiosity is performed and achieved in the context of a dialogue with a secular Other."[4] In relation to gender norms, women's gender performances may look conservative or traditionalist, but in relation to a "secular world" they conceive as other, they are "doing religion" via observance of particular practices that mark them out as Orthodox Jewish women. In relation to their performance of menstruation laws and rituals, "the performance of *niddah* enables alternatives to secular sexuality and femininity. One pathway to a distinctly orthodox femininity concerns an appreciation for the female body that *niddah* enables."[5] Thus unlike Mahmood's emphasis on piety and docility, Avishai emphasizes women's agency as active "observance."[6] A similar thing could be said for Orthodox Christian women, who adhere to a religion that sets itself up as different from the context around it—different from a communist nonreligious past and different from secularizing contexts where gender equality is prized.

Feminism and Religion: Why Aren't Orthodox Christian Women Feminists?

This book reveals Orthodox women's lack of interest in feminism; this strikes me, as a scholar of religion and feminism, as an interesting puzzle. Why are they not feminists? What accounts for Orthodox Christian women's disinterest in feminism? Is Orthodox Christianity a particularly gender-conservative religion?[7] Merdjanova discusses this in the Introduction. One answer may be that feminism has long been reviled in many countries where Orthodox Christianity is strong. Russia is a case in point: Pussy Riot emerged in strong opposition to the alignment they observed between the political regime and the Orthodox Church and their shared gender politics, and they were punished harshly. Praised in many countries as champions of freedom, the Russian population was critical of Pussy Riot, and this reflects the fact that, as Zabyelina and Ivashkiv explain, "Despite a solid intellectual tradition, the idea of feminism, for various reasons, has been discredited among the general population."[8] FEMEN, originally from Ukraine and even more controversial in their opposition to religion and their naked protest tactics, attracted even more negative reactions in Ukraine.

The "F-word" has a history of stigmatization, especially in Eastern Europe, where, as Jonathan Dean and I have argued, feminism did not follow the same pattern as it did in Western Europe.[9] Under communism, women's rights movements were nonexistent, and feminism was seen as a Western bourgeois ideology seeking to equalize women and men. Feminism, it was assumed, had no place in communist society, where equality between the sexes had been achieved with the granting to women of full voting rights, access to education, and paid work. Under communism, feminism was considered unnecessary and a threat to the state, and women's organizations were restricted. It was in the postcommunist 1990s and 2000s that a distinctive feminist movement emerged, challenging the erosion of women's economic position under the new capitalist economy and fighting for increased rights and freedoms for women. Yet after communism, feminism was—and is—often seen as a threat to national identity and the hallowed role of motherhood, both by those in power and by established Orthodox and Catholic Churches. Thus in contexts where feminism is disliked, the Church has been at the forefront of its rejection, and this has encouraged Orthodox Christian women to see feminism as antithetical to faith and associated with a morally questionable, decaying West.

Patriarchal gender discrimination within the Church gained renewed momentum after the fall of communism, with the emergence of the Orthodox Church after decades of marginalization, despite that women continued to form the majority of faithful. Under these circumstances, there was little receptivity for Western feminist theologies, which were renounced as a disregard of tradition and as "deficient and self-indulgent intellectual endeavors of women guilty of the sin of pride" (see Merdjanova's chapter). Today, this rejection of feminism continues. The Orthodox Church's "anti-ecumenism after 1990 curbed the spread of Western theological feminist ideas," Merdjanova argues in the Introduction. The Bulgarian Orthodox Church has also rejected international human rights frameworks and campaigned against the Istanbul Convention.

Feminism—or alignment with feminism as a mobilization connected to challenging sexism—has not emerged as a motivation for women's activism in the Orthodox Church. Some Orthodox women seem to be agitating for improved positions for women; others seem not to want them. "Gender equality" is a term that most of the Orthodox women discussed in this book would not aspire to, as Orthodoxy has a rich history of venerating femininity (Mary the Mother of God, female saints) and women's maternal role. Orthodox Christianity is a gender-essentialist religion—a religion that sees gender as biologically determined, not a social construct. But some Orthodox Christians see moving beyond gendered roles as spiritually necessary, prefiguring a heavenly or angelic state beyond gender, wifehood, and motherhood. Orthodox women's nonassociation with "feminism" relates partly, it seems, to Orthodoxy itself and partly to the negative position of feminism or "gender equality" in Orthodox-majority countries.

Certainly, there are Orthodox women who think and act in the spirit of feminism, that is, who seek gender justice and women's rights in the Church and in the wider society, even though they would very rarely call themselves feminists. The volume presents some examples of individual women challenging restrictions. One example is women seeking to study and teach academic theology, as Merdjanova discusses with reference to Bulgaria. Another is—unusually this is a group rather than discrete individuals—the Inochentist Turkish-speaking women's movement in Moldova (an ecstatic spiritual Orthodox movement birthed during the poverty and antireligious oppression of the 1950s and 1960s), where women renounced marriage and motherhood and still face rejection by the Orthodox Church (see Kapaló's chapter). A third is Orthodox women's Facebook groups, which are mostly occupied by conservatively religious women but with some liberal or feminist "dissenters" (see Riccardi-Swartz's and Sotiriou's chapters).

This presents Orthodox women as an interesting example of activism that can further the position of women within religion via religious, not secular, motivations. Religion can be the motivator for a sort of reformist "feminist" activism that does not seek to challenge the religion itself but to increase opportunities for women within it. This is a rich strand of religious feminism.[10] But it is a conservative version of reformism because it asks only (sometimes) for women to be deacons, not for them to be priests, and its agents are more likely to be individuals than working together as a collective or movement.

Some women contest male domination, but mostly in subtle and private ways, such as the Georgian women Gurchiani introduces who use "hidden transcripts" to undermine public forms of male power. This, Gurchiani says, "is a 'weapon of the weak' through which they constrain the powerful." We might see Orthodox women's work to expand opportunities for women to participate in Orthodoxy but within the terms of Orthodoxy as "feminist," as a form of hidden resistance to traditionalism, or as a new form of agency that simultaneously creates space while ceding space. To return to Avishai and Mahmood, agency resides in pious practices.

In Conclusion

This is an illuminating book, shining a light on Orthodox women's lives in many different contexts. It is also a brave book—it is unafraid to pinpoint patriarchal power relations in the Orthodox Church, and thus, for most of the authors who are Orthodox Christians or come from Orthodox backgrounds, this is a brave personal as well as intellectual challenge. It is also a sympathetic book, for it seeks to understand the agency of women who remain loyal to a Church that seems to disadvantage them.

Overall, this book presents an Orthodox Christian example of the centrality of gender to religion. It resonates with Dubisch's argument that there cannot be religion without gender, for "as long as gender is part of the world in which we live, it will be part of religion."[11] There also cannot be religion without women, Dubisch explains, even if "observer bias" leads women to be "seen as nonparticipants in religion or as marginal participants at best," for "such bias either stems from simply not looking at culture from women's perspective, and from accepting, in some cases at least, a dominant male viewpoint that denies or denigrates women's activities, or from definitions of religion that do not include what women do *as* religion."[12]

Dubisch gives an example from her fieldwork forty years ago, in a small village on a Greek island. This example, of Orthodox Christianity among Greek women, is a succinct case study of what this volume as a whole depicts, so it is worth quoting in full:

> Several months into my fieldwork, there was a funeral in the village. After the church service, I sat in the kitchen of one of the village houses with several women who were discussing the event and reminiscing about the elderly man who had died. Then they began to talk about death and the afterlife. "What happens after you die?" one of the women wondered. "Maybe it's like falling asleep," another woman suggested. "Maybe there is nothing," another offered. "You just cease to exist." They debated this issue for a few minutes and then finally shrugged. "Who knows?" they concluded.
>
> What struck me about this discussion was that these women would have been indignant if they had been accused of being anything but devout Greek Orthodox Christians. Yet they were debating the issue of an afterlife without even bringing up what was presumably a basic teaching of their religion—the idea of resurrection and eternal life. At the same time, it was women such as these who were responsible for the spiritual well-being of their families. They attended church services more regularly than men, lit votive lights in front of the family icons on the eve of saints days, offered prayers for the welfare of family members, and tended the dead. . . . Far from being distanced or alienated from their religion, these women were intimately

and actively involved, more so, for the most part, than village men. Indeed it was from such women that I learned much, if not most, of what I came to know about the doing of religion in rural Greece.[13]

Dubisch goes on to ask:

> Are the activities of Greek village women part of their religion, even if they are not overseen, and sometimes not even condoned, by the Orthodox Church? And are they themselves really Orthodox if they do not always see the formal teachings of their religion as central to their own religious practice and identity? The answers to such questions depend in part not only upon *how* we define religion but also on *who* defines it.[14]

To understand Orthodox Christianity, scholars must study Orthodox women, and this excellent volume illustrates this powerfully. Not only does this book help fill in the gaps, enabling us to see beyond the official theology and what male priests do and say, to include what women do as they practice faith within and beyond the church; it also directs us to see Orthodox Christianity as broader than its priests and institutions, as including even those manifestations that would be denounced as heretical or domestic. Women sitting in the kitchen discussing their doubts about the afterlife *is* Orthodox Christianity, and this book provides many illustrations of how this is so. Orthodox women *are* Orthodox Christianity, and this volume shows us the many ways this is so.

Notes

1. Elina Vuola, "Feminist Theology, Religious Studies, and Gender Studies: Mutual Challenges," in *Contemporary Encounters in Religion and Gender: European Perspectives*, ed. Lena Gemzöe, Marja-Liisa Keinänan, and Avril Maddrell (Basingstoke: Palgrave Macmillan, 2016), 324.

2. Kristin Aune, Mia Lövheim, Alberta Giorgi, Teresa Toldy, and Terhi Utriainen, "Introduction: Is Secularism Bad for Women?," *Social Compass* 64, no. 4 (2017): 449–80; Linell Cady and Tracy Fessenden, eds., *Religion, the Secular, and the Politics of Sexual Difference* (New York: Columbia University Press, 2013); Joan Wallach Scott, *Sex and Secularism* (Princeton, NJ: Princeton University Press, 2018).

3. Saba Mahmood, *Politics of Piety: The Islamic Revival and the Feminist Subject* (Princeton, NJ: Princeton University Press, 2005).

4. Orit Avishai, "'Doing Religion' in a Secular World: Women in Conservative Religions and the Question of Agency," *Gender & Society* 22, no. 4 (2008): 420.

5. Avishai, "Doing Religion," 424.

6. Avishai, "Doing Religion," 428.

7. Parallels might be made with Evangelical Christianity or Orthodox Judaism, both of which have strong feminist movements emerging from them (for example, in the United States, the Jewish Orthodox Feminist Alliance or Christians for Biblical Equality). Orthodox Christianity appears to lack a similar movement.

8. Yuliya Zabyelina and Roman Ivashkiv, "Pussy Riot and the Politics of Resistance in Contemporary Russia," *Oxford Research Encyclopedia, Criminology and Criminal Justice*, January 2017, doi:10.1093/acrefore/9780190264079.013.208.

9. Jonathan Dean and Kristin Aune, "Feminism Resurgent? Mapping Contemporary Feminist Activisms in Europe," *Social Movement Studies* 14, no. 4 (2015): 381–82.

10. Anne M. Clifford, *Introducing Feminist Theology* (Maryknoll, NY: Orbis, 2002), 32–38.

11. Jill Dubisch, "Can There Be Religion without Gender?," in *Contemporary Encounters in Religion and Gender: European Perspectives*, ed. Lena Gemzöe, Marja-Liisa Keinänan, and Avril Maddrell (Basingstoke: Palgrave Macmillan, 2016), 45.

12. Dubisch, "Can There Be Religion without Gender?," 46.

13. Dubisch, "Can There Be Religion without Gender?," 33–34.

14. Dubisch, "Can There Be Religion without Gender?," 35.

WOMEN AND RELIGIOSITY IN ORTHODOX CHRISTIANITY

INTRODUCTION

Ina Merdjanova

It would be wise to hear what an ancient church, newly charred and chastened by decades of oppression and martyrdom, considers essential to the regime of human rights. It would be enlightening to watch how ancient Orthodox communities, still largely centered on the parish and the family, reconstruct Christian theories of society. It would be instructive to hear how a tradition that still celebrates spiritual silence as its highest virtue recasts the meaning of freedom of speech and expression. And it would be illuminating to feel how a people that has long cherished and celebrated the role of the woman—the wizened babushka of the home, the faithful remnant in the parish pews, the living icon of the Assumption of the Mother of God—elaborates the meaning of gender equality.

—*John Witte Jr. and Frank S. Alexander*[1]

O rthodox Christianity, with its 250 million members worldwide, is the third-largest Christian denomination. Over a hundred million Orthodox Christians live in the countries of the former Soviet Union. The second sizable concentration is in Southeast Europe: Greece, Romania, Bulgaria, Serbia, Montenegro, and Cyprus are home to some 45 million Orthodox Christians. Significant Orthodox minorities live in Western Europe and in the Eastern Mediterranean, as well as in Africa, Australia, Canada, and the United States.[2] The context of Orthodox Christianity has varied significantly across the globe as a result of diverse historical legacies, particularly experiences of oppression and persecution of religion in the Soviet Union and in Eastern Europe during the Cold War, different legal systems of Church[3]-state relations, and divergent paths of modernization and secularization. The end of the communist regimes was a watershed moment for a majority of Orthodox Christians because it ended restrictions on their religious freedom.

For a long time, the social sciences failed to pay sufficient attention to Orthodox Christianity. A number of studies that appeared in the last fifteen years and examine various aspects of Orthodox Christianity in today's world began to reverse this trend. Researchers have started to focus on the Cold War and postcommunist developments from historical, political science, sociological, and anthropological perspectives, especially in terms of the power relations between Church and state.[4]

The place and roles of women in the Orthodox Church, however, have largely remained understudied, except in a dozen or so theological books, most of which focus on the contested issue of the ordination of women.[5] Discussions of how religion and the Church are profoundly gendered and of how gender constructs are applied in different Orthodox contexts have generally been missing from analyses of and writings on Orthodox Christianity. The same applies to debates about how gender regimes operate under specific geographical and historical conditions and at different levels of social and political life. It seems fair to say that the dominant theological, historical, and sociological frameworks of the study of Orthodox Christianity have remained gender blind. They have been slow to address the issues of women's rights, experiences, and aspirations, even though women in the Orthodox Churches typically outnumber men considerably. Gender aspects of lived Orthodoxy have remained underexplored: These include the subjectivity and agency of women related to their roles both in the sustaining of the faith and religious practice under the communist secularist regimes in Eastern Europe until 1989 and in the upsurge of religiosity after the fall of those regimes. Occasional sociological and ethnographic research, mostly article length,[6] and a recent edited volume titled *Orthodox Christianity and Gender Dynamics of Tradition, Culture, and Lived Practice*[7] reveal a slowly emerging positive shift. Overall, however, the field remains undeveloped in comparison to the extensive sociological, anthropological, and political science explorations of women in other Christian traditions or in Islam.

This volume therefore addresses a gap in the study of Orthodox Christianity that scholars have only recently and tentatively started to examine. It engages women's lifeworlds, practices, and experiences in relation to Orthodox Christianity in multiple, varied localities, discussing both contemporary and pre-1989 developments. The contributions included here critically engage the pluralist and changing character of Orthodox forms of institutional and social life in relation to gender by using feminist epistemologies and drawing on original ethnographic research to account for previously ignored themes, perspectives, knowledges, and experiences of women in Orthodox Christian contexts. The volume pushes out the understanding of Orthodox Christianity in new directions by looking at Orthodox women of diverse backgrounds in different settings, including parishes, monasteries, and the secular spaces of everyday life, and under shifting historical conditions and political regimes—and by offering new theoretical insights.

To be sure, the "women's question" emerges as one of the most, if not the most, contentious issue in the Orthodox Church. It connects with other important issues with which the Church has yet to deal in a consistent and in-depth matter: the challenges of modernity, secularization, neoliberalism, ecology, political ethics, global migration, sexuality, and relations with the members of other denominations and religions. More specifically, the relationship between Orthodoxy and women is a major aspect of Orthodoxy's struggle with the idea of human rights. It can be argued that religion is of great import to women's human rights given its influence on gender regimes and practices in societies: The justification for policies that limit human rights is often grounded in gender norms that religious institutions legitimate and even render sacred and thus above critique. An understanding of women's place and roles within a religion is crucial to the understanding of how this religion relates to human rights.[8] Therefore, the explorations of women's status and roles in Orthodox Christian contexts presented in this book implicitly touch upon the interplay between Orthodoxy and human rights.

The volume combines the depth of ethnographic analysis with geographical breadth. It starts with the context of Greece, where Orthodox Christianity has not suffered politically enforced secularization and has enjoyed a stable position since the establishment of the modern Greek state in the nineteenth century. The following six chapters look at the contexts of Bulgaria, Russia, Georgia, Moldova, Romania, and Serbia, predominantly

Orthodox countries with histories of communist oppression of religious institutions and practices after World War II. The last two chapters focus on Finland and the United States: places where Orthodox Christianity is a minority religion with long-term experience with the conditions of liberal democracy and religious freedom.

The volume brings issues of gender to scholars of Orthodox Christianity and scholarship on Orthodox Christianity to scholars of religion. It aims to broaden the appeal and accessibility of gender and Orthodox Christianity to a far wider audience: teachers and researchers, students, policy makers, and general readers. It is appropriate for courses on the anthropology and sociology of Orthodox Christianity, women's studies, religion, and gender studies.

Employing various research approaches and methodologies, the contributions engage two major intertwined lines of analysis—continuity and transformation—in social practices, demographic trends, and larger material contexts at the intersection of gender, Orthodoxy, and locality. To be sure, continuity contains the seeds of change, and transformation emerges within seemingly rigid structures and practices, in defiance to claims—coming both from within and without Orthodox Christianity—that Orthodox Christianity is immutable and fixed in time. Orthodox Christianity's emphasis on tradition and continuity, which distinguishes it from Protestantism (given Reformation) and Catholicism (given the sweeping reforms of Vatican II) goes hand in hand with a tremendous vibrancy of informal religious practices that are often unexamined theologically but well studied ethnographically.

Continuity

In my contribution, I look at patterns of continuity between the communist secularization and post-1989 developments in the Bulgarian Orthodox Church and society. After the communist regime purged religion from the public sphere, privatization and domestication of religion led to the feminization of Orthodox Christianity in Bulgaria. Women, especially elderly retired women, became the pillars of survival of the Orthodox Church. The fall of communism propelled religion back into the public space and reemphasized male domination in the religious sphere. Orthodox Christianity gained presence and visibility as an indelible marker of national identity, yet it produced no substantial impact on the social norms, public morality, and individual behavior of the people who identify as Orthodox. These complex dynamics of decline in the religious authority and social influence of the Orthodox Church are analyzed within the theoretical framework of neosecularization. Although genealogically distinct, both communist secularization and post-1989 neosecularization featured a feminization of Orthodox Christianity, as women remained the majority of practicing believers, coupled with a continuous subordination of women in the liturgical and institutional life of the Church.

Ketevan Gurchiani examines the role of women in the Orthodox Church in Georgia, analyzing how past legacies inform present realities. She discusses how the Soviet policies of militant atheism, on the one hand, and of indigenization, on the other, generated social practices of camouflaging, maneuvering, and domestication of religion. Restrictions imposed on the Orthodox Church inadvertently empowered women by making them the custodians of domestic religiosity. Ironically, this reasserted traditional views of women as belonging to the domestic arena. With the reinstitutionalization of religion in post-Soviet Georgia, women's acquired role of religious experts was rolled back. Nevertheless, by reappropriating the Soviet-era practices of camouflaging and maneuvering, women have sought to extend their housekeeping roles to church spaces and have exercised power not officially assigned to them. Drawing on James Scott's theory of domination and resistance as a complex interplay between the "public transcript" of the oppressors and the "hidden transcript" of the concealed critique of power by the oppressed,[9] Gurchiani interprets gender relations within the Georgian Orthodox Church along the lines of an official transcript legitimizing the existing subordination of women and a hidden transcript undermining male domination and empowering women.

James Kapaló looks at the persistence of the domestic sphere as an important aspect of the gendered dynamics in Orthodox Christianity in Moldova. Analyzing the testimonies of a group of women from the Turkish-speaking Gagauz Orthodox Christian minority, the author explores their responses to the Khrushchev-era antireligious campaigns of the 1950s and 1960s. At the time, many Gagauz women joined an underground Orthodox dissent movement commonly referred to as Archangelism. In Moldova, however, an Orthodox religious underground with strong female figures had already existed during the right-wing dictatorships that preceded Soviet rule. Kapaló suggests that our understanding of domestic religion during communism (the relocation of religion to the domestic

sphere and the enhanced role played in ritual and practice by women during this period) should be expanded to include an awareness of earlier forms
of Orthodox dissent in which the domestic sphere had become an important characteristic of the religious field.

Maria Bucur questions analytical frameworks that emphasize radical
change in the religious beliefs and practices among Orthodox Christians
in Romania, especially in relation to the communist takeover (1945–1949)
and the fall of communism (1989–1990). Instead, she suggests that the analytical framework of continuity better captures religion-related social processes in the twentieth century. It makes visible certain imbalances, gaps,
and faulty assumptions about the importance of the institutions in the daily
religious practices and beliefs in the historiography of Orthodoxy in Romania. The author argues that two aspects are crucial to the reevaluation
of Orthodox religiosity in Romania. First, the majority of the regular
churchgoers are a rural population, and, second, women have remained
central to the development and maintenance of religious practices in ways
that cannot be accounted for through an institutional analysis of the Orthodox Church, because of its implicit and explicit misogyny.

Milica Bakić-Hayden provides a multilayered portrait of Orthodox
women monastics and gives voice to their personal narratives of spiritual
encounters and growth. While monasticism in the past was the main acceptable alternative to married life for women, the author examines what
appeal it has today given the variety of lifestyles that exist for women in
contemporary society. Based on an ethnographic study done in the monasteries of the Serbian Orthodox Church, the chapter takes to task the continuity of female monastics' underrepresentation in the history of the Church.
The personal stories reflect the specific experiences and distinct agency of
the female monastics as members of a unique social group within the Church
as well as within the society at large and thus give the narrators voice and
empowerment both as monastics and as women. By juxtaposing stories of
certain female personages with important roles in the history of Orthodox
monasticism with contemporary examples from Serbia, the author highlights a continuity of marginalization, on the one hand, and a continuity of
willingness for monastic life among Orthodox women, on the other.

Transformation

Eleni Sotiriou discusses three major spheres of transformation at the intersection of economy, gender, and religion in Greece since the early 2000s.

The first one is linked to the impact of the recent "Greek crisis" on the religious practices and experiences of lay women as well as on gender relations within the religious sphere. After decades of economic growth in Greece and a tendency toward "detraditionalization" of gender roles between 2001 and 2008, the financial crisis that started in 2009 continued to spiral domestically, generating increasing female poverty and vulnerability and an escalation in male violence. Furthermore, an official Church discourse appeared that promoted traditional gender values as a means to deal with the crisis. Within this context, many devout women, particularly younger women "under forty," oppose ecclesiastic authority; their strong reaction against the rehabilitation of a dichotomous gender model of a male breadwinner and a female care provider demonstrates the emergence of critically minded devout female subjectivities. The second area of change is related to women's use of digital media, which provides a space and platform for them to express their views (including criticism of authoritarian clerical attitudes) and spiritual concerns publicly and to engage wider religious issues that previously were seen as the prerogative of men. The third area is related to an increased disparity between male and female monastics: While international nuns' convents are on the rise in Greece, where women combine spiritual service with social undertakings such as ecological activities and artistic projects, male monastics remain firmly oriented toward spiritual pursuits alone.

Detelina Tocheva explores the role of lay women in the post-Soviet transformation of Russian Orthodoxy. The involvement of thousands of devout women in a large variety of church-related activities, and particularly in the daily upkeep of parish life, has led to a de facto feminization of the parish structures of the Russian Orthodox Church. Parish priests hire women because of their professional skills and knowledge, especially as parish school teachers, pilgrimage and church event organizers, choir directors, and parish bookkeepers. A significant number of these women are single mothers. This has led to widespread unofficial recognition by both the priests and the congregations of single motherhood as a "normal" social specificity, something that does not impede women's professional service in the Church. The key roles of women, particularly of professionals who are single mothers, in the operation of the parishes are therefore generating a tentative cultural turn in the Russian Orthodox Church.

Helena Kupari and Tatiana Tiaynen-Qadir discuss how women participate in the process of making Finnish Orthodoxy a glocal religion: a religion that combines national identities (Finnish, Karelian, Russian, Ukrainian) with increasing transnational, multicultural, and multilingual interaction. The authors look in particular at the lived religiosity and experiences of two generationally set apart groups of Orthodox women: older Karelian women who along with their families were dislocated from the majority Orthodox eastern part of Finland during World War II and younger women of Finnish and migrant backgrounds (Russian, Ukrainian), some of whom are either "returnees" or converts to Orthodoxy. By focusing on three aspects of women's religiosity—liturgical experiences, family-making/domestic practices, and church-related activities—the authors demonstrate how these disparate groups of women seek to make Finnish Orthodoxy their spiritual and social home, wherein their practices feed into the uneven process of making Finnish Orthodoxy glocal.

Sarah Riccardi-Swartz examines the discourses and attitudes of Orthodox Christian women in the United States who participate in digital spaces. The digital religious landscape functions as a radically new arena of contestation and debate where women can freely express their views about faith and their secular concerns in a religious tradition that excludes them from positions of religious authority. Women are engaged in vital forms of social discourse that connect their religious values and practices to larger societal trends as part of "networked publics." The online articulations of Orthodox women therefore constitute a specific, recent form of female empowerment, whether women endorse or subvert the teachings of the Church. The author draws out the implications of continuity and transformation, showing how Orthodox Christianity in the United States employs the language of continuity but ultimately is being transformed by both conversion and technology.

A few notes are in order here. First, positionality and intersectionality in the relation between women and Orthodoxy form the general methodological framework of the volume. Positionality accounts for how women in diverse Orthodox geographies position themselves with regard not only to the institutionalized Orthodox Church but to various personal and social spaces as well: the family, the wider community of faithful, and the society at large. Intersectionality underscores women's relations to Orthodoxy as intersectional in the sense that their Orthodox female identities interplay with other identities related to their geographical location: rural versus urban, social class, education, age, and profession, among others. By taking into account the differences and fluidity in women's subjectivities, the approaches of positionality and intersectionality do not allow the treatment of Orthodox women as a homogeneous group and showcase the "women's perspectives" in regard to Orthodoxy as diverse and multiple. The contributions in the volume demonstrate the diversity of female Orthodox identities and the multiple ways that Orthodox Christianity has shaped gender-related social understandings and cultural experiences in different contexts.

Second, patriarchy forms an important tenet of Orthodox Christianity, and this has substantial effects on women's agency. Across the Orthodox world, politicized conservative circles have frequently opposed the principle of gender equality and denounced it as a tool of Western hegemony aiming to dislocate the local "values and traditions," that is, the established patriarchal status quo. The fusion of conservative religious and nationalist forces after 1989 has exerted a particularly negative effect on women. Nevertheless, Orthodox female subjectivities are complex and multilayered, as highlighted in this volume's chapters. Economic, political, and local cultural factors, in addition to religious commitments, shape and inform notions about the place and role of women in the Church, in the family, and in society. Generally, devout Orthodox women seem to be socially conservative; they conform to notions of gender complementarity rather than equality and rarely engage in open resistance to patriarchy, let alone in struggles to redefine traditional gender hierarchies. In practice, however, as discussed throughout the volume, they often tactically navigate complex terrains of patriarchal authority and religious conservatism to carve out or expand spaces for the expression of their gender-specific concerns and experiences and occasionally to engage in critical reflections. Therefore, Orthodox women—similarly to women in other religious traditions— oscillate between conformity to and resistance against unequal gender relations, subjugation to and bargaining with paternalistic masculinities, acceptance and subtle transformation of what conservative clerics extol as "traditional family values." In so doing, they both validate and reshape Orthodox notions of womanhood. Furthermore, as Kupari and Tiaynen-Qadir have usefully reminded us in their contribution to this volume, we should beware of representing conservative-minded religious women as passive victims who have internalized their own oppression within a patriarchal culture. Women's agency transcends simplistic juxtapositions of compliance versus resistance: It is also enacted through women's endeavors to follow the demands of the Orthodox faith and can be located in "their contemplative practices of liturgy, sensorial and corporeal experiences of religion, as well as in their nurturing and caretaking acts."

Last but not least, we might want to ask why Orthodox women rarely question the hierarchical gender order in the Church, let alone seek to subvert it, given that it was primarily through women that the faith was preserved in the Orthodox countries under communist rule. Orthodox women have both in the past and today pursued monasticism in greater numbers than men. In many parishes, women serve as chanters, choir directors, administrators, teachers, and council members. In the observations of Nadieszda Kizenko on Orthodoxy and gender in post-Soviet Russia—which are generalizable to other postcommunist countries as well—under communism "there was neither context nor an audience for discussing a greater role for women."[10] Today, a combination of factors contribute to the faint resonance of feminist agendas of opposition and resistance: Women seek in Orthodox Christianity a spiritual respite and are conscious of undermining their own work within the Church; antiecumenism after 1990 curbed the spread of Western theological feminist ideas; the search for spiritual fulfillment and a desire to resist the sexualization and commodification imposed on women by the new market culture has validated the spiritual and ethical message of the Church.[11] Notwithstanding these factors, according to Kizenko, the presence and voice of women in the Orthodox Church "are beginning to subtly alter Orthodoxy's patriarchal tradition."[12]

In other words, women's religious commitments are not necessarily adverse to personal autonomy, agency, and feminist interests, as many secular feminists would have us believe. It is important to avoid essentialist stereotyping and rejection of religion as directly responsible for "the eclipse of women's rights"[13] while at the same time paying attention to religiously endorsed sexist and patriarchal representations and practices that assign subordinate roles to women. Orthodox female authors have referred to historical evidence of women active in the early Eastern Church in various capacities, including as deaconesses up to the eleventh century, to justify struggles for the reinstitution of the women's diaconate today. However, little attention has been paid to the ways that religious teachings, values, and ongoing institutional and social practices have kept reinforcing a subordinate position for the female members of the Church. This is the larger background that still awaits in-depth interrogation, critical analysis, and visions of how gender injustices can be countered and liberal ideas of women's rights and gender equality can be contextualized. Both gender and religion are inherently linked to the unequal distribution of power: As Linda Woodhead has forcefully argued, "to take gender seriously in the study of religion means taking power seriously as well."[14] The study of women in Orthodox Christianity is, after all, a cultural and sociopolitical concern with power, an inquiry into structures of power and inequalities related to Church-supported and -promoted gender regimes.

When I started working on this volume, I remembered a small anecdote from my theological specialization in Oxford University in the early 1990s. During a tutorial, I shocked one of my mentors, a renowned Anglican theologian, when I expressed a firm opinion that maleness and femaleness are transcendental, God-given identities. This, according to the Russian religious philosophers whose work I was avidly devouring at the time, was the standard Orthodox understanding about gender, and I, still a neophyte, accepted it uncritically, not allowing myself the luxury of doubt. In his soft and polite, very English manner of going about things, my mentor did not try to argue with me, let alone to convince me of the opposite. He just nodded thoughtfully, yet by the end of the tutorial he asked me twice whether I really believed that gender is transcendentally defined. I wish he could ask me this question today.

This episode of days bygone humbles me but also fills me with hope that we keep developing and sometimes radically change our views and positions over the course of our lives. I wish to believe that transformational thinking and action on important social issues, such as the issue of women's equal rights and status, will one day become the order of the day in Orthodox Christianity—but those transformations need to be cultivated within, by women themselves, rather than imposed from the outside.

Notes

1. John Witte Jr. and Frank S. Alexander, "Introduction," in *The Teachings of Modern Orthodox Christianity on Law, Politics, and Human Nature*, ed. John Witte Jr. and Frank S. Alexander (New York: Columbia University Press, 2007), xvii–xxxiii, here xxvii–xxviiii.

2. For a classic primer on the history, theology, and contemporary aspects of Orthodox Christianity, see Timothy Ware, *The Orthodox Church* (London: Penguin, 1997).

3. The word "Church" in this volume is capitalized when it is used in the sense of an institutional, hierarchically organized structure. It is written with a

small letter when used in the sense of a community of past, present, and future generations of believers.

4. See, among others, Victor Roudometof, Alexander Agadjanian, and Jerry Pankhurst, eds., *Eastern Orthodoxy in a Global Age: Tradition Faces the Twenty-First Century* (Walnut Creek, CA: AltaMira, 2005); Victor Roudometof, *Globalization and Orthodox Christianity: The Transformations of a Religious Tradition* (New York: Routledge, 2014); Lavinia Stan and Lucian Turcescu, *Religion and Politics in Post-Communist Romania* (New York: Oxford University Press, 2007); Lucian Leustean, *Orthodoxy and the Cold War: Religion and Political Power in Romania, 1947–65* (London: Palgrave, 2009); Chris Hann and Hermann Goltz, eds., *Eastern Christians in Anthropological Perspective* (Berkeley: University of California Press, 2010); Victor Roudometof and Vasilios N. Makrides, eds., *Orthodox Christianity in Twenty-First-Century Greece: The Role of Religion in Culture, Ethnicity, and Politics* (Surrey: Ashgate, 2010); Irina Papkova, *The Orthodox Church and Russian Politics* (New York: Oxford University Press, 2011); Kristina Stoeckl, *The Russian Orthodox Church and Human Rights* (London: Routledge, 2014); Andrii Krawchuk and Thomas Bremer, eds., *Eastern Orthodox Encounters of Identity and Otherness: Values, Self-Reflection, Dialogue* (New York: Palgrave Macmillan, 2014); George E. Demacopoulos and Aristotle Papanikolaou, eds., *Christianity, Democracy, and the Shadow of Constantine* (New York: Fordham University Press, 2016); Kristina Stoeckl, Ingeborg Gabrial, and Aristotle Papanikolaou, eds., *Political Theologies in Orthodox Christianity: Common Challenges, Divergent Positions* (London: Bloomsbury, 2017); Vasilios N. Makrides and Sebastian Rimestad, eds., *Coping with Change: Orthodox Christian Dynamics between Tradition, Innovation, and Realpolitik* (Peter Lang, 2018).

5. Theological publications on women in the Orthodox Church include Elisabeth Behr-Sigel, *The Ministry of Women in the Church*, trans. Steven Bigham (Crestwood, NY: St. Vladimir's Seminary Press, 1991); Elisabeth Behr-Sigel and Bishop Kallistos Ware, *The Ordination of Women in the Orthodox Church* (Geneva: World Council of Churches, 2000); Elisabeth Behr-Sigel, *Discerning the Signs of the Times* (Crestwood, NY: St. Vladimir's Seminary Press, 2001); Gennadios Limouris, ed., *The Place of the Woman in the Orthodox Church and the Question of the Ordination of Women*, Interorthodox Symposium, Rhodos, Greece, 1988 (Katerini, Greece: Tertios, 1988); Kyriaki FitzGerald, *Women Deacons in the Orthodox Church* (Brookline, MA: Holy Cross Orthodox Press, 1999); Thomas Hopko, ed., *Women and the Priesthood* (Crestwood, NY: St. Vladimir's Seminary Press); Eleni Kasselouri-Hatzivassiliadi, Fulata Mbano Moyo, and Aikaterini Pekridou, eds., *Many Women Were Also There: The Participation of Orthodox Women in the Ecumenical Movement* (Geneva: World Council of Churches, 2010); Petros Vassiliadis, Niki Papageorgiou, and Eleni

Kasselouri-Hatzivassiliadi, eds., *Deaconesses, the Ordination of Women, and Orthodox Theology* (Newcastle: Cambridge Scholars, 2017); Gabrielle Thomas and Elena Narinskaya, eds., *The Ordination of Women in the Orthodox Church: Explorations in Theology and Practice* (Wipf & Stock, 2020).

6. See, among others, essays by Nadieszda Kizenko, "Feminized Patriarchy? Orthodoxy and Gender in Post-Soviet Russia," *Journal of Women in Culture and Society* 38, no. 3 (2013): 595–621; Jeanne Kormina and Sergey Shtyrkov, "St. Xenia as a Patron Saint of Female Social Suffering: An Essay on Anthropological Hagiology," in *Multiple Moralities and Religions in Post-Soviet Russia*, ed. Jarrett Zigon (New York: Berghahn, 2011), 168–90; Agata Ladykowska and Detelina Tocheva, "Women Teachers of Religion in Russia: Gendered Authority in the Orthodox Church," *Archives de sciences sociales des religions* 58, no. 162, L'orthodoxie russe aujourd'hui (Avril/Juin 2013): 55–74; Sonija Luehrmann, "Innocence and Demographic Crisis: Transposing Post-Abortion Syndrome into a Russian Orthodox Key," in *A Fragmented Landscape: Abortion Governance and Protest Logics in Europe*, ed. Silvia de Zordo, Joanna Mishtal, and Lorena Anton (New York: Berghahn, 2011), 103–22; Anastasia Mitrofanova, "Ortho-media for Ortho-women: In Search of Patterns of Piety," in *Digital Orthodoxy in the Post-Soviet World: The Russian Orthodox Church and Web 2.0*, ed. Mikhail Suslov (Stuttgart: Ibidem-Verlag, 2016), 239–60; Eleni Sotiriu, "'The Traditional Modern': Rethinking the Position of Contemporary Greek Women to Orthodoxy," in *Orthodox Christianity in Twenty-First-Century Greece: The Role of Religion in Culture, Ethnicity, and Politics*, ed. Victor Roudometof and V. N. Makrides (Farnham: Ashgate, 2010), 131–53; Eleni Sotiriou, "Monasticizing the Monastic: Religious Clothes, Socialization, and the Transformation of Body and Self among Greek Orthodox Nuns," *Italian Journal of Sociology of Education* 7, no. 3 (2015): 140–66; Aleksandra Djurić Milovanović and Radmila Radić, "Women in the Serbian Orthodox Church: Historical Overview and Contemporary Situation," *Occasional Papers on Religion in Eastern Europe* 39, no. 6 (2019); Vera Shevzov, "Women on the Fault Lines of Faith: Pussy Riot and the Insider/Outsider Challenge to Post-Soviet Orthodoxy," *Religion and Gender* 4, no. 2 (2014): 121–44. Jill Dubisch, *In a Different Place: Pilgrimage, Gender, and Politics of a Greek Island Shrine* (Princeton, NJ: Princeton University Press, 1995); and Helena Kupari, *Lifelong Religion as Habitus Religious Practice among Displaced Karelian Orthodox Women in Finland* (Leiden: Brill, 2016) stand out as book-length ethnographies that deal with aspects of women's lives in Orthodox contexts.

7. Helena Kupari and Elina Vuola, eds., *Orthodox Christianity and Gender Dynamics of Tradition, Culture, and Lived Practice* (London: Routledge, 2020).

8. Compare Julie Stone Peters, "Reconceptualizing the Relationships between Religion, Women, Culture, and Human Rights," in *Religion and Human Rights: Competing Claims?*, ed. Carrie Gustafson and Peter Juviler (London: Routledge, 1999), 140–44.

9. James Scott, *Domination and the Arts of Resistance: Hidden Transcripts* (New Haven, CT: Yale University Press, 1990).

10. Nadieszda Kizenko, "Feminized Patriarchy? Orthodoxy and Gender in Post-Soviet Russia," *Journal of Women in Culture and Society* 38, no. 3 (2013): 597.

11. Kizenko, "Feminized Patriarchy?," 614–15.

12. Kizenko, "Feminized Patriarchy?," 595.

13. See, among others, a polemic critique of all religious traditions as sexist and patriarchal in Sheila Jeffrys, *Man's Dominion: The Rise of Religion and the Eclipse of Women's Rights* (Abingdon: Routledge, 2012).

14. Linda Woodhead, "Gender Differences in Religious Practice and Significance," in *The Sage Handbook of the Sociology of Religion*, ed. James Beckford and N. J. Demerath III (Los Angeles: Sage, 2007), 569.

Women and Greek Orthodoxy in the Twenty-First Century

Charting Elements of Change

Eleni Sotiriou

Introduction

Orthodoxy, thus, is a religion which—to quote Shakespeare—"looks on tempests and is never shaken"—not even when it should be. Whatever changes may impact the world, the Orthodox Church refuses, for the most part, to accommodate itself to change, standing fixed in time, its bishops' gaze riveted on an "idyllic past" which serves as their beacon.[1]

This quotation encapsulates the widely held, stereotypical view of Orthodoxy as being immutable, particularly when it is compared to other branches of Christianity. As Hann and Goltz point out, such "orientalist" views can be internalized.[2] Specifically, Greek Orthodoxy, with its exaggerated emphasis on authenticity, continuity, and tradition, seems to offer little opportunity for the study of change, emphasizing mainly its personal, "soteriological" nature. Thus, in the normative Orthodox rhetoric, often heard from the ambo during religious services, sociocultural change is either bypassed or situated on the spiritual level, seen as stemming from personal change: a continuous striving of the individual to create a personal loving relationship with God, in imitation of the life of the saints. Even in outward aspects of the Church, change is viewed as emanating from looking backward rather than forward, in following the tradition of the Church Fathers.

Yet the Greek Orthodox tradition, even in its institutional forms, was and is neither changeless nor readily changeable, oscillating uncomfortably between rigidness and fluidity. Recent studies examining the different and sometimes innovative ways that Greek Orthodoxy responded to socioeconomic and political changes, both in the past and in the near present, provide ample evidence to support its flexibility and plasticity.[3] In spite of this, most of the researchers in these collective works agree that Greek Orthodoxy possesses an impressive ability to immerse changes, transformations, and innovations "in the springs of Orthodox tradition."[4] It is precisely this immersion that necessitates a scholarly excavation beneath the surface of seeming stillness in order to unearth the subtle changes, transformations, and innovations that can often go undetected under the blanket of tradition. This task becomes even more challenging when one looks at changes in the Greek Orthodox landscape through a gender-sensitive lens and, in particular, when one "zooms in" on female religiosity. This chapter endeavors to accomplish this task.

My aim, therefore, here is to identify and discuss what I think are the most important transformations, innovations, and elements of change in the way that lay and monastic women in Greece practice and experience Orthodoxy since the turn of the twenty-first century. This exploration falls under the category of "lived religion"[5] and accounts not only of women in relation to Greek Orthodoxy but rather of the "Orthodoxies" of different categories of women: younger women, older women, female bloggers, and female monastics. These "Orthodoxies" result from the interaction of tradition with globalization and different aspects of modernity (for example, digital media, global discourses, transnational financial circuits, enhanced mobility). This leads to varied articulations of tradition that include critical stances, opposition, adaptation, reformulation, or innovative acceptance. What becomes important, therefore, is the need to focus on the notion of women's agency beyond the "resistance-subordination" model of interpretation, examining "the motivations, desires, and goals" of women's religious practices, as many scholars of gender and religion have suggested.[6]

The chapter includes three sections, each of them devoted to three main developments of the last two decades that have had an impact on women's religious lives. The first section discusses still evolving changes brought about by the financial crisis on the religious beliefs, practices, and experiences of lay Greek Orthodox women of diverse age groups. Greek Orthodox female bloggers are the focus of the second section, exploring women's use of digital media to communicate their religion online and whether and how such media transform their relation to traditional patterns of authority. The third section deals with a novel phenomenon within Greek Orthodox monasticism, that of multiethnic convents, and examines how their members, mostly converts to Orthodoxy, "traditionalize" secular modern ecological discourses and practices to create their own distinct "brand" of Orthodox monastic life. The methods of investigation for each of these topics vary, ranging from ethnographic research to the use of information available on the internet, and are discussed in detail under each heading.

Finally, to my knowledge, these three topics have not been previously examined. Given the variety of the contexts and their complexity, I can only claim to offer some initial observations on the many facets of women's religious lives within Greek Orthodoxy. Thus, the reader must be warned against easy generalizations. More nuanced research on all of these topics is needed, and hopefully this chapter will trigger scholarly interest on issues of gender and Greek Orthodoxy, which largely remains a blind spot in academic research both in Greece and abroad.

"Doing Orthodoxy" under the "Greek Crisis"

The "Greek crisis" is an all-inclusive term describing the manifold and prolonged crises that Greece has undergone since 2008—a crisis often compared to the Great Depression. The initial financial and consequent economic, political, institutional, and societal crises were further exacerbated by the migration/refugee crisis in 2015. The impact of the Greek crisis is gendered in both its causes and consequences. There has been an explosion of studies on this crisis, and a number of authors have placed gender at the center of their analyses.[7] However, gendering the Greek crisis and Orthodoxy has remained mostly a missed opportunity.[8] My intention here is to provide an overview of the most important changes brought about by the Greek crisis on the religious beliefs, practices, and experiences of lay Greek Orthodox women.[9] My observations are based mainly on ethnographic data gathered during fieldwork conducted periodically from 2014 to 2017 in the city of Larissa, the capital of the Thessaly region, with a population of 144,651 (census 2011). Yet my engagement with gender and Orthodoxy began earlier, in the 1990s, and enhanced my ability to recognize the complex and "fluid" changes and transformations initiated and/or amplified by the Greek crisis. The Cathedral of St. Achillios became the focal point of my research. There I met my interlocutors, both men and women of different generations (from twenty-two to eighty-one years old), mainly university

graduates and of a middle-class social background. In the course of my ethnographic study, it became apparent that "women" and "men" cannot be
treated as homogenized and opposing categories. In the past, such treatment largely obscured important differences in the religious attitudes and
behavior both within these categories and between them. Studying male
and female religiosity under the crisis conditions required its exploration as
a dynamic process jointly and simultaneously defined by age and gender.
Thus, in this study, women and men are separated in two categories; the
category referred to as "younger" women and men includes those "under
forty years old," while the rest belong to the "older" generation.

In precrisis Greece, women's employment witnessed a rapid growth,
which started to undermine the prevailing male-breadwinner family model.
The crisis, however, not only interrupted such improvements but actually
reversed them.[10] High rates of unemployment; falling wages; longer working hours; loss of benefits; cuts in public services, welfare provisions, health
care, and pensions; and high taxation were the results of the austerity measures imposed on Greek men and women. These had a devastating impact
on the physical and mental health of the population and led to increased
rates of what was termed "economic suicide"[11] among men and to violence
against women, both in the domestic and public domain. Women, particularly young single mothers, retirees, and migrant women, were the ones
that suffered most under the crisis-austerity-recession conditions.[12]

The very conceptualization of the crisis was gendered and often evalu-
ated by my interlocutors in terms of the traditional values of "honor" and
"shame," for it was perceived as involving the loss of masculinity through
"sexual assault" (μας έχουνε γαμήσει) and an act of sodomy.[13] Greece was
feminized and assaulted by the external foreign politicoeconomic elites
through the imposition of what were seen by Greeks as extreme austerity
measures. This external victimization of Greece, however, was based on the
internal victimization of its women, who were often seen as the main spend-
thrifts and having a taste for luxuries.[14] Such perceptions called for a return to "traditional values," the articulation of a masculine nationalist
discourse, and an increase in right-wing extremism.

In the religious sphere, similar developments and attitudes were prevalent under the crisis. The modest gains made during the precrisis period
through discussions on "women's issues" and some limited actions by the
Church hierarchy on improving the position of women—in particular, the
attempted reactivation of the female deaconate in 2004 among monastic

orders by the then archbishop Christodoulos, which raised hopes for its possible extension among the laity—were totally abandoned.[15] Instead, the Church focused all its efforts on the fulfillment of its traditional role as the "mother of the nation" and also as "the people's mother."[16] Despite its decreasing finances, it became greatly involved in philanthropic activities throughout Greece, replacing some welfare services of the state and collaborating with secular actors. At the same time, crisis as a "theodicy," namely, as a "trial" and "pedagogical" punishment from God, became the most prevalent form of religious discourse, calling for a return to traditional values and for a legitimization of the preexisting gender inequalities. Repentance, avoidance of material excesses, and the protection of the three "Fs"—fatherland, faith, and family—were seen as the only way to Greece's restoration of its uninterrupted historical greatness.[17] Moreover, in the crisis environment elderism and propheticism received an even bigger impetus and became important mechanisms for the emotional management of the crisis, fueling collective imaginations of divine justice and victories that were to bring about a "golden age," making the austerity-imposed sufferings and sacrifices worthwhile.[18]

"Doing religion" in Greece today is significantly shaped by such secular and religious discourses. During my fieldwork in St. Achillios, service prayers, all-night vigils, and intercessory prayers to the Mother of God were multiplied in an effort to help people deal with the crisis. The most popular service, though, was the one dedicated to St. Luke the Surgeon (Άγιος Λουκάς ο Ιατρός), an Orthodox Russian saint from Crimea and medical practitioner who is believed to have performed healing miracles. This service prayer was first introduced in 2007, but its increased popularity drew unusually large crowds of people to the Church, pointing not only to the chronicity and pathology of the crisis and its detrimental effects on the health of the population but also to the existence of a corrupt state that could not "care" for its citizens, who had to surrender all hope to the domain of the supernatural.[19] Male saints cured and male elders prophesized, thereby becoming central figures in Orthodoxy's management of the crisis. Furthermore, while the typical churchgoers in the parish under study were older women, validating Woodhead's claim for the whole of Europe,[20] there was increased male church attendance and participation in the sacraments, in the Sunday school, and in various philanthropic activities.

This increased involvement in the religious sphere was particularly evident among my young male interlocutors. During the crisis, because of the

high unemployment rate among the young and the fact that many of them
had been forced to take menial jobs that did not match their qualifications,
younger males became more likely to get involved in spiritual work, which
they viewed as "work for the soul" and thus beneficial both spiritually and
emotionally. My younger male interlocutors felt they were "the prime victims of the crisis." They were stressed for not being able to provide for their
future families, and their engagement with the Church was used as a tactic to achieve not only spiritual and emotional benefits but also personal,
economic, and social ones. The Church provided them an opportunity to
extend their social circle and share their experiences with other men in similar economic and emotional hardship. Moreover, through closer contact
with the clergy they augmented their chances of finding jobs and financial support. The fact that there was a threefold increase of men joining
the priesthood since the beginning of the crisis further attests to the utili-
tarian motives of men's enhanced religious involvement.[21]

Given that practices and ideologies of caring in Greece remain strongly
feminized, during my time in the field I was surprised to discover that in
St. Achillios the care of the sick and the elderly was completely undertaken
by ten young men and that no women were involved. As women were feeling overburdened with care-related activities in the domestic sphere, many
of which had been the responsibility of female migrant workers during the
precrisis period,[22] their volunteerism in such philanthropic activities
decreased. The older women of my study, particularly those that were
housewives, retirees, or unemployed, were involved in philanthropic activities regarded as providing some pleasure, such as the soup kitchen of the
diocese. *Επιούσιος* (meaning, literally, "daily bread") was established by
the Diocese of Larissa in 2002, offering 150 daily meals to the destitute,
the homeless, and the lonely. In 2017, the number of meals distributed ex-
ceeded 450 per day. The soup kitchen was not seen by the older women as
a simple extension of their domestic roles but rather as a locus of female
sociability and support, as something done "out of choice," and as an agentic action that involved creativity and strategic planning. These women
were engaged with what the then local bishop called "the miracle of the
pot," as "mothers" feeding "the larger family of the poor." At the same time,
through their cooking they were correcting what they regarded as a great
social injustice and thereby providing a diffused critique both of austerity
measures and of the "greed" of the whole political system.[23] Younger men,
thus, were taking over the parts of philanthropic activity from which

women had withdrawn. Yet I would argue that this did not lead to a "masculinization" of Greek Orthodoxy but rather to a "feminization" of men. This is because older women still remain the religious virtuosi and the main lay actors in the religious sphere enabling lived Orthodoxy to maintain, even under the conditions of the crisis, its feminine character.

If one, however, zooms the generational lens in on younger women, a different picture emerges. The most intense critics of the Church and its management of the crisis among my interlocutors were the educated women under forty years of age. The Church's support of traditional gender values and its insistence on the domestication of women as one of the most important remedies for the hardships inflicted by the crisis were totally rejected by younger women as outmoded and degrading. They clearly articulated anticlerical sentiments, which, however, were not directed against specific individual priests, who were preaching against Greek women "emulating imported modern ideas of womanhood" and "idealizing work at the expense of the family" (the words of a priest). Their anticlerical feeling was broader; it was directed against the Church as an institution, against its leaders and their lack of political criticism of the state as being responsible for the country's financial collapse, and against the economic benefits that the Church was able to enjoy because of its close relationship to the state. Additionally, the increased philanthropic activity of the Church during the crisis was seen as inadequate in comparison to its alleged "vast wealth." These sentiments were not confined to the younger women of my study but were and still are widespread among the general population. Yet these sentiments, although also evident among the men and the older women of my research, did not affect their involvement in the religious sphere but were more related to general "crisis sentiments." In the case of men in particular, religious practice was directed more toward "orthopraxy."

Yet younger women's anticlericalism had brought about a rethinking of their relationship to the male Church hierarchy and to Orthodoxy more generally. Not only "orthopraxy" was out of the question; what became evident was an inclination toward a more individualized form of Orthodoxy and a fusion of Orthodox practices with other forms of spirituality that are categorized as New Age—particularly yoga, meditation, reiki, and veganism. With regard to such practices, scholars have talked about "a Greek spiritual revolution."[24] However, these practices were not only attributable to the official religious-crisis discourse. They also emanated from wider processes of globalization and secularization and resulted in a move from the Orthodox construction of relational personhood to "the imported construction of the individualistic human subject."[25] Before the crisis, the younger women of my study, feeling more positive about "women's issues" in the secular sphere and more empowered, exercised agency within the religious sphere in a more covert way, through the principle of *oikonomia*—a temporary and discretionary deviation from the strict application of church rules and prescriptions—thus placing themselves firmly within the bounds of Orthodox tradition. The crisis, however, increased their disenchantment with both secular and religious discourses that focused on their "essential" domesticity and brought about a transformation of their religious practices and beliefs. The younger women of my study did not participate in any philanthropic activities organized by the Church. They did, however, partake in the sacraments, such as that of the Holy Communion, and used religious objects, such as icons and holy water or oil from the church's oil lamps, to gain "positive energy."[26] Many of them had not baptized their children, though it is customary in Greece, and the unmarried ones were showing a clear preference for civil marriage. Orthodox baptisms and marriages were deemed "expensive and unnecessary." These women were thus either rejecting or reshaping the meaning of Orthodox beliefs and practices.

Given the enhanced participation of younger men during the crisis in religious practices previously dominated by women and the above-described changes in younger women's religious attitudes and practices, one can argue that lived Orthodoxy appears increasingly to be losing its "feminine touch."

Blogging My Orthodoxy

No critical discussion of gender and Orthodoxy in the twenty-first century can overlook the role of digital media in producing changing patterns of religious practice and experience. Media as a context for studying transformations in contemporary female religiosity has only started to attract scholarly attention in the last few years;[27] in the case of Orthodoxy, it has been discussed mainly in the Russian and the US contexts.[28] This section focuses on Greek Orthodox women bloggers and seeks to provide some initial observations on the way they engage with their religion online. The main question to be answered here is: Is the digital realm transformative of women's religious experience, beliefs, and practices, and if so, in what way/s? It has been widely accepted that new media have become powerful instruments to address and fight social, political, and gender inequalities. In the area of religion in particular, scholars have been debating the role that such media play in challenging and/or affirming traditional patterns of authority.[29] Following such discussions, Campbell pointed out the need to readdress the issue of "authority" and, in the case of religious blogs, to look at "what types of traditional roles, structures, belief, and text are primarily affirmed or challenged online."[30] Drawing on her argument, the second main question that this section seeks to address is: Do Greek Orthodox women's blogs pose a threat to traditional forms of religious authority and/or uphold and perpetuate them?

Orthodox blogs are a "space" well suited to the study of the transformative effects digital technology has on the religious lives of Greek Orthodox female believers because they are "spaces of religion"[31]—to use Evolvi's characterization—that exist between mainstream and alternative, public and private, and real and imaginary spaces.[32] This spatial "in-betweenness"[33] makes Orthodox blogs uniquely relevant to encapsulate the religious ambiguity and liminality of their owners. Greek women are at one and the same time insiders and outsiders in the Orthodox tradition, its religious virtuosi and perpetuators, yet they are precluded from leadership roles. Orthodox blogs as an extension of the offline religious beliefs and practices of women allow them to produce, spread, converse, and make public their own narratives of Orthodoxy. In this way, they connect with other like-minded believers, thereby creating a new sense of religious community.

Although the Church of Greece recognizes the increasing value of the internet as "a pastoral tool,"[34] the stance of its clerics has often vacillated between cautious use and total rejection, emphasizing more its risks than its benefits.[35] This attitude, coupled with the fact that the Church has always maintained a highly public profile in Greece and that—up until recently—it had the monopoly in the religious market, resulted in Greek Orthodoxy's relatively limited presence in the digital world, especially when compared to other forms of Christianity or, indeed, to other Orthodox traditions. The same holds true for Greek Orthodox women's blogs, which occupy a very small space in the Orthodox blogosphere.

I was unable to find data on exactly how many Orthodox women's blogs exist in the Greek blogosphere. Google and Blogger.com were used as search engines to identify a sample employing a combination of the terms "Orthodox," "Greek Orthodox," "blogs," "bloggers," and "women" in Greek.

Through this search, I was able to identify more than a dozen active blogs, as well as a few others that at points in the past have lapsed into inertia. While according to the National Centre of Social Research the gender gap in internet use in Greece is relatively small and rapidly decreasing (falling from 19 percent in 2016 to 7 percent in 2017),[36] the divide among male and female individual Orthodox bloggers seems to be far greater, with male bloggers dominating the scene both in terms of numbers and posting frequency. This could partly be attributable to the patriarchal nature of Orthodoxy, bestowing on male clergy and theologians the epistemic power and authority to write and converse on religious matters. The texts, therefore, of clerics and male theologian bloggers are prioritized and frequently reposted when compared to those of women bloggers, which—I would argue much like those offline—are treated more as "metatexts," that is, as a discourse on a preexisting male discourse.

Given the limited space of this section and the novelty of the investigation, I focus on three Orthodox women's blogs[37] in order to examine their online religious engagement. The study was conducted for a period of six months (from August 2018 to January 2019). Specifically, I paid attention to the profile, motivations, and blogging practices of these women; the responses and reactions, if any, that such practices elicited; and the topics they posted or reposted in their blogs. The blogs were all single-authored and were selected according to the nationality of the bloggers (all women were Greek), their place of residence (all women lived in Greece), the popularity of their blogs, their significance to other female and male Orthodox bloggers, their longevity, and the fact that all of them were written in Greek and therefore appealed to a Greek-speaking population. These three blogs described here seem to be among the most popular; they present interesting cases of digital religious identity and self-presentation and thus provide a ground for some preliminary observations and comparisons. Finally, the few inferences that follow are based on thematic analysis. Though all three bloggers used images and videos in their blogs that deserve to be closely scrutinized, given the iconicity of Orthodox Christianity, the emphasis here is on written texts, including comments and thematic categories.

Looking at the bloggers' profiles, two of them state their profession and/or role within Orthodoxy as a wife of a priest and as a Sunday school teacher and psychologist. Therefore, they are both related in some way to the Church's leadership and belong to mainstream Greek Orthodoxy. The third blogger does not identify her profession; her online name, Σαλογραία

(Salograia, meaning "Old Fool Woman"), is a neologism and an evident wordplay between the Greek word σαλός (fool), referring to the "Fools in Christ," a long-standing and influential Orthodox tradition among monastics, and the word for a female monastic (καλόγρια/καλογραία), alluding to her real and/or imaginary connection to Orthodoxy. Furthermore, though not directly stated, one can infer from her comments that she does not follow mainline Orthodoxy but belongs to the Old Calendarists, a branch of Greek Orthodox believers that follows the Julian liturgical calendar.[38]

As a blogger, Salograia provides quite an interesting case. Her long posts are emotional tales of private experiences, practices, and concerns, often presented as an imaginary dialogue between her "digital self," who appears to be old and well versed in matters of religion, and the "other"—the reader, whom she addresses using the language that a grandmother would use to speak to her grandchild. Employing this gender-specific style of communication, the blogger seeks to make her private experiences public in order to "socialize" the child-like reader into "authentic" Orthodox belief and practice, like the foremothers of Greek Orthodox believers have done for centuries in the offline space. Her narratives therefore are often nostalgic, and her intelligent and often humorous way of conversing on matters of religion and theology have gained her popularity and respect also among many male Greek Orthodox bloggers, despite her religious identity, which many Greek Orthodox view not only as "schismatic" but also as "heretic."[39]

My encounter with the Orthodox blogosphere left me with the impression that the most popular bloggers, gender notwithstanding, are very "traditional" in their religious attitudes. Thus, the abovementioned stance toward the blog of an Old Calendarist, particularly a female one, points to the formation of a supportive online religious community that denounces schismatic oppositions and social categories of exclusion in favor of a more inclusive body of Orthodox believers. Moreover, this online attitude poses a challenge to the Church hierarchy by putting the blame for the existing schism in the Greek Orthodox Church on the "unworthiness" and mistakes of some of its members.

This digital anticlericalism is also clearly exhibited by the abovementioned female blogger, who in her profile discloses one of her "interests": to oppose those she considers "bad priests." She also uses strong emotional language to describe the perceived materialism, authoritarianism, and tactics used by the clerical hierarchy to "police" the beliefs and practices of the laity.[40] The blogger's religious rigorism and her age—she seems to belong to the category that in this paper is referred to as "older women"—make her strong anticlerical sentiments somewhat paradoxical. Perhaps such sentiments are related to her religious identity as an Old Calendarist and thus to her feelings of marginalization and lack of recognition and power not only as a woman but as a member of a religious minority. Nonetheless, her blog appears to provide her with a safe public space to express her anticlerical feelings while opening new possibilities for empowerment and visibility that may result in helping her voice reach well-guarded male offline spaces, that is, those of the clergy in the higher echelons of the Church. Her popularity and support by mainstream male, female, and clerical Orthodox bloggers and readers are attributable to the affective power of her writings and the appearance of an honest and authentic "digital self" ready to invest in presumed shared religious values and practices.

While, as we have seen, certain religious roles, such as those of the ecclesiastical hierarchs, are harshly criticized in the online space of religion by some female Orthodox bloggers, the Orthodox blogosphere is mainly used by female "Orthodox professionals"—educators, theologians, and women belonging to Orthodox sisterhoods or women with a specific religious role, such as wives of priests. As such, they use their blogs more to support male religious authority than to oppose it.[41] I could hardly detect any traces of anticlerical sentiments in the other two blogs under study.

In fact, some of the blogs, and in particular the one most specifically directed to women readers, Ορθόδοξη Γυναίκα (Orthodox Woman), which is owned by the wife of a priest, not only uphold traditional male religious authority but appear to need its endorsement. Orthodox Woman as a blog has the formal appearance of a glossy religious magazine, whereas the blogger never authors or comments on the posts appearing. The posts are almost always reposts of texts, which—more often than not—are written by a Greek or Eastern European male Orthodox authority. These texts, as well as the visual material contained in the blog, have first appeared on blogs or other media forms of Orthodox clergymen or other male Orthodox bloggers, both laymen and lay theologians, whom this female blogger considers "authentic." Moreover, she states that Orthodox Woman is managed by both her and a priest (presumably her husband), and her chosen profile picture depicts both of them standing next to each other. Yet, on the full profile of the blogger(s), the information given is solely about her and her interests, and only her name appears below what is posted.[42]

I would therefore maintain that her intention is to create a digital identity very close to her "real" offline one and, additionally, to provide evidence to her readers that her blog is a trustworthy and legitimate space of authentic Orthodox faith.

Although the narratives, videos, and most of the images featured on *Orthodox Woman* are borrowed from other bloggers, websites, or books, they are not a simple reposting of things already written and seen but rather exhibit the agency of the blog's owner. Her posts are on a variety of issues of interest to women in relation to their Orthodox identity. These include matters of appearance; theological and canonical considerations concerning menstruation, abortion, and sexual abstinence; issues regarding marital relationships, motherhood, and the instruction of children in the Orthodox faith; domestic rituals; the lives of lesser-known female saints, women chanters, and deaconesses; and the role of the wife of the priest in parish life—to name but a few. By creating a blog primarily concerned with issues of proper female Orthodox piety, the blogger seeks to educate her readers (women and men) on such issues and to portray an ideal Orthodox lifestyle for women and subsequently for parents.

The role of the *presbytera* (priest's wife) in the offline context is, among other things, an advisory one, particularly in relation to the women of the parish, and her title points to her elevated role next to her husband.[43] Taking into account this and the fact that the blogger resides in a small village on a Greek island, her blog should not only be seen as a supplement to her offline role in the life of her husband's parish but also as a helpful tool to extend her *diakonia* to a much larger "parish," namely, that of the Greek Orthodox population all over the world. In fact, her blog has 458,937 visitors from 144 countries.[44]

An additional point of interest for the purpose of this section is the fact that the blogger's posts, by promoting a very traditional model of Orthodox female piety that many religious women in contemporary Greece find outdated, simultaneously provide a critique to the mainstream culture of late modernity and secularism and especially their concomitant feminist agenda. In particular, in one of her chosen posts on the position of women in Orthodox Christianity, written by a male clergyman, secular feminism is labeled as "antifeminist feminism," which is regarded as "unhealthy," antispiritual, degrading for women, and responsible for the disintegration of the family through such practices as civil marriage, civil partnership, and "automatic divorce." Secular feminism is further contrasted to "Orthodox

Christian feminism," which is termed as its "healthy" version.[45] The latter is viewed as the only version of feminism that secures the "moral and spiritual" equality of women and men, as opposed to their "material" (occupational) equality advocated by secular feminism. Orthodox Christian feminism, according to its supporters, extols the position of women both in church and society through their equal but essentially different role to that of the opposite sex: as mothers, housewives, and custodians of the traditional family model.[46]

The pathology of secularism is also implicitly exhibited in the blogger's posts on the use of digital media, where the total picture portrayed is a hazardous one. The posts are mainly articles that appeared in newspapers, enumerating the dangers that the use of such media entails, particularly for children, offering advice and advocating avoidance and "digital detox."[47] Such posts, apart from highlighting the already mentioned "real" and "digital" advisory role of the blogger as *presbytera*, also point to the ambiguous position that she, as a female Orthodox blogger, occupies between mainstream and alternative spaces of religion. By completely endorsing "traditional" male viewpoints of female Orthodox religiosity while using "modern" technological means to disseminate such views, she is able to achieve a far greater agency than the one she has in the offline religious sphere.

Active resistance to secularism also appears to be the message that the third blogger wants to transmit to her readers. This message is contained in the name of her blog, *Aένaη ΕπAνάσταση* (*Ceaseless Revolution*). In explaining the name given to her blog, she declares that *Aένaη ΕπAνάσταση* is the Church as communion and reunion with Christ, the unabated effort needed to transform oneself and society in the Orthodox Christian sense, as Christ did through his sacrificial blood for humanity's redemption from sin.[48] The Greek word ΕπAνάσταση (revolution) includes the word Ανάσταση (resurrection), and the blogger plays with these two words to indicate the revolutionary spirit of her blog against what she terms "asocial individualism" and, indirectly, against nominal Orthodoxy. In her blog, polemical words abound, and as she maintains on the post "The Terrorist Saint: the mysterious life of a Saint (20 Jan. Alexander the first of Russia)," real change comes from those that are marginalized, thereby criticizing the believers that do not make their Orthodox faith present in their everyday lives.[49] Her view of Orthodoxy appears to favor well-established beliefs and practices and promotes traditional gender values and roles. In addition, her narratives often contain comments on national issues and encourage political activism against decisions reached by the government that may threaten either Greece or Orthodoxy by taking away certain privileges perceived as belonging to them.[50]

The blogger's attitude toward religious authority is an affirming one, but in a different way from that of the owner of *Orthodox Woman*. She regularly posts texts written by certain clerics or male theologians, whose sermons or writings she regards as spiritually valuable. But at the same time, perhaps given her institutionally endorsed role as a Sunday school teacher, she feels qualified enough to provide her own supplementary narrative. On many occasions, she also presents evidence supporting her viewpoints, evidence drawn not only from religious authorities but from various other sources, such as the scientific community, trying to make them more attractive to a wider and more sophisticated and skeptical audience. Interestingly, the blogger does not only follow male religious authorities but also male lay thinkers, and she presents their views and opinions on a variety of themes, including matters of faith.[51] She does not, therefore, challenge male authority either in the religious or in the secular sphere but rather uses it as a source to gain authenticity and, consequently, more like-minded followers and readers. Yet, in spite of her traditionalist views on many Orthodox issues, she does not seem to support the following of Orthodoxy in a strict and non-negotiable way. Rather, she emphasizes a form of social justice grounded in Orthodox tradition and the continuous individual and collective transformation needed to attain it.[52] This blog also contains numerous links to other social network platforms, such as Twitter, Facebook, and Pinterest, pointing to what I would call a "digital religious activism" that appears to criticize and challenge certain social practices, government policies, and decisions and to defend what is assumed to be traditional Orthodox praxis.

It is important to note that a thematic category that all bloggers in this study extensively post on is that of "Saints." The lives of both male and female saintly figures are narrated in an effort to acquaint Orthodox believers especially with those saints that are more unfamiliar, thereby adding new role models to the long list of Orthodox saints for them to emulate and/or ask for help on specific issues. Many times these saints, who are overwhelmingly male, are imported into the Greek Orthodox tradition from other Eastern Orthodox contexts, and most of them have been canonized in the last two centuries.[53] I would argue that this chronological proximity and the fact that such figures under communism were either annihilated from the collective memory or were physically persecuted and suffered for their Orthodox faith render them—in the eyes of the bloggers under study—ideal role models for the Greek Orthodox believers today, who should make their faith pervasive in an increasingly secular society. Mitrofanova, in her study of digital media and Russian Orthodox women, argues that such media are looking to external traditions, and especially to the unbroken tradition of the Greek Orthodox people, for role models of female piety.[54] On the other hand, the female bloggers of this study turn to the external traditions of Eastern Europe for relatively new role models of "strong faith" and true Orthodox piety. The fact that these role models are mainly male has more to do, I suspect, with the patriarchal nature of Orthodox Christianity.

In blogging their Orthodoxy, these three bloggers follow clearly different approaches to religious authority, ranging from blind acceptance to open criticism. Yet the three bloggers also share traits in common. First, they do not seem to blog for fun; they treat their blogs as "windows" to true Orthodox belief and practice. As personal bloggers, and as women participating in a religious tradition that denies them formal roles, they try hard to create an online Greek Orthodox community based on trust and credibility within a space where deception and false information are abundant. Thus, the affirmation of certain traditional Orthodox beliefs and practices and the religious discourses of male charismatic figures and religious leaders are considered important by the bloggers, for they authenticate their own religious views and ensure their success as bloggers.

Second, by blogging they all publicly communicate their objection to an Orthodoxy weakened by secularism and to the nominal Orthodox beliefs and practices prevalent among Greeks today. To this end, they all seem to support traditional gender values and roles as prescribed by the patriarchal hierarchy of the Church. However, concentrating on gender issues is not the sole motive or even a motive at all for becoming bloggers. Digital media provide them with an opportunity to educate themselves and their followers/readers on matters of Orthodoxy beyond gender and open new ways of creating connections and community with both men and women.

Third, their blogging practices and religious identities online seem to be based on their offline ones, being either "Orthodox professionals" or members of Orthodox minority groups. Blogging does not substitute for offline religious activity but complements and extends it. Nonetheless, the absence from the Orthodox blogosphere of the voice of ordinary lay Greek Orthodox women that are not in any specific way bound to Orthodoxy, as those under study are, is conspicuous. Although I can only speculate about the age of the Greek Orthodox women bloggers from my own limited research, I assume from their narratives that most of them seem to belong to the "over-forty" category. Such observations may attest to the fact that women of the younger generation become disinterested in this particular space of the blogosphere, preferring to publicize their own more fluid and individualized forms of religiosity on other digital venues.

Finally, and perhaps more importantly, while the female bloggers of this study defend religious tradition, they also break tradition. This is not done through the discursive articulation of their faith but by the very fact of blogging their Greek Orthodox faith and drawing public attention to themselves. Having no official voice and no formal religious leadership, they blog, and their "digital voice" is reaching larger audiences (as seen by the numbers of visitors to *Orthodox Woman*) than those reached by either the male clerics or their catechist sisters in offline spaces.[55] However, in this way they unintentionally blur the boundaries between "experts" and "followers." Their blogs become "windows" to authentic Orthodox beliefs and practices that many Orthodox women outside the geographical boundaries of Greece look upon as exemplary patterns of Orthodox female piety. One can thus argue that the blogging of "Orthodoxy" creates a new form of "digital elderism." Despite their still limited number in comparison to the Orthodox male bloggers, women bloggers are slowly becoming "digital elders," thus closing the gap with the Church's ordained members.

Converts, Missionaries, and Ecologists: The Changing Face of Greek Orthodox Female Monasticism

Digital technology was also the doorway to Greek Orthodoxy for some of the nuns of the Holy Monastery of the Honorable Forerunner in Greece. A number of the non-Greek nuns had their first encounter with the convent while "spiritually hunting" on the internet and, in the words of one of the sisters, revealing that in their case "even God used digital pastoral science."[56] In this section, I seek to describe some of the transformations taking place within Orthodox female monasticism in Greece in the last two decades by concentrating on two convents that are the principal agents of such changes.[57]

The convent of the Honorable Forerunner is distinct from other convents in Greece for two main reasons that at first sight might appear disconnected:

first, because of its demographics. The convent is one of the two female monastic communities in Greece the membership of which is currently overwhelmingly international (μονές αλλοδαπών). The twenty-five nuns, who live in the convent under the care of a Greek abbess, have different ethnic backgrounds and come from a diverse range of countries, including Austria, Australia, the United Kingdom, Armenia, Germany, Cyprus, Lebanon, Russia, the United States, Estonia, Greece, and Japan.[58] Many of the nuns were not raised as Orthodox and are converts to Orthodoxy. Second, the distinctiveness of the convent derives from the nuns' unique relationship to the environment. Indeed, the nuns, alongside their "spiritual calling," have developed what I would term an "ecological calling," which resulted in the convent's presentation by various travel journalists as the "green Ark"[59] and the "ecological convent."[60] These two distinct characteristics of the convent greatly increased its attractiveness not only to religiously motivated visitors but also to those with more secular, ecological mindsets, both from within and outside of Greece.

The convent is located at an altitude of 1,080 meters, on the top of the southern slopes of Mount Kissavos, in Thessaly, central Greece. It boasts 482 years of history, having been built by the monk-martyr St. Damianos in the sixteenth century. The monastery was closed in 1889, and its buildings were completely abandoned to decay after the Greek Civil War (1946–1949). In the 1980s, some monks from Mount Athos reopened the monastery, only to dissolve the monastic community a few years later. In 2000, the current female monastic community settled in the convent, grew in members, and began restoring its old buildings. The first few nuns that founded the current monastic community came from the sister convent[61] of the Holy Hesychasterion of the Apostle of St. Paul in Attica, while in 2009 a few sisters left the convent in order to establish, in the spirit of missionary work, a sister convent in Saaremaa, Estonia.[62] All the nuns are educated; they speak various languages, and their ages range from the late twenties to the late sixties. Although the common language of communication between the nuns (and their main liturgical language) is Greek, parts of the liturgy are held in some of the nuns' own languages. The nuns' high educational level allows them to participate in various conferences and events on a wide range of Orthodox issues, including the position of women in Orthodoxy and the equality of the sexes, especially as these pertain to the monastic context. The sisters' views on the subject are of interest here; they are also portrayed in the monastic community's self-representation to the outside world, which can be found on the official website of the convent and reads as follows: "The multiethnic monastic community enables a special kind of missionary work, and at the same time demonstrates in practice that in essence, *in the Orthodox Church there is no discrimination on the basis of language, race, and gender.*"[63] This point is better elaborated by Sister Theodekti, the abbess of the convent, in her paper "Ἰσότητα τῶν δύο φύλων καὶ γυναικεῖος μοναχισμός" (Equality of the two sexes and female monasticism).[64] According to her, the Church, through the institution of female monasticism, granted an opportunity to women to become equal to men both at the spiritual and the social level. The female monastic is free from male custodianship and from housework, she can work to sustain herself and her community, and above all she can compete with male monastics for spiritual perfection. While the biological differences between male and female monastics cannot be denied, as monastics they liberate themselves from their gender at the spiritual level through their common goal of *theosis*, namely, deification, and their common vows of chastity, poverty, and obedience.[65]

It emerges, therefore, that the sisters treat Orthodox monasticism as a reality beyond gender. In fact, if one considers the liminal position of both male and female monastics as being of this world and dead to the world, their genderless angelic status donned by their Great Schema, their similar monastic habits and the hard physical toil needed to sustain their communities, it can be argued that such groups become "agents of a gender variant status"[66] that challenges the dominant gender models of the secular world. Yet in practice, female monastics, even as abbesses, are almost always under the supervision of a spiritual father or ecclesiastical hierarch in the diocese of whom the monastic community resides. At least in our times, unmediated wisdom from God seems to be more the prerogative of "holy" men than women. Moreover, the spiritual geography of Greece is hierarchically structured, with the all-male monastic community of Mount Athos at the top.

Although the words of Sister Theodekti point to a necessity for rethinking the concept of gender in the context of Orthodox monasticism, the case of the convent of the Honorable Forerunner complicates matters even further given its multiethnic character. Indeed, the synergetic effect of conversion, gender, and monasticism in contemporary Greek Orthodoxy remains unexplored. Generally, the issue of gender is largely overlooked in studies of conversion, and there are few existing studies that emphasize the

importance of gender-related experiences in the conversion process.[67] In
recent years, the center of attention has mainly been on female converts
from North America and Europe, including Greece, to Islam.[68] Even studies focusing on the wider phenomenon of conversion to Orthodoxy are
rare,[69] and there is only a very limited number of studies that peripherally
touch upon the issue of gender by examining intermarriage conversion in
Orthodox Christian parishes, mainly in North America.[70] As far as I am
aware, studies of female converts from other religious traditions or from
atheism to Orthodoxy in the Greek monastic context are totally absent.
Nevertheless, if one considers this issue within Greece today, apart from
the foreign monasteries of Mount Athos, there are no male monasteries
where the majority of monks are foreign converts to Orthodoxy; the novel
phenomenon of convents with a strong multiethnic character deserves to
be studied extensively.

In the convent of the Honorable Forerunner, every non-Greek Orthodox nun has undergone her own unique and individual inner (in terms of
spiritual) and outer (in terms of somatic) journey to Orthodoxy, and their
stories of conversion range from being drawn by the exotic smells and
sounds of Orthodox Liturgy, to gazing into faith through the painting of
icons, and to an intense "spiritual hunt" for authenticity and inner perfection. The non-Greek nuns as converts, therefore, share many common
characteristics with other young, educated, and "cosmopolitan" converts,
who, living in the era of late modernity, view religion as a matter of personal choice and for whom "the aesthetics, perceived authenticity, and alternative nature of the Orthodox Christianity are profoundly appealing."[71]
Examining their individual narratives would require a paper of its own.
What I want to stress here is the fact that these nuns, the majority of whom
are neither culturally nor ethnically Greek, in their quest to form an Orthodox monastic self transform the Orthodox monastic experience both
within the walls of the convent and outside it. This transformation is best
captured by the convent's intense ecological ethos and praxis. I would argue that the ecological ideals and practices of the nuns not only reflect Orthodox monastic values and practices but also incorporate patterns of the
nuns' own cultural distinctiveness and secular knowledge. In this way, they
become an important vehicle of ensuring the unity, continuity, and growth
of the multiethnic monastic community, but also its distinct identity within
the monastic topography of Greece. The convent describes its ecological
activity in both spiritual and economic terms as "one of the forms of mo-

nastic service, as a way of glorifying God and making an offering of thanks-giving, and as a concrete expression of respect for His creation, and the primary source of income for the building and maintenance of the coenobium."[72]

The basic objective of the ecological activities of the nuns is therefore material: the sustenance of the nuns' bodies and the preservation of the monastic community. However, this is not reduced to an end in itself but is spiritualized by being seen as monastic service (*diakonia*), as part of the everyday labor of the nuns performed under the simultaneous and con-tinuous recitation of the Jesus Prayer ("Lord Jesus Christ, son of God, have mercy on me"). Orthodox monastic communities are primarily commu-nities of prayer devoted to the worship of God. The emphasis thus should always be on spiritual activity. Any other activity, which may lead to ma-terial gains, may invite extensive condemnation or even be regarded as *hy-bris*. Consequently, the nuns are careful to fix their ecofriendly agricultural activities within the frame of Orthodox tradition, which regards humans as stewards (*oikonomoi*) of God's material world, caring for it, maintain-ing it in its integrity, and offering it as a sacrament to God. This is most evident in the Eucharist, "in which fruits of the Earth shaped by human skill are offered up in thanksgiving, to be returned to [humans] again as God's gift of Himself."[73] Historically, Orthodox monastic communities had lived in total harmony with the environment, both in terms of their architecture fitting in with the surrounding landscape and in terms of the use of available resources. Thus, Orthodox monasticism and ecology have a long and lasting relationship, which is epitomized by the Ecumenical Pa-triarch Bartholomew of Constantinople, who is often referred to as the "Green Patriarch."[74] The nuns place firmly their ecological practices within the bounds of Orthodox tradition, as well as on human necessity, and thus avoid the danger of overwriting complex and diverse ascetic practices with secular ecological and environmental ones.

Since the establishment of the Holy Monastery of the Honorable Fore-runner, the idea of being fully self-sustainable was at the very heart of the community of the nuns: "Without depending on subsidies or grants by any third party so they can have freedom of choice and no obligations to any-one."[75] The nuns grow their own vegetables in the convent's gardens and greenhouse, which during the cold winter months is kept warm by heat-ing vats filled with water, using the remainders of candles burned in nearby churches. The nuns grow an orchard, maintain an apiary and collect honey, and cultivate different types of herbs and medicinal plants using not only "indigenous" traditional methods but also experimenting with "external" ones coming from the various countries of their origin. For example, the nun from Japan offered her knowledge on cherry trees, since her country is famous for their cultivation and the adoration of cherry blossoms, and the Armenian nun taught her fellow sisters the cultivation of topinambur, or Jerusalem artichoke, a variety of sunflower with a lumpy, brown-skinned tuber that often resembles a ginger root.[76] Organic agriculture, therefore, mirrors the multiethnic and multicultural composition of the convent and becomes a significant part of its identity.

This organic produce provides the food shared in the common *trapeza* (dining hall) by the nuns and, on feast days, by a growing number of pilgrims visiting the convent. Additionally, it is utilized to make other products, such as jams, natural soaps, oils, and ointments, which are sold by the nuns to increase the convent's income. However, the biggest pillar supporting the convent's economy comes from traditional livestock raising. The convent is famous for its dairy products, which are sold in the convent's shop, local markets, and even abroad. Finally but even more importantly, the nuns are the first among the monastics to engage with "the production, conservation, and distribution of natural seeds" free from hybridization or genetic manipulation. They exchange them with other growers and seed savers in exchange meetings held both within the walls of the convent and in various other exchange gatherings.[77]

The planting, production, conservation, and distribution of seeds may be viewed metaphorically as the best exegetical images for the establishment, maintenance, and growth of the monastic community, as well as for the relation of the nuns with one another and with the outside world. The sisters in the convent descend neither from the same family nor from the same nation and thus are not coming from "a common seed."[78] At the spiritual level, they are united by their common Orthodox faith and ascetic practices, and they are connected with heaven and with one another through the Eucharist by sharing the blood of Christ. At the material level, they are attached to their monastic land, their new country, by planting seeds and seeing them grow, holding the same hope for their monastic community and the one they have "planted" in Estonia. Conserving the seeds ensures the maintenance of their community, and their exchange strengthens the ties, which the community builds with lay people, not only with those from the vicinity but also with those from abroad and from the countries of origin of the nuns. Seeds, therefore, become the link in the chain of relatedness.[79]

Moreover, over the years, the nuns have become specialists in organic farming and pass the knowledge they amass for free to other organic farmers as well as to the younger generation by educating pupils on issues concerning ecology and the environment. The "ecological mission" of saving seeds and spreading ecological awareness through education is coupled with the mission of spreading the word of the Bible. The nuns, particularly the English native speakers, through the use of digital media, teach English to nonbelievers or non-Orthodox in various parts of the world by using texts from the New Testament and by explaining "the meaning of Orthodoxy."[80] Orthodox monastic practices, cultural diversity, and modern ideas and technologies are all pieced together to create a new form of female Orthodox monasticism that enables the nuns to elevate their position not only within the Greek Orthodox monastic world but also globally.

The second convent under study is that of the Sacred Monastery of St. George "Karaiskakis." The convent sits at an altitude of 530 meters on the south side of the Pindus mountain range in Thessaly, central Greece. It was founded in the twelfth century, and during the Ottoman occupation it served as a school for Greeks, which kept the Greek language alive. Its present name "Karaiskakis" derives from the hero of the Greek Revolution Georgios Karaiskakis (1780–1827), who was born in a nearby cave and used the convent as his headquarters during the War of Independence (1821–1829). The current female monastic community was established in 2003,[81] having previously resided in the convent of the Exaltation of the Holy Cross in Boeotia, near the town of Thebes, central Greece.

The most striking common feature that the two convents under study share is their multiethnic status—most of their members are of non-Greek origin and are converts to Orthodoxy. Fifteen nuns from different countries, including Germany, Greece, the United States, England, Ukraine, Russia, Norway, Israel, Bangladesh, and France, live in the convent of St. George "Karaiskakis" today.[82] The nuns are highly educated, all have at least a university degree, most have studied theology, and all are multilingual. Their ages range from twenty to eighty years. Although more than ten languages are spoken within the walls of the convent, the main language of communication is Greek.

The second shared characteristic of the two convents is their ecological character. The convent owns forest land and uses wood for heating, furniture, woodcarving, and construction. The convent's orchard, vegetable garden, and herb garden are completely organic and provide the raw materials for ointments and herbal tinctures. Sheep and goats graze freely in the fields owned by the convent and provide the milk for the dairy products from the modernly equipped dairy barn, which are sold widely. Volunteers of all ages, but particularly young teenagers and adults, are invited to stay in the convent to help the nuns with their many everyday activities. The nuns in return introduce them to monastic values and practices.[83] The main objective of the environmentally friendly forms of energy and the organic agricultural activities is not only the self-sufficiency of the convent but also the formation of a space for spiritual activity, the dissemination of monastic values, and eventually the increase in the size of the monastic community.

Thus, in spite of the common ecological preoccupation of the two convents, both the character and intensity of this preoccupation differ. In both convents, ecology is primarily regarded as a spiritual activity. Yet in the convent of the Honorable Forerunner, ecological activities are more clearly organized and separated from missionary work, while in the convent of St. George "Karaiskakis" the two activities are closely related. The latter convent draws its distinctiveness more from its missionary endeavors than from its ecological ones. This is also attested by the fact that the convent of St. George "Karaiskakis" is part of an expanding network of monastic communities, both male and female in Greece and abroad, that are loosely connected as "spiritual children" of the same *gerontas* (elder/spiritual father).[84]

Additionally, while in the convent of the Honorable Forerunner the abbess is Greek and its multiethnic community fully embraces Greek Orthodox monasticism, in the convent of St. George "Karaiskakis" the abbess is of German origin and converted to Orthodoxy from Protestantism. This community maintains a form of Orthodox monasticism that is not typically Greek but embraces different elements of monastic traditions of various Orthodox types. It exhibits an "openness" to certain areas uncharacteristic of traditional Orthodox monastic practices. These distinctive elements can clearly be seen in the slightly differing habits of the nuns, particularly in the style of their head covering, in the religious attires of the abbesses on ceremonial occasions, and in the ways the nuns connect to the outside world. The convent is open to visitors all day, there are no restrictions on how or when one can enter the convent (such restrictions are typical of other Greek monasteries/convents), and the main entrance to the convent remains for most of the day unlocked. This "openness" can also be witnessed in the amiable relations of the abbess with leaders of Western Christian churches such as the pope. At the same time, however, such practices and attitudes have caused serious problems for the convent within the Greek Orthodox religious space, in particular with certain fundamentalist male theologians and clerics, who consider this novel monastic trend as a "Trojan horse" that may lead to an adulteration of Orthodoxy.[85] Conflicts exist also between the bishop of the Metropolis of Thessaliotis and Fanariofersala, to the jurisdiction of which this convent and its sister community of the Monastery of the Twelve Apostles "Kokkini Ekklisia" belong.[86] These conflicts are probably more the result of a clash between male ecclesiastics, namely, the bishop and the elder Dionysios, the spiritual father of these convents.[87] However, it may also be a case of male inability to deal with female charisma.

One of the most valuable assets of the convent of St. George "Karaiskakis," along with the beautiful hagiographies of its sixteenth-century church, is its abbess, Diodora. Diodora became Orthodox during one of her visits to Greece in 1987. According to her journalist friend Ilka Piepgras, who wrote a book about her, Diodora compared her decision for favoring Orthodoxy over Protestantism to the eating of a candy: "In the West faith is like putting a wrapped candy in the mouth; in Orthodoxy the candy is unwrapped. The intensity of Christian faith back home was for me very anaemic. . . . Protestantism is theory, Orthodoxy is praxis."[88] Holding degrees in fine arts, theology, and law from various European universities and speaking nine languages, the abbess is a charismatic woman not only intellectually but also spiritually, a pole of attraction for many females from all over the world who want to come into contact with the Orthodox faith, as her missionary work demonstrates. Abbess Diodora is, together with her elder, the founder of Orthodox monastic communities in the United States, Norway, France, Slovenia, and Germany.[89]

In this section, I was able to describe only the most quintessential features of these two multiethnic convents. Their vibrancy and uniqueness could fill many books. What I hope became evident is that these female monastics are not a simple appendage to the Greek monastic landscape but its real transformers. The world of Greek Orthodox monasticism is not insular, and in this time of late modernity, secularization, and globalization, ideas such as ecofriendly practices and environmental awareness are projects with which different Greek monasteries and convents are engaged. Moreover, missionary work is undertaken by many monastics either independently or within an official Church context. Yet these convents, because of their multiethnic identity, are able to carve their own special niche, one not easily pressed into a fixed Greek Orthodox monastic mold.

Conclusion

Greek Orthodoxy up until now has been characterized by a high level of "feminization" in terms of church attendance, participation in the sacraments, various philanthropic activities, pilgrimage, and religious education, with women as catechists, school teachers, academic theologians, and members of monastic communities. Yet it remains a patriarchal religion on the clerical level. Women's issues are almost always dismissed given the obsessive insistence on the part of most clerics to consider them as foreign to the Orthodox tradition by stressing the common humanity of men and women and their "different" yet "equal" and "complementary" roles within the Church. The rapid global changes and their attendant discourses are taken into account by the Greek Church hierarchy reluctantly, if at all, and much later than by other Christian churches and denominations, and they are always treated with caution and suspicion, for they might defile the Holy Grail of Tradition. It is almost like the tortoise chasing the hare. Though, unlike in Aesop's fable, the end of the story remains open.

Orthodoxy avails of an important practice of negotiation and adjustment of religious rules in view of a specific context, situation, or experience, namely, the principle of *oikonomia*.[90] It is like "a magic wand" that other forms of Christianity do possess but do not apply in the way that Orthodoxy does. As a nun convert to Orthodoxy once told me: "*Oikonomia* is Orthodoxy's most beautiful asset." Indeed, some of the women of this study used *oikonomia* to update certain elements of tradition and make them more applicable to their lives. I described these women elsewhere as "the traditional modern."[91] Yet in the world of globalization and late modernity, *oikonomia* might not be enough. For Orthodoxy also has a big disadvantage, its "nationalization." As we have seen under the conditions of the "Greek crisis," women, particularly the younger ones, became openly anticlerical because of the Church's support of traditional gender models and its close relationship to the state. These women, because of their connection to Orthodoxy since childhood,[92] maintained some elements of Orthodox practice but mixed them with elements from various forms of spirituality and gave them new meanings. In that sense, they became "the spiritual postmodern."[93] This chapter demonstrates that in the domain of the "everyday" where the real lives of Greek Orthodox women are enacted and their beliefs and practices are embodied and expressed, a wide variety of interpretations of, and relations to, tradition exist that point to what Simion Pop called an "Orthodox complex space,"[94] where both polymorphism and continuity are allowed. Women, as we have seen, constantly negotiate their religion between the changeless and the changing, and in doing so they use patterns of religious authority to gain authenticity while at the same time either overtly or covertly or even unintentionally challenging those patterns. Their religion is future-oriented and tradition-bounded. In this chapter, I avoided giving a clear definition of tradition. I left that to the women I studied, thus questioning the emphasis on the "institutionalist perspective"[95] with regard to women's position within Orthodoxy at the expense of the larger picture of everyday lived religiosity. In any case, the rapid rhythm of social change in late modernity might not even necessitate "the blessings" of the ecclesiastical hierarchy. As we have seen, at least in the digital domain there is a potential for women to undertake some roles and positions within Greek Orthodoxy that were previously the prerogative of men. Given the entanglement between the digital and the real world, the future position of women within Greek Orthodoxy may look very different.

Notes

1. Sabrina Ramet, "The Way We Were—and Should Be Again? European Orthodox Churches and the 'Idyllic Past,'" in *Religion in an Expanding Europe*, ed. Timothy A. Byrnes and Peter J. Katzenstein (New York: Cambridge University Press, 2006), 148.

2. Chris Hann and Hermann Goltz, "Introduction: The Other Christianity?," in *Eastern Christians in Anthropological Perspective*, ed. Chris Hann and Hermann Goltz (Berkeley: University of California Press, 2010), 2.

3. See Victor Roudometof and Vasilios N. Makrides, eds., *Orthodox Christianity in Twenty-First-Century Greece: The Role of Religion in Culture, Ethnicity, and Politics* (Farnham: Ashgate, 2010); Trine Stauning Willert and Lina Molokotos-Liederman, eds., *Innovation in the Orthodox Christian Tradition? The Question of Change in Greek Orthodox Thought and Practice* (Farnham: Ashgate, 2012).

4. Dimitris Stamatopoulos, "Holy Canons or General Regulations? The Ecumenical Patriarchate vis-à-vis the Challenge of Secularization in the Nineteenth Century," in *Innovation in the Orthodox Christian Tradition?*, ed. Trine Stauning Willert and Lina Molokotos-Liederman (Farnham: Ashgate, 2012), 160.

5. See Meredith B. McGuire, *Lived Religion: Faith and Practice in Everyday Life* (Oxford: Oxford University Press, 2008); Nancy T. Ammerman, "Finding Religion in Everyday Life," *Sociology of Religion* 75, no. 2 (2014): 189–207.

6. For a discussion of Mahmood's argument about the need to "uncouple the notion of agency from that of resistance," see Lena Gemzöe and Marja-Liisa Keinänen, "Contemporary Encounters in Gender and Religion: Introduction," in *Contemporary Encounters in Gender and Religion: European Perspectives*, ed. Lena Gemzöe, Marja-Liisa Keinänen, and Avril Maddrell (Cham: Springer International Publishing/Palgrave Macmillan, 2016), 1–28, esp. 7.

7. For some indicative studies on the crisis, see Dimitris Dalakoglou, Georgios Aggelopoulos, and Giorgos Poulimenakos, eds., *Critical Times in Greece: Anthropological Engagements with the Crisis* (Abingdon: Routledge, 2018); Daniel M. Knight and Charles Stewart, "Ethnographies of Austerity: Temporality, Crisis, and Affect in Southern Europe," *History and Anthropology* 27, no. 1 (2016): 1–18; Daniel M. Knight, "The Greek Economic Crisis as Trope," *Focaal—Journal of Global and Historical Anthropology* 65 (2013): 147–59. On the effects of the crisis on gender, see Alexandra Bakalaki, "Crisis, Gender, Time," *Allegralab*, August 19, 2015, http://allegralaboratory.net/crisis-gender-time/; Heath Cabot, "The Chronicities of Crisis in Athens's Social Solidarity Clinics," *Hot Spots, Cultural Anthropology Website*, April 21, 2016, https://culanth.org /fieldsights/860-the-chronicities-of-crisis-in-athens-s-social-solidarity-clinics; Phaedra Douzina-Bakalaki, "Volunteering Mothers: Engaging the Crisis in a Soup Kitchen of Northern Greece," *Anthropology Matters* 17, no. 1 (2017): 1–24.

8. To my knowledge, so far only two articles have looked at Greek Orthodoxy, gender, and the crisis from a feminist theological perspective: Spyridoula Athanasopoulou-Kypriou, "Die Krise, die Frauen und die Orthodoxe Kirche in Griechenland," *Junge Kirche* 75, no. 1 (2014): 16–18; Spyridoula Athanasopoulou-Kypriou, "The Gender Perspectives of the Economic Crisis in Greece and the Greek-Orthodox Church's Witness in Troubled Times: Charity Meals or a Quest for Justice?," *Journal of the European Society of Women in Theological Research* 23 (2015): 117–29.

9. This section has appeared in a more extensive form in Eleni Sotiriou, "On Saints, Prophets, Philanthropists, and Anticlericals: Orthodoxy, Gender, and the Crisis in Greece," in *Orthodox Christianity and Gender: Dynamics of Tradition, Culture, and Lived Practice*, ed. Helena Kupari and Elina Vuola (London: Routledge, 2020), 171–89.

10. Maria Karamessini, "Is the Sex of Austerity Female? Evidence from the Greek Great Depression," *Travail, Genre et Sociétés* 33, no. 1 (2015): 141–47.

11. See Pam Harrison, "Greek Debt Crisis: Tragic Spike in Suicide Rates," *Medscape*, June 23, 2015, https://www.medscape.com/viewarticle/846904#vp_2a.

12. Bakalaki, "Crisis, Gender, Time."

13. Bakalaki, "Crisis, Gender, Time."

14. My observations on this point are also in agreement with those of Bakalaki, "Crisis, Gender, Time."

15. For a discussion of the precrisis religious discourses on women's issues, see Eleni Sotiriu, "'The Traditional Modern': Rethinking the Position of Contemporary Greek Women in Orthodoxy," in *Orthodox Christianity in Twenty-First-Century Greece: The Role of Religion in Culture, Ethnicity, and Politics*, ed. Victor Roudometof and Vasilios N. Makrides (Farnham: Ashgate, 2010), 131–53.

16. See Gerasimos Makris and Vasilios Meichanetsidis, "The Church of Greece in Critical Times: Reflections through Philanthropy," *Journal of Contemporary Religion* 33, no. 2 (2018): 247–60.

17. See Efstathios Kessareas, "The Greek Debt Crisis as Theodicy: Religious Fundamentalism and Sociopolitical Conservatism," *Sociological Review* 66, no. 1 (2018): 125–26.

18. Discussions of prophesies and particularly those of Elder Paisios (1924–1994), a recently (2015) canonized saint and widely revered hermit from Mount Athos, were taking place more often among the male interlocutors of my study than among women. In the Greek Orthodox context, prophesies are gendered and often connected to charismatic elders of Mount Athos.

19. For a discussion on the chronicities of the crisis and their normalization, see Cabot, "The Chronicities of Crisis."

20. Linda Woodhead, "Gendering Secularization Theory," *Social Compass* 55, no. 2 (2008): 188.

21. See Yannis Stamos, "Greece in Crisis: Culture and Politics of Austerity. Workshop Review," *Journal of Greek Media & Culture* 1, no. 2 (2015): 359–63.

22. See also Evthymios Papataxiarchis, Pinelopi Topali, and Angeliki Athanasopoulou, *Worlds of Domestic Work: Gender, Migration, and Cultural Transformations in Athens of the Early Twenty-First Century* (University of the Aegean and Alexandria Publishers, 2008) (in Greek).

23. For a similar analysis, see Douzina-Bakalaki, "Volunteering Mothers."

24. See Eugenia Roussou, "Spirituality within Religion: Gendered Responses to a Greek 'Spiritual Revolution,'" in *Gender and Power in Contemporary Spirituality: Ethnographic Approaches*, ed. Anna Fedele and Kim E. Knibbe (New York: Routledge, 2013), 48.

25. Renée Hirschon, "Indigenous Persons and Imported Individuals: Changing Paradigms of Personal Identity in Contemporary Greece," in *Eastern Christians in Anthropological Perspective*, ed. Chris Hann and Hermann Goltz (Berkeley: University of California Press, 2010), 306.

26. For a discussion of improvised and intermittent forms of religious practice and the use of religious objects by Orthodox believers and nonbelievers

alike to generate "positive energy" in the Ukrainian context, see Catherine Wanner, "An Affective Atmosphere of Religiosity: Animated Places, Public Spaces, and the Politics of Attachment in Ukraine and Beyond," *Comparative Studies in Society and History* 62, no. 1 (2020): 68–105.

27. For one of the most important publications up to date discussing the interplay of media, gender, and religion, see Mia Lövheim, ed., *Media, Religion, and Gender* (London: Routledge, 2013). For a discussion on the impact and significance of new media on women and religion from a feminist perspective, see Gina Messina-Dysert and Rosemary Radford Ruether, eds., *Feminism and Religion in the Twenty-First Century: Technology, Dialogue, and Expanding Borders* (New York: Routledge, 2015).

28. On the greater involvement of women in religious publications on Russian Orthodoxy, see Nadieszda Kizenko, "Feminized Patriarchy? Orthodoxy and Gender in Post-Soviet Russia," *Signs* 38, no. 3 (2013): 595–621. On the role of digital media in the creation of new modes of pious behavior among Orthodox women in Russia today, see Anastasia Mitrofanova, "Ortho-Media for Ortho-Women: In Search of Patterns of Piety," in *Digital Orthodoxy in the Post-Soviet World: The Russian Church and Web 2.0*, ed. Mikhail Suslov (Stuttgart: ibidem Verlag, 2016), 239–59. On Eastern Orthodox women in the United States and their use of Facebook groups as a platform to voice and spread their religiopoliti-cal beliefs, see the chapter by Sarah Riccardi-Swartz in this volume.

29. For a discussion of how authority is challenged or/and affirmed in the blogosphere, see Heidi A. Campbell, "Religious Authority and the Blogosphere," *Journal of Computer-Mediated Communication* 15 (2010): 251–76.

30. Campbell, "Religious Authority and the Blogosphere," 252.

31. For a discussion of blogs as hypermediated spaces of religion rather than religious spaces imbued with a sense of sacredness, see Giulia Evolvi, *Blogging My Religion: Secular, Muslim, and Catholic Media Spaces in Europe* (New York: Routledge, 2019), 66.

32. Evolvi, *Blogging my Religion*, 64.

33. Evolvi, *Blogging my Religion*, 65.

34. See the paper by Archimandrite Simeon Venetsianos at the Conference of Ecclesial Press Officials (June 6, 2006), "The Internet in Service Submission of the Church: From the Zeal of the Mission to the Responsibility of Balance" (in Greek), http://www.ecclesia.gr/greek/holysynod/commitees/press/venetsianos.htm.

35. This attitude of "digital anxiety" is not only characteristic of the Greek Orthodox ecclesiastical hierarchy and its clergy but is also shared by other Orthodox traditions and some fundamentalist groups that distrust digital technologies, considering them as profane and a threat to the religious authority of their hierarchy. See Mikhail Suslov, "The Medium for Demonic Energies: 'Digital Anxiety' in the Russian Orthodox Church," in *Digital Orthodoxy in the*

Post-Soviet World: The Russian Orthodox Church and Web 2.0, ed. Mikhail Suslov (Stuttgart: ibidem Verlag, 2016), 21.

36. National Centre for Social Research, *The Internet in Greece: Final Report* (Athens: EKKE, May 2017), 18, https://www.iis.se/docs/WIP-2017-english -Version-EKKE.pdf.

37. Due to the volume of the material and the lack of space in this section, only the respective blog URL is cited as a source. Moreover, in my view, blogs are public spaces, freely accessed, and therefore permission from the author should not be deemed necessary: http://orthodoxigynaika.blogspot.com, http://www.sophia-ntrekou.gr, https://salograia.blogspot.com.

38. Since 1924, the Greek Orthodox Church follows the revised Gregorian liturgical calendar except for the calculation of the date of Easter. This caused an internal schism in the Greek Orthodox Church, which finally led to the formation of different Old Calendarist groups. The Julian calendar is also followed to this day by the monastic community of Mount Athos.

39. See the comments written under the post on "Orthodox Women's blogs" on the blog "Νεκρός για τον Κόσμο," November 22, 2013, http://o-nekros .blogspot.com/2013/11/blogpost_19.html. The blogger is male.

40. See the "full profile," https://www.blogger.com/profile/17283178488 194923234; and the category "priests," https://salograia.blogspot.com/search/label /παπάδες.

41. My argument supports Campbell's wider study on Christian bloggers as inclined to affirm rather than challenge traditional religious authority. Campbell, "Religious Authority and the Blogosphere."

42. See https://www.blogger.com/profile/12765286774801982724.

43. This exalted role is symbolically depicted on the profile picture of the blogger. For the role of *presbytera* as a trusted advisor on religious matters, see Dimitris Salapatas, "The Role of Women in the Orthodox Church," *Orthodoxes Forum* 29, no. 2 (2015): 177–94.

44. FlagCounter data retrieved on December 14, 2019.

45. For the blogger's posts on the position of women in Orthodox Christianity, see https://orthodoxigynaika.blogspot.com/search/label/χριστιανισμός%20 και%20γυναίκα.

46. For an interesting discussion on the position of Greek Orthodox clergy and lay theologians regarding feminist theory and feminist theology, see Spyridoula Athanasopoulou-Kypriou, "The Reaction of Greek Orthodox Theology to the Challenges of Feminist Theologies," in *Gendering Transformations. Conference Proceedings*, ed. Giota Papageorgiou (Rethymno: University of Crete, 2005), 10–18.

47. See https://orthodoxigynaika.blogspot.com/search/label/διαδύκτιο.

48. See http://www.sophia-ntrekou.gr/2013/05/blog-post_2034.html.

49. See http://www.sophia-ntrekou.gr/2013/06/blog-post_1355.html.

50. See, for example, her position on the Macedonian issue: http://www .sophia-ntrekou.gr/2018/01/zHtw-makedonia.html.

51. See http://www.sophia-ntrekou.gr/search/label/Νίκος%20Λυγερός.

52. See, for example, http://www.sophia-ntrekou.gr/2017/06/blog-post_2 .html. Although this blogger is against abortion and posts texts written by the clergy on the subject, at the same time she reappropriates posts on research material arguing that abortion is largely the result of poverty.

53. Among the saints often referred to in the blogs under study are: (1) Seraphim of Sarov, who was canonized by the Russian Orthodox Church in 1903. Under Soviet rule his relics were confiscated, and his biographer was arrested and executed. His relics were rediscovered in 1991, causing excitement all over the Orthodox world; (2) Saint John of Shanghai and San Francisco, referred to in the blogs as St. John Maximovitch, who was glorified by the Russian Orthodox Church in 1994 and is considered a miracle worker. While in China, he refused to submit to the authority of the Soviet-dominated Russian Orthodox Church. He later served the archdiocese of Western Europe and after that the one of San Francisco; (3) Saint Luke the Surgeon, Archbishop of Crimea, canonized by the Russian Orthodox Church in 1966 and, as already mentioned in the first section of this chapter, especially venerated in Greece for his healing miracles.

54. See Mitrofanova, "Ortho-Media for Ortho-Women," 252–53.

55. The need to focus on the digital lives of Orthodox women in order to hear their important yet often "unheard voices" and gain a greater understanding of them as social actors is also emphasized by Riccardi-Swartz in this volume.

56. See Sister Theoktisti's speech on the First Conference on Digital Media and Orthodox Pastoral Care, http://www.saintjohns-monastery.gr/index.php/video/ ?lang=en.

57. Information about the convents mentioned in this section derives mainly from the official websites of the convents, videos produced by the nuns made available either on the convents' official websites or on YouTube, their written brochures, and journalistic accounts on the convents found on the web. Although over the years I have visited both convents and had discussions with some of the nuns, I prefer to base my analysis on material available in the media, as I am more interested in the way the nuns present themselves to the general public and publicly construct the identity of their monastic communities, as well as in how others perceive them.

58. The number of the nuns and therefore the countries of their origin are often fluctuating for several reasons, one of them being the convent's missionary work outside the geographical boundaries of Greece.

59. See https://www.elliniki-diatrofi.gr/index.php?/magazine/article/67-Moni -Timiou-Prodromou-I-Prasini-Kibotos-Tou-Kissabou.

60. See https://www.ypaithros.gr/anatoli-larisas-ena-oikologiko-kai -polyethniko-monastiri/.

61. A sister monastery is a dependency designating the relationship of a monastic community with a newly created one founded in another place within the same country or abroad.

62. For a more detailed history of the convent, see its official website in English: http://www.saintjohns-monastery.gr/?lang=en.

63. See http://www.saintjohns-monastery.gr/index.php/tautothta/?lang=en. Emphasis is in the original.

64. See Sister Theodekti, "Equality of the Two Sexes and Female Monasticism," in *Gender and Religion: The Position of the Woman in the Church*, ed. Pantelis Kalaitzidis and Nikos Ntontos (Athens: Indiktos), 407–31 (in Greek).

65. Sister Theodekti, "Equality of the Two Sexes and Female Monasticism," 424–27.

66. See Aaron Raverty OSB, "Monks as Model Men: Gender Anomalies or Heroic Ideal?," *Open Journal of Social Sciences* 5 (2017): 110.

67. See, for example, the chapter on gender and conversion in Ines W. Jindra, *A New Model of Religious Conversion: Beyond Network Theory and Social Constructivism* (Leiden: Brill, 2014), 161–82.

68. For female converts to Islam in the West, see Karin van Nieuwkerk, ed., *Women Embracing Islam: Gender and Conversion in the West* (Austin: University of Texas Press, 2006). For the case of female converts from Greek Orthodoxy to Islam, see Alexandros Sakellariou, "Female Converts from Greek Orthodoxy to Islam and Their Digital Religious Identity," *Journal of Women of the Middle East and the Islamic World* 13 (2015): 422–39.

69. For studies in the North American context emphasizing an element of continuity in conversion rather than a rupture with the past and present religious self, see Daniel Winchester, "Converting to Continuity: Temporality and Self in Eastern Orthodox Conversion Narratives," *Journal for the Scientific Study of Religion* 54, no. 3 (2015): 439–60. For a study of conversion to Orthodoxy from the point of view of converts as consumers shopping in a religious marketplace, see Amy Slagle, *The Eastern Church in the Spiritual Marketplace: American Conversions to Orthodox Christianity* (DeKalb: Northern Illinois University Press, 2011). In the North European context, for a study problematizing the concept of "convert" and arguing for the examination of conversion from atheism to Orthodoxy and not only from Western forms of Christianity, see Berit Synøve Thorbjørnsrud, "Who Is a Convert? New Members of the Orthodox Church in Norway," *Temenos* 51, no. 1 (2015): 71–93.

70. See Amy Slagle, "In the Eye of the Beholder: Perspectives on Intermarriage Conversion in Orthodox Christian Parishes in Pittsburgh, Pennsylvania," *Religion and American Culture* 20, no. 2 (2010): 233–57.

71. See Jeffers Engelhardt, "Right Singing and Conversion to Orthodox Christianity in Estonia," in *Conversion after Socialism: Disruptions, Modernisms, and Technologies of Faith in the Former Soviet Union*, ed. Mathijs Pelkmans (New York: Berghahn), 92.

72. See http://www.saintjohns-monastery.gr/index.php/kthnotrofikh -monada/?lang=en.

73. See Elizabeth Theokritoff, "The Divine Economy: Ecology and the Orthodox Church," *Green Christian* 86 (2018): 17.

74. For the ecological theology of Patriarch Bartholomew, see John Chryssavgis, ed., *On Earth as in Heaven: Ecological Vision and Initiatives of Ecumenical Patriarch Bartholomew* (New York: Fordham University Press, 2012).

75. See http://hist.stagona4u.gr/index.php/look-fresh-quotes/item/347-35 -nuns-on-the-kisavos.

76. See http://hist.stagona4u.gr/index.php/look-fresh-quotes/item/347-35 -nuns-on-the-kisavos.

77. See http://www.saintjohns-monastery.gr/index.php/sporoi/?lang=en.

78. For a discussion of gender and kinship within the context of Greek Orthodox monasticism, see Marina Iossifides, "Sisters in Christ: Metaphors of Kinship among Greek Nuns," in *Contested Identities: Gender and Kinship in Modern Greece*, ed. Peter Loizos and Evthymios Papataxiarchis (Princeton, NJ: Princeton University Press, 1991), 154.

79. For Catholic nuns creating seed sanctuaries, see Sarah McFarland Taylor, *Green Sisters: A Spiritual Ecology* (Cambridge, MA: Harvard University Press, 2007), 210–30.

80. See the interview with Sister Theodekti in 2012 at http://www.saintjohns -monastery.gr/index.php/video/?lang=en.

81. See https://www.karaiskakimonastery.org/history.

82. See (1) the official website of the convent, https://www .karaiskakimonastery.org/about; and (2) https://diablog.eu/el/taxidevontas/agios -georgios-karaiskakis-ena-enallaktiko-monastiri/. The number of the nuns has not been updated, but in my visit in January 2019 there were fifteen nuns.

83. See https://diablog.eu/el/taxidevontas/agios-georgios-karaiskakis-ena -enallaktiko-monastiri/.

84. The influence of elders, particularly those considered as charismatic, on individuals, monastic communities, and larger society, is a widespread yet much criticized phenomenon in the Orthodox world. In Greece, elderism has produced influential religious discourses that have increased in popularity in the years of the "Greek crisis." At the same time, elderism is often connected with excesses in religious attitudes and behavior such as fundamentalism and propheticism. Especially in monastic communities, it has in some cases resulted in a form of "cultish culture," in which the elder is worshipped and obeyed

above all. See "Elderism, Futurism, and Prophetism," *National Herald*, January 31, 2017, https://www.thenationalherald.com/148846/elderism-futurism -prophetism/. For elderism in Greece, see Stratis Psaltou, "The Elders of Mount Athos and the Discourse of Charisma in Modern Greece," *Critical Research on Religion* 6, no. 1 (2018): 85–100. I do not want to suggest here that this is the case with the particular monastic community under study, but I simply want to point out general popular perceptions.

85. For such claims that resulted in lawsuits against the abbess of the convent of St. George "Karaiskakis," see https://www.koutipandoras.gr/article /ieros-polemos-tessaron-eton-gia-mia-fotografia.

86. See https://www.romfea.gr/diafora/14819-athoothikan-monaxes-gia -upothesi-me-tin-iera-mitropoli.

87. This view is supported by the account of events given by the journalist, friend, and classmate of Abbess Diodora. See Ilka Piepgras, *Meine Freundin, die Nonne* (München: Droemer Verlag, 2010), 171–79.

88. Piepgras, *Meine Freundin, die Nonne*, 167.

89. See https://www.in.gr/2017/02/11/greece/synantisi-toy-proedroy-tis -dimokratias-me-tin-gerontissa-diodwra/.

90. See Richard Potz and Kyrillos Katerelos, eds., *Oikonomia, dispensatio, and aequitas canonica* (Hennef: Edition Roman Kovar, 2016).

91. Sotiriu, "'The Traditional Modern.'"

92. Here Hervieu-Léger's study of "religion as a chain of memory" is relevant. Danièle Hervieu-Léger, *Religion as a Chain of Memory* (New Brunswick, NJ: Rutgers University Press, 2000).

93. For a more detailed analysis, see Sotiriou, "On Saints, Prophets, Philanthropists, and Anticlericals."

94. Simion Pop, "Eastern Orthodox Christianity as Anthropological Object: Conceptual and Methodological Considerations," *Studia UBB Sociologia* 56, no. 2 (2011): 98.

95. Pop, "Eastern Orthodox Christianity," 95.

Women, Orthodox Christianity, and Neosecularization in Bulgaria

Ina Merdjanova

Introduction

When hearing about my project on women and Orthodox Christianity, Father Alexander (pseudonym) sighed: "This project is for the Department of Oriental Studies." I was puzzled. "Why?" "Because our Church is oriental, and most of our clergy and lay people are oriental. They don't even want to reflect on this issue." I offered Father Alexander a copy of the book *The Ordination of Women in the Orthodox Church*, by Bishop Kallistos Ware and Elizabeth Behr-Sigel, which I had translated into Bulgarian and published back in 2004. "I know this book," he said. "I read it carefully, and I thought it was a timely publication. But do you have any idea of the turmoil it stirred among the clergy?" No, I did not have any idea, as I had left for a visiting fellowship abroad immediately after the book's publication. I only noticed the silence with which it was met, even though I had omitted the frightening reference to "ordination" in the Bulgarian translation by shortening the title simply to *Women in the Orthodox Church*. It sold relatively well for Bulgaria's sluggish book market, but nobody talked publicly about it. The only review it received was written by a feminist literary professor and published in *Kultura*, a weekly with a long tradition and popular among Bulgarian intellectuals. The ecclesiastic circles remained mute, and I assumed they hadn't noticed it or didn't want to discuss the topic, which I knew many saw as controversial. "Most of the clergymen qualified the book as meaningless and provocative, while some rejected it outright as nonsensical," clarified Father Alexander. Being a female, like most of the participants in Bulgarian Orthodox Church–related practices, as well as Western educated and therefore no longer "oriental" enough, prompted me to joke: "I hope I was not excommunicated in absentia."[1]

In this chapter, I propose new directions for rethinking the relationship between women and Orthodox Christianity in Bulgaria after the end of communism by introducing the theoretical framework of neosecularization. I argue that communist secularization between the end of World War II and 1989 inadvertently led to a feminization of Orthodox Christianity caused by the privatization and domestication of religious practice. The collapse of the communist regime propelled religion back into public space and reestablished male domination in the religious sphere. The euphoria of religious freedom generated a mass interest in and (re)turn to the Orthodox Church, which proved short-lived due to both historical legacies and newly emerged sociopolitical realities. Orthodox Christianity has been present and visible as an indelible marker of national identity, but it has produced no substantial impact on the social norms, public morality, and individual behavior of the people who identify as Orthodox (around 76 percent of the population). These complex dynamics of decline in religious authority can be described as neosecularization. Rather than focusing on discontinuity with the communist past and the "revival" of religion after 1989, the perspective of neosecularization explicates patterns of continuity both in terms of the feminization of Orthodox Christianity, evident in the fact that women remain the majority of practicing believers, and in terms of the circumscribed social influence of the Orthodox Church.

The methodological approach I take in this chapter combines historical and sociological analysis. My account draws on insights from my participant observation during religious services, informal interviews and conversations with clergy and lay people, examination of official Church documents, statements of Church leaders, and blogs and other publications in printed and online media related to women and Orthodox Christianity in Bulgaria. For the purpose of protecting the identities of my interviewees, I either anonymize them or use pseudonyms when quoting from our conversations, save for a few cases.

Generally, I see women's relations with Orthodox Christianity as diverse, multiple, and intersectional. Orthodox female identities intersect with other identities related to women's social status, education, rural versus urban place of living, age, and profession, among others. Last but not least, I do

not see Orthodox Christianity as a unified discursive tradition. Both clerics and lay followers differ in how they view women's status and rights, as
becomes evident from my fieldwork conversations.

Secularization, Desecularization, Neosecularization

Secularization in this chapter is understood as a process of social modernization that renders the secular spheres (the modern state, the capitalist market
economy, and modern science) functionally differentiated and emancipated from the religious sphere.[2] Secularization is thus a process by which
religion "ceases to be significant in the working of the social system."[3] In
a secularized world, religion is no longer the unifying system of meaning
and ethical norms, what Peter Berger called the "sacred canopy" of society;[4]
it becomes one sphere among multiple other spheres of a differentiated
social reality. The decline of religion as a meaning-organizing system, which
permeates and influences all spheres of life, often leads to religion's aligning
with political and other secular forces, through which it can retain at least
some of its social impact. It "lends" its symbolic capital and functions
to worldly ideologies and systems of social organization, such as various
political movements, among which nationalism figures prominently.[5] Importantly, as Peter Beyer has reminded us, religion loses the "specifically
religious in the process of respecifying the religious."[6]

I interpret neosecularization[7] as a complex process wherein, after a period of desecularization of already secularized societies and a rise of religious authority at individual, social, and/or political levels, the pendulum
swings back to a condition in which the significance of religion decreases
and the hold of religious authority over the social system declines.[8] A
neosecular society is not a society without religion but a society in which
religious injunctions and prescriptions have very little influence on the
individual and collective life of its members.

In Bulgarian society, Orthodox Christianity has remained an important aspect and a marker of national identity and thereby has retained its
public visibility. Yet it does not have a substantial impact on the worldviews and behavior of those citizens who define themselves as Orthodox.
Neosecularization in Bulgaria is not a reincarnation of the communist secularization, even though the historic legacies of a pervasive atheist ideology and practice cannot be discounted. It is rooted in new sociopolitical
conditions related to globalization and the neoliberal paradigm, which re-

inforce and perpetuate the prevalence of individualistic discursive practices and erode communal bonding. Importantly, after 1989 the Bulgarian Orthodox Church was unable to respond to the spiritual searchings of
Bulgarian society. This, alongside squabbles and splits within the Church,
the lack of willingness on the part of the ecclesiastics and theologians to
confess and repent for their cooperation with the secret services of the communist state, and the controversial behavior of certain clerics, prompted a
postcommunist decline of religious authority.

Instead of interpreting the recent history of Orthodox Christianity in
Bulgaria as a straightforward radical break with communist secularization,
I propose to look at patterns of continuity. I focus in particular on women's
central role in keeping the Church alive by participating in its liturgical
life and by informally transmitting religious faith and practices to younger
generations.

The communist secularization aimed to emasculate the Orthodox
Church institutionally and socially, on the one hand, and to appropriate it
in the upkeep of a national ideology by validating it exclusively as a custo-
dian of "Bulgarianness" during the "five centuries of the Turkish yoke,"
on the other. The communist government abolished religious education,
confiscated Church property, and launched attacks on the clergy, thereby
overtaking completely the management of the Church. The Church was
gradually marginalized and turned into an obedient tool of the new regime. Despite official church-state separation, the state paid the salaries of
the clergy and thus co-opted and controlled them. People who attended
services were placed under the surveillance of the secret police, and persistence in churchgoing came at a price. Believers gradually started to be seen
as second-class citizens; they could not join the Communist Party, which
in itself barred them from pursuing prestigious careers such as doctors,
teachers, and so on. The communist regime rigorously imposed the doctrine of "scientific atheism," which proclaimed religion a remnant of bourgeois society, a system of superstitions that functioned as an "opiate" and
supported the ignorance and manipulation of people. Religion was expected
to die away with the advancement of communist society.

As Bulgaria emerged from communism, the Orthodox Church gained
an opportunity to recover from its spiritual and institutional stagnation.
In 1991, the ecclesiastical Spiritual Academy was restored to its pre-1950
standing of a theological faculty within Sofia University. A second theological faculty, at Veliko Turnovo University, was established, and theology was

also introduced as a discipline at the universities of Shumen and Plovdiv. However, the Church was confronted with the challenges of a society transitioning to a market economy, liberal democracy, and cultural pluralism at a moment when its strength was sapped. The communist regime had crippled and corrupted the leadership of the Church by co-opting it and preventing anybody with higher-than-average grades from enrolling at the ecclesiastical academy; it had also infested the rank-and-file clergy with state security pawns. According to His Eminence Gerasim, secretary of the Holy Synod, "We never had a revival of Orthodox Christianity in Bulgaria, because it was destroyed under communism. In Russia, they had an underground church, and Christianity flourished after 1990, but here we did not have anything to revive."[9]

The Bulgarian Orthodox Church was torn apart by heated debates over the ties of its hierarchy to the former regime. In 1992, the Directorate of Religious Affairs at the Council of Ministers declared the election of Patriarch Maxim in 1971 invalid because of the interference of the communist regime in it and appointed an alternative Synod led by Metropolitan Pimen. The priests split between the two synods and shocked parishioners by engaging in fistfights on several occasions and repeatedly hurling abuse and anathemas at one another, until a new Religious Denominations Act in 2002 pronounced the alternative Synod illegal. Two years later, the police forcibly evicted its priests from the Church properties they used. The state therefore continuously strove to control the Church by various means, including by interfering in intrachurch affairs. During the rift within the Church it registered and thus legitimated an alternative Synod and later proceeded to ban this Synod.

The Church failed to address constructively the disastrous consequences of its internal split, which left many of its followers resentful. Moreover, lacking a strong connection to contemporary theological discourses, human capital, and experience in democratic practice, it was ill-equipped to come to terms with Bulgaria's burgeoning cultural and religious pluralism, which it saw as a threat. This prompted it to further align with the political powers in search of a privileged position. The 1991 Constitution reaffirmed church-state separation but followed an accommodationist approach by defining Orthodox Christianity as the traditional religion of the Bulgarian nation. The state allocates funds for the upkeep and repair of church buildings and exempts the Church's production and trade in candles from taxes, among other subsidies. Recent amendments to the 2002 Religious

Denominations Act, which came into effect in 2019, provided for increased government funding for the Bulgarian Orthodox Church (and for the Muslim community). According to the revised law, the clergy's salaries are paid from the state budget—a return to a controversial communist-era practice.

The transition to democracy reversed the marginalization of the Church and restored its visibility in the public sphere. Yet the Church was unable to offer the spiritual and moral leadership expected by the people who flocked to it. Most of its attempts to have a say in political and social life, for example by launching a struggle to introduce an obligatory catechetical religious education in public schools, were unsuccessful. There was neither a reversal of the differentiation between distinct social spheres nor a growth in the levels of religious practice, even though Orthodox Christianity garners significant symbolic capital as a key element of national identity. According to the national censuses, the number of people in the country who identify as Orthodox fell from 86 percent in 1992 to 84 percent in 2001 and to 76 percent in 2011.[10]

Data from the 2006 World Values Survey reveal the ongoing process of neosecularization. They indicate that only 5.6 percent of Orthodox Christians go to church each week, and 8.6 percent attend service once per month, wherein the number of women among the churchgoers is over two times that of men. Some 39.5 percent of the respondents visit church only on major religious feasts, 6.4 percent visit only once a year, and 23.1 percent report never going to church. Around 46.8 percent think the Church does not offer adequate answers to their problems, and only 27.8 percent find the Church's answers adequate. Some 63.2 percent of the surveyed consider the Church's response to social problems inadequate, and only 13.7 percent value positively the social positions of the Church. Only 24.3 percent report that they pray in their daily life—17.4 percent of men and 30.7 percent of women—while 75.2 percent say they don't pray. The majority of respondents think that religious leaders should not try to influence people's vote (74 percent) or the government's policies (68 percent). Most of the surveyed consider divorce justifiable, while people are evenly divided on the issue of abortion.[11]

The results of a 2017 study by the Pew Research Center on religiosity in the Orthodox countries are also symptomatic. Only 15 percent of Bulgarian Orthodox report that religion is very important in their lives; in comparison, in Greece 59 percent of Orthodox see religion as very important;

in both Romania and Georgia religion is very important to 50 percent of
Orthodox. Just 5 percent of Bulgarian Orthodox attend church weekly,
and 11 percent pray daily, the lowest rates among Orthodox populations;
for comparison, in Romania 21 percent attend church weekly and 42 percent
pray daily, while in Greece the numbers are 17 percent and 31 percent respectively. Most strikingly, 22 percent of those who identify as Orthodox
in Bulgaria do not believe in God; for comparison, the relevant numbers
in Russia and Serbia are 13 and 9 percent. Only 17 percent of Bulgarians
fast during Lent, as opposed to 68 percent of Greeks, 64 percent of Serbs,
and 58 percent of Romanians.[12]

In other words, surveys and polls reveal not only a dynamic of progressive "unchurching"[13] among Orthodox Bulgarians but also a condition that
can be described sociologically as "belonging without believing."[14] Apart
from a small number of parishes with charismatic priests, who attract larger
congregations of younger people and who are being consulted by parishioners on a more regular basis because of their moral integrity, intelligence,
and openness, the overwhelming majority of the parishes have few regular
communicants. Most people tend to see the Bulgarian Orthodox Church
as a "community cult" linked to the national identity and history rather
than as a Eucharistic religion of salvation.[15]

Yet a paradox emerges: The Church continuously outranks Bulgaria's
secular institutions in surveys of trust. The 2006 World Values Survey found
that the Church is the second most trusted institution in Bulgarian society, with 59.1 percent expressing trust in it, second to the army, which gar-
nered the trust of 68.1 percent of responders. According to a 2016 survey
of the Open Society Institute on Bulgarians' attitudes toward institutions,
the European Union and the Bulgarian Orthodox Church ranked the highest, with 55 percent of the respondents expressing trust in them, while
Parliament and the political parties ranked the lowest, with 22 percent and
17 percent. The army was trusted by 50 percent, on par with universities.[16]

The relatively high trust of Bulgarians in the Church seems to reflect a
profound social disappointment with other institutions and especially with
the political parties and Parliament. To be sure, the World Values Survey
showed that the majority of people are rather ambiguous about the ways
that the Church responds to the problems in their social and individual
lives. Consequently, very few people orient their lives according to religious
injunctions. My conversations with practicing believers indicate that they
tend to decide individually, according to their personal situation, which

religious prescriptions to follow and which to ignore, especially when it comes to marriage, divorce, abortion, and sexual life.

Neosecularization is also evident in the growing isolationism of the Bulgarian Orthodox Church. The Church withdrew from the ecumenical movement, leaving the World Council of Churches in 1998. Furthermore, it gradually alienated itself from other Orthodox denominations, with the notable exception of the Russian Orthodox Church. It was particularly striking that it refused to take part in the historical Pan-Orthodox Council in Crete in 2016, an important event organized by the ecumenical patriarch to consolidate an Orthodox position on pressing contemporary issues such as the mission of the Orthodox Church in today's world and its relations with the rest of the Christian world, among others. More broadly, the Bulgarian Orthodox Church regularly expresses "traditionalist"[17] negative attitudes toward modernity, the West, liberalism, the rights of women, sexual minorities, and the "sects,"[18] among other things. However, it has never voiced a critique of the neoliberal economic restructuring Bulgaria went through and its disastrous social costs, the rise of poverty, endemic corruption,[19] inequality, or discrimination against ethnic and religious minorities, among other important issues. In the rare cases when it takes a public stance on urgent social problems, it raises eyebrows among many of its followers. During the refugee crises in 2015–2016, the Holy Synod called on the government to stop admitting more refugees, even though it expressed compassion for those already in the country. It pointed out that accepting more refugees from the Middle East could threaten Christianity and "raises questions about the stability and existence of the Bulgarian state in general."[20]

Overall, the Orthodox Church in Bulgaria has succumbed to the neoliberal subjectivization, marketization, and commodification of postcommunist culture and societal life, instead of offering a viable spiritual alternative—which further enhanced the process of neosecularization.

Women and Orthodox Christianity: The Missing Debate

Paradoxically, until today, the relation between women and Orthodox Christianity has not been a subject of discussion in Bulgaria. Even though the secretary of the Holy Synod told me that "women are a main human factor in Orthodoxy, because of which the Church survives,"[21] there has never been an official recognition of women's role in keeping the Church alive. Furthermore, the majority of priests do not seem to think they need to address the gender imbalances in their parishes. "We have not thought about women in the Church," admitted Father Marin (pseudonym), adding: "We don't think there is a discrimination against women; my parish, for example, appoints four priests and six women." He did not clarify that the women's jobs are limited to candle selling, baking the *prosphora* (the leavened bread used in the Orthodox liturgy), and cleaning the building. When I pressed him with questions about gender equality, Father Marin made clear his view that "women are not equal to men and therefore should not work male jobs; women and men have different characteristics, and nature separates them."[22]

"There are no debates on the role of women, human rights, modernization, ecumenism," Father Stoyan (a pseudonym), one of the few well-educated and critically minded priests in the Church, told me. "It is very difficult to involve the clergy in such debates; most of them are mainly interested in the business affairs into which they have turned the Church. Clerics who suffer from a deficit of knowledge are easy to manipulate and to mobilize around conservative causes. They don't recognize the fact that women are the basis of the parish life."[23]

Indeed, the clergy entered the postcommunist transition with low levels of education; they lacked both the knowledge and rhetorical skills necessary for participation in meaningful public debates on important contemporary issues. But more importantly, it seems that thirty years after the end of communism Bulgarian clerics and theologians still do not consider the "woman question" worth even a debate. This missing debate also reflects the silencing of feminist themes and discussions in society at large, which consistently perceives feminism as a foreign ideology irrelevant to the local context. The dominant understanding is that the modernization of society carried out in communist times emancipated and liberated women; the continued subordination of women within family life is rarely mentioned.

Since post–World War II processes of industrialization and modernization required an increased workforce, women were enlisted en masse in the building of communism. New legislation promoting compulsory education of all citizens and gender equality streamlined women's participation and professional advancement in the public sphere. According to Tatyana Kmetova, executive director of the Center for Women's Studies and Policies, by the 1980s Bulgaria had the highest percentage of working women both among the socialist countries and in the West, and women were represented in almost all walks of life.[24] The communist system, however, was riddled with contradictions. The authoritarian state was based on male supremacy, as was evident in the overwhelmingly male Communist Party leadership and in the low representation of women in politics. Despite the advancement of equality between the sexes and of the economic and social rights of women, the deeply ingrained patriarchal relations remained untransformed in the sphere of family life, where the unequal distribution of domestic roles and duties persisted. Women continued to bear the primary responsibility for housework and raising children while also working full-time in paid jobs outside the household. "Emancipation of women under communism in the job market and in education had nothing to do with gender equality," noted Kmetova. "We did not have a women's movement because of the idea that all women's issues had been resolved from above. We haven't changed much in this regard after 1989. We have the lowest culture of what gender equality means, and we don't understand the content of women's rights."[25]

Under communist secularization, the surviving vestiges of religious practice and beliefs were confined to the domestic sphere. This led to a de facto feminization of Orthodox Christianity. Women became the sole conveyors of the basics of Orthodox beliefs and practices to children and grandchildren, in however fragmented and limited forms, because no other sources of religious knowledge were available. They kept performing the traditional family customs and rituals associated with faith. They thus served as the primary, though unofficial and unrecognized, guardians of religious tradition. Women, particularly elderly women, continued to attend church on major Christian feasts and to prepare at home the ritual meals, to pray and communicate to their families the spiritual meaning of the holy days, and to perform domestic religious customs related to birth, death, and marriage. They would often secretly have their grandchildren baptized, an act that could have serious consequences, including job loss, for younger working parents.

Each year on the night of December 24, my grandmother used to say: "In the past, we called this night Christmas Eve." She would prepare the unleavened bread and vegetarian meals required for the feast and tell us about the birth of Jesus. It all sounded like a fairy tale. Christmas was never mentioned in public parlance; instead, New Year was the official seasonal holiday, celebrated with a decorated fir tree and the arrival of the Grandfather Frost—the communist replacement of Santa Claus—with gifts for the kids.

In 1984, during my studies at Sofia University, my landlady, who had a wide network of connections, obtained a special permit for me to attend the Easter service at the nearby St. Aleksander Nevsky Cathedral. The building was cordoned off by police, who kept away those onlookers without permits. We were ushered into the nave of the cathedral, which was full of worshippers and plainclothes policemen. This was my first attendance of a church liturgy, and everything looked otherworldly: the iconostasis, the clergy in bright garments with golden epitrachelions, the magnificent choir. The service was in Old Slavonic, and I understood little of it. I still vividly remember the ritual of lighting the candles at midnight after the patriarch pronounced the words "Christ is risen" and the ceremonial circling of the worshippers around the church building with lit candles in their hands. The majority of the worshippers were solemn elderly women dressed in their best clothes.

The fall of the communist regime ended the severe restrictions on religious freedom, and the Church reemerged into the public sphere. The linkage of national and religious identities reinforced the social standing of Orthodox Christianity. At the same time, the economic liberalization and adjacent structural adjustments seriously challenged the preexisting officially enforced gender parity and led to female marginalization as a result of women's decreased access to the labor market, the disappearance of family-oriented social benefits, and rising social and domestic violence.[26] The masculinization of culture in the process of democratization[27] was supported by religious teachings about the "natural" difference between the sexes, the "traditional" gender roles, and the validation of women exclusively through their motherhood.

In the conditions of neosecularization, Orthodox Christianity in Bulgaria has remained largely feminized. "Some 90 percent of our regular parishioners are women," pointed out Father Zachary (pseudonym), who serves as a priest in a small provincial town.[28] My visits to a number of congregations in Sofia showed that at least two-thirds of the faithful are women. Recent tendencies toward a wider participation by young people of both sexes in the liturgical and social life of the Church seem to be limited to rare parishes with charismatic priests in the capital and in a few larger cities.

A glance at the modest monastic life in the country reveals that female monastics outnumbered the male monastics both under communism and after it. In 1987, there were 135 monks and 170 nuns serving in 120 monasteries.[29] Today, a total of two hundred monastics serve in the 205 monasteries in the country—and the number of nuns remains higher than that of monks, according to the secretary of the Holy Synod.[30] The situation in Bulgaria is markedly different from that in other Orthodox countries such as Romania and Greece, where both male and female monasticism have been thriving. The decrease in the number of monastics by one-third since the end of communism can be read as another sign of neosecularization.

The inherent contradiction between the official masculine domination and the unofficially feminized spaces in Orthodox Christianity has caused anxiety among conservative ecclesiastics and theologians. Orthodox female subjectivities have been restricted, and a more equal status of women has been denied by continuous discursive practices emphasizing women's traditional roles as wives, mothers, and caregivers. A number of women work as secretaries and accountants at the administrative institutions of the Orthodox Church,[31] but women are barred from decision-making and leadership roles. They don't serve as readers in the church, and certain ecclesiastics have gone so far as to ban the singing of women in the church choir, even though female chanters remain overrepresented in the Bulgarian Orthodox Church because of the steep decline in the numbers of male chanters.

Women and the Study of Theology

The negative reversal of the overall status of women in postcommunist society dovetailed with a growing female participation in the life of the religious community. Women take part in the liturgical life and are occasionally active in charitable, cultural, and educational initiatives. Importantly, since the fall of communism, women gained access to religious education alongside men in the theological faculties that emerged. In the first fifteen years after 1989, women flocked to study theology in greater numbers than men, and only the application of gender quotas kept their share at 50 percent of the theological students. When gender quotas were not applied (different faculties applied them at their own discretion), women made up over 60 percent of the theological students. Very few of these women, however, worked in the field of theology after graduation, and only those who took a second major had decent chances of finding a job after leaving the university. The failed attempts by the Bulgarian Orthodox Church to introduce mandatory religious education in public schools quashed hopes that female theological graduates would find professional realization as teachers in religion.

A theological alumna shared her frustration with the high unemployment rates among the estimated three thousand women who had completed theological studies since 1991:

> We were given a resource, and this resource remained unused. When we raise this issue with the Church hierarchy, the casual advice to us is to find realization as mothers, wives of priests, or nuns. We are doomed to poverty. Despite the efforts we have made to learn, we remain unnoticed and left behind, with wasted lives that could have been so useful. If a woman is not married to a priest, or if she is not a metropolitan's protégée, she would not receive even a basic job in the Church.[32]

This situation confirms that a religious-education training system that is open to women does not necessarily translate into a female presence in the religious job market that is anything more than symbolic.

Furthermore, women have been deterred in various ways from teaching positions in the institutions of higher religious learning. When I returned to Bulgaria from my theological specialization at Oxford University in 1993, I offered to deliver a course of lectures on modern Christian theology to the theological students at Sofia University. I had in mind presenting major contemporary writers from the Catholic and Protestant traditions, on the one hand, and modern Western Orthodox thinkers, on the other. However, I was discouraged even to submit my project for consideration at a faculty meeting. The theological professor with whom I discussed my idea pointed out: "There is no such thing as modern theology!" When I embarked on an argument that I had studied "such a thing" for a whole year at Oxford and that it was a necessary subject because Bulgarian students should have a basic knowledge of Western Christian schools of thought, I was bluntly told: "You obviously have forgotten that you are a woman."

It took the strong will of a sympathetic dean before the first woman was appointed to teach theology at Sofia University in 2002. Currently, only four women teach at the theological faculty of Sofia University, out of twenty-five academic staff. The ratio is similar in the second-largest theological faculty, at Veliko Turnovo University. Some female theologians complained that although the negative attitude toward women's academic ambitions has considerably subsided among the older professors, it has been, alarmingly enough, taken on by members of the junior male faculty.

Since the mid-2000s, the number of theological students declined dramatically, to the point that the theological faculties have struggled increasingly to enroll the cohort of students necessary to keep them running. Recently, with the help of nationalists in government, theology acquired the status of a "protected discipline," to be funded by the state budget irrespective of the number of students it attracts. This development is yet another example of the ongoing neosecularization in Bulgaria.

It is important to point out that the dissemination of religious knowledge among female students at Orthodox theological faculties did not result in the questioning of the traditional male authority structures, let alone in the production and circulation of feminist religious discourses. There have not been any discussions about the historic, cultural, and theological underpinnings of the construction of specific, secondary roles of women in the liturgical and material spaces of the Church. To be sure, female theologians have minimal participation in knowledge production. Furthermore, a theological education that features literalist and conservative religious teachings and relies on outdated pedagogies does not enable women to engage critically with sacred texts and established practices from a female perspective. It instead supports women's internalizing of secondary, complementary roles. My conversations with female theological alumni indicate that they rarely question the traditional male-dominated and male-oriented order in the Church. It seems that the majority of them study, accept, and transmit uncritically gender-discriminative theological discourses. Religious knowledge acquisition at the theological faculties therefore reaffirms asymmetrical gender relations in the family and society and socializes women in nurturing, serving, and caregiving roles.

In rare cases, some female theological graduates are sensitive to the perpetuation of outdated religious teachings about women's supposed inferiority, and these women are typically marginalized. A critically minded alumna complained of the educational process at her theological faculty and particularly of the practice of "most professors reading out outdated lectures by old-time theologians." She noted that women who had studied theology lack critical thinking: "Most of us accept the Church restrictions toward women. Women are deliberately kept in the dark; their questions are not answered in a comprehensive manner. This has to change; the attitude to women should be the same as the attitude to men. We need to return to the early centuries of the Church when women were treated with more respect. There is an acute need for reforms, but it is unclear how these reforms can be carried out."[33] Another alumna concluded: "There is an important place for the pious women's activities in the Church and in society, but women have to claim this place. Unfortunately, those who graduated theology, like most of the observant women, are often too passive and submissive."[34]

Antifeminism

Texts related to "women's issues" in Orthodox Christianity rarely appear in Bulgaria. They are mostly limited to various Orthodox websites that publish occasional translations of (mainly Russian) Orthodox authors. The latter typically emphasize biologically determined and gender-differentiated "gifts and services" in the Church and attack feminism by presenting it in a skewed, generalized way. Feminism is typically seen as a function of female pride, disregard of tradition, willingness to take up male roles, and forgetfulness that a woman's most sacred and elevating role is supposedly motherhood.

The only public discussion on the Church and feminism I was able to locate was organized in 2015 by the Orthodox NGO Pokrov Bogorodichen (The Veil of the Mother of God). I will summarize some of the views expressed during the discussion in order to illustrate the level and content of what seems to be a standard theological conversation on feminism in Bulgaria. The three discussants, a nun and two university theologians, one male and one female, missed a rare opportunity to engage with the topic in a consistent, critical, and in-depth manner. The male theologian deplored feminism, alongside other "-isms" such as "colonialism, racism, sexism, Nazism," as a compensatory mechanism of Western societies related to their colonial and slaveholding pasts. In such societies, averred he, the issue of rights becomes an issue of compensations; therefore "this is not our debate, because we didn't have in the past a traumatic experience, which requires compensation." In his view, "the Christological debate, which positions Christ at the center of all themes, resolves the problem of feminism." He noted that "our debate should be about the human being, not about women and men," while ignoring the fact that in an environment of male supremacy, any supposedly universalist or neutral perspective expresses the dominant male position. The female theologian repeatedly emphasized her great concern that feminism might be arriving in Bulgaria. "Even though we don't yet have problems with feminism, there exist some signs, such as the disintegration of the family, that feminism is making inroads," she suggested. She picked out random quotations by two Western feminist theologians to create a boogeyman image of feminism. She went on to fault women in general for undermining their husbands' authority, which to her was "indicative of how we [women] relate to God." The theologically educated nun noted that women were given the roles of mothers and assistants to the apostles and that these roles are equally important as male roles in the church, so "women should not ask for more." To her, the feminist question par excellence was "Why women can't be priests?" and it revealed women's pride and inferiority complex. "Such is the order of things that has been given to us. Each society requires hierarchy, and this does not go in the way of democracy," she concluded.

This discussion is symptomatic of how Bulgarian Orthodox circles view feminism. It demonstrates not only a lack of knowledge of the basics—let alone the complexities—of feminism but also a conspicuous lack of interest in earnestly engaging the subject.[35] When pressed with questions about women's status, Bulgarian theologians of both sexes emphasize that women in the Church are revered on par with men as martyrs and saints, and they invoke the exalted position of the Mother of God as the New Eve and as a preeminent model of womanhood, celebrated for her obedience to God's will.[36] They also, however, steer clear of issues with which Orthodox women struggle today in the Church and in the larger society, failing to engage what Eleni Sotiriu calls "the ambiguities and contradictions inherent in the tradition" and the "gap between theology and praxis" regarding women's status in Orthodox Christianity.[37] They would reject Western feminist theologies wholesale as deficient and self-indulgent intellectual endeavors of women guilty of the sin of pride. Thus we could say about Bulgaria what Spyridoula Athanasopoulou-Kypriou diagnosed in nearby Orthodox Greece: "Greece has seen the development of an anti-feminist theological discourse before even the formation of a feminist one."[38]

The Orthodox encounter with feminism and feminist theology has occurred mainly through the involvement of Orthodox churches in the ecumenical movement.[39] Consequently, the fact that the Bulgarian Orthodox Church left the World Council of Churches over twenty years ago has no doubt supported further theological stagnation and perpetuated stereotyped and biased representations of and anxious hostility toward feminist ideas. There has hardly been any public mention of the several pan-Orthodox meetings since 1976 that sought to articulate an Orthodox position on the issue of women's roles and service in the Church and argued for the reintroduction of the order of deaconesses.[40] Meaningful debates about women's ordination never happened in Bulgaria, where theologians and clergy continue to frame women's exclusion from ordination through references to the maleness of Jesus Christ and associated biological arguments. This is in contrast to Greece, for example, where in 2002 the Orthodox Church created a synodal committee, with women included, to improve women's roles and participation in ecclesiastical life and to reinstitute the order of deaconesses.[41] The clerics and theologians in Bulgaria have not even started to think in this direction, let alone to deliberate on how religion and the Church are profoundly gendered.

The Backlash against Gender Equality

The Bulgarian Orthodox Church occasionally expresses publicly conservative opinions on gender-related debates such as reproductive rights, abortion, and homosexuality. In 2008, the Church launched a campaign to roll back the country's liberal abortion laws. A gynecologist was denied communion by a priest who appeared on various TV stations to communicate the Church's position that abortion is homicide. The case failed to generate public debate on abortion, which continues to be available on demand.[42] It is indicative, however, of how the Church sees gender equality more generally and women's bodily autonomy more specifically. In terms of reproductive rights, the Bulgarian Orthodox Church rejects most methods of assisted reproduction and surrogate motherhood under the pretext that "they contravene the integrity of marriage."[43]

Furthermore, the Church sees itself as a guardian of so-called traditional values and frequently calls for their legal protection. Addressing a conference on the twenty-fifth anniversary of the adoption of the first postcommunist constitution in the country, Patriarch Neophyte stated in 2018 that "the laws in Bulgaria should be based on traditional values" and asserted that even though the Bulgarian Orthodox Church is separated from the state, it is not separated from the people.[44] This focus on "traditional values" closely mirrors a contemporary ideological narrative dominant in the Russian Orthodox Church, which, in the observation of Stoeckl, invokes "tradition" as a "provider of rules for social and moral behavior and as a source of limitation to individual human rights."[45] Moreover, "traditional values" are used synonymously with patriarchal social and family norms (strictly defined gender differences and roles, a divinely ordained male-female hierarchy) in an ongoing effort to reframe patriarchal order as tradition.

In 2018, the Bulgarian Orthodox Church vehemently opposed government plans to ratify the Council of Europe Convention on preventing and combating violence against women and domestic violence, also known as the Istanbul Convention. It formed an alliance with ultranationalist activists and scored a rare success by focusing the debate on the concept of gender identity. In an unprecedented, well-coordinated action, conservative ecclesiastics and theologians appeared on televised discussions and public debates and even organized a conference to denounce the convention as a "vicious conspiracy" by the West to destroy traditional values and norms in Bulgarian society by spreading "gender ideology" and spearheading "the implantation of an alien value system." They castigated the notion of "gender" as foreign imposed, godless, and hostile to a posited Christian moral order. According to the Holy Synod, "the Istanbul Convention raises concern about the future of the European Christian civilization because it includes a new understanding of human beings as absolute masters without God, who follow their wills and passions to the extent of self-defining their own gender. This understanding opens the gates of moral destruction." The Synod said it supported efforts to root out violence, especially violence against women, but condemned "the Istanbul Convention's ideas of gender and criticism of religion, traditions, customs, and education, as contradicting the traditional understandings of the Bulgarian nation about faith, nationality, morality, honor, dignity, upbringing, family."[46]

In its official statement, the Synod insisted that the convention tried to introduce "a third gender," but "sex can be only biologically defined because man and woman are a creation of God." It expressed concerns regarding the convention's Article 12, which calls for the eradication of "prejudices, customs, traditions, and all other practices which are based on the idea of the inferiority of women or on stereotyped roles for women and men"[47]—thus inadvertently displaying its attitude toward women's equality. The Church hierarchy's take on the document leaves an impression that they do not see violence against women as a serious social issue, even though they have condemned it in general terms. Furthermore, in a baffling effort to denounce the convention, the Synod ordered parish priests to serve a special prayer

called the "Canon of the Holy Mother of God" so that it wouldn't be ratified. "It is shameful that we were decreed to pray against the Istanbul Convention instead of praying for women who have been battered and suffered
various forms of violence," Father Alexander told me.[48]

The other mainline religious communities—the Muslims, the Catholics, and several Protestant churches—joined the position that femininity
and masculinity can only be biologically defined and rejected the notion of
"gender" as a socially defined sex. They shared concerns about a perceived
threat to "traditional morality" and the "traditional family," in terms borrowed from the increasingly visible and audible discourse of transnational
conservative-fundamentalist religious alliances.[49] Major political parties fell
in line, wary of losing votes, and the convention was ultimately rejected
after the Constitutional Court pronounced it unconstitutional. The voices of
intellectuals, feminist academics, and NGOs who insisted that the document aimed to prevent and reduce violence against women were stifled by
what looked like a well-coordinated propaganda campaign.[50] There was
no in-depth social debate about women and children who had suffered violence; a substantial and much-needed discussion was thus replaced by rhetorical antigender statements about traditional values, social norms, and
national identity, statements in which the Church took an active role.
The Church itself did not offer any practical help to women and children
traumatized by violence by, for example, opening safe houses or organizing free consultations for them in conjunction with psychologists and
lawyers.[51]

"Only three or four of the clerics read the text of the convention; most
people in the Church discussed something they did not really know. Even
though the article about the social construction of gender was awful, the
rest was acceptable, and the document should have been ratified save for the
gender part," Father Marin told me. In his view, "violence against women
is related to the decline of the traditional family, and the fight against this
violence is possible only through the promotion of the 'small church': a
harmonious family in the spirit of the tradition we have inherited."[52]

A female lawyer, who is also a practicing Orthodox Christian, commented:

> From a legislative perspective, we already have a legal regulation to de-
> fend women and children against violence, but it is not being applied.
> I mediate family disputes, and I have stories of battered women who

turned to the police for support and were ridiculed by the psychologists hired by the police. There are shelters for battered women, but they are not advertised, and the society knows very little about them. Therefore we have problems on a structural level, with the mentality and mechanisms of application rather than with a lack of legislation. The Church plays a role in making women think of themselves as subordinate to men, in supporting a mentality of gender discrimination.[53]

Conclusion

Unable to overcome fully its communist legacies and to respond adequately to the challenges of democratization and the attendant neoliberal market reforms in the aftermath of 1989, the Bulgarian Orthodox Church entangled itself in internal arguments and splits. It failed to provide spiritual and moral guidance to its followers and to act as a meaning-creating agency, a failure most apparent during the hardships of a painful economic and sociopolitical transition. Consequently, it lost much of the authority it had recovered with the fall of communism. "Symphonic" alliances of the Bulgarian Orthodox Church with political power,[54] the focus on ritual and ceremonial performances, and the neglect of social service[55] led to a growing distancing of the Church from the life and concerns of its adherents. Consequently, the overwhelming majority of people who self-identify as Orthodox do not coordinate their lives with the church calendar, even though many attend Christmas and Easter services and a couple of other major feasts. Very few accept unconditionally or comply fully with religious prescriptions. This is especially true of issues related to sexual and marital life, abortion, and divorce. Even when Orthodoxy is interiorized by its observant followers, it is rarely seen as a comprehensive doctrine, one that defines all major aspects of life.

Under the conditions of neosecularization, women continue to be the major constituency that keeps the church alive. Despite mass detachment of Orthodox Bulgarians from the institutionalized Church, Orthodox Christianity is an important part of the historical heritage and national identity. This is how the Bulgarian Orthodox Church remains a factor in the social organization of difference, including in the sphere of gender. There hardly exist any depoliticized and denationalized forms of Orthodox Christianity, which emphasize the personal relationship with God and deemphasize the role of Orthodoxy as a marker of national belonging.

Under the pretext of "defending tradition," the Bulgarian Orthodox Church has supported conservative social norms and gender-distinct roles in the Church, the family, and in the job market, thus perpetuating a gender-complimentary model based on structural patriarchy. It has not conducted a debate on the status of women in the Church or developed women-sensitive interpretations of exclusivist statements in the Bible and in the texts of the Church Fathers. Orthodox discourses of binary gender relations, male dominance, and auxiliary female roles have played an important part in what Kizenko calls "the cultivation of a non-liberal femininity"[56] among female theological students and a larger body of devout female constituencies.

Patriarchal attitudes and practices remain an important tenet of Orthodox Christianity and have a limiting effect on women's agency.[57] Conservative ecclesiastics and theologians have continuously aligned themselves with secular patriarchy by supporting nationalist ideologies and opposing gender equality, something that was particularly prominent during the 2018 public debates about the ratification of the Istanbul Convention. However, Orthodoxy is not the sole factor determining female subjugation; it intersects with political, social, cultural, and economic forces, all of which need to be taken into consideration when explaining how women operate under specific historical conditions and how gender regimes are formed and transformed. The continued marginalization of women in Orthodox Christianity post-1989 has correlated with larger processes of rising gender asymmetry and male domination in society.

Even though women are consistently silenced in ecclesiastical spaces and in the theological faculties, there exist observant women who are critical of gender discrimination. Their positions, nonetheless, remain marginal and are hardly ever publicly expressed, which accounts for the lack of female religious voices seeking gender justice, equality, and women's advancement in the Church and in the wider society. Activists in the secular feminist scene insist that the Church is sexist and inherently patriarchal and write off any dialogue with it. "Feminists are hostile to us; they think religion is a source of evil, and they never come to talk with us," complained the secretary of the Holy Synod.[58] Religious feminism is nonexistent, and even the mention of it sends tremors of apprehension among clerics and theologians, who are quick to denounce it as irrelevant to the local conditions.

To be sure, practicing Orthodox women come from all walks of life; they pertain to widely differing ideological, professional, social, and economic profiles; and their faith commitment varies and shifts in different stages of their lives. They sometimes comply and sometimes don't comply with official Church pronouncements. They often approach religion in an individualized manner, according to their personal life situations and concerns. Furthermore, the realities of neosecularization considerably curtail, even though they do not obliterate, the influence of the Church on gender relations in society.

Notes

The final revisions of this chapter were done during my visiting fellowship at the Leibniz Institute for East and Southeast European Studies in Regensburg, Germany, in early 2020. I am grateful to my colleagues at the institute for their comments and feedback.

1. Personal communication, July 1, 2018.

2. Cf. Jose Casanova, "Secularisation Revisited: A Reply to Talal Asad," in *Powers of the Secular Modern*, ed. David Scott and Charles Hirschkind (Stanford, CA: Stanford University Press, 2006), 12.

3. Bryan Wilson, *Religion in Sociological Perspective* (Oxford: Oxford University Press, 1982), 150.

4. Peter Berger, *The Sacred Canopy: Elements of a Sociological Theory of Religion* (New York: Doubleday, 1967).

5. For interpretations of nationalism as a political religion, see Ina Merdjanova, *Religion, Nationalism, and Civil Society—The Postcommunist Palimpsest* (Lampeter: Edwin Mellen, 2002), 71–78.

6. Peter Beyer, *Religion and Globalization* (London: Sage, 1994), 107.

7. For a detailed discussion of neosecularization as a sociological paradigm, see Vesna Malesevic, "Ireland and Neo-secularisation," *Irish Journal of Sociology* 18, no. 1 (2010): 22–42.

8. See Mark Chaves, "Secularization as Declining Religious Authority," *Social Forces* 72, no. 3 (1994): 749–74. The author calls for a new approach to secularization, which situates religion and religious change in a concrete historical and institutional context and focuses on the decreasing or increasing scope of religious authority rather than on the decline or resurgence of religion.

9. Personal communication, September 19, 2018.

10. According to data from the national censuses, there has been a decline of both historic religions of Bulgaria: Orthodox Christianity and Islam. The latter shrank from 13 percent in 1992 to 12.2 percent in 2001 and to 10 percent in 2011. http://www.nsi.bg/census2011/PDOCS2/Census2011final_en.pdf. The data is based on the numbers of the people who answered the question about

the religious affiliation, which in the 2011 census was optional, and 21.8 percent of the total population didn't answer it.

11. World Values Survey, Bulgaria 2006, http://www.worldvaluessurvey.org /WVSDocumentationWV5.jsp.

12. Pew Research Center, Religion in Public Life, Orthodox Christianity in the Twenty-First Century, November 8, 2017, http://www.pewforum.org/2017 /11/08/orthodox-christianity-in-the-21st-century/.

13. I use the antonym of Casanova's term "churching" when he speaks about the "progressive churching" of the American population. Casanova, "Secularisation Revisited," 16.

14. "Belonging without believing" is the opposite condition to what Grace Davie described as "believing without belonging." See Grace Davie, "Believing without Belonging: Is This the Future of Religion in Britain?" *Social Compass* 37, no. 4 (1990): 455–69.

15. Compare Weber, who distinguishes between "cultic communities" and "genuine religions of salvation." Max Weber, *The Sociology of Religion* (Boston: Beacon, 1993).

16. OSI, "Democracy and Civil Participation: Public Attitudes towards Democracy, the Rule of Law, and the Fundamental Human Rights in 2016," Sofia, February 28, 2017, http://osi.bg/downloads/File/2017/Democracy%20 Survey%202016%20ENG.pdf.

17. For an illuminating discussion of "traditional Orthodoxy," see George Demacopoulos, "'Traditional Orthodoxy' as a Postcolonial Movement," *Journal of Religion* 97 (2017): 475–99.

18. New religious movements, which spread in the country after 1989, are viewed rather negatively by the Church and pejoratively called "sects." See the subchapter "Traditional Churches and New Religious Movements" in Merdjanova, *Religion, Nationalism, and Civil Society*, 33–48.

19. Bulgaria is the most corrupt member state in the EU, according to Transparency International. "Transparency International: Bulgaria Is the Most Corrupt Country in Europe," *Sofia Globe*, January 25, 2017, https://sofiaglobe .com/2017/01/25/transparency-international-bulgaria-is-the-most-corrupt -country-in-europe/.

20. Извънредно съобщение на Св. Синод на БПЦ по повод кризата с бежанците [Special announcement of the Holy Synod of the Bulgarian Orthodox church with reference to the refugee crisis], November 26, 2016, http://www.bg-patriarshia.bg/news.php?id=184530.

21. Personal communication, September 19, 2018.

22. Personal communication, September 18, 2018.

23. Personal communication, July 4, 2018.

24. Personal communication, September 19, 2018.

25. Personal communication, September 19, 2018.

26. Shocking statistics in 2010 indicated that every fourth woman in Bulgaria is a victim of domestic violence. "Всяка четвърта българка - жертва на домашно насилие" ["Every fourth Bulgarian woman—victim of domestic violence"], *Vesti*, March 6, 2010, https://www.vesti.bg/bulgaria/obshtestvo/25 -ot-bylgarkite-zhertva-na-domashno-nasilie-2819211. However, not only do very few women in Bulgaria seem to report domestic violence, but violence against women as such is rarely discussed in the public sphere.

27. Mary Hawkeswarth argues that democracy is most often understood as "a Euro-American model of male-male-dominant democratic elitism," and thus the gendered democratic process reaffirmed male-biased gender regimes both within the household and within the public, political sphere. Mary E. Hawkeswarth, "Democratization: Reflections on Gendered Dislocations in the Public Sphere," in *Gender, Globalization, and Democratization*, ed. Rita Mae Kelly, Jane Bayes, Mary E. Hawkeswarth, and Brigitte Yung (Lanham, MD: Rowman and Littlefield, 2001), 223–36.

28. Personal communication, September 21, 2018.

29. *Bulgaria: A Country Study*, ed. Glenn E. Curtis (Washington: GPO for the Library of Congress, 1992), "Religion," http://countrystudies.us/bulgaria/26 .htm.

30. Personal communication, September 19, 2018. It was not possible to find agreed-upon statistics for the number of functioning monasteries and the number of monastics in the country today. The 205 monasteries quoted here obviously include both functioning and nonfunctioning sites. Twenty of the monasteries are nonfunctioning because of a lack of monastics. For example, a 2013 PhD study on the functioning Bulgarian monasteries by Atanas Kazakov lists ninety-seven such monasteries. Атанас Казаков, "Действащите български манастири: перспективи за туристическо развитие," PhD diss., Sofia University, 23–29. However, estimates from various sources converge on the fact that the number of nuns is higher than that of monks.

31. According to the secretary of the Holy Synod, in the Synod itself, out of the seventy-two administrative staff, forty-eight are women who work as secretaries and accountants. Personal communication, September 19, 2018.

32. Personal communication, September 19, 2018.

33. Personal communication, July 15, 2018.

34. Personal communication, July 13, 2018.

35. The discussion (in Bulgarian) can be found at https://www.pravoslavie.bg /пол/църквата-и-феминизмът/.

36. About similar theological discussions in Greece, compare Eleni Sotiriu, "Contested Masculine Spaces in Greek Orthodoxy," *Social Compass* 51, no. 4 (2004): 499–510, esp. 501.

37. Sotiriu, "Contested Masculine Spaces," 502.

38. Spyridoula Athanasopoulou-Kypriou, "The Reaction of Greek Orthodox Theology to the Challenges of Feminist Theology," in *Gendering Transformations*, ed. Yota Papageorgiou (Rethymno: University of Crete, 2007), 16.

39. Sotiriu, "Contested Masculine Spaces," 500.

40. In 1988, an All-Orthodox Symposium held in Rhodos, Greece, declared that the ancient order of female deacons, which existed until the eleventh century, should be revived. A number of follow-up international Orthodox meetings held around the world discussed and reiterated this decision, which, however, was not put into practice, mainly because of fears that it could be a first step toward the future ordination of women as priests.

41. Eleni Sotiriu, "'The Traditional Modern': Rethinking the Position of Contemporary Greek Women in Orthodoxy," in *Orthodox Christianity in Twenty-First-Century Greece: The Role of Religion in Culture, Ethnicity, and Politics*, ed. Victor Roudometof and Vasilios N. Makrides (Surrey: Ashgate, 2010), 140.

42. This antiabortion campaign is described in Lavinia Stan, "Eastern Orthodox Views on Sexuality and the Body," *Women's Studies International Forum* 33 (2010): 38–46, esp. 45.

43. The Church blesses only artificial inseminations in which material from the married couple is used and embryos are being implanted in the wife's body. See *Становище на Св. Синод на Българската православна църква за методите на асистирана репродукция и заместващо майчинство* [Statement of the Holy Synod of the Bulgarian Orthodox Church on the methods of assisted reproduction and surrogate motherhood], http://www.bg -patriarshia.bg/index.php?file=attitude_6.xml.

44. "Законите да стъпват на традиционните ценности" [The laws should be based on traditional values], *Стандарт* [*Standard*], July 13, 2018, http://paper.standartnews.com/bg/article.php?d=2016-07-13&article=258237.

45. Kristina Stoeckl, *The Russian Orthodox Church and Human Rights* (London: Routledge, 2014), 73.

46. Обръщение на Св. Синод относно процедурата по приемане и ратифициране в България на Истанбулската конвенция [Address of the Holy Synod regarding the procedure for the adoption and ratification of the Istanbul Convention], January 22, 2018, http://www.bg-patriarshia.bg/news .php?id=254118.

47. Становище на Светия Синод по повод Истанбулската конвенция [Statement of the Holy Synod regarding the Istanbul Convention], January 22, 2018, http://www.bg-patriarshia.bg/news.php?id=254101.

48. Personal communication, July 1, 2018.

49. Some feminist activists in Bulgaria with whom I talked observed that the conservative campaign against the Istanbul Convention might have been

inspired and financially supported by outside organizations such as the Christian right-wing group World Congress of Families (WCF) through its Russian links. For an analysis of the WCF's activities worldwide, see L. Cole Parke, "Natural Deception: Conned by the World Congress of Families," *Public Eye*, January 21, 2015, https://www.politicalresearch.org/2015/01/21/natural-deception-conned -by-the-world-congress-of-families. I am not able here to prove or disprove this observation. It seems, however, that the successful campaign against the Istanbul Convention marked the beginning of an antigender *kulturkampf* of a sort in Bulgaria, which is also fueled by para-Church actors (NGOs and lay theologians) and which follows in the step of similar antigender wars already raging in several postcommunist majority-Catholic countries, such as Slovakia, Poland, Croatia, and Slovenia, as well as in Russia.

50. About the debate on the Istanbul Convention, see, among others, Stanislav Dodov, "It Was Never about the Istanbul Convention," *LeftEast*, August 2, 2018, http://www.criticatac.ro/lefteast/it-was-never-about-the -istanbul-convention/#.W6ubWHZjT5U.

51. Plamen Ivanov, "Istanbulskata konvenciya u misionerskata deinost na Balgarskata pravoslavna carva" [The Istanbul Convention and the missionary activity of the Bulgarian Orthodox Church], *Hristiyanstvo i kultura*, March 28, 2018, http://www.hkultura.com/articles/detailed/130.

52. Personal communication, September 18, 2018.

53. Personal communication, July 20, 2018.

54. "Symphony" is a theologicopolitical principle in Orthodox Christianity, which was developed in the sixth century by the Byzantine emperor Justinian I. According to it, the Church and the state function in a symphonic interdependency, wherein the former takes care of divine matters and the latter of worldly affairs.

55. As His Eminence Gerasim, the secretary of the Synod told me, "Orthodox Christianity takes care of the afterlife, and its social role is secondary." Conversation, September 19, 2018.

56. Nadieszda Kizenko, "Feminized Patriarchy? Orthodoxy and Gender in Post-Soviet Russia," *Journal of Women in Culture and Society* 38, no. 3 (2013): 602.

57. This observation corroborates the findings of wider studies such as the analysis of the World Values and European Values Surveys for the period of 1995–2001 by Inglehart and Norris, according to which cultural factors, especially religious outlooks, influence gender equality in societies. Ronald Inglehart and Pippa Norris, *Rising Tide: Gender Equality and Cultural Change around the World* (Cambridge: Cambridge University Press, 2003).

58. Personal communication, September 19, 2018.

LAY WOMEN AND THE TRANSFORMATION OF ORTHODOX CHRISTIANITY IN RUSSIA

Detelina Tocheva

After the disintegration of the Soviet system and the replacement of atheist policies by state-sponsored pro-Orthodox stances, women's multifaceted participation in the life of the Orthodox Church has been instrumental for both the promotion of Orthodoxy and the consolidation of the place of the Russian Orthodox Church (Patriarchate of Moscow) in Russian society. Women are engaged in a wide variety of church-related activities. In most parish churches, women clean and sell candles and books. At a higher level, women teach the faith and other subjects to youth and adults in parishes and in private Orthodox schools. Women participate in church choirs, an essential component of Orthodox liturgical life, as singers and choir directors. While some contribute to modest parish newsletters and websites, others run major Orthodox media outlets.[1] Some women run departments and organizations placed under the authority of the Church. A national Union of Orthodox Women was established in 2010 with the blessing of Patriarch Kirill.[2] Lay initiatives with marked female participation, such as Orthodox pilgrimages, Orthodox antiabortion advice services, and special expiation prayers have become popular, as have lay intercessory prayers, ordered in a church or a monastery or performed by lay faithful, predominantly women, as a form of care for significant others.[3] The Blessed Kseniia of Petersburg and Saint Matrona of Moscow are the two most popular female saints in contemporary Russia, known for their capacity to help with the problems with which most Russians, especially women, struggle. The Church canonized them as part of its efforts to regain popularity after seven decades of militant atheism.[4] As

76

Nadieszda Kizenko has put it: "The two groups traditionally missing in Orthodox Christianity's power circles—women and parish clergy—have together risen to positions of new prominence in the postperestroika era."[5] Even though, as Kizenko has suggested, the post-Soviet feminization of Orthodox Christianity would hardly undermine the patriarchal structures of the Church, important transformations are underway. This chapter discusses the transformations of Russian Orthodox Christianity related to women's participation and work in church parishes.

A substantial post-Soviet novelty is that thousands of devout women have made local churches, pilgrimage services, and parish schools their workplace, and thus women play important roles in the everyday functioning of the parishes. Given the feminization of parish staff, both officially and informally, it might seem strange that theological arguments about the ordination of women advanced by Orthodox theologians based in the West have not been discussed in post-Soviet Russia—either by female believers or by clergymen.[6] Locally, gender disparities between the dominant male clergy and subordinate female staff in the parishes have never been questioned. The lower material reward for women as parish workers even when they are full-time employees has never been interrogated. One can argue that in addition to doctrinal teachings, patriarchal culture, or what Rivkin-Fish calls justification of local knowledge in cultural common sense,[7] is key to the reproduction of embedded gender inequalities in the Church.

However, despite that patriarchal local knowledge and common sense have supported the reproduction of gender inequality within Church structures, at the same time they have also authorized, and even encouraged, a discreet cultural turn in the Church. While doctrinal positions have remained essentially attached to the patriarchal principle, the fundamental role of women in the operation of the parishes has prompted tentative change. Parish priests hire women because of their professional skills and knowledge. Women serve as parish school teachers and school leaders, pilgrimage and church event organizers, choir directors, and parish bookkeepers. Many of these parish employees are single mothers; they are de facto the heads of their households—and parish priests have thus tacitly recognized their single motherhood as a "normal" social specificity that does not preclude women's professional service in the Church. This recognition has been neither a conscious decision nor a reappraisal of certain canonical rules. Neither has it occurred as a result of feminist advocacy. It has rather been the corollary of navigating the mundane technicalities and the challenges of everyday parish operation. This tacit recognition has been prompted by the clergy's search for pragmatic solutions to ordinary parish problems. However, it also reveals how women have acquired key roles in the transformation of Orthodoxy at the parish level.

In what follows, I provide a background discussion of women as professionals and single mothers in Russia, and I describe the official positions of the Church regarding women, work, and the family. Further, I investigate the process of the feminization of parish structures by looking at the life trajectories of two Orthodox women who are parish workers. The first acts as the head of a parish school and contributes to the parish website and newsletter. The second has worked for many years as a parish bookkeeper. The two are single mothers. Their life trajectories and their views of themselves as parish workers and of the reasons why they were drawn closer to the Church provide useful illustrations of the process of feminization of the parish staff and of how this feminization both reasserts patriarchal relations and brings about change. The data about the post-Soviet processes at the parish level of the Church are drawn from my ethnographic fieldwork conducted mainly, but not only, in the parishes of a small city located in the region of Saint Petersburg, in northwestern Russia, which I call here Ozerovo.[8]

Women as Professionals and Single Mothers

If the prominence of women in the contemporary Church has no precedent in history, women were by no means absent or unrepresented in the past. Throughout the history of Russian Orthodoxy, women have played important roles as religious practitioners, supporters of the Church, monastics, and saintly figures.[9] Women have borne witness to the powers of miracle-working icons and relics, which led to the recognition of those powers by the wider community of faithful and by the clergy.[10] Since the demise of the Soviet system, the Soviet and post-Soviet legacies regarding women's professional occupations, motherhood, and gender relations have given an original twist to the role of women in the Church and have surreptitiously reshaped the Church from within. Being skilled professionals and single mothers are two widespread sociological characteristics of women in Russia. Their acceptance as "normal" is part of the "common sense." They do not really clash with the basic Church positions about women and the family. Nonetheless, their silent recognition by the Church indirectly challenges two key Russian Orthodox ideological standpoints. The first posits that women are primordially mothers and that their professional lives are of secondary importance. The second defines the family as a patriarchal unit with a husband-father as its head. In this section, I discuss these two sociological characteristics of women in Russia, looking at how they relate to the Church's official position.

Women in the Labor Market

In order to grasp the characteristics and dynamics of women's participation in the life of the Church as parish workers, it is important to understand the wider context of Russian society. In contemporary Russia, women's mass participation in the labor market continues an entrenched Soviet practice. Another Soviet legacy is the continuous assignment to women of lower positions and lower salaries than those of men, even when they have the same qualifications and skills. The post-Soviet politics of gender, however, is not a mere continuation of the Soviet practices. The demise of the Soviet system prompted the emergence of "state patriarchy," which manifested in part in the promotion of "Russian traditional values" by both the state and the Church. As Anna Temkina and Elena Zdravomyslova have put it,

> The reaction to the Soviet legacy and its patriarchal model turned traditional patriarchy, with its naturalization of gender roles, into an appealing alternative to the Soviet notions of masculinity and femininity and its hypocritical policy of gender equality. Ideologies of gender equality and gender freedom seemed ever more out of place as the rhetoric of getting back to national traditions infiltrated public discourse and set the terms of choice.[11]

Since 2000, when Vladimir Putin came to power, the improvement of fertility rates has been a top political agenda. Neotraditionalist images of the nuclear family surfaced, reasserting the primordial role of the woman as birth giver and care provider.[12] The Russian Orthodox Church, in alliance with the political powers, played a key role in promoting these ideas. This powerful patriarchal and pronatalist political discourse has not affected the level of women's employment, and women's participation in the labor market has reached levels similar to those for men. But the overall cultural and political patriarchal bent has had an effect at the level of wages. Women's

salaries have steadily remained lower than men's. A large-scale study conducted by the NGO Oxfam Russia found that, on average, "women are paid
64 percent of the pay of men for their work."[13] The realities of women's
official and informal employment at the parish level therefore reflect the
larger situation with women's work status in Russia.[14]

Recognizing a woman as a good professional is not at odds with the basic theological positions regarding women and the family as reflected in
the "Basis of the Social Concept of the Russian Orthodox Church," the
most important recent theological document adopted by the Church.
Adopted in 2000, the "Basis of the Social Concept" aimed at updating the
Church's positions on a wide range of issues in order to respond to the societal challenges of the postcommunist era. In a chapter titled "Personal,
Family, and Public Morality," this document extensively argues that male
dominance is the only acceptable principle of gender relations and that
women are intrinsically defined by motherhood. The position regarding
women's employment outside of the family home is expressed in the context of a warning to both women and men against the neglect of motherhood and fatherhood in the pursuit of professional careers:

> The living continuity of generations, beginning in family, is contin-
> ued in the love of the forefathers and fatherland, in the feeling of
> participation in history. This is why it is so dangerous to distort the
> traditional parents-child relationship, which, unfortunately, has been
> in many ways endangered by the contemporary way of life. The di-
> minished social significance of motherhood and fatherhood com-
> pared to the progress made by men and women in the professional
> field leads to the treatment of children as an unnecessary burden, con-
> tributing also to the development of alienation and antagonism be-
> tween generations.[15]

The argument is interwoven with nationalistic considerations. The professional life of women is addressed in general terms expressing concern
that their professional careers might take precedence over their maternal
duties. The document fails to attend to the fact that, under the conditions
of Russia's neoliberal market capitalism, the work market is highly demanding to women, who are likely to be judged with more rigor and inflexibil-
ity than their male colleagues. It ignores the fact that some of the most
physically and mentally demanding jobs, in sectors such as healthcare, education, and public services, which also pay poorly, are predominantly

filled by women. The document does not provide a spiritual guidance of how women are to combine their extremely demanding jobs with a motherhood that matches the high standards set by the Church. Finally, the Church hierarchs leave aside a contradiction internal to their own institution: the fact that thousands of women are employed in parishes first and foremost for their professional skills yet on salaries lower than those of the men, especially the clergy, with little consideration of how those women manage to make a living and support their family. In practice, the task of harmonizing professional careers and motherhood is left to women, who seek guidance from spiritual advisors, in various Orthodox publications, and from lectures of priests available on the internet, online journals, and forums.[16] It is also revealing that in the bemoaning of "the diminished social significance of motherhood and fatherhood compared to the progress made by men and women in the professional field," motherhood comes first and fatherhood second. It looks like the emphasis on motherhood, over that on fatherhood, echoes a secular, commonsense view in Soviet and post-Soviet Russia that mothers are the pillars of the family while fathers are of secondary importance and in many cases simply unimportant. This consideration brings us to the issue of single motherhood.

Single Motherhood

Among the contemporary lay Orthodox believers, single mothers are as common as married mothers and mothers who live with a partner. Around one-third of Russia's children are born out of wedlock. Single motherhood, from being socially stigmatized yet widespread in Soviet times, became, in the post-Soviet era, culturally accepted and considered "normal" by both the single mothers themselves and wider society. Some single mothers are divorced, others are widowed, and others were never married. A common characteristic is that they raise their children aged under eighteen without a father or partner. The support provided by their own aged mothers is often instrumental, but some have to rely on their own capacity to earn a living and care for their children.[17] Being a single mother is a widespread condition also among women who are parish workers, whether they hold a permanent or an occasional position as a parish employee. Married mothers with more than two children have progressively become more represented among parish workers in recent years. Their families reflect the Orthodox ideal of large patriarchal families. But they have remained marginal in comparison to mothers with one or two children and in comparison to single mothers.

The ideal of the large patriarchal family endures among the committed Orthodox. In the post-Soviet era, a new popular imaginary appeared, one densely populated by romanticized portraits of noble men and women from a historically vague period commonly referred to as "before the Revolution." For many post-Soviet Orthodox believers, this was an idealized era of political harmony, elevated morality, and strong faith. In the 1990s, it provided a counterimage to the current political and economic turmoil, the abrupt collapse of the Soviet social hierarchies, and the widespread social distress.[18] During my field research in Ozerovo, I encountered numerous mothers and grandmothers, but also some fathers and uncles, who frequented the main parish school with some regularity. While accompanying their children and staying to chat sometimes for hours during the Sunday classes, some of them carried out their own religious socialization. More knowledgeable and observant Orthodox parents also enjoyed socializing during innumerable tea-drinking afternoons in this school. Conversations often revolved around pre-Revolutionary Orthodox piety and the Soviet-era ignorance of religion. Many did not hesitate to speak of their own lack of knowledge about Orthodoxy at the beginning of the post-Soviet transformations. In the eyes of these Orthodox believers, the family of the last tsar, Nicolas II, provided a model for family relationships and piety. Canonized in 2000 as "passion bearers," meaning persons who suffered bloody repression (the tsar and his family were murdered by the Bolsheviks in 1918) but not killed because of their faith, this type of saint represents a model of elevated morality and spirituality. In the context of the deep social, economic, and political transformations after the fall of the Soviet regime, the last royal family has been considered by sympathizers as a model family profoundly attached to the Orthodox principles of patriarchy, mutual love, and love for the Lord.[19] A teacher even embellished the walls in his school's dining room with portraits of Russia's Romanov-dynasty royal families. As my interlocutors from the parish school admired those moral-spiritual portraits, I could not help but notice not only the gap between their own social worlds and that of the model persons they admired but also the discrepancy between the family models of those idealized persons and the realities of present-day Russian society. Many of the pupils and half of the parish school teachers who admired the royal family and taught children that the father is the legitimate head of the household lived in families without adult men to perform the idealized, pivotal role of the father-husband.

In the frame of female parish activism and Orthodox education, being a single mother is not a minority condition, either. Among most of the female parish school workers and mothers of pupils whom I have encountered over the years, this is a typical situation that no one, including the priests, finds out of order. There is a striking contrast between the image of the patriarchal family that women engaged in Orthodox education are prone to praise highly and those women's actual families, where men are absent because of early death or because they have left, often shortly after the birth of a child. Middle-aged women working for local churches told me that after having lived for a short period with a man they actually preferred not to repeat this experience in order to avoid problems of, in their words, drinking and "typical male laziness." They considered it a better option to remain "without men" and rely on the support of their own trustworthy, elderly mothers. For most of them, the ideal epitomized by the last royal family is a romantic picture of the old times but is confined to books and posters, like the one hanging on the wall of the dining room in Ozerovo's main parish school.

The Church has ignored the normalization of single motherhood that emerged during the Soviet era and became culturally accepted in contemporary society. The Soviet and post-Soviet transformations transfigured family models, too. Family models on the ground have become extremely dynamic and fluid, as real families evolve and transform over the life trajectories of their members. The multiple forms of single-mother families and the various ways these mothers experience their situation, far from the stereotypical image of the suffering, weak woman, is what Jennifer Utrata called "a quiet revolution." Utrata's study demonstrated that single motherhood is frequently defined by those mothers in terms of choice, and when it is not, it is often considered as a lesser evil than having to support a (drinking) man in addition to assuming the double burden of domestic and salaried work.[20] Parish priests and every single church worker are aware of these realities. Most clergymen know from personal experience that nearly a third of Russia's children, including those in their parish, come of age in families where the de facto head of the household is the mother. Yet the Church has not reflected on these facts. The "Basis of the Social Concept" totally ignores them and instead insists on the principle of male dominance in the family:

**While appreciating the social role of women and welcoming their
political, cultural, and social equality with men, the Church opposes
the tendency to diminish the role of woman as wife and mother.
The fundamental equality of the sexes does not annihilate the
natural distinction between them, nor does it imply the identity of
their callings in family and society.** In particular, the Church cannot
misconstrue the words of St. Paul about the special responsibility of
the husband, who is called to be "the head of the wife" who loves her
as Christ loves His Church, and about the calling of the wife to obey
the husband as the Church obeys Christ (Eph. 5:22–23; Col. 3:18).[21]

In her research on Orthodox female psychologists who participate in
the antiabortion campaigns of the Church, Sonja Luehrmann has noted
the stunning discrepancy between the conservative, so-called pre-
Revolutionary male-centered family ideal promoted by Orthodox female
activists and the realities of practical life: "For the family values activists
themselves, the past is a source of authoritative models rather than alternative trajectories."[22] In championing conservative family values, these urban, educated, and self-confident women mobilize the Soviet legacies that
made Russian women part of the public space and led to the cultural recognition of women as professionals. As therapists and counselors, they
"make assumptions about actually existing support networks that often emphasize matrilineal descent and female inter- and intragenerational solidarity
over male progenitors or providers."[23] A longing for social and political
order in Russia and for a distinctively Russian self-assertion vis-à-vis the
West lurks behind the promotion of such values and models. Priests, parish
workers, and Orthodox activists can continue to further sustain this discrepancy as long as the arrangements they find in navigating the practical
challenges of contemporary Russian society and politics help them adver-
tise their messages and reach out to a wider public. But more importantly,
I take inspiration from Luehrmann's findings and bring my own data
from ethnographic fieldwork to argue that the pragmatic acceptance of
real-life norms and values within Church structures has far-reaching reper-
cussions because it has set the conditions for a tacit cultural, even though
not doctrinal, turn in the Church.

The engagement of lay women in parishes, which are the basic territorial
units of the Church, has been instrumental to the everyday operation of
the churches after 1991. In exploring this feminization of the parishes,

I argue that female professionalism and single motherhood have become intrinsic characteristics of contemporary parish life. I look at the cases of two women who are single mothers and who have worked for their respective parishes since the mid-1990s. I was able to witness their family and professional trajectories over more than ten years, since 2006 and 2007, respectively. The first sees herself as a skilled professional, indispensable to her parish, who works simultaneously as a journalist and a parish school director. To her, being a single mother was not the incentive to pursue a career in the Church structure. The second points to her situation as a single mother as the main motivation bringing her closer to the church, where she has also taken a bookkeeping job. Despite this difference between the two cases, they are nonetheless representative in two respects. Single motherhood among parish workers is as common as it is in Russian society at large. Similarly, within the parish microcosm and in the country's job market, education and bookkeeping are typically female occupations. By using the example of the lives of these two women, I seek to illustrate two of the multiple ways that women have participated in creating a cultural turn in post-Soviet Orthodoxy and, more particularly, in normalizing within the Church a situation that has already been socially accepted.

Claiming Professionalism

Parish schools illustrate particularly well the participation of women as skilled professionals in the operation of Orthodox education and in church life more broadly. The team of teachers in the largest parish school in Ozerovo is composed of women and, despite occasional staff changes from the opening of the school in the early 1990s to the present moment, the situation has not changed in terms of gender makeup. One can distinguish between the official and the unofficial but immensely important hierarchies. The official director of the school is the church rector (*nastoiatel'*); the spiritual leader (*dukhovnik*), who comes second on the formal scale of importance, is also a priest in the same church. The portraits of these two clergymen appear first on the website of the school. The top of the informal hierarchy begins with a third photograph, of the woman who is the actual head of the school, officially hired by the parish as a "deputy director." All the teachers, without exception, are women. They teach "The Law of God," a basic subject included in all formal Orthodox courses; Church Slavonic; the history of the Church; Orthodox singing; and technical and art classes such as sewing, drawing, pottery, and photography. The female composition of the school's staff is not a local peculiarity but a widespread condition. With the Orthodox revival, women have assumed important new tasks in the sphere of religious education both by teaching at the parish level and by bringing Orthodox education to secular schools when they are employed there as professional school teachers.[24] Besides education, at the parish level women work as church cleaners and church shop sellers, perform gatekeeping functions, organize pilgrimages for the parishes, and provide bookkeeping services. Women are not ordained and cannot be recognized as "servants of the sacred"; therefore, they do not belong to the official clerical hierarchy. However, the multiple roles they play are organized in formal and informal hierarchies, based on embedded material and symbolic inequalities among these women.[25] Some have salaried jobs. Other church workers are granted various sorts of material compensation. Still others work on a completely voluntary basis. The overall lower payment and often informal work arrangements for women in parish structures reflect the persistent unfavorable conditions for women in Russia's work market since the early 1990s. Under such circumstances, for women who come from the lower and middle classes, working for the Church offers a job opportunity, social integration, and the possibility to enjoy social recognition by fellow church workers, clergy, and the laity. Here, I take the example of Irina Antonovna, the female head of the main parish school in Ozerovo, and trace her rather typical trajectory, experiences, and aspirations. Drawing on her case, I argue that the common sociological profile of such women has effectively transformed the ecclesiastic organization at its basic territorial level, from the very beginning of their involvement in the 1990s. Women like Irina Antonovna have helped integrate the Soviet social norms of female professionalism and single motherhood within the Orthodox Church not necessarily as values professed by those who teach religion or by the priests but as social norms integral to the functioning of the Church.

Irina Antonovna is currently the official deputy director and informal head of the parish school. I first met her in 2006; I receive updates about her activities to this day. She was born in 1955 in Arkhangelsk, where she lived until she moved to Ozerovo in 1996. In between, she spent five years as a student in late-Soviet Leningrad (today Saint Petersburg). When she decided to leave Arkhangelsk in 1996 with her daughter, who was a child at the time, a university friend living in Ozerovo helped her settle there.

Irina Antonovna said that she first bought a small flat but then succeeded in buying, in her words, a large two-room apartment. Irina Antonovna has a common Soviet background. Her parents had typical Soviet professions for women and men respectively: Her mother worked as a teacher in a kindergarten; her father was an army officer. Her parents obtained an apartment in the usual Soviet way, that is, thanks to a system that allocated accommodation through the employing institution of one of the family members. Irina Antonovna's parents were in a way privileged because her father's position provided easy access to accommodation in an apartment block. After the completion of her high-school education, Irina Antonovna left for Leningrad to study journalism at the university and graduated successfully in five years. She later completed a second degree in political science. During the late Soviet period, women saw a massive increase in their access to some areas of professional activity previously considered to be reserved for men, in spite of the official emancipation discourse. Journalism was one such area.[26] Irina Antonovna married during the last year of her studies, just before her graduation. According to her, this was a happy marriage. Her daughter was born in 1984.

In 1995, after eleven years of love, mutual understanding, and support, in Irina Antonovna's words, her husband unexpectedly passed away at the age of thirty-nine. With the early loss of her husband—she became a widow when she was thirty-nine herself—Irina Antonovna turned into one of the innumerable Russian "women without men" and into a single mother. In Irina Antonovna's narrative, both the happy life with her husband and the brutal event that brought it to an end are definitive moments in her life experience. But from a sociological point of view, the early death of her husband and her experience of being a single mother are by no means exceptional, as single motherhood has become a widespread sociological pattern in Russia since the collapse of the USSR.[27] In 1996, shortly after her husband's death, Irina Antonovna decided to leave Arkhangelsk with her daughter. This was a bold decision. In Russia, the 1990s are usually remembered as a period of chaos and turmoil. But in Irina Antonovna's recollections, material hardship and job insecurity do not loom large. She did not speak of single motherhood as a special challenge to her at that time. She stressed that she was determined to rely on her professionalism; she was not afraid of moving away from her native city and was quite confident about her capacity to find a new job. Her work experience as a journalist in Arkhangelsk helped her immediately find a job at a large weekly local newspaper based in Ozerovo. She recollected that she thought of herself in this decisive moment above all as a good professional journalist.

Like the overwhelming majority of Russians in late Soviet times, neither Irina Antonovna's parents nor her parents-in-law went to church. But unlike most of my informants, who asserted that they had started learning about their own religion during the very last years of Soviet rule and often later, Irina Antonovna said that she had realized the importance of icons and prayers in her early childhood. She remembered that her parents had icons in their home. These icons were kept hidden in her parents' room so that, she said, guests visiting the family could not see them. She explained that her mother performed prayers and was one of the few persons who knew how to pray (*molitvennitsa*) during the era of militant atheism. Irina Antonovna liked to point out that she had a strong sense of being Orthodox even as a child, a rarity for her generation. Yet a closer examination of the trajectory of her religious socialization as a practicing and knowledgeable Orthodox believer shows that this was a secondary socialization, which is the most widespread type for her generation. Irina Antonovna took the initiative of baptizing her daughter, an act her husband approved of. This happened during the second half of the 1980s, under Mikhail Gorbachev's rule, when the reform period known as perestroika was initiated. One aspect of the reforms consisted in a slightly weakened control over religious practice, although there was no real liberalization. Later, in 1988, the year when the whole country celebrated the state-initiated Millennia of the Baptism of Russia, Irina Antonovna decided to get baptized, on the eve of her thirty-third birthday. But, as she said during one of our conversations, she became really interested in religious matters when she moved to Ozerovo and, more precisely, when she was offered a job in the main local parish. The baptism of her child, followed by her own baptism, as well as her assuming a completely new job in a church milieu in the mid-1990s, pertain to a general pattern whereby typical Soviet female trajectories started to be smoothly integrated into the ongoing religious revival. Intimately interwoven with this process is the opening of new, distinctively female career paths as part of the post-Soviet growth of the Church.[28]

In the 1990s and 2000s, these two processes were deeply interrelated, and Irina Antonovna's case provides a good illustration of this. She stressed in a conversation that her deepening engagement with the Orthodox Church and faith and her self-assertive attitude as a professional journalist not only unfolded simultaneously but reinforced each other. Irina Antonovna's integration in the Church provides an example of one of the ways that, from the early 1990s onward, women like her have confidently brought Soviet-era social norms into the Church. Their valuable professional skills and expert knowledge in areas such as education, group leadership, and the organization of collective events have been recognized by both the clergy and lay believers. Irina Antonovna is particularly representative of this group. When she was employed as a journalist at Ozerovo's weekly newspaper, she interviewed the rector (*nastoiatel'*) of the main parish on the occasion of an important church celebration. They also were able to chat informally. During their conversation, they found out that they had common acquaintances in Arkhangelsk. They liked each other. When the interview was published, the rector contacted Irina Antonovna to tell her he appreciated her work very much. But he did much more: He offered her a job as a journalist and staff member of his parish. At that moment, the parish was trying to launch a monthly newsletter, but the lack of knowledge and experience among the available church staff was an obstacle. Shortly after this offer, Irina Antonovna had to resign from her job at the local newspaper, following a conflict with the chief editor. She then readily accepted the job at the parish. Irina Antonovna described her new job to me as a place of personal and professional autonomy within the microcosm of parish workers. In her words, the rector did not simply show respect for her professional competence but explicitly demanded she be autonomous: "He told me immediately: 'Irina Antonovna, I am a theologian, you are a journalist [*ia bogoslov, a Vy zhurnalist*]. Let's separate these two activities. If you have questions, of course you can approach me and you can approach any other priest from our parish.' In fact, nobody among my readers and among the clergy has ever made any critical remarks about my articles."

Irina Antonovna was self-assertive and confident about her professional skills. In her words, the rector did not claim to be an all-knowing person— he relied on her professionalism and was reluctant to intervene in her work. He delimitated his sphere—theology—and left Irina Antonovna free to act in her own sphere of competence. Thus Irina Antonovna's role in the parish was legitimized without any struggle or argumentation on her side: It was the rector who asked her to work for the parish. The priest knew she had received appropriate training and that her professional experience would allow her to perform her duties. The priest's role, in this case, had been to give his blessing as an expression of his spiritual authorization. Her

professional competence included skills that priests do not have. Irina
Antonovna was given a desk in the library of the parish school.

After a year, she asked the rector if she could enroll in a three-year Orthodox course specifically designed to train women at the Spiritual Academy in Saint Petersburg. Several of my female informants from Ozerovo
received formal Orthodox education in this way. The academy did not issue
to women its usual diplomas, which are reserved for men; women received
special certificates. The rector offered that the cost of this course be paid by
the parish, even though he worried that after receiving the certificate Irina
Antonovna might feel attracted to higher positions in the Church. But after
graduation, Irina Antonovna resumed her work at the parish newsletter. In
addition, she started teaching Orthodox subjects to children, drawing from
her newly acquired academy knowledge. Shortly after, she was promoted to
informal deputy head of the school and worked under the authority of the
informal female director. Irina Antonovna also began organizing pilgrimages, an activity she also presented as her response to a demand initially
formulated by priests.[29] "I do it for a 'thank you,'" she said, meaning that
she received no payment for her work as a pilgrimage organizer and guide,
"but I feel a real pleasure." Her reward was the positive emotions she received from a social interaction in which she played a leading role. The payment for her salaried functions—the newsletter, teaching, and organizing
parish and school events—was rather meager. Women's jobs at the parish
level are rarely well paid. But public recognition and integration in a social
milieu in which her professional skills were highly valued were priceless. In
2010, thirteen years after her first steps as a regular parish employee, Irina
Antonovna assumed office as the informal head of the school, following the
departure of the woman who had been her unofficial boss at the school.
Today, she continues to write for the newsletter. She also actively contributes
to the website of the parish by writing short reports about school and parish
events almost on a daily basis. In official photographs taken during important ceremonies, she always occupies a prominent place close to high-
ranking clergy invited from Saint Petersburg and Moscow. The trajectory of
this woman journalist trained in Soviet times demonstrates that the Church
has readily offered her a place, obviously in part because she is devout but
above all because of her professional skills. Journalism, the primary source
of her professional pride and self-confidence, was later supplemented with
new organizational and teaching skills.

Irina Antonovna felt privileged in spite of her low remuneration in comparison to the rector's salary. She found a workplace and a community of fellow church workers, pupils, and parents where she felt respected. Moreover, she held a position of authority that gave her satisfaction and confidence. She was close to the rector and occasionally met high-level officials, clergy, and laity. Moreover, she was surrounded by women teachers who generally are well educated and polite and who, since 2010, became her subordinates. Parents, too, tended to treat Orthodox teachers respectfully, especially so as the school's head. Irina Antonovna also felt respected as a professional journalist. With Russia's job market being particularly harsh for women, Irina Antonovna's place in the parish was in fact a valuable one.

But seen from a different perspective, women like Irina Antonovna have virtually no further career prospects; avenues for economic and social upper mobility are curtailed at the parish level, to say the least. From this point of view, the triumphant integration of ordinary women in the making of post-Soviet Orthodox parish life means that these women are very likely to remain within the typical limits of Russia's mainstream female existence, facing low payment even while feeling that their professionalism is needed and valued.

Above All, Being a Good Single Mother: Another Parish Worker's Point of View

Irina Antonovna has always been self-assertive regarding her professional competence. Given the way she developed her career and how she presented herself to outsiders and closer acquaintances, single motherhood for her occupied the background of her life; professional self-fulfillment was always front and center. This, however, did not mean that she neglected motherhood. But she spoke and behaved in a way that implied that being a good worker was a necessary prerequisite for being a good mother. She explained on numerous occasions how proud she was of the fact that her daughter had graduated from a prestigious university. Recently, she mobilized her (female) networks, established over the years through the parish school, in order to search for a stable and well-paid job for her daughter, as my acquaintances reported to me. Being a mother, no matter how old her daughter was, was and had always been important to her. Yet, in her own eyes, work identity was what defined her above all.

In this respect, Irina Antonovna differed from another single mother and long-term parish bookkeeper. At the parish level, besides education, there are other occupations that, in addition to being official jobs, receive symbolic recognition from the male clergy and from female coworkers. This is, in particular, the case of parish bookkeepers. Bookkeeping is a highly feminized profession in Russia, including at the basic territorial level of the Church. Unlike heads of parish schools and teachers, bookkeepers remain largely unknown to believers who do not belong to the insider circles of parish management. They are invisible to those numerous casual religious practitioners who drop by the churches to light a candle or order a prayer. Although invisible from the outside, bookkeepers are of critical importance to every single parish. Church rectors tend to entrust the bookkeeping of their parish to women whom they consider pious, trustworthy, and experts in their professional field. In church life, bookkeeping is a sensitive area, since each parish is required to deliver reports to the deanery and to the eparchy to which it belongs on a regular basis. How much the parish should contribute to the higher levels is defined on the basis of these reports.

I met Elena Ivanovna for the first time in 2007. She was then the book-keeper of the smallest parish in Ozerovo. She was born in Ozerovo in the mid-1960s and had a younger sister. Her parents, both of them university graduates, raised them in Ozerovo. Immediately after her graduation from high school, Elena Ivanovna enrolled in a technical university in Saint Petersburg (then Leningrad). She graduated as an engineer in 1991 and immediately took a job in a factory in Ozerovo. She then married a young man with whom she had fallen in love. After having worked as an engineer for a year, she got pregnant. Her daughter was born in 1993, and Elena Ivanovna chose to take a three-year maternity leave. She gave birth to a son in 1996. Her husband had a job, and the family did not seem to have suffered excessively from the overall poverty of those years. Elena Ivanovna's parents and her sister also helped Elena Ivanovna's family cope with the material difficulties everyone in Russia was experiencing at that time. Elena Ivanovna had been confident that she could return to her job after her maternity leave and thus had taken advantage of her entitlement to a long-term leave. In 1998, she got pregnant for a third time. When she announced the news to her husband, he was unhappy. "He did not want us to have a third child," she said. She wanted to keep the child; her husband refused. When it became clear that they could not find a compromise, he decided to leave. They divorced; a few years later, he met another woman, with whom he had a child. To the three children he had had with Elena Ivanovna he became a father whom the children knew but saw rarely. When Elena Ivanovna gave birth to her son, her parents and her sister's family strongly supported her. After retirement, her parents had moved to a small village located in the region of Saint Petersburg, where they bought a house. They took to beekeeping. The honey they produced became a success, and their production expanded and thrived. Over the years, Elena Ivanovna kept telling me, "We practically live on the honey they produce."

During her pregnancy with her third child and right after the departure of her husband, Elena Ivanovna became interested in Orthodoxy. Faced with her new and challenging situation, she needed a moral beacon. In a trajectory typical of many during the post-Soviet period, she started reading and learning about her own religion. Her parents were not believers and had not transmitted any religious knowledge to their daughters. Her sister had gotten married by then. Elena Ivanovna, her sister, and her sister's husband together started to frequent a local church in Ozerovo. The priest, whom I interviewed in 2007, had come from his native Ukraine to serve in this church in 1996. He was known for his amiable relationships with everyone but also for his religious rigor. His parishioners described him as a strong supporter of Orthodox values and that he expected strict canonical observance.

Approximately at the same time, Elena Ivanovna learned that she could not return to the factory that previously had employed her. Times had changed, and the new market system in its local version meant that jobs were no longer guaranteed. Everyone had to find new ways to make a living. Elena Ivanovna decided to reorient her professional career. Like many women, she learned bookkeeping, registered as an entrepreneur, and started providing bookkeeping services to the private enterprises that were mushrooming in the late 1990s (and many of which collapsed soon after). She was not the only woman engineer who sought to establish her own business during this period. In the first decade of Russia's post-Soviet transition to capitalism, "the first wave of women thinking about business opportunities were overwhelmingly engineers and other technical specialists."[30] Although she never stopped relying on her parents, she had her own work, which was important to her. It was difficult organizing her time between housekeeping, cooking, and checking whether her children had done their homework. Elena Ivanovna was particularly invested in providing a good

psychological environment for her children. Besides Orthodox education—
she never forced her children to attend church and Sunday classes, and
indeed they did not—she found out that contact with animals had a positive effect on them. She bought two budgerigars and let them live cage
free in one of the rooms of her apartment. When I visited her in her home,
she explained that her life took place in the midst of flying birds, cooking,
cleaning, and supervising her children's homework. She tried to do her own
work as a bookkeeper in the evening, after the children had fallen asleep.
These were exhausting years for her but also years of satisfaction, as she
realized that she was indeed able to make ends meet.

When Elena Ivanovna registered as a bookkeeper in the second half of
the 1990s, the parish priest asked her if she could take care of the parish
bookkeeping. He needed a competent bookkeeper versed in the technicalities of parish life. She gladly accepted, and the parish became one of her
clients. Simultaneously, Elena Ivanovna and her sister's family became part
of the tiny minority of those self-identified Orthodox believers who observe the religious ceremonies and rituals of the parish regularly. Her bookkeeping service, for which she was paid a wage, was for Elena also part of
her duty to the parish. For nearly fifteen years, she fulfilled this task with
the greatest possible accuracy, she said. But the practical demands of parish bookkeeping sometimes clashed with her high moral standards, as she
suggested to me in 2007. More recently, when we met in November 2019,
she told me that she had never liked bookkeeping. This work had provided
a solution because it had secured a relatively good income when her children
needed food, clothing, and so on. In addition, she could work at home in
the evenings and make herself available for her children and domestic work
during the day. Eventually, however, she gave up this job in 2013 and felt
relieved.

In 2013, Elena Ivanovna called me to announce in a quavering voice
that the parish rector had passed away shortly after being diagnosed with
cancer. Elena Ivanovna was deeply shaken by this unexpected loss. The new
rector brought with him a new (female) bookkeeper. This was a decisive
moment in Elena Ivanovna's life. She decided to give up bookkeeping. Her
teenage sons were causing her great worries: "They became troublemakers
[*razboiniki*]," she complained. She decided to devote even more time to her
sons than before. Liberated from the burden of bookkeeping, she had to
search for another job. Having lived in Ozerovo all her life, she knew a
few well-off families who needed somebody to take care of their houses

and provide everyday help with shopping and other practical tasks. She thus became a cleaning lady, or, rather, a "helper to wealthy families," as she put it. She no longer needed to stay up at night completing accountancy tables and reports. Since then, she has become a much less regular church-goer. Before the death of the previous rector, she would hardly miss a Sunday service, but from 2013, she started going to church once every two weeks and even less often sometimes. Her attendance of the liturgy has become even less frequent since 2017, when her daughter gave birth to a boy. Elena Ivanovna feels obliged to provide childcare support to her daughter and son-in-law almost on a daily basis. Over the years, Elena Ivanovna rearranged her work in order to devote more time to her children, her family duties, and now to her grandson. The financial and other support from her parents was instrumental in reaching that goal. The situation started to change recently. Her parents had developed health problems and could not keep as many beehives as they earlier had. But her children were becoming more autonomous too, so supporting them financially was not as necessary as it used to be. As of this writing, one of her sons is studying at the university; the other is off for his one-year mandatory military service. Even though Elena Ivanovna has more time now than ever before, she has adopted some of the modes of practicing religion typical of the innumerable casual Orthodox believers, such as infrequent participation in parish life and search for spiritual advice on the internet. She particularly appreciates the online lectures of a relatively liberal priest. In her parish, she helps on Sundays by serving the tea at the parish school where her best friend gives Sunday lessons.

For Elena Ivanovna, the most intensive period for her as professional bookkeeper and committed churchgoer coincided with the period when she was the head of a household in which she had to provide for her three children. During this period, which lasted almost fifteen years, the rector appreciated her professional skills, devotion, and piety. Single motherhood has never been an obstacle to Elena Ivanovna's spiritual-professional career in the parish. Nor was it considered a mark of inferiority. Elena Ivanovna has always given precedence to motherhood over professional work, before and after her involvement in Orthodoxy, which was made possible thanks to the help received from her parents. An important part of her responsibility as a single mother of three was to establish rules at home. Everybody in her parish community understood that she was the head of the family.

Conclusion

In the 1990s, the life trajectories of many women intersected with the post-Soviet resurgence of the Russian Orthodox Church. Such women not only became practicing believers; they also turned into major actors in the daily operation of parishes. Their trajectories became an integral part of the process of consolidation of the place of the Church in Russian society. Statistical data about such women are unavailable. However, field observations support arguments that this process is ubiquitous in the Church, at least at its basic territorial level, the parishes. The historically unprecedented importance within the Church structures of women who provide professional work and of women who are single mothers demonstrates the embeddedness of the contemporary Russian Orthodox Church within Russian society. These two features have been "normalized" in parish life, similar to their "normalization" in society at large. The pragmatics of post-Soviet parish management rather than articulated feminist claims led to the recognition of Orthodox women as heads of households and as skilled professionals, that is, an aspect independent of their maternal roles. This informal recognition bespeaks a cultural turn even though it has not been reflected in the doctrinal positions of the Church, which have remained conspicuously ill-attuned to the overall societal changes in relation to women and the family. However, beneath the surface of the rigid canon and patriarchic axiological positions, transformation does take place. This transformative process has been mutually beneficial. On the one hand, in three decades, the Church has grown and moved into new spheres: Orthodox schooling, Orthodox publishing, online media, and the offer of pilgrimages have skyrocketed. On the other hand, thousands of women have found simultaneously spiritual and professional fulfillment within parish structures at some point in their lives. It is difficult to judge if this cultural turn has some emancipatory potential for Orthodox women and, if so, to predict how precisely such potential will develop in the future. It is nonetheless true that transformation, not stagnation, is the hallmark of contemporary Orthodoxy as it is lived on the ground.

Notes

1. Nadieszda Kizenko, "Feminized Patriarchy? Orthodoxy and Gender in Post-Soviet Russia," *Signs* 38, no. 3 (2013): 595–621; Anastasia Mitrofanova, "Ortho-Media for Ortho-Women: In Search of Patterns of Piety," in *Digital*

Orthodoxy in the Post-Soviet World: The Russian Orthodox Church and Web 2.0, ed. Mikhail Suslov (Stuttgart: Ibidem, 2016): 239–59.

2. See the website (in Russian): http://союзправославныхженщин.рф/. The existence of this organization is meant to express the top-level symbolic recognition of women as part of the Church, even though, as Anastasia Mitrofanova pointed out, "this organization does not function at the grassroots level and does not affect the lives of average female parishioners." Mitrofanova, "Ortho-Media for Ortho-Women," 244.

3. Jeanne Kormina, *Palomniki: Etnograficheskie Ocherki Pravoslavnogo Nomadizma* (Moscow: Vysshaia Shkola Ekonomiki, 2019); Sonja Luehrmann, "'God Values Intentions': Abortion, Expiation, and Moments of Sincerity in Russian Orthodox Pilgrimage," *HAU: Journal of Ethnographic Theory* 7, no. 1 (2017): 163–84. Jeanne Kormina and Sonja Luehrmann, "The Social Nature of Prayer in a Church of the Unchurched: Russian Orthodox Christianity from Its Edges," *Journal of the American Academy of Religion* 86, no. 2 (2018): 394–424.

4. About Saint Ksenia of Petersburg, see Jeanne Kormina and Sergey Shtyrkov, "St. Xenia as a Patron of Female Social Suffering: An Essay on Anthropological Hagiography," in *Multiple Moralities and Religions in Post-Soviet Russia*, ed. Jarrett Zigon (New York: Berghahn, 2011), 168–90; Sergei Shtyrkov, "The Unmerry Widow: The Blessed Kseniia of Petersburg in Hagiograhy and Hymnography," in *Holy Foolishness in Russia: New Perspectives*, ed. Priscilla Hunt and Svitlana Kobets (Bloomington, IL: Slavica, 2011), 281–304; Nadieszda Kizenko, "Protectors of Women and Lower Orders: Constructing Sainthood in Modern Russia," in *Orthodox Russia: Belief and Practice under the Tsars*, ed. Robert H. Greene and Valery A. Kivelson (University Park, PA: Penn State University Press, 2003), 189–218. About Saint Matrona of Moscow, see Jeanne Kormina, "Canonizing Soviet Pasts in Contemporary Russia: The Case of Saint Matrona of Moscow," in *A Companion to the Anthropology of Religion*, ed. Janice Boddy and Michael Lambek (Chichester: Wiley Blackwell, 2013), 409–24; Jeanne Kormina and Sergey Shtyrkov, "The Female Spiritual Elder and Death: Some Thoughts on Contemporary Lives of Russian Orthodox Saints," *State, Religion, and Church* 4, no. 2 (2017): 4–24.

5. Kizenko, "Feminized Patriarchy," 598.

6. See Kyriaki Karidoyanes FitzGerald, "The Ministry of Women in the Orthodox Church: Some Theological Presuppositions," *Journal of Ecumenical Studies* 20, no. 4 (1983): 558–75; Vassa Kontouma, "Women in Orthodoxy" in *The Orthodox Christian World*, ed. Augustine Casiday (London: Routledge, 2012): 432–41; for an overview, see Valerie A. Karras, "Orthodox Theologies of Women and Ordained Ministry," in *Thinking through Faith: New Perspectives from Orthodox Christian Scholars*, ed. Aristotle Papanikolaou and Elizabeth H. Prodromou (Crestwood, NY: St. Vladimir's Seminary Press, 2008), 113–58.

7. Michele Rivkin-Fish, "Pronatalism, Gender Politics, and the Renewal of Family Support in Russia: Toward a Feminist Anthropology of 'Maternity Capital,'" *Slavic Review* 69, no. 3 (2010): 703.

8. My research began with one year of fieldwork in 2006–2007 as a member of the project group "Religion and Morality in European Russia" at the Max Planck Institute for Social Anthropology, Halle, Germany. Since then, I have made further shorter trips and maintained a friendly relationship with some people through visits, phone calls, and emailing. Most recently, in October 2019, I resumed fieldwork in the same locality. Over the years, I have conducted direct and participant observation and open and semi-structured interviews with numerous churchgoers, clergy members, church workers, and casual religious practitioners on church premises, in parish schools, during pilgrimage trips, and during daily activities in my informants' homes and in their workplaces. Long-term contact with some of my acquaintances, including the two women whose cases are discussed in this chapter, has been a key to a better understanding of female positionality in the Church. I have replaced the name of the city and the individual names with pseudonyms in order to protect the privacy of my informants.

9. Isolde Thyrêt, *Between God and Tsar: Religious Symbolism and the Royal Women of Muscovite Russia* (DeKalb: Northern Illinois University Press, 2001); Brenda Meehan, *Holy Women of Russia: The Lives of Five Orthodox Women Offer Spiritual Guidance for Today* (San Francisco: Harper, 1993); Elina Kahla, *Life as Exploit: Representations of Twentieth-Century Saintly Women in Russia* (Helsinki: Kikimora, 2007); Vera Shevzov, "The Russian Tradition," in *The Orthodox Christian World*, ed. Augustine Casiday (London: Routledge, 2012), 15–40; William G. Wagner, "Paradoxes of Piety: The Nizhegorod Convent of the Exaltation of the Cross, 1807–1935," in *Orthodox Russia: Belief and Practice under the Tsars*, ed. Valerie A. Kivelson and Robert H. Greene (University Park, PA: Penn State University Press, 2003), 211–38; William G. Wagner, "'Orthodox Domesticity': Creating a Social Role for Women," in *Sacred Stories: Religion and Spirituality in Modern Russia*, ed. Michael D. Steinberg and Heather J. Coleman (Bloomington: Indiana University Press, 2007), 119–45.

10. Dorothy C. Weaver, "Shifting Agency: Male Clergy, Female Believers, and the Role of Icons," *Material Religion* 7, no. 3 (2011): 394–419; Isolde Thyrêt, "Muscovite Women and the Politics of the Holy: Gender and Canonization," *Russian History/Histoire Russe* 35, nos. 3–4 (2008): 447–61.

11. Anna Temkina and Elena Zdravomyslova, "Gender's Crooked Path: Feminism Confronts Russian Patriarchy," *Current Sociology* 62, no. 2 (2014): 259.

12. Rivkin-Fish, "Pronatalism, Gender Politics, and the Renewal of Family Support in Russia."

13. See Oxfam, "After Equality: Inequality Trends and Policy Responses in Contemporary Russia," discussion paper, 2014, 21, https://www.oxfam.org/en/research/after-equality.

14. It would be misleading, however, to define men as the winners of what has been termed "the post-Soviet transition." In Russian society, men as husbands and fathers are often described as absent from the family life and uninterested in their children. In the context of rampant unemployment and inadequate wages throughout the 1990s and later, post-Soviet models of hypermasculinity advertised in commercials and in the state-driven promotion of the image of man as the family's breadwinner have exacerbated the existing gender tensions. Sociological research shows that men's lived experiences are far more complex than the alleged lack of interest in family life or the easy escape in alcoholism. See Rebecca Kay, *Men in Contemporary Russia: The Fallen Heroes of Post-Soviet Change?* (London: Routledge, 2006).

15. "The Basis of the Social Concept of the Russian Orthodox Church," https://mospat.ru/en/documents/social-concepts/kh/.

16. Kizenko, "Feminized Patriarchy?"; Mitrofanova, "Ortho-Media for Ortho-Women."

17. Jennifer Utrata, *Women without Men: Single Mothers and Family Change in the New Russia* (Ithaca, NY: Cornell University Press, 2015).

18. Olga Shevchenko, *Crisis and the Everyday in Postsocialist Moscow* (Bloomington: Indiana University Press, 2009).

19. Kathy Rousselet, "Constructing Moralities around the Tsarist Family," in *Multiple Moralities and Religions in Post-Soviet Russia*, ed. Jarrett Zigon (New York: Berghahn, 2011): 146–67. The Church celebration in Ekaterinburg in July 2018 of the hundredth anniversary of the killing of the last emperor, Nicolas II, and the members of his family by the Bolsheviks revealed the growing public activism of groups of monarchists and "venerators of the Tsar as God." See Kathy Rousselet, "Les enjeux de la Célébration du Centenaire de l'assassinat des Romanov," https://www.sciencespo.fr/enjeumondial/fr/odr/les-enjeux-de-la-celebration-du-centenaire-de-l-assassinat-des-romanov.

20. Utrata, *Women without Men.*

21. Emphasis in the original. "The Basis of the Social Concept of the Russian Orthodox Church."

22. Sonja Luehrmann, "'Everything New That Life Gives Birth to': Family Values and Kinship Practices in Russian Orthodox Antiabortion Activism," *Signs* 44, no. 3 (2019): 771.

23. Luehrmann, "'Everything New That Life Gives Birth to,'" (773).

24. About the post-Soviet rise of lay women's authority as teachers of religion in the schools belonging to the Church and in the secular state schools, see Agata Ladykowska and Detelina Tocheva, "Women Teachers of Religion in

Russia: Gendered Authority in the Orthodox Church," *Archives de Sciences Sociales des Religions* 162 (2013): 55–74.

25. See Detelina Tocheva, *Intimate Divisions: Street-Level Orthodoxy in Post-Soviet Russia* (Berlin: LIT, 2017), 99–119.

26. During the Soviet period, for the first time in the history of Russian society, technical and scientific professions became highly feminized. However, the level of women's salaries remained lower than men's salaries in all sectors and at all levels of the professional hierarchy. Barbara Alpern Engel, *Women in Russia, 1700–2000* (Cambridge: Cambridge University Press, 2004).

27. Utrata, *Women without Men.*

28. See Detelina Tocheva, "Rupture systémique et continuité éthique: l'orthodoxie russe postsoviétique," *ethnographiques.org* 28 (2014), http://www.ethnographiques.org/2014/Tocheva; Sonja Luehrmann, *Secularism Soviet Style: Teaching Atheism and Religion in a Volga Republic* (Bloomington: Indiana University Press, 2011).

29. Numerous women acting within the frame of parish education hold a position that is in reality a combination of several jobs. Ladykowska and Tocheva, "Women Teachers of Religion in Russia."

30. Sue Bridger, Rebecca Kay, and Katheryn Pinnick, *No More Heroines? Russia, Women, and the Market* (London: Routledge, 1996), 122.

WOMEN AND THE GEORGIAN ORTHODOX CHURCH

Ketevan Gurchiani

Introduction

Women in the Georgian Orthodox Church clearly comprise the majority of adherents: Female members visibly outnumber men during church services.[1] The Church, however, assigns women a subordinate status: During the liturgy, women can only serve as chanters and Holy Book readers; in the church spaces, they are supposed to take a place to the left side of the priest; during the sacrament, men come first; no female can enter the altar; a woman is regarded as unclean on her days of menstruation and during the first forty days after giving birth. Even chanting in choirs is divided along gender lines: There are debates surrounding female and male chanting and implying the lesser importance of female choirs.[2]

Women's subordinate role is continually reinforced by the head of the Church. Patriarch Ilia II stated: "Nowadays it is an accepted view that men and women are equal. The Holy Scripture says that man is the head of the family. The family is one whole body, and the body cannot have two heads."[3] Still, the Church has its important women exerting their power from behind the scenes. They employ what has been called "hidden transcripts" to negotiate their spaces and adjust to the sociopolitical changes.[4]

This chapter interprets the relations of power as having "dual transcripts": "public transcripts" and "hidden transcripts," wherein "official" male dominance is undermined by informal agendas. This power relation is elusive and relational, and both transcripts are interrelated. The use of hidden transcripts is a "weapon of the weak," through which they constrain the powerful and exert their agency. It is enacted individually.[5] The subordinated have their areas of strength and power. They try to play their role in a way that maximizes their benefits, and through this they actively negotiate their power vis-à-vis the more powerful.[6] I see the informal power exerted by women in the Church as a legitimate part of Church power relations.[7]

This chapter asks how the role of women in the Georgian Orthodox Church evolved as a result of the domestication of religion under the atheistic communist regime and argues that the current status of women is a continuation of both their empowerment and the reinforcement of traditional gender roles during the communist period. At the same time, it looks at how women exert power through ritual practice in domestic areas or exert agency in Orthodox Christianity as domestic religious experts. The chapter looks at women as "religious virtuosi," in the Weberian sense; that is, women carry the "expert knowledge" of being properly Georgian and truly Christian, being dominated and powerful at the same time.[8]

With Talal Asad, I see religion and culture as intertwined, continuously affecting each other, while at the same time I acknowledge the role of religion as a dominant power in shaping traditions and in establishing discursive conventions.[9] Women's position in the Georgian Orthodox Church is culturally constructed and reflects a specific history of institutional arrangements and social practices. In what follows, I discuss how women's roles in the private and public realms interact and influence each other, and more specifically I discuss how the roles performed in the domestic arena and in the Church resemble each other. Women live out in the Church what they are in their domestic space, and vice versa.[10] This similarity also extends to the ways women negotiate and exert agency. Culture is not immutable: Power relations are shifting, roles are adjusting, and meanings are changing. Women's status in the Georgian Orthodox Church today is a hybrid mixture of Soviet legacies and post-Soviet realities. I seek to show the different layers in this mixture.

I consider women in the Georgian Orthodox Church as mediating figures who surpass binary descriptions such as strong-weak, visible-invisible, domestic-public, rational-irrational. Gender is performed and negotiated.[11] In order to demonstrate the hidden power of women, I start with a discussion of women and their ambiguous place in the Georgian Orthodox Church as an institution. Second, I look at Soviet atheism and at the important role women played and still play in domestic religiosity, albeit under changed circumstances. Next, I analyze women who expand their domestic space to include functions of the institutional religion, thereby playing a powerful role from backstage. Finally, I focus on women operating in the gray zones of religiosity as healers, fortune-tellers, and clairvoyants. In all three cases I highlight how women assemble their identities through seemingly contradictory practices.

The Ambiguous Role of Women in the Georgian Orthodox Church

The dual transcript of male/female power relations is embedded in the discursive practices of the Georgian Orthodox Church. The Patriarchate, with its very name signaling the gendered world of Orthodox Christianity, acknowledges the central importance of female figures in the Georgian Orthodox Church. The main female figure defining the identity of Georgians is the Mother of God, Mariam. A popular myth claims that Georgia is a "Chosen Land" belonging to the Mother of God. Moreover, the history of the Georgian Orthodox Church is particularly connected with female figures: The land was Christianized by a female saint, Saint Nino. Nino arrived in the fourth century and converted first Queen Nana and then King Mirian to Christianity.[12] She is venerated as the patron saint of Georgia, along with St. George. Another important female figure in the construction of Georgian national identity is the medieval female king Tamar.[13] Georgian mythology assigns to her cosmological powers: She created this land, and she divided the sea from the land.[14] Historians in the Middle Ages regarded her as the second Messiah. Mariam, Nino, and Tamar stand as three pillars of Georgian identity. As the Mother of God, Mariam symbolizes their being "Orthodox" in the sense of "rightly believing Christians"; Nino symbolizes Georgia's antiquity and continuity from the fourth century to the present; and King Tamar symbolizes Georgia's golden age.[15] Most churches in Georgia are dedicated to the Mother of God or St. Nino, and most of the shrines, where the local customs are a syncretic mix of Christian and pagan beliefs, are dedicated to Tamar (along with St. George).[16] The three names Nino, Mariam, and Tamar are the most popular female names in Georgia.

The elevated position of women in the Georgian Orthodox Church is also signified by the fact that the first Christian martyr was St. Shushanik, a woman belonging to the Georgian Orthodox Church. As in many other traditions, women commissioned the first churches and monasteries. Nuns traditionally played a significant role in community life.[17] Historical accounts speak of nuns who helped establish educational centers and collected funds for the building of cloisters and churches.[18] Still, historically, women have always been limited to lesser roles in the Church hierarchy.[19] Nuns and abbesses have largely played a backstage role,[20] though there are some notable exceptions.[21] This chapter focuses on women who are perceived as "weak" and as lacking agency but who nevertheless try to negotiate their ways as devout parishioners.

Religion in Georgia is a vastly researched topic because of the importance Orthodox Christianity has in people's everyday life and in the public sphere. According to a recent survey, the Church is the most trusted institution in the country.[22] When it comes to women in the Georgian Orthodox Church, some feminist authors perceive religion as a source of gendered roles and stereotypes, which shape cultural tradition.[23] Others, such as Tsopurashvili,[24] Machabeli,[25] and Javakhishvili,[26] see the demoted status of women as a departure from the more equal position of women in early Christianity in general and in the Georgian Orthodox Church in particular.[27] While most clergymen assign women a subordinate role,[28] others agree that the diminished role of women is a sign of regression.[29] The position of women in the Georgian Orthodox Church is similar to the position of women in other Orthodox churches struggling with the challenges of the postcommunist transition.[30]

This chapter examines the role of women parishioners in the Orthodox Church in Georgia from a genealogical perspective, looking at different layers of the past constituting the present. It also tries to show that the role of women exists beyond clear-cut binaries. It joins a growing body of research on the lived religion of Orthodox women in Georgia by scholars such as Gavashelishvili, Tserediani, Tuite, and Bukhrashvili. In a recently published volume on shared sacred spaces, focusing on syncretic practices and the important materiality of shrines, Tserediani, Tuite, and Bukhrashvili present a detailed analysis of gendered practices in the mountainous region of Svaneti as a specific development of local Christianity there.[31] Gavashelishvili focuses on the importance of religion on the lives of female practitioners. Her work shows a creative assemblage of meanings and practices and depicts women as skillful bricoleurs.[32] My aim here is to show women's agency and contestation in a seemingly subordinated realm.

Women and Soviet Atheism in Georgia

The role women play in institutional religion today is closely linked to their role in domestic religion during Soviet times, when domestic space became the primary domain for the performance of religious rituals. The question of religion during the Soviet era in Georgia is closely linked to questions of identity and symbolic meanings attached to religion. In the Soviet Union, two policies dominated the management of religion: indigenization (*koreni-zatzia*) and militant atheism. In the case of Georgia, where national identity was closely linked to claims of an ancient statehood and of the ancient history of the Church, these two policies were in conflict. The Soviet politics of indigenization was rooted in an essentialist or primordial approach to identity.[33] Orthodox Christianity maintained its great importance in Georgia as a proxy for ethnonational identity and as a symbolic sign of the antiquity and historical continuity of Georgianness. Throughout the Soviet era, Orthodox Christianity underwent "museumification" in the public realm but remained important in daily lives via the agency of women. Women were considered essential in preserving the national identity. They were also seen as guardians of local traditions. The term "traditions" incorporated many aspects of religion during the period of Soviet ideological atheism.

Militant atheism entered Georgia in the early years after the Bolshevik annexation in 1921.[34] The first years of communism were marked by brutal attacks against church buildings, the clergy, and the customs associated with everyday religiosity. The assault on the institutional religion has been profound: Out of the over 2,500 churches functioning in Georgia before 1917, only forty remained open by 1975.[35]

Women used their high societal status, their academic skills, or their domestic expertise to avail themselves of more freedom to practice religion. They combined secular and spiritual lives using their successful careers or social prestige to pursue their religious callings. As Wynot points out: "The closure of monasteries led to a phenomenon of 'monasteries without walls' and 'monasticism in the world.'"[36]

The Domestication of Religion and Domesticity of Women

This section looks at how women mold practices to play major social roles from a place unlikely to foster dominance: the domestic realm. They obey and disobey at the same time. As Hegland points out, "Any action contains aspects of agency and resistance as well as control and accommodation, and, even within the confines of ritual, people can find creative and agential opportunities."[37] Women emerged in the Soviet times as both ritual practitioners and guardians of religious practices in the domestic arena, while at the same time they continued to play the traditional role of "domestic" women. Since the realm of the home was and remained the domain of women throughout the Soviet era,[38] the domestication of religion was especially empowering for women who practiced religious customs. Ironically, this empowerment at the same time reasserted women's traditional roles as family guardians.[39]

Like other communist countries, Georgia introduced gender-equality measures, yet the official policies did not alter gender roles in the household. This, in the words of Gomel, "created a paradoxical reality of women's full participation in the labor force while they remained burdened with the traditional domestic roles as well. The gender politics of the Soviet utopia seem, at first glance, simply to reflect this duality: women are, of course, present in the future Communist society and ostensibly equal, yet they mostly appear as the protagonists' wives and girlfriends."[40] In Soviet Georgia, the narrative about women was neatly tied to the extolment of women as heroines, including in the domestic sphere. The tendency to intermingle Georgianness and heroism in idealized narratives played out in the discourse about "the true Georgian woman." This discourse was linked to a nineteenth-century romanticized image of the Georgian woman whose utmost priority was motherhood and the service to her family and country. Often she was the heroic mother of heroic sons. During the Soviet era, the sacrificial and heroic nature of the Georgian woman was tightly linked to the national history. The ideal of the woman hero-laborer, introduced by the Soviet policies for the increase of labor productivity, was less significant than the *mother hero*: an official status given to women who gave birth to more than ten children, which was introduced in 1944 for Soviet women and was used by the republics for their own ends.[41] In Georgia, the *mother hero* was seen as a key figure in the preservation of the national identity and was closely linked to religious traditions.

Religious Practice in the Domestic Arena

The restrictions imposed by the atheist Soviet regime resulted in the shifting of the sacred space into the domestic sphere. The practice of religion was relocated to the household (Figure 1). It has often been camouflaged

Figure 1. "Apartment Crisis," *Satirical Journal of Militant Atheists*, Tartaroz, 1928, N-148, 8. The image depicts the Church functioning as a club sporting Soviet symbolism. The clergy members are losing their space, forcing them outside. *Source*: Shmagi Liparteliani, "Antireligious Soviet Posters in Georgian Media (1921–1945)," MA thesis, Ilia State University, 2018.

as "folklore," "traditions," and "superstitions." The policy of indigenization stressed the importance of ethnic belonging and consequently played an important role in keeping traditional customs alive; it even revived some forgotten rituals or created new ones.[42] As Dragadze notes, people had to find a way to practice and to frame these practices; thus religious customs were referred to as "Georgian traditions" and imbued with moral character and stability.[43] Domestic religiosity became so commonplace that even the Communist Party leaders had to participate in main celebrations in order to remain "good Georgians," as my fieldwork (2015–2018) in Imereti, in rural western Georgia, showed.

The domestication of religion was often empowering for laywomen. As most places (urban or rural) were left without priests and as religious practices shifted to the household, women took over the functions of organizers of religious rituals. Despite state atheism, Easter celebrations, christenings, and Christmas were widely practiced at home throughout the Soviet era.[44] In places without a priest, the religious rituals and celebrations were relocated entirely from the church to the home. Women were "virtuosi" who knew how to perform the rituals. They became ritual practitioners with high social prestige. Furthermore, the religious celebrations involving larger *supras* (traditional parties) reaffirmed women's social networks. At the same time, they reinforced women's role as keepers of traditions in the face of the Soviet (often also perceived as colonizing Russian) other.[45] Celebrations were places where the past met the present.

When priests were available and could be involved in the rituals performed in the houses, women were mostly in charge of negotiating and organizing their visits or organizing a visit to a nearby church to help the priests in the performance of the religious ritual. By emerging as skilled virtuosi, women also enhanced their traditional role as guardians of the moral code and of the "Georgianness" attached to it. They employed tactics to undermine the subordinate role the traditions assigned to them. The domestic realm became an arena to challenge this role and to exert agency. Religiosity became part of their everyday, mundane chores, and it was imbued with purity and morality. Women knew when to wash according to religious prescriptions, when to clean, how to keep the fast, and when to avoid certain food. Many of the celebrations maintained their symbols in culinary ways. At present, the rules of how to celebrate holidays such as the Assumption of Mary, the Ascension of Mary, and the more locally significant Barbaroba (the day of St. Barbara) or Giorgoba (the day of St. George) are closely linked to the

Figure 2. Food prepared for Ascension, 2017. Photo by the author.

home and more specifically to the kitchen. In my ethnography I often encountered women being proud of knowing exactly what to do during Mari-
amoba (the Ascension of Mary): They have to place all kinds of fruit on the
table and prepare *kverebi* (small breads filled with cheese) with a cross pattern
on them. The families held on to the "stamps" to make the cross pattern
throughout the Soviet era. Someone in the village had kept manufacturing
them at home for the families to make the preparation of religious food
easier. Different forms of proper religious dishes emerged (Figure 2).

Veneration of the Deceased

The post-Soviet revival of institutional religion changed the significance of domestic religiosity and the importance of women as religious virtuosi. The role of women in performing religious rituals is disappearing. Still, women try to negotiate their function as ritual experts and to bring their domestic expertise to the institutional religion. Some rituals and religious practices involve women more than others and are still mostly practiced at home. With the revival of the institutional religion, the contestation between domestic female roles and official male priestly roles follows a hidden transcript: There is no open discussion between female congregation members and priests about the subordinated roles. Still, ethnographic research shows a hidden transcript that, according to Scott, "consists of those offstage speeches, gestures, and practices that confirm, contradict, or inflect what appears in the public transcript."[46]

A good example of the continuities, changes, and adaptations is the complex and extensive ritual surrounding death. The elaborate rituals involve taking care of the corpse, preparations for the funeral, lamenting, and the burial rite. This is followed by an at least yearlong observation of rituals on marked days. Rituals before a funeral involve certain collaborations of men and women, but women's symbolic place in the rituals of veneration of the dead is central. The women act as mediators between the dead and the living; they stay closer to the corpse—that is, they grieve on the front stage. The demeanor expected from the grieving family is gendered, with women taking on the expressive role of loud lamentation.[47] As grieving members of the family, they command a special power and authority. Furthermore, in the rituals surrounding the dead, women again come out as "virtuosi," as ritual practitioners with expert knowledge. This role was especially enhanced during the Soviet period, when women were the sole practitioners and no priest was present.

The preparation for a funeral was and still is a lengthy process in which the private homes of people play a crucial role. The house as the domain of women becomes an open stage where the performance of grief takes place. It invites a closer look to see how the perceived backstage becomes the front stage. During communism, the home became a place to mediate the transition from the world of the living to that of the dead. Dying at home guaranteed a proper (meaning religious) farewell and a proper funeral, with rituals asserting the status of the family, knitting closer ties in the community, and helping loved ones overcome their grief.[48]

For at least three days the deceased person is laid out at home. During this time (two evenings, called *panashvidi*, and the burial day) some formal condolences and farewells take place. A *panashvidi* is meticulously organized when kin and friends visit the house of the deceased.[49] The usual order of things is lifted; normality is inverted. The house, a space for the living and the dead, is liminal, between and betwixt.[50] The door of the house, usually kept locked, remains open day and night; the furniture is moved and rearranged differently; all the mirrors are covered with white sheets; the chairs are arranged around the coffin in the center of the largest room; and only women sit around the coffin mourning the deceased.[51] Women own the place.[52] They are the ones who display grief and take condolences. Farewells are expressed; there is wailing or storytelling and often a recollection of dreams as visions. The men stand outside and take condolences there, mostly remaining silent.

Social roles and rules of hospitality are inverted: Female hosts become honored guests, and guests become hosts. Female neighbors cook and serve food for the family, take care of everyday chores, and escort guests to the door. Any distinction between day and night is lifted. There is no sleep anymore. Someone must stay awake in honor of the dead body during the night. Close kin or friends keep them company. Days and nights are filled with different rituals and preparations: Women take care of the corpse, arrange flowers, and place small cups filled with wheat grains, wine (sometimes water), and oil on a small table behind the corpse. Candles are stuck into the wheat. Female members take care to keep the candle lit day and night. On the day before the funeral, a special dish is prepared at home to be served during the wake to bid farewell. The preparation for burial also often includes choosing objects to accompany the deceased.[53] After leaving the house, the corpse is relegated to the men. The burial itself is more of the men's domain.

The entire year following the burial is filled with rituals that see women as experts. Giving proper honor to the deceased is an honor that Georgian families try to earn. Women take the sole responsibility of observing all the rituals. Most rituals revolve around preparing meals in a special order and form. These take place on the day of the burial, the wake after the funeral, and on the ninth day, fortieth day, and anniversary of the death. During the year, there are at least seven days when women cook (mostly the favorite food of the deceased) a kind of repast in the name of the dead family member and say "*miuva*" (it will reach him/her). During the Soviet period, this ritual was entirely carried out at home. The food would be placed in front of the picture of the dead person, along with wine, and would be shared with kin or people who needed it most.

In the 1990s, one of the first decrees issued by the Patriarchate of the Georgian Orthodox Church tried to regulate and thus institutionalize the practices connected with the funeral and veneration of the dead. It short-ened the number of the days of mourning and established the priority of the church-performed practices over the domestic ones. It also limited the expressive aspect of the mourning (for example, wearing black for years). The reinstitutionalization of the funerals reintroduced priests as the main ritual practitioners and dispensed with the expertise of women.

Consequently, today a hybrid mixture of domestic and institutional prac-tices can be observed in funerals. The functions are negotiated: The bodies are cared for at home, but usually priests are invited to perform the Office at the Parting of the Soul from the Body. The helping hands in such rituals are now exclusively the men of the families. For the duration of the chants and prayers at this service, the traditional "antistructure" of the Georgian *panash-vidi* is lifted, and men remain in the house next to the women.

The lengthy farewell period has been split between the house and the church. Practices that were previously confined entirely to the domestic realm have been partly relocated to the church. As of recently, mostly in ur-ban areas, it is becoming more common to have at least one *panashvidi* (a day for condolences) in a church space and to have a church service before the funeral there. With the return of funerals to the church, the gendered func-tions change, with "spiritual expertise" now provided by a more distant and always male priest. Nevertheless, efforts to keep the domestic and familiar together through the restored or invented institutional traditions continue.

The Georgian Orthodox Church insists on the futility of some of the rituals, especially those where women were the main actors. Some of the rituals remain in the hands of women, and most of them are the subject of negotiations where women try to use manipulative tactics to undermine the imposed rules. The Church stresses the importance of the sacred space of churches and of conducting the rituals there. Women try to negotiate this. There is an attempt to combine their domestic importance and the institu-tional change: They prepare the meals, bring part of the repast to the church, let priests bless it, take small parts back home to purify the rest of the meal, and serve it to the family and loved ones at home.[54] Most importantly, they bring their domestic expertise to the institutional realm of churches, thereby playing their domestic roles and exerting agency there.

The Informal Power of Women

This section discusses how women perpetuate and extend their domesticity to the institutional realm. While performing their constructed "nurturing" role, women in the Georgian Orthodox Church rely on the transcript of a traditional, devoted woman. At the same time, they are employing hidden transcripts to exert power from backstage.

In present-day Georgia, female members of a congregation play a variety of roles. Some operate in the background, and others perform important roles as shadow leaders of the parishes. Helping the needy and taking care of a household are the main functions that laywomen fulfill today. By so doing, they can exert their power. The most common task assigned to women in a church today is to be a "helper": a cleaner, candle and icon seller, and bookkeeper.[55] Still, they operate beyond the assigned role and mold these practices to their own ends.

Almost every church in Georgia has at the priest's right hand an important female figure who runs the household. This important backstage role manifests the dual transcripts of power relations.[56] By employing everyday tactics and skillfully performing their gendered role, women become matriarchs in a patriarchate. Recently, these women acquired a term, *mdivan-referenti*, meaning a secretary who helps in the technical details. This kind of manager, exclusively female, mostly takes care of the priest's schedule and his availability, thus having significant power in the eyes of the parishioners and commanding the trust of the priest.

The self-appointed female managers also manage the income of the church, greatly enlarging the domain of their power. They make sure that everyone pays according to the customary rules for different services. These rules are established locally with the active involvement of the female assistants.[57] The "manager" usually stands near the donation box, tells the "consumer" the amount of money to be put in the box for the provided service, and makes sure that the right amount is given. She also compiles lists of those who have paid. This kind of management increases the church income and is assigned to the woman by the priest himself.[58] In their function as helpers of the priest, women emerge as church managers, remaining mostly offstage but being very influential. In taking care of the household, women also connect with the community: They raise funds and collect products such as oil and wine for the services. They also attend local schools and organize church visits for the students.[59]

The female church managers act as guardians of moral codes and sartorial habits. In recent years, rules on bodily practices were introduced for worshippers.[60] The Church increasingly sees the body of women as susceptible to aberration. The Orthodox priests try to discipline the female body and advise women on acquiring a typical, obedient appearance.[61] To mediate between visitors and priests and to minimize conflicts, female managers make sure that there are some spare scarves to be used in the sacred space. While the priests advise, the female managers are there to see how the words of a priest are followed in the space of the church. It is hard to escape their watchful eye. Female churchgoers often rely on the mercy of the female managers. Male churchgoers can be instructed as well when wearing short pants or other "inappropriate" clothing. Gratifying the female manager is increasingly important.[62] While the priest performs on stage, the interaction with parishioners is almost exclusively left to women managers. Such a distribution of roles opens up a space for the seemingly powerless to command certain amounts of influence and control.

Female managers in local churches have a role model: Shorena Tetruashvili, the secretary-referent of the Georgian patriarch. She is not a cleric but is regarded as one of the most influential persons in the Patriarchate's inner circles. As a shadow figure who exercises power and leaves the impression that she "runs the Patriarchate," she is a matriarch in an exclusively male world. A powerful figure operating next to the Patriarch for over thirty years, she is famous for her skills of persuasion and tacit influence.

Shorena Tetruashvili runs the everyday life of the Patriarchate, largely remaining backstage. She shunned the public eye for many years. The beginnings of her career have been shrouded in secrecy. Recently, Tetruashvili made headlines as a target of a plot, the so-called Cyanide Case, planned by a high-ranking official in the Georgian Orthodox Church. Giorgi Mamaladze, an archpriest and head of the Patriarchate's Property Management Service, was detained on February 10, 2017, at Tbilisi International Airport before his departure to Germany. The media reported that "according to the Prosecutor's Office, a poisonous substance, sodium cyanide, kept in a concealed manner, was seized upon a search of his luggage. Mamaladze is charged for having attempted to murder Shorena Tetruashvili."[63] The media also highlighted Shorena's importance as a shadow figure with undeniable influence in the Patriarchate. She was believed to hold a strong sway over the archbishops and the Patriarch himself. One of the bishops accused her of being a corrupt and powerful figure who treats the bishops as her servants and calls them her "golden fish" if they accede to her requests.[64] A sign of her power is that she is the only person from inside the Patriarchate to mention openly in a court trial a mistake made by the Patriarch, who is highly respected.[65] Her signature appeared on official letters submitted to the prosecutor's office, which forced the Patriarchate to answer questions about her formal and informal power.

The public imagination combines her female domesticity and her hidden power. It is telling that Shorena Tetruashvili is also known as a skilled hostess. The Patriarchate has been her only home for more than seventeen years. Visiting the Patriarchate is like visiting her house. Only the chosen ones can arrange a meeting with the Patriarch through negotiations with her.[66] A towering figure in the Georgian Orthodox Church, called a "gray cardinal" leading a "shadowy government,"[67] this powerful woman has smaller counterparts in almost every church. The latter largely rely on the domestic role of women as guardians of traditions and as powerful backstage figures.

The Gray Zones of Religiosity and Their Continuation

A field of religiosity in which female religious practitioners operate mostly for female members is related to practices of fortune-telling and clairvoyance. This section describes how the subordinate role assigned to women is circumvented and how women, as ritual practitioners employing creative tactics, take over the stage. Some of the practitioners are associated with the Church, whereas others operate in gray zones of religiosity. The fieldwork I did between 2013 and 2017 showed that some practitioners are tolerated and incorporated into the Church, while others are defined as "sorcerers," as not being properly religious, and even as dangerous. There is also a linguistic divide: *mkurnalebi* (healers) and *natelmkhilvelebi* (clairvoyants) are more acceptable; *mkitkhavebi* (fortune-tellers) are outside proper religious practices. While the practices of removing spells and of clairvoyance are often conducted in an ecclesiastical environment or are loosely associated with clerical figures (a nun or more seldom a priest), fortune-tellers operate more independently. Clairvoyants and fortune-tellers are almost exclusively women.

Since being Orthodox Christian is one of the most important national identity markers for Georgians,[68] there is understandably a certain tension and anxiety when Christians engage in forbidden activities and resort to fortune-tellers. Usually traditional Orthodox Christian clients consider visits to fortune-tellers as episodes in their lives when something demonic overcomes the "orthodox" in them. "Whenever I have a problem, I always ask myself whether it is connected with my taking part in those crazy sessions. But I could not help myself: I was afraid, but I wanted to know and to see. I felt so torn apart," a woman, Nutsa, age fifty, told me.[69]

Many believers first consult priests who counsel against their visits to fortune-tellers, but some manage to overcome this injunction by negotiating their participation, hiding their practices, or even by accepting consequent punishment. After their visits, the most devout often seek atonement for their sin. Many of the believers cleverly manage to combine both practices in a specific way. The difference between the symbolic capital of the Church and the "lower" practice (called "magic" or "occult" by the Church) helps as well. Because the domain of institutional religion is understood as being hierarchically "higher" than the practice of fortune-telling, it becomes possible for the clients to engage in both. Fortune-tellers and their clients typically use the term "religion" as something more elevated than the practice of prediction. The word that describes a believer in Georgian is *mortsmune*, derived from the word *rtsmena*, or "faith" in a general sense. The Orthodox Church calls its members either *mortsmune* or *religiuri* ("religious"). The words for fortune-teller in Georgian are *mkitkhavi* ("reader") and *marchieli* ("one who guesses"). The fortune-telling is therefore a process of reading and interpreting. In order to function under the conditions of Church dominance, fortune-tellers often employ tactics of camouflage. In the words of de Certeau, "Everyday life invents itself by poaching in countless ways from the properties of others."[70] Creative "poaching" is most apparent in the fortune-tellers' organization of the spaces where fortune-telling is done. As many Georgians increasingly regard the display of their Christian identity as a "front-stage" matter, fortune-tellers and their clients pay close attention to the display of Christian material symbols.[71] Usually a fortune-teller represents herself—they are most often women—as a member of the mainstream religion, not as an outsider. Subsequently, by demonstrating her Orthodox identity, she places her practice under the alleged patronage of the Church.

Natasha, one of the fortune-tellers I visited, was a former wrestler with a commanding personality, always altering and enlarging her services and learning new techniques. She freely reflected on the changing circumstances and the challenge to her practice under an influential Church. "It becomes harder and harder because of the Church. It was much easier in Moscow [where she also worked]. We try to show that we are not dangerous."[72]

An alignment with the official religion is especially visible in the organization of the spaces where such rituals are housed. These sites often bear the mark of implicit negotiations with the acknowledged hierarchy. Usually, fortune-tellers work from their homes. The typical location has an entrance, which serves as a waiting room, followed by the main room. The entrance is structured to enable a smooth transition from the public to the private realm. Clients in the waiting room are surrounded with familiar symbols of identity, alluding to the specific fusion of "Georgianness" with Christianity: They encounter Christian icons, predominantly those of Georgian saints. The picture of the current patriarch, Ilia II, who enjoys great popularity and whose photographs have become a part of home shrines in recent years, is present as a rule. Pictures of old Georgian churches and beatified kings as well as of modern saints famous for their miracles are also displayed. This display prepares clients and helps them feel less anxiety when stepping inside. Clients also encounter a wall with Christian religious symbols in the main room. Often the wall is further decorated with pictures of the fortune-teller, aiming to demonstrate her link with the Church. On these pictures, the fortune-teller is usually receiving a blessing, standing in front of a church, or humbly kissing the hand of a priest. For a client entering the room, the fortune-teller belongs to the domain of icons and priests. This is how a fortune-teller presents herself as sharing an Orthodox identity with (most of her) visitors and thus legitimates her practice. Fortune-tellers signal their belonging with the help of other adjustment tactics as well: They don't work during Lent, actively participate in congregational life, and have a priest counselor, usually referred to as a *modzgvari* (pastor) or *mamao* (father).[73]

Practices such as cloaking or camouflaging are not out of the ordinary for an Orthodox client. They look like a continuation of the familiar tactics of adjusting and maneuvering that Soviet citizens practiced during the seventy years of Soviet hegemony. Camouflaging or disguise was one of the most widespread Soviet tactics to deal with power.[74] This tactic was maybe the most creative and widely used of the everyday practices for concealing anti-regime attitudes or deviations from the official narrative promoted in Soviet films and literature. It involved the "cloaking" of stories and images, telling something else by using allusions, hints, and hidden meanings.[75] It required that the intended audience or reader watch and read between the lines.[76] Some mutilated texts were produced, however, and as Gomel has suggested, this "new strategy of reading" enriched rather than impoverished "the semantic potential of the text."[77] The forms of concealment widely used in self-representation in Soviet everyday life at the same time positioned creative users between conformism and nonconformism. Only those who cloaked their messages in acceptable forms, by changing the main message in a subtle way, would succeed.[78] It was a way to survive: People applied forms of creativity that allowed them to "remain in line" with the dominant power. However, the adjustment tactics also reproduced the system of control. They allowed people "to translate a text from something incorrect to correct, from forbidden to permissible" within it, thus reproducing the system.[79]

This kind of survival by camouflage is often visible in practices that operate on the periphery of the dominant. In this case, fortune-telling faces strong religious pressure either to disappear or assimilate. By using such tactics, they react, play along, and maintain some space; at the same time, they become more dependent, for the habitual use of such tactics locks a nondominant religious or so-called occult practice into the existing hierarchy. Camouflaging as an acknowledgment of power shows that occult practices in Georgia do not develop independently but are instead absorbed by the dominant Church.

This development is a product of a specific history and context. Church followers, fortune-tellers, priests, and clients of fortune-tellers alike create a web of interdependence in which the more powerful are directors and the less powerful are directed but not entirely subordinate. They create certain ways to survive and exert their power, but they also imitate one another to a certain extent. Skilled in manipulation, they "poach the properties of each other in countless ways."[80] The way that both the "dominant" and the "weak" work makes this appropriation possible. Fortune-tellers display themselves as believing Christians and as part of the larger Christian hierarchy. The especially skilled practitioners manage to be associated with priests or nuns and thus to offer remedies for everyday needs from inside the institutional religion.

There are certain cloisters that bless the activities of clairvoyants, spell-removers, and healers. Some monasteries or individual nuns even facilitate their meetings with "clients." This is the case with a church in Tbilisi, where a nun invites a renowned spell-remover from Kutaisi (the second-largest city in Georgia). This female clairvoyant is famous for her ability to deal with curses. Her legitimization derives from a story told to the numerous clients waiting outside the church: Many years ago, she found that a spell had been put on Catholicos-Patriarch Ilia II. The nun, Mother Johanna, facilitates her visits to Tbilisi and ensures that possible clients are informed. A line of clients forms in front of the newly built church. The first step is called the "diagnosis"—finding out if someone has received a curse or a spell. Each person buys candles and enters a room. The clients usually have pictures of their loved ones for the diagnosis. Marina, the fortune-teller, says a prayer. She then looks at the client, then at the icons, and utters her diagnosis, determining whether the person is affected by a spell or not. If there is a spell, then she, accompanied by a nun, visits on an agreed-upon date the house of this person to remove the spell. The rather lengthy process of finding the exact location of the spell is supported by prayers. The fortune-teller and the nun bring icons, pray, and light candles. This process itself is a mix of spirituality and materiality: The fortune-teller looks for and eventually finds a doll-like figure somewhere in a dark storeroom. The ritual, reminiscent of media images of voodoo, is closely intermingled with Christian rituals. A canonical and Christian prayer is performed in Old Georgian. An instruction is issued by the fortune-teller on how to get rid of the spell: The doll must be burned. But the ritual will not be complete without a Christian priest, she advises. The place will only be fully purified if the family asks a priest to visit and bless the house.

For fortune-tellers, clairvoyants, and their practicing Orthodox clients, the Soviet experience serves as a readily available frame, which allows different content to be presented under Christian terms. In such gestures we simultaneously find a maneuver to survive and an acknowledgment of power but also a way to maintain one's own way of practice. Female practitioners are especially skilled in employing these tactics. There is also a certain level of acceptance of the "eccentric" female spirituality that has been kept alive throughout the Soviet era. The figure of an exceptional woman carrying out ritual functions has its place in Georgian mythology and poetry. It is not confined to the literary genre only. In 2016, during my fieldwork in Bojorma, in eastern Georgia, I witnessed how a laywoman took over the functions of a local priest, who was overwhelmed with too many visitors. On that day, St. George was being celebrated by surrounding villages in an old church on a hill. The church has no Christian Orthodox priest, only a local spiritual leader called a *khevisberi*. The woman was one of the many visitors regarded by fellow men and women as "knowing best what to do." Because the *khevisberi* was very busy, worshippers asked her to carry out a ritual prayer invoking Tamar and the Mother of God, drink some wine, and perform a libation. This event once again demonstrated a level of flexibility and freedom to transgress in a structure defined along gendered distinctions.

Conclusion

This chapter looked at women and the Orthodox Church in Georgia from a historical perspective, analyzing how different layers of the past have a strong presence in the present. It focused on how contradictory discourses and practices shape the role of religious women in Georgia and the attitudes toward them. First, it focused on the conflicting Soviet policies of atheism and indigenization that led to an acceptance of the importance of domestic religiosity. It analyzed how the restrictions imposed by the ideological atheism in Soviet times empowered women in domestic religious practices. The two conflicting policies of militant atheism and of indigenization supported trends in which the camouflaging, maneuvering, and domestication of religion gained an upper hand.[81] Under the conflicting Soviet policies, there were different groups of women: those who took a leading role in domestic religion and those who successfully operated in the gray zone as healers, fortune-tellers, and keepers of practices and rituals identified as "folkloristic" and thus tolerated. The roles women performed in the sphere of domestic religiosity were and are still based on the view of women as traditional guardians of a specific moral code and preservers of Georgianness. At the same time, they have given women agency, enlarged their domain, and empowered them. The current religiosity of women incorporates those layers from the past. The informal practices and negotiations of meanings and functions within the Church and in the gray zones of religiosity are the main fields of both obedience and power for women.

Women are part of the Church as novices, nuns, and superiors of cloisters; they function as unofficial deaconesses, Holy Book readers, churchwardens in monasteries, members of choirs, and helping hands in the church households. Even though women are officially subordinated in all their positions and functions to men in the Church, they find ways to exert power, which turn individual members into shadow matriarchs. Scott's concept of "dual transcripts"—an official one legitimizing the existing subordination and a subtext, or hidden transcript, empowering the subordinate and undermining the existing domination—can be applied to understanding the role of the subordinate but still powerful women in the Georgian Church.

Notes

1. About the exceptional popularity of the Church as an institution and its involvement in civil society, see a policy brief: Salome Minesashvili, "The Georgian Orthodox Church as a Civil Actor: Challenges and Capabilities," 2017, http://gip.ge/wp-content/uploads/2017/05/Policy-brief-8-Salome -Minesashvili.pdf.

2. Online Orthodox forums give insight into the debates surrounding female and male chanting. Churchgoers discuss if two choirs in churches are necessary, implying the lesser importance of female choirs. For a forum discussion that sees female choirs as a temporary solution and not of the same quality as male choirs, see http://church.ge/index.php?showtopic=2440&st=20.

3. "Ilia II: The Husband Is the Head of a Family," *Tabula*, April 9, 2012, http://www.tabula.ge/ge/story/59228- ilia-meore-ojaxshi-mtavari-aris-qmari.

4. James C. Scott, *Hidden Transcripts: Domination and the Arts of Resistance* (New Haven, CT: Yale University Press, 1990).

5. Scott, *Hidden Transcripts*, 119, 188.

6. Andrea Cornwall and Nancy Lindisfarne, "Dislocating Masculinity," in *Dislocating Masculinity: Gender, Power, and Anthropology*, ed. Nancy Lindisfarne and Andrea Cornwall (London: Routledge, 2016), 27–61.

7. Edwin Ardener, "Belief and the Problem of Women and the 'Problem' Revisited," in *Feminist Anthropology: A Reader*, ed. Ellen Lewin (Malden, MA: Wiley-Blackwell, 2006): 47–65. Susan Carol Rogers, "Female Forms of Power and the Myth of Male Dominance: A Model of Female/Male Interaction in Peasant Society 1," *American Ethnologist* 2, no. 4 (1975): 727–56.

8. Max Weber, *Wirtschaft und Gesellschaft: Grundriss der verstehenden Soziologie* (Mohr Siebeck, 2002).

9. Talal Asad, "The Construction of Religion as an Anthropological Category," in *Genealogies of Religion: Discipline and Reasons of Power in Christianity and Islam* (Baltimore, MD: Johns Hopkins University Press, 1993), 27–54.

10. Robert A. Orsi, *The Madonna of 115th Street: Faith and Community in Italian Harlem, 1880–1950* (New Haven, CT: Yale University Press, 2010).

11. I align myself with the scholars who analyze gender as a cultural product, which is not a stable category. Compare Judith Butler, *Gender Trouble and the Subversion of Identity* (New York: Routledge 1990); Faye D. Ginsburg and Anna Lowenhaupt Tsing, eds., *Uncertain Terms: Negotiating Gender in American Culture* (Boston: Beacon, 1990); Aihwa Ong and Michael G. Peletz,

eds., *Bewitching Women, Pious Men: Gender and Body Politics in Southeast Asia* (Berkeley: University of California Press, 1995); and Marjorie Harness Goodwin, *The Hidden Life of Girls: Games of Stance, Status, and Exclusion*, vol. 1 (Malden, MA: Blackwell, 2006).

12. Stephen H. Rapp Jr., "Georgian Christianity," in *The Blackwell Companion to Eastern Christianity*, ed. Ken Parry (Malden, MA: Wiley-Blackwell, 2010), 137.

13. She has been crowned as king and was called the Georgian equivalent for king, not queen.

14. Zurab Kiknadze, *Georgian Mythology* (Tbilisi: Ilia State University Press, 2016).

15. Compare Charles King, *The Ghost of Freedom: A History of the Caucasus* (Oxford: Oxford University Press, 2008); and Paul Manning, "Materiality and Cosmology: Old Georgian Churches as Sacred, Sublime, and Secular Objects," *Ethnos* 73, no. 3 (2008): 327–60.

16. For a more detailed analysis, see Kevin Tuite, "The Meaning of Dael. Symbolic and Spatial Associations of the South Caucasian Goddess of Game Animals," in *Language, Culture, and the Individual: A Tribute to Paul Friedrich. Lincom Europa* (Munich, 2006), 165–88. See also Nino Tserediani, Kevin Tuite, and Paata Bukhrashvili, "Women as Bread-Bakers and Ritual-Makers: Gender, Visibility, and Sacred Space in Upper Svaneti," in *Sacred Places, Emerging Spaces: Religious Pluralism in the Post-Soviet Caucasus*, ed. Tsypylma Darieva, Florian Mühlfried, and Kevin Tuite (Berghahn, 2018), 17:46–70.

17. The first mention of a female scribe is from the twelfth century: Abbess Ekaterine of the Deltavi Convent. Since the sixteenth century, the corpus of manuscripts regularly lists women as scribes. Out of more than 122 Georgian female scribes, many were nuns in convents. Nana Khazaradze, "Women and Scholarship in History of Georgia," in *Gender Problems in Georgia* (Tbilisi: International Centre of Education and Information for Women, 2002).

18. Regarding some prominent nuns, see publications of monasteries available at http://samtavro.ge/index.php?m=377.

19. The subordinate place of women in the Church concerned activists fighting for women's rights as early as the beginning of the twentieth century. Relying on the discourse of the significance of female saints and women being the pillar of the Georgian Orthodox Church, those activists demanded expanded roles and rights for women in the Church. Speaking at the meeting of the main Church assembly in Tbilisi on September 15, 1917, a Georgian public figure, Mariam Dadiani-Anchabadze, stressed the importance of involving women as preachers. "Speech Made by Mariam Anchabadze at the Meeting of the Church Assembly in Tbilisi on September 15, 1917," *Voice of Georgian Women* 27 (October 19, 1917).

20. This chapter will not focus on the activities of nuns. Today, nuns continue mostly to play their traditional roles: they excel in reviving and reinventing crafts and in pioneering food technologies; they have an impact on surrounding communities through the jobs and support they offer. At the same time, they are skilled managers of monasteries, raising funds and running shelters for women and children or a mercy center: e.g., http://www.mercycenter.ge/ge/. The typical activity of such monastic centers includes the running of a vocational college, a hospice, and home care services. Yet there is a widespread perception that the Church can do more for society. Nongovernmental organizations often criticize the Church, including its monasteries, of not doing enough for the poor and the needy given the amount of funding it receives from the state.

21. Human rights often point out that the Church promotes homophobia and xenophobia among its members. An important development came about when an Orthodox nun, Mother Sidonia, became an avid defender of human rights. The Center for Tolerance at the office of the Ombudsman of Georgia awarded Mother Sidonia with the title of Advocate of Tolerance of 2018. So far, she is the only person representing the Georgian Orthodox Church to receive this award. See an interview with Mother Sidonia: http://www.tabula.ge/ge/tv/religion /76226-deda-sidonia; https://www.radiotavisupleba.ge/a/29608896.html. The activist role of this nun was however criticized by the Patriarchate as a pursuit of public life. Protest of the Patriarchate: https://1tv.ge/news/sapatriarqo -deda-sidonia-ar-moqmedebs-arc-saberdznetis-da-arc-saqartvelos-eklesiis -kanonmdeblobit-da-mis-sajaro-qmedebebtan-arc-ert-eklesias-kavshiri -ar-aqvs.

22. The survey was commissioned by Transparency International Georgia and conducted by the Caucasus Research Resource Centers (CRRC) in the period from February 20 to March 5, 2019. See https://www.transparency.ge/en /post/majority-respondents-say-judges-history-succumbing-political-pressure -should-leave-judiciary. Its results corroborate the findings of Caucasus Barometer Georgia 2017, according to which 70 percent of people fully trust or trust the religious institutions they belong to.

23. Elene Japaridze, Maia Barkaia, Nina Zhghenti, and Mariam Amashukeli, *The Study of Georgian Youth's Awareness, Perceptions, and Attitudes of Gender Equality* (Tbilisi: Center for Social Sciences, 2014), 28.

24. Tamar Tsopurashvili, "Myth about the Domestic Place of Woman in Christianity," in *Detector of Myths*, https://mythdetector.ge/ka/myth/miti-imis -shesakheb-rom-kalis-adgili-martlmadidebluri-scavlebis-mikhedvit-sakhlshia.

25. Apart from the female pillars of the Christian identity in Georgia, some researchers have noted the importance of women in Georgian cosmology expressed linguistically in forms such as *deda eklesia* (Mother Church), *dedamica* (mother earth), *dedaena* (mother tongue), *dedakalaki* (mother city, i.e., capital),

dedaazri (mother meaning, i.e., the primary definition), *dedabodzi* (mother pillar, i.e., the main pillar). Kitsi Machabeli, "The Historical Role of Georgian Woman," in *Gender Problems in Georgia* (Tbilisi: International Centre of Education and Information for Women, 2002).

26. Manana Javakhishvili, "Woman and the Christian Tradition," part 1, in *Gender Problems in Georgia* (Tbilisi: International Centre of Education and Information for Women, 2002).

27. Rusudan Gotsiridze, "Ordination of Women in Christian Churches," MA thesis, Ilia State University, 2011.

28. For a detailed discussion, see Elene Gavashelishvili, "Childless Women in Georgia: Between Religious Restrictions and Medical Opportunities," *Anthropology of the Middle East* 13, no. 1 (2018): 24–42.

29. The priest Bidzina Gunia emphasized the importance of increasing the involvement of women in leading positions during a 2006 conference in Tbilisi, while the historian Abashidze stressed that the diminished role of women in Georgian Orthodoxy is a degradation of the tradition. See "On the Role of Women in Traditional Religious Doctrines," https://www.radiotavisupleba .ge/a/1548011.html.

30. For the case of Russia, see Nadieszda Kizenko, "Feminized Patriarchy? Orthodoxy and Gender in Post-Soviet Russia," *Signs: Journal of Women in Culture and Society* 38, no. 3 (2013): 595–621. Kizenko, too, acknowledges the importance of tactics employed by women. When dealing with the dominant power they try to acquire their position by negotiating the new terrain "whether as casual parishioners, as 'virtuosi,' as priests' daughters who become priests' wives and church choirmasters, as church lawyers and heads of parishes, or in the new religious publications industry" (601).

31. Tserediani, Tuite, and Bukhrashvili, "Women as Bread-Bakers and Ritual-Makers."

32. Gavashelishvili, "Childless Women in Georgia," 24–42.

33. The rise of militant atheism coincided with the introduction of another Soviet policy, *korenizatsiya* (indigenization or nativization), announced in April 1923. This policy implied a kind of revival of national roots and a building of titular nations in every republic. In Georgia it revived ideas that national history is closely linked to Christianity. Efforts to build a titular nation were accompanied with claims of linearity and antiquity. The *korenizatsiya* policy had important implications for historiography and ethnography. The early Christianization of Georgia in the fourth century played a major role in the national historiography and became one of most important markers of linearity.

34. Militant atheism in Russia starts as early as 1922. In a letter of March 19, 1922, Lenin addresses members of the Politburo, charting the actions against

the "Black Hundreds" clergy and their followers. See the exhibit "Revelations from the Russian Archives," Library of Congress, https://www.loc.gov/exhibits /archives/anti.html.

35. See Peter Reddaway, "The Georgian Orthodox Church: Corruption and Renewal," *Religion in Communist Lands* 3, nos. 4/5 (1975): 14–23; Shmagi Liparteliani, "Antireligious Soviet Posters in Georgian Media (1921–1945)," MA thesis, Ilia State University, 2018.

36. Jennifer Wynot, "Monasteries without Walls: Secret Monasticism in the Soviet Union, 1928–39," *Church History* 71, no. 1 (2002): 66.

37. Mary Elaine Hegland, "Shi'a Women of Northwest Pakistan and Agency through Practice: Ritual, Resistance, Resilience," *Political and Legal Anthropology Review* 18, no. 2, (1995): 69.

38. Compare Gavashelishvili, "Childless Women in Georgia."

39. About the significance of domestication for women, see Ketevan Gurchiani, "How Soviet Is the Religious Revival in Georgia: Tactics in Everyday Religiosity," *Europe-Asia Studies* 69, no. 3 (2017): 508–31. The special role of women in domestic religion has been observed by other authors as well; see Meredith B. McGuire, *Lived Religion: Faith and Practice in Everyday Life* (Oxford: Oxford University Press, 2008), 143.

40. Elana Gomel, "Gods Like Men: Soviet Science Fiction and the Utopian Self," *Science Fiction Studies* 31, no. 3 (2004): 365.

41. Instructions on awarding different degrees of the honorable status and the order of the "Hero Mother" had been issued in Tbilisi in 1945.

42. Vera Bardavelidze, *Afmosavlet sakartvelos mtianetis t'raditsiuli sazogadoebriv-sak'ult'o Zeglebi* [Traditional cultic monuments of the East Georgian mountain districts], vol. 1: *Pshavi* (Tbilisi: Metsniereba, 1974). Kevin Tuite, "Real and Imagined Feudalism in Highland Georgia," *Amirani* 7 (2002): 25–42.

43. Tamara Dragadze, *Rural Families in Soviet Georgia: A Case Study in Ratcha Province* (London: Routledge, 1988), 73.

44. Some rituals, such as christening children, were performed, when possible, in a church but more frequently at home in collaboration with former or reinstalled priests. My ethnographic fieldwork between 2014 and 2018 gathered life stories of priests who had been stripped of their status in the early 1920s, shaved of their beards as a sign of resignation from priesthood, and sent to work as swineherds instead of being spiritual pastors. Still, throughout the years they continued to perform rituals, especially baptisms at homes, by invitation. In this way, the tradition of baptizing continued in Georgia.

45. Compare Dragadze, "Rural Families"; and Helga Kotthoff, "Gender, Emotion, and Poeticity in Georgian Mourning Rituals," *Gender in Interaction: Perspectives on Femininity and Masculinity in Ethnography and Discourse* 93 (2002): 283.

46. Scott, *Hidden Transcripts*, 4–5.

47. For a detailed analysis of lamenting as a gendered activity and its social meaning see Kotthoff, "Gender, Emotion, and Poeticity," 283ff.; and Lauren Ninoshvili, *Wailing in the Cities: Media, Modernity, and the Metamorphosis of Georgian Women's Expressive Labor* (Ann Arbor: University of Michigan Library, 2012). Ninoshvili points out how women became symbols of "woundedness." It has been noted by different scholars how funeral rites, especially laments, are an opportunity for women to let the larger society hear their voice. Charles Briggs, "'Since I Am a Woman, I Will Chastise My Relatives': Gender, Reported Speech, and the (Re)Production of Social Relations in Warao Ritual Wailing," *American Ethnologist* 19, no. 2 (1992): 337–61.

48. Dragadze has observed in Soviet Georgia that villagers preferred dying at home rather than in a medical institution. Dragadze, "Rural Families," 73.

49. For a more detailed description of a ritual from Soviet times, see Dragadze, "Rural Families," 149.

50. Victor Turner, "Liminality and Communitas," in *The Ritual Process: Structure and Anti-structure* (Chicago: Aldine Transaction, 1969): 94–130.

51. In some places, the days of condolences are accompanied by wailing women. Only in Svaneti do men perform the ritual wailing.

52. In her research among mountain Jews in Azerbaijan Sasha Goluboff found the contrary to be the case and interpreted the mourning as display of emotion that "validates patriarchy." Sascha L. Goluboff, "Patriarchy through Lamentation in Azerbaijan," *American Ethnologist* 35, no. 1 (2008): 83.

53. How the objects are chosen and what they reflect is a larger topic not to be discussed here.

54. Discussed elsewhere; see Gurchiani, "How Soviet Is Religious Revival in Georgia." Another tradition is to invite priests to bless houses and/or meals at homes. The efforts to keep both institutional and domestic spaces important for religious practices are also visible in the practice of hosting icons.

55. Typically, women are tasked with the upkeep of churches; preparation of fine embroideries, baking, and the like are also significant in parish life. There is a difference between rural and urban areas, however. Whereas in urban areas working in a church is not very desirable and is mostly associated with being poor, in rural areas it provides some forms of employment for women. The church is also an important arena where women can perform their gendered identity outside their homes.

56. Scott, *Hidden Transcripts*.

57. Diana Modebadze, "The Gift in Georgian Orthodox Church," MA thesis, Ilia State University, 2017.

58. For more examples of this kind, see Modebadze, "The Gift in Georgian Orthodox Church."

59. Author's interview with a schoolteacher in Tbilisi, 2016.

60. Ketevan Gurchiani, "Georgia in-between: Religion in Public Schools," *Nationalities Papers* 45, no. 6 (2017): 1100–17. A similar situation is described in Kizenko, "Feminized Patriarchy," 606.

61. For some priests, any manifestation of physical embellishment is unacceptable. For example, the clergy who responded to various questions by the laypeople warned women that those who use makeup "will be punished severely, as they are transforming a human being which is flawless and does not need any correction." Question 664 in *1000 Questions to the Mother Church*, 180. The book is available at http://sibrdzne.ge/7364.

62. Female churchgoers are also bargaining: They readily put on a dress or a skirt but take it off when they leave the sacred space. This dressing and undressing are in a metaphorical sense a sign of poaching: taking from the church what is needed but not completely obeying. They are negotiating meanings and practices as skilled jacks-of-all-trades. Gavashelishvili, "Childless Women in Georgia."

63. "Shorena Tetruashvili Being Questioned at the Court," *Channel 1*, July 14, 2017, http://old.1tv.ge/en/news/view/169678.html.

64. Bishop Petre Tsaava on *Rustavi 2* (TV channel), February 14, 2017.

65. "Shorena Tetruashvili: 'Patriarch Ilia II violated the constitutional agreement,'" https://digest.pia.ge/post/153713-sorena-tetruasvili-ilia-meore -konstituciur-motxovnebs-ascda-.

66. The coffee she prepares was described to me on so many occasions as something magical, so when I got the chance to try it, I made sure to enjoy it as something special.

67. More about her: https://dfwatch.net/tag/shorena-tetruashvili; Joshua Gold, "Geopolitical Implications of Georgia's Orthodox Church and Its Religious Nationalism," *Hemispheres* 41 (2018): 105–129, esp. 118.

68. See data available at Caucasus Barometer Georgia for different years. Caucasus Research Resource Centers, http://caucasusbarometer.org/en/.

69. Author's interview in Tbilisi, 2014.

70. Michel de Certeau, *The Practice of Everyday Life* (Berkeley: University of California Press, 1984), xii.

71. Compare Erving Goffman, *The Presentation of Self in Everyday Life* (1959; Garden City, NY: Doubleday, 2008).

72. Author's interview in Tbilisi, 2014.

73. Gurchiani, "How Soviet Is the Religious Revival in Georgia."

74. Sheila Fitzpatrick, *Tear Off the Masks! Identity and Imposture in Twentieth-Century Russia* (Princeton, NJ: Princeton University Press, 2005); Gurchiani, "How Soviet Is the Religious Revival in Georgia."

75. Serguei Alex Oushakine, "Crimes of Substitution: Detection in Late Soviet Society," *Public Culture* 15, no. 3 (2003): 448.

76. Olga Klimova, "Soviet Youth Films under Brezhnev: Watching between the Lines," PhD diss., University of Pittsburgh, 2013.

77. Elana Gomel, "The Poetics of Censorship: Allegory as Form and Ideology in the Novels of Arkady and Boris Strugatsky," *Science Fiction Studies* 22, no. 1 (1995): 87.

78. Alexei Yurchak, "Soviet Hegemony of Form: Everything Was Forever, Until It Was No More," *Comparative Studies in Society and History* 45, no. 3 (2003): 480–510.

79. Stephen Kotkin and William Richardson, "Magnetic Mountain: Stalinism as a Civilization," *History: Reviews of New Books* 24, no. 1 (1995): 37–38.

80. Certeau, "The Practice of Everyday Life," xii.

81. Domestication, as theorized in Tamara Dragadze, "The Domestication of Religion under Soviet Communism," in *Socialism: Ideals, Ideologies, and Local Practice*, ed. C. M. Hann (London: Routledge, 2003), 188–98.

WOMEN AND ORTHODOX DISSENT: THE CASE OF THE ARCHANGELIST UNDERGROUND MOVEMENT IN SOVIET MOLDAVIA

James A. Kapaló

Introduction

Soviet rule in Moldavia transformed the religious landscape and deeply affected gender dynamics within Orthodox Christianity. This chapter explores these changes by drawing on the testimonies of a group of women from the Gagauz minority, who are Turkish-speaking Orthodox Christians from villages in the south of today's Republic of Moldova.[1] The rapid Sovietization of society, the mass deportation of class enemies and religious minorities, and the closure of Orthodox places of worship caused massive disruption to the lives of ordinary Moldovans. This took place against a backdrop of widespread famine and starvation among the rural population in 1946–1947. Women responded in a variety of ways to these harsh circumstances, including exploring the potential of their Orthodox faith to provide purpose and a sense of certainty and security. The term "domestication" has been used by a number of scholars of religion to describe the relocation of religion to the domestic sphere during communism, when women played a greater role in ritual and practice. In Soviet Moldavia, however, an Orthodox religious underground with strong female figures had already emerged during the right-wing dictatorship that preceded Soviet rule. In this chapter, I point to the ways that our understanding of domestic religion during communism should be expanded to include an awareness of the significance of earlier forms of Orthodox dissent in which the domestic sphere had become an important dimension of what is known commonly as the religious underground. In so doing, I highlight some of the diverse ways that the agency of Orthodox women shaped the religious field in Moldavia in the twentieth century.

Historical Context

The territory we know of today as the Republic of Moldova has an extremely complex history of occupation and reoccupation and of shifting borders. This history brought about changes in both political and religious jurisdiction. Bessarabia, which constituted the eastern part of the medieval Principality of Moldavia (one of the two Romanian principalities that later, in the 1860s, formed the fledgling Romanian state, the other being Wallachia), had been a vassal of the Ottoman Empire since the sixteenth century before it was integrated into the Russian Empire following the Russo-Turkish War of 1806–1812. From this point on, the population was gradually incorporated culturally and religiously into the Russian Empire and its Church. The distinctive character of Moldavian Orthodox culture was eroded through the imposition of Russian hierarchs and ritual practice but not entirely eradicated. These lands, populated by a majority of Romanian-speaking ethnic Moldovans, maintained close cultural affinities with the Moldavian lands to the west of the river Prut that went on to form part of the new Romanian nation-state. The southern part of the newly occupied Russian lands, referred to as the Bugeac, had been sparsely populated by seminomadic Tartars. They were expelled by Russia to Crimea and Dobrudja, and the land was settled with Orthodox Christians from the eastern Balkans, mainly Bulgarians and Gagauzes. The 1897 Russian Imperial census, which was conducted on the basis of native language, reported that Moldovans constituted 47.6 percent of the Bessarabian population, with the remainder comprising Ukrainians (19.6 percent), Jews (11.8 percent), and Russians (8 percent), plus a number of other smaller groups such as Germans, Gagauzes, and Bulgarians, especially in the south.[2]

In this ethnically diverse context, between 1812 and 1918 the Russian Orthodox Church, following its assimilation of the local Moldavian Orthodox community, intermittently and sometimes vigorously pursued a policy of Russification of the local Moldavian Church. Starting with the Russian annexation of Bessarabia in 1812, the territory became a "battleground between Orthodox Churches,"[3] with Russia and Romania competing to define Orthodox Christian culture. The Russian Orthodox Church set up its own eparchy in Bessarabia in 1813 and, following a period of relative autonomy under the local-born bishop Gavriil Bănulescu-Bodoni, exercised control of the Church through a succession of bishops appointed to the new diocese of Kishinev-Khotinsk (Chişinău and Hotin in Romanian) from the imperial center. Gradually, under Bănulescu-Bodoni's successors, the Moldavian character of the church was eroded as Romanian-language liturgical books were removed; ethnic Russians, Ukrainians, and Belorussians took over positions of authority; and monastic institutions were headed by abbots brought in from outside the territory. In 1856, when Russia lost three southern districts of Bessarabia at the Treaty of Paris following her defeat in the Crimean War, the policy of Russification of the remaining territory was accelerated. When Russia won back the southern districts in 1878, they too were subjected to rapid measures to ensure the Russian character of the church life there.[4]

Following World War I, Bessarabia was united with Greater Romania and was subject to an intense nation-building process largely intended to undo the previous century of Russification. The Romanian interwar period is characterized by policies aimed at the centralization of the state and the nationalization of culture, driven by the desire to transform all of the newly acquired multiethnic and religiously diverse territories of Bessarabia, Bukovina, and Transylvania into integral parts of a unified nation-state. The new provinces and their populations, including Moldovans, were viewed through cultural-imperialist lenses. What is more, Romania was a society made up of an overwhelmingly agrarian population that her political and intellectual elites were fixated on transforming into citizens of a modern state, even as they considered those they labeled "peasants" to be the "cultural and social backbone of the nation."[5] Of all the new territories, Bessarabia was considered the most problematic not only because of its diverse ethnic, linguistic, and religious makeup (only 56 percent of the population was ethnic Romanian in 1930) but also because it was the most rural, with only 13 percent living in urban centers.[6]

Following the defeat of the Axis in World War II, Romania was compelled to cede Bessarabia to the Soviet Union, with the territory henceforth named the Moldavian Soviet Socialist Republic (MSSR). Mainstream Romanian Church historiography up to this point tends to frame the history of the territory up to 1944 almost exclusively in terms of the national struggle of the Romanian-speaking majority for control of the local church dominated by Russian hierarchs.[7]

The Repression of Religion in Soviet Moldavia

The period following the reoccupation of Bessarabia by Soviet forces in
August 1944 (Romania had been forced to cede Bessarabia and northern
Bucovina to the Soviet Union in June 1940 before joining the Axis inva-
sion and recapturing the lost territory in the following year) up to Stalin's
death in March 1953 was perhaps the harshest and most brutal of the
twentieth century for the local population. The rapid Sovietization of society, the mass deportation of class enemies and religious minorities,[8] and
the closure of Orthodox places of worship massively disrupted the lives of
ordinary Moldovans. This took place against a backdrop of widespread
famine and starvation among the rural population in 1946–1947, with estimated deaths of between 123,000 and 200,000.[9]

With the advent of World War II, Stalin was forced to reconsider his
attitude toward the Russian Orthodox Church because he needed to gal-
vanize and strengthen the solidarity of the Soviet population. The new attitude culminated in the famous meeting between Stalin and the bishops
of the Orthodox Church that took place on September 4, 1943, at which
a concordat was reached that normalized church-state relations and allowed
the Church to conduct its normal activities, with worshippers freely attending church, performing services, and taking part in religious processions.[10]
In parts of the Soviet Union that had experienced the antireligious campaigns of the 1920s and 1930s, an underground movement had taken shape
composed of dissenting groups of Orthodox believers and members of other
religious communities that refused to register, in protest at state interference in church life. The so-called underground or catacomb churches included groups such as the True Orthodox Church of Russia and the
Ionnites, followers of Father John of Kronstadt, who operated clandestinely
outside of official Orthodox structures.[11]

The Orthodox religious underground in Soviet Moldavia, however, had
been shaped by the policies of the Romanian state in the interwar period
and especially by the right-wing dictatorship of Marshal Antonescu, who
had attempted to suppress various Orthodox dissenting movements that
were considered both heretical and antinational in sentiment. These included the Old Calendarists and the Inochentists, two movements characterized by the important role that women played in mobilizing religious
opinion and defending their communities from state interference.[12] The Romanian Orthodox Church's introduction of the Revised Julian calendar[13]

in 1924 provoked a religious crisis, especially in the western part of the former principality of Moldavia (which had been part of the Romanian state since unification in the 1860s) and the newly acquired territory of Bessarabia, both of which had influential monastic institutions with a strongly traditionalist outlook. Resistance to the new calendar resulted in violent confrontations in the 1930s between the Romanian gendarmerie and the Stiliști, or Stylists, the term used to refer to those who continued to adhere to the old-style calendar. For the Romanian Church and state, the calendar was a question related to the social, moral, and religious order of the new nation-state,[14] but for large portions of the Orthodox population it represented a cataclysmic break with tradition and with liturgical time itself and marked a sign of the impending End of Days. The Inochentists also resisted the introduction of the new calendar. Inochentism had emerged in the last decade of the Russian Empire in the western provinces populated by ethnic Moldovans, especially Bessarabia. Initially the movement centered on a pilgrimage and on the charismatic preaching of a Moldovan Orthodox monk, Inochentie of Balta; however, once the movement attracted the negative attention of the Orthodox Church and state authorities, it was transformed into a dissent movement that critiqued the hierarchy of the Church and preached the impending End of Days.[15] These two groups, the Old Calendarists and the Inochentists, had formed clandestine networks in Bessarabia before the Soviet occupations of 1941 and 1944 and had two decades of experience in operating underground.

Unregistered and unrecognized religious groups were, by their nature, difficult to keep track of and to control. The Inochentists, who occupied a liminal space between Orthodoxy and open schism with the Church, were especially elusive. In the MSSR, the secret police was able to draw on the information and records of the previous regime, which had been meticulous in collecting data on the Inochentists and others in preparation for their eventual internment and deportation, thus facilitating swift intervention and arrests in 1945–1946. Alexandru Culiac, one of the main leaders of the Archangelist branch of the movement, was arrested for the first time by the Soviet authorities in 1945 and sentenced by a special session of the NKVD to five years of exile in Kazakhstan for anti-Soviet sectarian activity.[16] Several other leaders of the movement were arrested and deported between 1946 and 1948, accused of "anti-Soviet agitation among the population" aimed against participation in the kolkhozes, Komsomol, and the Communist Party.[17]

Following the death of Stalin, with the exception of a brief Hundred
Days antireligious campaign in 1954, there was a general liberalization of
policy toward religions, and most mainstream churches and registered communities could function without too much state interference. Although
the state still worked actively to ensure that they not thrive, religion gradually began to regain some ground, and many religious leaders were re-
leased from the Gulag.[18] This period of relative calm, however, came to an
end when, at the height of the Cold War between 1958 and 1964, Khrushchev initiated an antireligious campaign that replaced the mass repression
of the past with a return to the policies of the 1930s. He sought to revive
aspects of early Soviet culture, in part to mark a clear break with the Stalin-
ist era, and was a passionate believer in the importance of "scientific atheism" in the construction of a modern communist future.[19] A Central
Committee report of September 13, 1958, in response to a perceived rise in
the activity of religious groups, proposed a campaign that would focus on
education led by trained cadres, the media, and the production of specialist antireligious literature effective for a modern socialist society; shortly
after, on October 4, the Central Committee launched an extensive antireligious campaign.[20] Khrushchev's new religious policy was based on the
revival of two principles devised in the 1920s; the first, which emphasized
the principle of Soviet legality,[21] saw the creation of a clear distinction between registered congregations, which would be offered concessions, while
dealing extremely harshly with unregistered and underground groups; and
the second encouraged prioritizing the repression of clergy and preachers in
an attempt to isolate them from society, while persuading believers through
education and agitation to embrace atheism.[22]

This dramatic shift in policy carried a number of implications for both
the official Orthodox Church and the underground dissenting communities. First, responding to a call by the party to tailor propaganda to local
needs,[23] there was a marked increase in the number of antisect, and specifically anti-Inochentist, publications in Moldavia from the spring of 1958
onward; these included a volume discussing Inochentism, Jehovah's Witnesses, and Murashkovites entitled *Preachers of Obscurantism*, by Aleksan-
drov (1958), and a sourcebook for teachers of atheism entitled *Materials to
Assist Teachers of Atheism*, which included testimonials from ex-Archangelists,
followers of Alexandru Culeac.[24] Both of these were published in Romanian
in order to reach the ethnic majority-Moldovan population. There was
also a series of articles in both Russian- and Romanian-language newspa-

pers and magazines such as *Sovetskaya Moldavia* (Soviet Moldavia), *Sovetskaya Kultura* (Soviet Culture), *Femeia Moldovei* (Women of Moldavia), and *Tinerimea Moldovei* (Youth of Moldavia). The large number of articles in women's and youth magazines reflects the Soviet authorities' view that women and young people were especially vulnerable to the pernicious influence of the superstitious Orthodox underground. And finally, to ensure that the message about the dangers of Inochentism reached the widest possible audience, a documentary film was also produced in 1959 by Moldova Film entitled *Apostles Unmasked.*

The rapid closure of many Orthodox churches and nearly all monasteries in Soviet Moldavia in this period directly affected Orthodox believers, whether members of the Inochentist dissent movement or not, in unintended ways. Between 1954 and 1958, the number of Orthodox churches in operation had remained more or less stable, but in 1958 closures gradually began to increase. According to the official figures of the Council of Orthodox Church Affairs, in 1960 alone 138 Orthodox churches were deregistered in Moldavia.[25] The Orthodox Church had already lost a significant number of priests in 1944: Several hundred had fled as refugees to Romania when Soviet forces reentered the country,[26] and many of the churches these priests had served, around 350, were dropped from the registration roll.[27] The sudden closure of Orthodox places of worship left entire regions with no easy access to priests. The number of functioning Orthodox churches fell dramatically from over 1,100 to just over two hundred by 1988,[28] with most former religious buildings transformed into cinemas, storehouses, hospitals, or museums. Of the twenty-five functioning monasteries in Bessarabia in 1945, fifteen remained open in 1956, but by 1964 all but one had been closed.[29] Although the removal of priests and the closure or destruction of buildings visibly demonstrated the end of the old social order, "superstition," as religious belief and practice was routinely termed, proved extremely tenacious.[30]

Domestic Religion and Dissent

The forced retreat of religious actors, institutions, and communities in the face of state repression, which took various forms, from propaganda campaigns to mass deportations, achieved varied results depending on the specific context. There was an appearance of success as "the transmission of religion was confined to the domestic sphere."[31] Soviet authorities, however,

were aware that despite church closures the religious population, "left to
its own devices," congregated at informal worship services and numerous
house churches.[32] In a previous article, where I discuss the phenomenon of
domestic religion, I outline some of the consequences of Orthodox church
closures, such as the redistribution of religious materials, publications, icons,
bibles, and ritual objects rescued from churches into homes and the daily
lives of believers.[33] This dispersion of material religious charisma into homes
following the closure of churches was accompanied by profound fear among
individuals and communities for their spiritual and physical well-being as
ritual protection, obligations, and taboos were compromised. This, as Kononenko points out, in turn prompted "substitute religious activity during
the Soviet period."[34] In this sense, the destruction of religious institutions
gave new impetus to practices that could replace them.

Gender was, of course, highly significant in this process; as Viola discusses, older women in village society, who were "seen as outside Soviet control" and freer from many of the pressures to conform to Soviet ideals,[35] took
on the role of keepers of Orthodox tradition and knowledge. Because of their
age, these women were also considered "not fully feminine" in vernacular
Orthodox belief. Consequently, this "combination of political reality and
folk belief" led to the feminization, and also the geriatricization, of religious
activity.[36] Similar tendencies can be observed not only among mainstream
Orthodox but also among certain religious minorities or Orthodox dissenting groups. In his anthropology of Russian Old Believers, Douglas Rogers
recounts that in the Soviet era, "their pastors were nearly universally spiritual
mothers rather than fathers, and services took place in domestic spaces that
had themselves become more closely associated with women than with
men." As Rogers goes on to explain, this process came to characterize all
societies in the Soviet bloc, with "the disassociation of men from religious
life as they identified more closely with public party positions, waged labor
in the state farm, and the pervasive networks of socialist society."[37]

Earlier waves of religious dissent and repression in the Russian Orthodox world from the seventeenth century onward had resulted in a similar
phenomenon of domestic religious ritual replacing or supplementing public worship among groups such as the Old Believers,[38] the Skoptsy,[39] and
the Stundists.[40] In the Soviet era, these groups were joined by new underground "catacomb" churches that mirrored earlier patterns of domestic
practice and hidden worship. Many of these groups transformed domestic

space into sacred safe havens where liturgical life could continue in seclusion. In addition, with the closure and the forced laicization of tens of thousands of monks and nuns across the Soviet Union and communist Eastern Europe, former members of religious orders set up households in towns and villages and continued to pursue a private religious life in the midst of socialist society.[41]

These expressions of domestic religion should be understood therefore as the product not only of communist repression but also of centuries of dissenter tradition from within the Russian Orthodox Church. In the context of Soviet Moldavia, domestic forms of religion drew on or grew out of earlier traditions of Inochentist and Old Calendarist Romanian Orthodox dissent established in the interwar period. These two groups, rather than relying on the agency and commitment of older women, drew their strength from devout younger women who pledged their lives to the salvation of their souls and disappeared into the religious underground.

Women in Inochentism

Women and young girls played central roles in the emergence and spread of Inochentism in a number of ways. Pilgrims to Balta, the home monastery of the monk Inochentie, participated in mass confession in a similar way to that practiced by John of Kronstadt,[42] which frequently resulted in the ecstatic possession of large numbers of believers. The many young women and girls who experienced possession became known as "young martyrs," who were seen as taking on the sins and suffering of others and were also considered to be prophetesses.[43] The possession cult that emerges from the contemporary accounts bears one of the key hallmarks of Lewis's category of "peripheral possession,"[44] which identifies certain forms of possession, those that are most often found among women and that are initially considered as an illness, as "thinly disguised protest movements," a kind of "clandestine ecstasy" that can be targeted against the dominant sex.

Inochentie, as a monk of the Russian Orthodox Church, also extolled the virtues of leading a life according to monastic rules. In Orthodox Christianity, monastic life was regarded as coming closest to the ideal spiritual life, one free from the temptation of original sin, which was supposedly linked to sexuality. Inochentie, like John of Kronstadt before him, in preaching the renunciation of marriage and sexual relations, wished to unburden his followers of material concerns and obligations to family to allow them to prepare through prayer and repentance for the End of Days. For women, the rejection of the model of bride, mother, and housewife was especially transformative: This not only relieved them of all such duties and their associated inferior social status; it also served as a marker of their spiritual equality with men.[45]

Free from the traditional roles of wives and mothers, women gained an opportunity to take on leading roles within the new community that Inochentie had gathered around him. Women took on administrative tasks, served as missionaries, and took charge of the collection of charitable offerings on behalf of the community. According to early reports, women wandered the villages spreading news of the movement and seeking new adherents: "Women appeared to be leading the whole movement: collecting money, gathering people together for prayer at night, helping to dig 'miraculous' wells, intervening with the local parish to conduct communal memorial liturgies."[46] The "wise virgins" that flocked to Inochentie had the important task of gathering offerings; this practice allowed the movement to grow and amass considerable wealth.[47] The Romanian theologian Botoşăneanu claimed that it was thanks to "the preaching of women, so-called sisters, that the movement spread over the river Prut" into the rest of Romania.[48] Among these women followers were also Orthodox nuns from some of the monasteries in Bessarabia.

A special place was also reserved within the movement for Inochentie's mother, who is said to have been recognized by his followers as having "superiority in religious questions and as having their deep respect: they kissed the ground near her house, received blessings from her and kissed her hand"; she was referred to by his followers as *măiculiţa Domnului*, "dear little mother of God," or *născătoare de Dumnezeu*, "Mother of God."[49] The use of this honorific title for important women, which was also a feature of other Orthodox dissent movements,[50] continued in later Inochentist communities.

The important role of women, and especially young women, in the early Inochentist movement gave a distinctive character to Orthodox dissent that emerged in interwar Bessarabia. In some branches of the movement, especially among the so-called Archangelists, women took on some priestly functions, and young women were especially important as missionaries. From bulletins issued by the Romanian police it is evident that a large proportion of those wanted by the authorities for "religious crimes" were

Figure 1. Three Inochentist women, including Maria Sârbu, from Sireţi, in the county of Lăpuşna, who was sentenced to three months' imprisonment on September 22, 1938, for conducting Inochentist propaganda. She confessed to having lived a "vagabond" life traveling from village to village preaching Inochentie's message of repentance. *Source*: *Archiva Naţională a Republicii Moldova* fond. *Tribunalul militar al Corpului III armată, Chişinău* [National Archive of the Republic of Moldova—Military Tribunal of the Third Army Corps, Chişinău], dosarr. 738-1-6846, 21 © National Archive of the Republic of Moldova.

young women. They were all reported to be dressed in black like nuns, which is one of the reasons given for why Inochentist women were sometimes hard to detect. Following a series of raids on Inochentist groups in Soroca county in September and October 1941, the gendarme commander described the appearance of the Inochentists to help others identify them by sight: "The men wear long beards, and the women 'experienced women proselytizers' wear on their heads large black headscarves, which cover the front [of their heads] and back (uniformly)."[51] The fact that the women were described as "experienced proselytizers" demonstrates the important role that these mainly young women were playing in these communities. The archival record gives the impression of a cat-and-mouse game in which these young women played with the authorities as they traveled from village to village in Bessarabia, even crossing the Dniester into Soviet territory. The vital role that women had played in promoting the pilgrimage to Balta in the 1910s continued in the 1920s, 1930s, and 1940s under Romanian rule.

The harsh policies of the Antonescu regime toward religious dissenters, which included internment in labor camps, imprisonment, and the threat of deportation to concentration camps alongside Jews and Roma, drove Inochentism underground, and the movement became increasingly secretive and elusive. Inochentist communities began to construct for themselves alternative religious spaces, secret hideouts dug under their homes and gardens, thus transforming the material conditions of their Orthodox religious practice decades before the advent of Soviet communist rule in Moldavia. Women's agency and leadership within the religious underground was both an important resource and source of strength as well as one of the principal factors that the authorities could use to attack the movement. The domestic forms of religion and the religious underground in Soviet Moldavia, therefore, were shaped by this earlier period of Orthodox dissent and set the context for Orthodox dissent during the Soviet era.[52]

Orthodoxy and the Archangelist Underground in Soviet Moldavia

The Soviet antireligious campaigns of the 1950s and 1960s are gradually passing from living memory, but they have left a lasting stamp in the Moldovan religious psyche. Between 2005 and 2014, I conducted a series of interviews with women members of the Archangelist branch of Inochentism[53] in the village of Hadjiovca (I have changed the name of the village and have given the women pseudonyms to protect the identity of my informants) and neighboring villages. These villages are mainly populated by members of the Gagauz minority, Turkish-speaking Orthodox Christians who migrated to the region at the beginning of the nineteenth century.[54] Both Inochentism and its later iteration Archangelism were and still are predominantly ethnically Moldovan (and Romanian speaking) in character, with members of the Gagauz minority only having joined from the 1950s onward during the Soviet antireligious campaigns.

Since the collapse of the Soviet Union and Moldovan independence, the Archangelist community has gradually moved above ground, both metaphorically and literally, although they are still not a registered religious community and do not have official places of worship. They hold their Sunday meetings in the homes of members of the community, which they do on a rotating basis. The movement, however, remains very secretive, and they are wary of outsiders. I first encountered members of the Archangelist movement by chance when I was living in Comrat, the capital of the Gagauz Autonomous Region in the Republic of Moldova, researching Orthodox religion among the Gagauz minority there. While speaking to a group of village women a friend of mine had gathered together with the purpose of talking about their religious writing practices, one of the women suddenly outed her neighbor by declaring, "She doesn't eat meat at all; she's an Inochentist!" The woman took her neighbor's comment in good humor explaining that she follows the monastic rules, like a true Christian. Over the following weeks and months, little by little, more and more bits of information filtered through about this group, and I gradually came to realize that their story was more than some curious local anomaly but a widespread and neglected aspect of religious diversity in that part of the Orthodox Christian world.

I met most of my interviewees in their homes or chatted with them on the benches arranged on the porch or veranda. In Hadjiovca, locals estimate that there are around forty members of the community with perhaps twenty more in the neighboring villages. The overwhelming majority of Gagauz are Orthodox Christian, with small but significant numbers of Baptists and Adventists. As Archangelists do not feature in any official statistics, it is difficult to estimate their numbers, but a conservative estimate for Archangelists in the whole of Moldova may be in the region of two thousand to four thousand members, some more active than others, the vast majority of whom belong to the Moldovan majority.

The Archangelists in Hadjiovca trace the origins of their community back to the 1960s. As Maria explained:

> I was six years old when we started, I am fifty-four years old now. My father used to eat meat, he would give it to us secretly! He started later than us, two years later; honey, fish, eggs are what we eat. When I was six we became stronger [in our faith]. People came from the monasteries from that place, first they taught in the Moldovan villages and after they came here [to the Gagauz villages], they came to my grandmother, then my mother, and after other people came and they liked it, they saw that there is nothing new here, it is Orthodoxy like in a monastery.
>
> (Maria, August 13, 2011)

Like Maria, Ana also linked the arrival of Archangelism with the closure of Orthodox institutions.

> Here, in Hadjiovca, it started in the 1960s, when all the churches and monasteries were destroyed. All the monks and priests were made homeless. There were people that used to travel further afield to monasteries, some to Russia and to other places, wherever they could find. So when the churches were closed people began to gather together to pray. The people that came from the monasteries said that we have to be stricter, you need to keep all four fasts, Wednesday, Friday, Sunday, if you want good health, and on feast days. Keep Sundays, do not do any major jobs, there should only be religious service, you can feed animals but you shouldn't do anything else. . . . My grandmother was very involved with the Orthodox Church, she sang in the choir, she was in the Church committee, so when in 1959 they closed the Church, she had always been there. When the Church was closed, she wanted to go somewhere, to find a way to save her soul, so she went to Kiev, to the Lavra, at that time it was open, and told them there that in our village there are people, monks, who came from monasteries that had been closed, and they say you have to do like this, how to observe the fast, Sundays, feast days, Wednesdays, and so on. We have to do it this way to save our souls, and they [the monks in the Lavra] said don't look for something more correct than

this, the way they tell you to observe it, keep it, follow them because maybe the churches will open again one day but they will not be open soon; if you want to save your soul they are not teaching you incorrectly, stick to it!

(Ana, July 8, 2013)

The central factor in these accounts of the beginning of the community is the closure of the monasteries and churches, which in turn is intimately related to the need to maintain Orthodox traditions, the most basic and important element of which was the keeping of fasts. As Ana went on to describe:

I don't keep them all, but at least I am afraid and I feel bad about it if I don't keep them all. With my friends who are Orthodox and are good Christians, if someone invites them to eat something that is not allowed, they will find an excuse and eat it anyway. For example, if it is Wednesday or Friday and someone invites you to eat they will eat, but we won't. That is the way this system works, that's the way it was established and we want to follow it. We decided to make the rules of our life like this and that's the way we want to follow them.

(Ana, July 8, 2013)

Fasting became not only a question of personal commitment and penance but also a boundary marker between the faithful and those "in the world." A woman from the neighboring village of Cavarlâc (a pseudonym) reinforced this same theme: adherence to the rules of Orthodoxy that were threatened by the way of life that communism and the closure of the churches had brought.

I was a child and we went to the fields during the summer, we heard that in the neighboring village there were people that never went to work when there was a holy day, I was attracted to this, I liked it, and then I finished school and went to study, and I came here to do my work experience, I am from another village. I came here when I got married, and later I met these people here, my husband's brother. . . . I started to read, I liked it a lot, my parents fasted, but when they came from church on Sunday they prepared food and lit the fire, but here when I came . . . we don't do any such thing.

(Evghenia, July 10, 2013)

Strict fasting and the keeping of the Sundays and of the complex calendar of holidays and feasts, regardless of obligations to the state, became a marker of Archangelist identity vis-à-vis the lapsed Orthodox community: the preservation of the authentic, monastic route to salvation in the midst of an atheist world. The closure of the churches in Hadjiovca and the neighboring villages also left people with a sense of anxiety for their well-being and their souls.

As Kononenko describes, all across the Soviet Union similar processes had been unfolding since the 1930s. The people particularly active in preserving local religious culture, whom she refers to as "culture keepers," became custodians of both intangible and material elements of their traditions. As ritual protection, obligations, and taboos were compromised by the disappearance of churches and the liturgical calendar, "fear of the consequences of violation prompted substitute religious activity."[55] In this way, the unintended consequence of the Orthodox Church closures of the late 1950s and 1960s was the appearance of a new layer of the religious underground in Moldavia and an expansion of Inochentist ideas to communities and areas of the country that had not been reached during the interwar or wartime periods, largely because of ethnic and linguistic differences. Douglas Rogers describes the domestication of religion that happened in the Soviet Union in the following terms: "First, religious practice often slipped from public view into the spaces of the home; and second, believers began to domesticate religion, to claim for themselves some of the ritual and even theological competencies formerly arrogated to specialist clerics."[56] Religious materials, publications, icons, bibles, and ritual objects were hidden or rescued from churches condemned to closure and were thus dispersed into communities. These materials found their way into the homes and daily lives of believers. Sometimes large collections of items were hidden to prevent confiscation; other less conspicuous items were used in the domestic setting, where they were employed in healing practices, added to the icon corner, or read on Sundays in place of attending the liturgy. In the homes of Archangelists, numerous rare and valuable liturgical books, icons, and pieces of church furnishings now adorn domestic ritual spaces. Echoing an earlier chapter of Russian Orthodox dissent, the Archangelists, like the priestless Old Believers centuries before them, took over the "transmission of spiritual power, sacrament and knowledge" from a fallen church.[57]

When Maria's family joined the community, she was still at school. She remembers vividly how she was treated because of her family's refusal to conform to Soviet norms.

> At that time the leaders of the kolkhoz were very much against us. The kolkhoz chief here in Hadjiovca was against us because we were not going . . . we were keeping our faith strictly, and this was his character, he was a very bad man, he was a very cruel man, he behaved very badly toward us, cruel, but after he died things changed, people were not so, you know. . . . Our parents did not put the [pioneer] tie on us, we were not wearing the star either, they pulled my hair, they beat me very much, but I didn't put it on, neither the badge nor the tie, I didn't put them on; they pulled my hair, I cried, they beat me up, also slapped my cheeks, but it was like that and that's all. The teacher beat us, others too, the pupils beat me up, they were hitting me, so many things happened, but all for the sake of God.
>
> (Maria, August 13, 2011)

For Maria, her suffering in school was for her faith. Those older than Maria, like her relative Domnica, who became one of the "sisters" living in the underground, recalled how their houses were kept under constant surveillance: "Everyone was against us, the kolkhoz . . . they knew which houses were Inochentist, and they posted people to watch the gates to check that no one went to visit them during the night" (Domnica, June 15, 2014). But this kind of treatment, according to Domnica, was part of their path to salvation. "When we were persecuted, it made our faith even stronger; it was a sign of the truth of our faith." Some of the sisters were arrested multiple times. Domnica told me the story of Vasilisa, who faced a Comrades Court in the 1960s and was sentenced to three years in what was described to me as a relatively "open" prison farm. She escaped several times, and when she reappeared in the village yet again, the other members of the group would ask her why she had escaped, as it would only bring the authorities' attention back on the community, and they would pick her up and return her. Her reply, which Domnica relayed to me with a smile, was, "Because I can." Domnica, too, had been arrested several times. "I was even in the newspaper with my photograph, but usually we managed to disappear again before our trial dates came round." The young women often operated far from their home villages, passing through the capital, Chişinău, where they could be

relatively anonymous. On this occasion, however, they were unlucky enough
to be spotted by someone from Hadjiovca, who handed them over to the
authorities. But as Domnica explained, the sisters were experienced at dealing with their captors and used their wits to evade trial and prison.

> Because we were very well behaved when we were arrested, very meek
> and compliant, we could earn the trust of our prison guards, and they
> gave us chores in the prison, such as cleaning and making food. We
> were innocent young girls. But we knew that on the twentieth day
> after our arrests we would have to be officially charged and stand trial,
> so we worked out which day to give the guards the slip and disappear
> back into the crowds in Chişinău.
>
> (Domnica, June 15, 2014)

Domnica and the other women who were present one Sunday afternoon
in June 2014 remembered with some humor the lives they used to live avoid-
ing detection and defying the best efforts of the authorities to stop their
preaching. These Archangelist women had challenged Soviet society and
had also overturned traditional gender roles. The Archangelist women I
spoke to in Hadjiovca were unmarried, following the tradition laid down
by Inochentie one hundred years earlier, mostly living with their unmarried siblings or sometimes alone. As young women, they had rejected marriage to become "sisters" of the Archangel Michael and had entered a new
spiritually purposeful religious life. The underground community, as they
described it to me, relied on the faith, commitment, and strength of purpose of the young, especially young women.

Today, the Archangelist community in Hadjiovca is aging but still active. Unlike some other groups that originated from the teachings of Inochentie, the sisters in Hadjiovca embrace the term that others have used to
classify them: "We like it, we like it. . . . He [Alexandru Culiac, the founder
of Archangelism] endured for us, to teach us about God." As well as embracing the term "Archangelist," Domnica also openly displays images of
Alexandru Culeac, the Archangel Michael, in her home, something that
would have warranted arrest during Romanian and Soviet rule.

With the end of the Soviet Union came the return of the Orthodox
Church to Hadjiovca. Archangelists, however, have not returned to the
fold. The priest of the village is scornful of the Archangelists and condemns
their practices, especially the role that women play in the community; the
most common accusations leveled at them no longer relate to orgies or

human sacrifice but instead refer to their practice of allowing women to serve at communion. The community in Hadjiovca is similarly scornful of the Orthodox Church and its hierarchy, which they consider to be hopelessly compromised by a lack of true faith.

> When the Romanians came with the *novy stil* [referring to the calendar reform of 1924], they were the first; when the Communists came, they were first; and when the Church opened again, they were first again. You want to know why we don't go to Church? The foundation of the Church is there, it is belief, there is belief. The Church doesn't sin, but who is inside the Church? If the shepherd is good, the flock will be fine, but if the shepherd isn't concerned with them they will scatter and become the food of wolves.
>
> (Domnica, June 15, 2014)

As Domnica went on to explain, "The Church doesn't like us because we follow God's law more strongly than they can. They cannot accept us back because we will show them up for what they are." Domnica draws a strong distinction between Christians who follow God's word and the Orthodox who, despite having the right credentials in terms of ritual and belief, have become corrupted, fickle, opportunistic, hypocritical, and proud. She refers to herself as a Christian first. "I am a Christian, and Orthodox yes, this is necessary. But being Orthodox is not enough to make you a Christian." But both Maria and Domnica were quick to draw a distinction between themselves and sectarians such as local Baptists or Adventists.

> We don't teach anything new; everything we do is from the monastic tradition, we just maintain things the way they should be, and we follow the words of Father Inochentie, we follow what he taught us.
>
> (Maria, August 13, 2011)

The community in Hadjiovca relies on their own ritual specialists, "our own people," as Maria describes them, from Chişinău, the capital.

> There are men and women who never got married, and they only serve for this purpose. Of course they don't just sit around, they have normal jobs, but on Sundays and feast days they don't work, for example now it is six o'clock and from now on we don't work, we don't light fires, nothing. After Saturday evening nothing, there is only evening prayer.
>
> (Maria, August 13, 2011)

The boundaries between the Orthodox and members of the Archangelist community are both ritual and somatic. Their critique, although sometimes verbalized, is enacted through their bodies, which they are able to master more successfully than are the custodians of the Orthodox Church, and through ritual separation.

Moldova, which was catastrophically affected both politically and economically by the breakup of the Soviet Union, is often cited as the poorest nation in Europe, and the Gagauz minority is further marginalized linguistically, economically, and socially within Moldovan society. Gagauz women and men, since the 1990s, have engaged in labor migration on a large scale to Russia, Turkey, Greece, and Western Europe. Leyla Keogh, in her study of Gagauz women's practices of labor migration, has highlighted the "economic resourcefulness" of Gagauz women in postsocialism and how they have contested the "gendered social order" in a context in which "motherhood" is central to women's identities.[58] Archangelist women, like their Orthodox neighbors, also travel to find work outside of Moldova; Maria worked for many years in Greece as a housekeeper, and this has similarly provided them with more autonomy and economic security. Unlike the often younger Orthodox women migrants described by Keogh, however, for whom being a "better mother" by securing an income for the family is the way to expand "their imaginations and desires, and even help them construct new lifestyles,"[59] for the older generation of Archangelist women, the traditional domestic social role as carers and mothers had long been overthrown when they were young women in the religious underground.

Conclusion

The changing names of the borderland known as Bessarabia, Soviet Moldavia, and Moldova reflect the ever-shifting political and religious realities that shaped Inochentism in the region. It was this borderland status that also ensured that religious dissenters, under both Romanian and Soviet rule, became important targets in both states' aim of transforming the social order. Following the radical monastic tradition first advocated by the Orthodox monk Inochentie of Balta in the first two decades of the twentieth century and then continued in the underground communities in Antonescu's Romania, young Orthodox women in Soviet Moldavia were attracted by life in a religious underground that received new impetus as an unanticipated consequence of the Khrushchev antireligious campaigns and Orthodox Church closures of the late 1950s and 1960s. Domestic forms of Orthodox religious practice in Soviet Moldavia were shaped not only by older women, as was common in many parts of the Soviet Union, but also by the young, who broke the commonly understood pattern of the feminization of religion during communism described by Rogers, Kononenko, Viola, and others. These young women engaged in high-risk, clandestine religious activities that contributed to a recasting of aspects of traditional religious authority structures that had started in earlier decades.

The ideal of celibacy in Inochentism helped establish a symbolic parity between men and women, which in turn empowered women to take on important new roles in religious life as priests and living saints, some honored as Mothers of God. Inochentism, especially in its more radical Archangelist form, required social disobedience from young women: They were expected to act differently and to reject the civic duty of giving birth and of offering the state future citizens, workers, and soldiers. The Romanian state, the Orthodox Church, and the Soviet Union all shared one idea about womanhood; women should be marshaled for the good of the state and the nation. The centrality of young women in the Inochentist movement, who took identities that challenged Orthodox Christian tradition, peasant societal norms, and the reproductive expectations of the state, fueled the extreme accusations of sexual and moral degeneracy that appeared in the Romanian press in the interwar period and in Soviet antireligious propaganda materials. As the testimonies of Domnica, Ana, and Maria demonstrate, opting to join the Inochentist underground in the Khrushchev years was in part driven by anxiety at the loss of Orthodox institutions, rituals, and ritual specialists. The radical beliefs of Inochentist dissenters, however, had been shaped earlier by the upheavals that befell the tsarist state and the modernizing and nationalizing projects of Romania. Women in Bessarabia, Soviet Moldavia, and contemporary Moldova have been important actors in reshaping Orthodoxy as practiced at home and in the community in the face of the successive states' attempts to reshape religious, social, and political realities.

Notes

Some elements of this chapter appear in my monograph *Inochentism and Orthodox Christianity: Religious Dissent in the Russian and Romanian Borderlands* (London: Routledge, 2019). I would like to thank Catherine Wanner for the opportunity to participate in the conference Public Religion, Ambient Faith: Religion and Socio-Political Change in the Black Sea Region, Kiev, 2016, and for her insightful comments, which helped shape some of the points I make here. The research for this chapter has received funding from the European Research Council (ERC) under the European Union's Horizon 2020 research and innovation programme No. 677355.

1. The Moldavian Soviet Socialist Republic (MSSR) consisted of most of the territory of the historical province of Bessarabia plus lands to the east of the river Dniester formerly part of Ukraine. Soviet Moldavia, apart from a brief period from June 1940 to June 1941, existed from 1944 to 1991. Following the breakup of the Soviet Union in 1991, the leadership of the former Soviet Republic declared the independence of the Republic of Moldova, adopting the Romanian spelling of the name of the territory. In this chapter, I refer to Moldavia during the Soviet period and Moldova for the post-Soviet period. I refer to the inhabitants of both as Moldovans.

2. G. Murgoci, *La population de la Bessarabie. Étude démographique avec cartes et tableaux statistiques* (Paris, 1920).

3. Nicholas Dima, "Politics and Religion in Moldova: A Case Study," *Mankind Quarterly* 34, no. 3 (1994): 175–94.

4. J. Eugene Clay, "Apocalypticism in the Russian Borderlands: Inochentie Levizor and His Moldovan Followers," *Religion, State, and Society* 26, nos. 3/4 (1998): 251–63.

5. Sorin Radu and Oliver Jens Schmitt, "Introduction," in *Politics and Peasants in Interwar Romania: Perceptions, Mentalities, Propaganda*, ed. Sorin Radu and Oliver Jens Schmitt (Newcastle: Cambridge Scholars, 2017), 1.

6. Irina Livezeanu, *Cultural Politics in Greater Romania* (Ithaca, NY: Cornell University Press, 1995), 9–10.

7. See, e.g., Nicolae Popovschi, *Istoria Bisericii din Bassarabia în veacul al XiX-lea sub Ruşi* [The history of the Church of Bessarabia in the nineteenth century under the Russians] (Chişinău: Museum, 1931); Ion Nistor, *Istoria Basarabiei* [The history of Bessarabia] (Bucharest: Humanitas, 1991); Mircea Păcarariu, *Basarabia: Aspecte din Istoria Bisericii şi a Neamului Românesc* [Bessarabia: aspects of the history of the Church and the Romanian nation] (Iaşi: Trinitas, 1993); and Dima, "Politics and Religion in Moldova."

8. On April 6, 1949, the Council of Ministers of the USSR took the decision to begin Operation South, the mass deportation from Moldavia of a wide spectrum of anti-Soviet elements but especially the *kulaks*. Mass deportation was a tried-and-tested method by 1949 deployed to remove troublesome populations from sensitive border regions, to eliminate resistance to collectivization, and

to remove economic and political elites. Emily Baran, *Dissent on the Margins: How Soviet Jehovah's Witnesses Defied Communism and Lived to Preach about It* (Oxford: Oxford University Press), 60). Between July 6 and 9, 35,796 people were deported to Siberia, constituting the largest deportation in the history of Bessarabia. Of these, 7,625 families were classified as *kulaks*; the remainder were accused of being collaborators with the "German-fascist occupation." Igor Caşu, *Duşmanul de Clasă: Represiune politice, violenţă şi resistenţă în R(A)SS Moldovenească, 1924–56* [Class enemy: political repression, violence, and resistance in the SSR of Moldavia, 1924–1956] (Chişinău: Cartier, 2014), 234. This second category included 345 families of sectarians, mainly Jehovah's Witnesses. Jehovah's Witnesses were subject to a further mass deportation from Moldavia in April 1951, when they were exclusively targeted in Operation North. The total number of Jehovah's Witnesses deported in this operation was 2,724. Caşu, *Duşmanul de Clasă*, 298.

9. Caşu, *Duşmanul de Clasă*, 189–90.

10. Tatiana A. Chumachenko, *Church and State in Soviet Russia* (Armonk, NY: M. E. Sharpe, 2002), 190.

11. William Fletcher, "Underground Orthodoxy: A Problem of Political Control," *Canadian Slavonic Papers* 12, no. 4 (1970): 363–94.

12. On the role of women in Inochentism, see James A. Kapaló, "Wise Virgins and Mothers of God: Women, Possession, and Sexuality in the Early Inochentist Movement," in *Marginalised and Endangered Worldviews: Comparative Studies on Contemporary Eurasia, India, and South America*, ed. Lidia Guzy and James A. Kapaló (Lit Verlag: Berlin, 2017), 137–61; on women in the Old Calendarist movement, see Iuliana Cindrea-Nagy, "Femeile stiliste în arhivele politiei secrete" [Stilist women in the archives of the secret police], *Magazin Istoric* 1 (2019): 66–70.

13. The Revised Julian calendar was adopted by the Orthodox Churches of Constantinople, Alexandria, Antioch, Greece, Cyprus, Romania, Poland, and Bulgaria at a congress in Constantinople in May 1923. Russia, along with Ukraine, Georgia, and Jerusalem, rejected its introduction.

14. See D. Croitoru, "Pericolul stilismului şi inochentismului din Basarabia" [The danger of Stilism and Inochentism in Bessarabia], *Misionarul* 8, nos. 1/2 (1936): 120–21.

15. On Inochentism, see Kapaló, *Inochentism and Orthodox Christianity.*

16. ASISRM-KGB 022997, 2:209–10.

17. Pavel Moraru, *Urmaşul lui Felix Dzerjinski: Organele Securităţii Statului în Republica Sovietica Socialistă Moldovenească* [Follower of Felix Dzerzhinsky: organs of state security in the Soviet Socialist Republic of Moldavia] (Bucharest: Institutul Naţional pentru Studiul Totalitarismului, 2008), 109.

18. Baran, *Dissent on the Margins*, 71.

19. Catriona Kelly, *Socialist Churches: Radical Secularizatioon and the Preservation of the Past in Petrograd and Leningrad, 1918–1988* (DeKalb: Northern Illinois University Press, 2016), 190.

20. Kelly, *Socialist Churches*, 191.

21. Sonja Luehrmann, *Secularism Soviet Style: Teaching Atheism and Religion in a Volga Republic* (Bloomington: Indiana University Press, 2011), 98.

22. Baran, *Dissent on the Margins*, 70–71.

23. Baran, *Dissent on the Margins*, 72.

24. *Materiale în Ajutorul Lectorului-Ateist* [Material for the support of teachers of atheism] (Chişinău: Societatea pentru răspîndirea conoştinţelor politice şi ştiinţifice a R.S.S. Moldoveneşti, 1959).

25. Nathaniel Davis, "The Number of Orthodox Churches before and after the Khrushchev Antireligious Drive," *Slavic Review* 50, no. 3 (1991): 613.

26. Romeo Cemîrtan, "Situaţia şi evoluţie vieţii bisericeşti din RSSM în periodă 1945–1962" [The situation and evolution of the life of the Church in the MSSR in the period 1945–1962], in *Destine individuale şi collective în comunism*, ed. Cosmin Budeancă and Florentin Olteanu (Iaşi: Polirom, 2013).

27. Davis, "The Number of Orthodox Churches," 612.

28. Dima, "Politics and Religion in Moldova," 184.

29. Iurie Babii et al., eds., *Locaşuri Sfinte* [Holy places] (Chişinău: Alfa şi Omega, 2001)

30. Kelly, *Socialist Churches*, 3.

31. Chris Hann, "Introduction: Broken Chains and Moral Lazarets: The Politicization, Juridification, and Commodification of Religion after Socialism," in *Religion, Identity, Postsocialism: The Halle Focus Group 2003–2010*, ed. Chris Hann (Max Planck Institute for Social Anthropology, 2010), 12.

32. Fletcher, "Underground Orthodoxy," 383.

33. James A. Kapaló, "Domestic Religion in the Soviet and Post-Soviet Moldova," in *Religion im Kontext/Religion in Context: Handbuch für Wissenschaft und Studium*, ed. Annette Schnabel, Melanie Reddig, and Heidemarie Winkel (Baden-Baden: Nomos, 2018), 305–21.

34. Natalie Kononenko, "Folk Orthodoxy: Popular Religion in Contemporary Ukraine," in *Letters from Heaven: Popular Religion in Russia and Ukraine*, ed. John Paul Himka and Andriy Zayarnyuk (Toronto: London: University of Toronto Press, 2006), 47.

35. Lynne Viola, "бабьи бунты and Peasant Women Protest during Collectivization," *Russian Review* 45, no. 1 (1986): 23–24.

36. Kononenko, "Folk Orthodoxy," 48–49.

37. Douglas Rogers, *The Old Faith and the Russian Land: A Historical Ethnography of Ethics in the Urals* (Ithaca, NY: Cornell University Press, 2009),

174. See also James Kapaló, "'She read me a prayer and I read it back to her': Gagauz Women, Miraculous Literacy, and the Dreaming of Charms," *Religion and Gender* 4, no. 1 (2014): 3–20, 175.

38. See Irina Paert, *Old Believers, Religious Dissent, and Gender in Russia, 1760–1850* (Manchester: Manchester University Press, 2003); and Rogers, *The Old Faith and the Russian Land*.

39. Laura Engelstein, *Castration and the Heavenly Kingdom: A Russian Folk Tale* (Ithaca, NY: Cornell University Press, 1999).

40. See S. I. Zhuk, *Russia's Lost Reformation: Peasants, Millennialism, and Radical Sects in Southern Russia and Ukraine, 1830–1917* (Baltimore, MD: John Hopkins University Press, 2004).

41. J. J. Wynot, *Keeping the Faith: Russian Orthodox Monasticism in the Soviet Union, 1917–1939* (College Station: Texas A&M University Press, 2004).

42. Nadieszda Kizenko, *A Prodigal Saint: Father John of Kronstadt and the Russian People* (University Park: Pennsylvania State University Press, 2003), 60.

43. Clay, "Apocalypticism in the Russian Borderlands," 251–63.

44. I. M. Lewis, *Ecstatic Religion: A Study of Shamanism and Spirit Possession* (London: Routledge, 1989), 26.

45. Kapaló, "Wise Virgins and Mothers of God."

46. Nicolae Popovschi, *Mișcarea de la Balta său inochentismul în Basarabia* [The Balta Movement or Inochentism] (Chișinău: Tipografia Eparhială— "Cartea Românească," 1926), 110.

47. Petre Cazacu, *La mănăstore, la părințelul* [To the monastery, to the father] (1938; Chișinău: Noua Galilee, 2001), 33.

48. Grigore Leu Botoșăneanu, *Confesiune și Secte* [Confessions and sects] (București: Tipografia Cărților Bisericești, 1929), 53.

49. Popovschi, *Mișcarea de la Balta său inochentismul în Basarabia*, 110.

50. Zhuk, *Russia's Lost Reformation*, 130.

51. *Archiva Naționale Istorice Centrale*—fond. *Inspectoratul General al Jandarmeriei* (Romania) [Central National Historical Archive—General Inspectorate of the Gendarmerie], dosar. 22/1941, 209.

52. For a fuller account of the role of women in Inochentism, see Kapaló, "Wise Virgins and Mothers of God"; and Kapaló, *Inochentism and Orthodox Christianity*.

53. The Archangelist movement grew out of the earlier Inochentist movement in 1920s Bessarabia (the present-day Republic of Moldova) under Romanian rule and is one of the main surviving branches of the movement. Formed around a family of brothers, most prominent of whom was Alexandru Culiac (b. 1891), the movement venerated its leaders as various heavenly or saintly persons returned to earth to battle Satan at the End of Days. Alexandru Culiac was venerated as the Archangel Michael on earth, which is how the name of this branch of the Inochentist movement originates.

54. On Gagauz history, identity, and religion see James A. Kapaló, *Text, Context, and Performance: Gagauz Folk Religion in Discourse and Practice* (Leiden: Brill, 2011).

55. Kononenko, "Folk Orthodoxy," 47.

56. Douglas Rogers, "Old Belief between 'Society' and 'Culture': Remaking Moral Communities and Inequalities on a Former State Farm," in *Religion, Morality, and Community in Post-Soviet Societies*, ed. M. D. Steinberg and C. Wanner (Bloomington: Indiana University Press, 2008), 124.

57. Paert, *Old Believers, Religious Dissent, and Gender in Russia*, 39.

58. Leyla J. Keogh, "Globalizing 'Postsocialism': Mobile Mothers and Neoliberalism on the Margins of Europe," *Anthropological Quarterly* 79, no. 3 (2006): 455.

59. Keogh, "Globalizing 'Postsocialism,'" 455.

GENDER AND RELIGIOSITY IN COMMUNIST ROMANIA: CONTINUITY AND CHANGE

Maria Bucur

Of Continuity and Change

Some of my oldest memories from childhood are linked to the dark tall cupolas, strong incense, and cold, drafty air of the churches where my grandmother, who had been raised as a deeply religious person in her small village near Oradea, would take me on Saturday mornings to have *colivă* blessed by the priest.[1] I knew close to nothing about Christianity, but I loved eating *colivă* and knew it was special and that I should say a prayer[2] and the name of our relative for whom it had been prepared when accepting it. I also knew to be quiet and lower my head before the priest. Starting at age seven I often went into churches on my own, especially on the way home from school. My school was five minutes from the Patriarchy and from another old church in downtown Bucharest, Sf. Vineri (St. Friday), located across the street from the Theological Institute.[3] Most of the time, these churches were practically empty. At most a few older women dressed in black would sit on the hard seats along the walls of the *pronaos*[4] (seldom anywhere close to the altar) or would be in the area where candles for the living and the dead would burn, praying, lighting a candle, or standing around crying. Had I not been introduced to religion by my grandmother and thus become comfortable with and curious about Orthodoxy, I probably would have never known or cared much about this aspect of life in Romania. My city-dwelling parents were both nonreligious and at most engaged in the once-a-year ritual of going to Easter midnight mass, an event more social and culinary (the mass would always be followed by a great feast) than spiritual in how they approached it.

The experience of religious life and institutions of the urban generations growing up under full-fledged Romanian communism (those born in the 1960s) was similarly mediated by either the presence of an older relative—most likely a grandmother who, being retired,[5] had the time both to see to religious rites and take care of small children—or by the absence of such an important force and thus only vaguely aware of religious customs and beliefs.[6] Religious rites and self-identification existed somewhere within the normal range of referents in one's life, an institution one could easily comprehend and accept in terms of important rites of passage and ritual. Yet for many children growing up in urban environments during this period, Orthodoxy was not powerfully present or clearly situated in relationship with other aspects of our life—playing, friendship, school, dreams for the future, vacations. Religiosity, however, was a different business. One learned (or not) to pray at home and to identify principles of belief—faith in God, fear, respect, love—rather informally and through one's family circle. Sunday school, weekly church attendance, and a programmatic relationship to the Church as an institution and to learning its theology and internalizing its principles were not things I experienced or saw evidence of among most of my urban co-generationists, who were officially Orthodox, meaning that they had actually been baptized in an Orthodox church (most often before the age of two).[7]

Therefore, the growing presence of the Orthodox Church since 1990 in the daily lives of all citizens in Romania, from ritual and personal involvement in activities of the Church to compulsory religious education and a vast presence of the Church in mass media,[8] seems like an important change in religion and religiosity in postcommunist Romania.[9] Many scholars, from theologians to political scientists and anthropologists, have viewed the end of communism as a break in the development of Orthodoxy in the former Soviet bloc. They identify the post-1990 period as one of radically greater freedom in religious matters as well as greater religiosity on the part of the population.[10] This study questions this claim, made both explicitly and implicitly in some of the existent scholarship,[11] and instead suggests that continuity better encapsulates much of the development of religiosity—religious beliefs and their embodiment in specific practices—among Orthodox Christians in Romania in the twentieth century.[12] My argument also implies that secularization in this country has not been as closely tied to the relationship between the communist regime and the Orthodox Church as some have claimed.[13] I also make visible important imbalances, gaps, and faulty assumptions about the importance of institutions in the daily religious practices and beliefs of most Orthodox populations in the historiography on Orthodoxy in Romania. Because of the inadequate focus on practices on the ground, scholars have failed to see continuities and have embraced analytical frameworks that stress change, especially around the communist takeover period (1945–1949) and the fall of communism (1989–1990). Central to reevaluating this trajectory are two aspects of Orthodoxy in Romania: (1) most believers live in the countryside; and (2) women have remained central to the development and maintenance of religious practices in ways that cannot be accounted for through any institutional analysis of the Orthodox Church because of its both implicit and explicit misogyny.[14] My study suggests an agenda for further research on this topic.

The History and Historiography of Orthodoxy in Romania before 1945

Continuity as a trope of understanding religiosity during the communist period can only be fully articulated by looking at a longer period of time preceding 1945. The history of the Romanian Orthodox Church identifies it as one of the oldest markings of "Romanianness" north of the Danube, starting in the seventh century AD.[15] Much of the history of the Church during the Middle Ages and early modern period stresses the importance of continuity under duress of the institution and also of the practices linked to it. Evidence of such continuity is often linked to the presence of religious funerary symbols, to oral history and folklore, and to rituals described in historical sources starting in the early modern period, focusing especially on birth, marriages, and death.[16] Such claims and evidentiary bases served the nationalists of the nineteenth and early twentieth century well.[17] These intellectuals, many of whom were clergy or educated through religious institutions, wished to craft a sense of Romanian identity closely linked to the Orthodox Church, through a Janus-faced process of separating ethnic Romanians from other religious-linguistic groups living in the Romanian principalities and Transylvania (such as Bulgarians, Jews, Russians, Roma, Germans, Protestants, Catholics, Ukrainians, and Hungarians) and unifying them around a common set of beliefs and practices.[18]

For a majority of Orthodox Christians, themselves overwhelmingly illiterate until the mid–twentieth century, religious identity was linked
mostly to traditional rituals learned locally from the older generation and
passed down primarily by lay believers through food, clothing, and feasting, which women generally coordinated among rural communities.[19] The
gendered aspect of religious acculturation and transmission of rituals from
one generation to the next has not been the focus of much interest in Romania, though scholars of Orthodoxy elsewhere (especially anthropologists
and folklorists) have drawn attention to the central role women played in
everyday religiosity.[20] For Romania, a handful of studies have begun to draw
attention to how women were central in both enacting and educating younger
generations about rituals centered on religious holidays and rites of passage
(birth/baptism, marriage, death) and in blending pagan and dogmatic
elements.[21] Food in particular, as a central component of both proper engagement with the liturgy and the cult of the dead, has continued to be
women's domain. The priest played an important role in blessing food in
order to endow it with its symbolic Christian meaning, but in most rural
areas, until the twentieth century, the priest was not always there to perform
this role. Yet ritualistic food, as suggested by ethnographic evidence from
the turn of the twentieth century, was an integral part of how Orthodox
Christians in Romania understood religious rituals and norms.[22]

Traditionally, other elements of the cult of the dead, such as wailing, preparing the body for the funeral, and proper memorial rituals that continue
for seven years after a person's death, were also overwhelmingly the responsibility of women, both customarily and normatively. In the most impressive
analysis of rites of passage among populations living in Romania and Transylvania (and focusing almost exclusively on Orthodox Christians) published
at the turn of the twentieth century, the author identified women's participation in death rituals as an art—something to be learned and perfected from
one generation to the next—as well as something exclusively female.[23] For
instance, wailers were to be only women, and if the deceased did not happen
to have any immediate female kin, female neighbors and friends were to
perform this role. Considering the fact that most of the people involved in
the complex rituals and incantations to be performed were illiterate, the continuity of such precise and normatively inscribed gender roles is striking. It
points to the centrality of such issues in the everyday life of a rural community and in particular in women's lives, who, as described by the Romanian
scholar Simion Florea Marian, seemed to have spent a great deal of their lives
learning and performing such religious rituals, taught primarily by the older

generation of women that surrounded them. In addition, the process of learning and teaching such rituals to subsequent generations becomes an even more impressive feat when placed in the context of patrilocality. Most women tended to follow their husbands after getting married so would have to leave behind some learned rituals and traditions and learn new ones to pass them down to their own daughters and daughters-in-law, in a lifelong learning process of engaging with religious rituals and local traditions.[24]

The fate of the Orthodox Church as an institution central to the politics of modern Romania was closely related to its own long-standing principle of *symphonia*—the harmonious coexistence of the Church as an institution of spiritual authority alongside the institution of the Byzantine emperor as representing state authority in the pre-Ottoman period (before 1453).[25] Under the Ottoman millet system, the Orthodox Church continued to retain important elements of autonomy by working with the sultan. In the Romanian principalities (Wallachia and Moldova), which were never directly under Ottoman control, by the 1860s the Orthodox Church was the largest single landowner and greatly benefited from tax exemptions and other legal privileges. Rulers adamant about curbing the great power of this institution, especially Alexandru Ioan Cuza (r. 1859–1864), succeeded only in part in reducing the Orthodox Church's privileges. Cuza forced the Church to close down many monasteries and nationalized the lands they controlled, but he was soon ousted.[26] Subsequent rulers, including the first king of Romania, Charles I (r. 1864–1916), adopted a more respectful attitude of noninvolvement in internal Church affairs, together with paying homage to the Church as an important national institution.

Romania's victory at the end of World War I enabled King Ferdinand (r. 1914–1927) and especially Queen Marie (r. 1914–1938), both converts to Orthodoxy, to position themselves as overseers and embodiments of Orthodoxy as the national religion in Romania.[27] The Liberal and Peasant parties worked to include nods toward religious toleration in the postwar Constitution (1923), as both parties had sizeable non-Orthodox populations (especially Jews and Greek Catholics, respectively) among their ranks.[28] The dynastic and official commemorations of the interwar period marked the close connection between the Romanian state and Orthodoxy and reinforced it, cleverly incorporating many elements of popular religious practice, as a means to gain support among the population and sustain legitimacy through such cultural-religious alignments.[29]

Yet even as the religious institutions of Greater Romania afforded the Orthodox Church a central privileged position, there is evidence that, especially in rural areas, religious customs of Orthodox believers continued unabated and at times in tension or even conflict with centrally mandated practices. The transformation of certain religious holidays—most prominently the Ascension—into national holidays brought about various reactions on the part of Orthodox believers. Although some participated compliantly in these commemorations, others paid only scant attention or ignored the Bucharest dictates regarding the specific types of ceremonies to be performed on that day.[30] Many saw the superimposition of the Heroes Day onto the clearly demarcated holiday of the Ascension as simply an addition of names of those who fell in World War I to the commemoration of the local dead that was customary for Ascension. This minimized any significant change in ritual, religious practice, and signification of the holiday along any martial nationalist lines.[31] In other words, seeing the growing prominence of the Orthodox Church in state rituals is to some extent a misleading indicator of general changes in patterns of behavior among the population. There is more evidence of substantial impact among religious minorities, who were offended by this two-tiered relationship with the Romanian state and resented having to bow to the Orthodox Church through presumably secular rituals such as Heroes Day. Catholics, Jews, and Protestants often resisted the Romanian state's mandates to treat what were Orthodox religious holidays as their own civic holidays and often chose simply to ignore orders to participate in such rituals.[32]

Another equally important aspect of the relationship between the rising prominence of the Orthodox Church as a state-supported institution and religiosity among believers is church attendance. After 1918, the Romanian state spent a lot of money to build and restore churches and to train a sufficient number of priests for the large Orthodox population in the country.[33] By 1940, even with over ten thousand churches and other places of worship in place, and with more than 8,500 priests and 10,500 cantors employed by the Church, church attendance among Orthodox believers was low. Only 10 percent of the flock attended church at least once a week.[34]

The meaning of this statistic is difficult to ascertain qualitatively (and even quantitatively) with any degree of nuance, as we are not privy to the methods employed to arrive at this number or to the breakdown of the population along regional, gender, class, and rural/urban lines. However, based on my own research on the commemorative practices developed and continued during the interwar period, I posit that the rural population had a rate of attendance higher than 10 percent, for reasons that pertain to existing traditions, work patterns, and proximity of the place of worship. Women tended to attend church on Saturdays, for services dedicated to the memory of dead relatives, and for regular mass on Sunday. They also tended to participate in baptisms, weddings, and funerals, often for people who were not members of their own families, in part because of the specific ritualistic roles they were asked to perform. Men would more often attend Sunday mass and some of the rites of passage, but less often than women.

In the meantime, urban dwellers, especially given their small percentage of the total population (between 15 and 20 percent), had a significantly lower than 10 percent rate of attendance for reasons that have to deal with accessibility and comfort with specific settings. Many urban inhabitants were first generation and were more comfortable attending services that looked and felt like their rural homes. The Village Museum, inaugurated in Bucharest in the 1920s, served as an alternative for some newcomers to the metropolis. Young men and women could be seen on Sunday mornings making their way to the remote location of the museum, but this was not an option for those with small children and the poor, as public transportation was for the relatively privileged in that era.[35] The urban rate can be gleaned anecdotally also from the scarce mention in newspapers and personal accounts of religious events.[36]

Historians of religion in Eastern Europe have generally been uninterested in the phenomenon of popular religion in terms of the gender dimensions of specific practices.[37] Evidence to consider this question is sparse at best. Yet the issue of how particular traditions and the meanings ascribed to them became entrenched and continued to be so over a long period of time into the twentieth century is one that needs to be addressed. We cannot assume that Orthodoxy existed as a living religion in the Romanian lands in the premodern periods simply because there was a metropolitanate in Bucharest, Iasi, or Sibiu or because a sizeable number of priests served in churches throughout the country. One has to look at the local level and in the area of material culture and ethnographic/folkloric evidence to understand this phenomenon of continuity.

The Orthodox Church under Communism (1945–1989)

The communist takeover has to be seen within the larger narrative of the modern period, in terms of both institutional relations with the state and of the differentiated declining religiosity evident at the beginning of World

War II. The narrative of the Orthodox Church under communism has varied greatly depending on who has crafted it and on whose behalf. Theologians and opponents of the communist regime in Romania as a brutal atheist state have focused on the aggressive curbing of religious freedom in Romania by looking at the imprisonment of large numbers of priests, monks, and nuns and at the infiltration of the clergy by the secret police and demolition of places of worship, especially in the 1980s.[38] Critics of the Orthodox Church prefer to focus on the large degree of compliance with the Securitate on the part of priests. Other critical voices also focus on the takeover by the Orthodox Church of all assets of the Uniate Church after the latter was folded into the Orthodox Church in 1948.[39]

A more balanced view of the relationship between the Church hierarchy and the communist regime has begun to develop in recent years. In its 2006 *Final Report*, the Presidential Commission for the Study of the Crimes of Communism provides a narrative of religious oppression and compliance in communist Romania. The report highlights the early abuses of the Romanian Communist Party against priests and religious institutions and also makes visible the extent to which the Romanian Orthodox Church was able to achieve a more autonomous and stable position by the 1960s, in clear contrast to other religious denominations such as the Baptists or the Uniates.[40] More recently, Lucian Leuştean has offered an even-handed and well-documented analysis of how Orthodox Church leaders negotiated this position of autonomy.[41] Leuştean sees the techniques used and results achieved by the Orthodox Church in harmony and continuity with the tradition of *symphonia* rather than as a break with the past.

Everyday Religiosity and Gender under Communism

Missing from these accounts and from much of the scholarly framing of studies on the fate of the Orthodox Church under communism is the question of what happened to everyday religiosity among Orthodox believers in the institutional context of early violence against outspoken believers or later in the context of compliance and even active work with the secret police. The Presidential Commission is silent on this matter, preferring to focus only on the exceptional fate of well-known priests and religious dissidents.[42] Leuştean frames his questions in terms of institutional relations between the Church and the communist regime. We are, therefore, left wondering what was happening on the ground.

Some evidence about religiosity among Orthodox Christians comes from anthropological research such as Gail Kligman's outstanding *Wedding of the Dead*. Her research shows a great degree of continuity (while acknowledging significant change) from before the communist period in terms of rural practices surrounding the cult of the dead among the Orthodox: "Although the state operates according to Marxist principles, village life continues according to traditional principles, among which religion is a guiding force."[43] Katherine Verdery's *Political Lives of Dead Bodies* also hints at continuities in religious practices.[44] The many Romanian ethnographers who wrote about "popular traditions" under the communist regime, as they could not write openly about popular Christianity, also attested to the continuity of such practices.[45] In addition, a growing oral history literature since 1990 has enriched the picture of localized religious practices.[46] The Museum of the Romanian Peasant, created in 1990, and the more traditional Village Museums in Bucharest, Sibiu, and Cluj are all products of the interwar period's obsession with the "vitality" of peasant culture. They have focused significantly on religious rituals and practices in the countryside and have visually narrated these practices as continuously sustained—even during the communist period—through grassroots local traditions rather than via any specific institutional links with the Church or political regime.[47]

These studies and visual narratives suggest that the countryside remained somewhat removed from the struggles over authority and integrity that the Orthodox Church engaged in at the center of political power.[48] This is not to say that villagers were ignorant of or uncaring about, for instance, the imprisonment of priests or the infiltration of the clergy by the Securitate. In many informal conversations I have had over time with Orthodox believers, I heard strong opinions about the local priest, whom many suspected of being a collaborator of the Securitate and thus avoided personally. But that seldom meant outright rejection of Orthodoxy.[49] Uniates who had been forced to go underground or, as an alternative, to attend Orthodox Churches were far more critical of the Church as an institution.[50] Yet they were not speaking on behalf of secularization but on behalf of a different kind of religiosity. My own grandmother occasionally "shopped around" churches in Bucharest in search of priests who were less overtly compliant, but she never quit attending church on the grounds of the priest's corruption by the communist regime.

In an oral history project conducted in 2009–2010, together with three other collaborators, I interviewed over a hundred women from urban and rural backgrounds in Hunedoara county.[51] They ranged in ages from the mid-forties to the mid-eighties and in educational/professional/economic backgrounds from barely literate peasants to doctors, business entrepreneurs, and teachers. Of this cross-section of Romanian society, a majority not only self-identified religiously (overwhelmingly Orthodox) but also expressed strong opinions about what the Church was and is or is not doing right. In other words, religiosity and the Orthodox Church were topics they wanted to engage with and obviously thought about. Although these interviews took place twenty years after the end of communism and it is obvious that these two decades have influenced the respondents' views on religiosity and the Orthodox Church in particular, some of their references suggested a longer process of self-identification with the Church:

> Back then [under communism] we weren't allowed but I made time, I made time to go [to church], my husband would take me, but somehow he wasn't really all that . . . religious, but he liked to take me; if I said, "you know, I would like to go to Easter mass somewhere," he would get in the car and drive me, so he respected my religious beliefs. . . . Back then we used to go in hiding. . . . When I had to join the Party, we were forbidden to go to church, but if I felt like it, I would still go who knows where and I didn't care, I would go more seldom, but still went.[52]

In addition to underscoring the difficulty and fear associated with church attendance in relation to Communist Party membership, this statement also exemplifies gender differences in church attendance. An interesting aspect of this narrative, which is not atypical of other personal reflections on the ways the Party attempted to curb religiosity, is that the description reflects a remembrance of fear of retribution, even as documentary evidence from Party archives suggests that such retribution was not as common from the 1960s on as it had been before. Most of the people we spoke with were in fact of generations that had not lived through the 1940s and early 1950s.

Other respondents also suggested interesting cross-religious attendance and traditions. A couple who were Protestant (he) and Catholic (she) spoke of keeping two Easters (Catholic and Orthodox) and participating in funerals and baptisms in the local Orthodox Church because their neighbors were Orthodox.[53] By contrast, one respondent spoke about self-identifying as an Orthodox but attending a specific Catholic church in Hunedoara "because many years ago I was searching, I think I was sixteen [that would have been in 1985], and I was searching for a path and I wanted to find answers to some questions, and this was the church that gave me the answers I needed at that time."[54]

Overall, those who self-identified as regular churchgoers spoke of difficulties in practicing religious traditions in public under communism and of greater church attendance since then, but they also identified religious holidays (of which there are at least one per week in the Orthodox calendar) as important times when they used to go to church, in addition to Sundays. In terms of gendered involvement in religious holidays, they also identified men as being far less involved than women in keeping traditions alive both at home and in any kind of public fashion.[55]

These observations help us better understand an apparently surprising statistic. In 1990, after half a century of tough atheistic communist dictatorship, church attendance of at least once a week among the Orthodox in Romania was at 20 percent, up 10 percent from 1940.[56] It is not clear what methods were used to measure attendance and how to disaggregate this number. But even if we allow for a wide margin of error and for differences between the methods employed in the 1940 statistics and the 1990 ones, church attendance went up, not down, under an aggressively atheist regime that placed thousands of priests in prison.

Other important numbers can enhance our understanding of religiosity under the communist regime, with a pronounced gendered quality, as shown in Table 1. The table highlights some little-known developments that no scholar, to my knowledge, has tried to analyze in terms of gender differences. To begin with, most evidently, the number of people embracing religious orders grew significantly in the two decades from 1938 to 1957. At the height of the purges in the communist bloc, the number of monks and nuns allowed to take religious vows was growing. It is hard to analyze this data in terms of the motivations of the people joining monasteries. But it is clear that, despite outspoken atheism and purges among the clergy, the Orthodox Church had a great deal of autonomy in replenishing the numbers of its dedicated clergy.

Second, and least known and analyzed of all, the number of nuns in Romanian monasteries grew much faster and was far larger than the number of monks. In addition, one is struck by how this significant disparity (a ratio of more than 2:1 nuns to monks by 1957) is reflected negatively in the number of monasteries dedicated to nuns versus monks. The number of monks stayed relatively flat over the two decades, as did the number of

Table 1. Orthodox Monasteries in Romania (1938–1957)

Year	1938	1949	1957
Monks	1,638	1,528	1,773
Nuns	2,549	3,807	4,041
Male monasteries	119	122	113
Female monasteries	35	56	77

Source: Lucian Leuştean, *Orthodoxy and the Cold War* (London: Palgrave, 2009), 204.

monasteries where they resided, so that the occupancy ratio goes from 14:1 to 16:1 between 1938 and 1957. This ratio also indicates that monks lived in relatively small monasteries and were likely assisted by the local population. By contrast, the ratio of nuns to monasteries declines from 73:1 to 53:1 during the same time period. Even with this decline, it is clear that far more nuns crowded into individual monasteries than monks. The declining ratio also suggests, if we take into account the actual rise in total number of nuns, that in fact more nunneries were opened under communism, again raising the question of how we understand the atheistic and religiously oppressive nature of that regime.

The disparity in occupancy rate is so huge that it begs for an explanation. The size of monasteries may be such an explanation, though not all or even a majority of nuns' monasteries were larger in size than those inhabited by monks. On the contrary, some of the largest and best-known monasteries in Romania are occupied by monks. Another possible explanation would be the inability of the Orthodox Church to obtain approval for building more women's monasteries to keep up with the growing number of women taking the veil.[57]

I would venture to suggest a few other important elements, all pointing toward the masculinist privileges that have defined many institutional practices of the Orthodox Church over time. Privacy has been deemed essential to monks' ability to focus on their religious practices of meditation, praying, and writing; however, the same has not been the case with nuns.[58] They are more often asked to reside in shared lodgings (several nuns in a cell), and their religious practice is more directly identified with active, public, and communal activities. Nuns are expected to prepare food, work in the fields, sew, and do artisanal work (especially textile and decorative arts, such as weaving, embroidery, and painting eggs, but rarely icon painting).[59] These may be important reasons why solitary living is not considered important for and by nuns and why they tend to live in much larger communities than monks. Of course, the issue of personal safety, being protected from the threat of sexual assault, was also a prominent reason for nuns' placement in communal quarters.[60] However, a solid understanding of the reasons behind these gendered disparities demands more sustained ethnographic and sociological research.

The exponential growth of women taking the veil during the communist period may be viewed by some as a discontinuity. I choose to interpret it differently and to connect it to the existing religiosity among women especially in the countryside, in connection to some of the problems of adjustment of the rural population to the communist regime's economic and social policies. Obviously, a desire to serve the Church and live a religiously committed life was an important component. Yet other socioeconomic elements with pronounced gendered aspects played roles as well. Educational and economic opportunities did indeed open up a great deal for women under communism, but these opportunities were not always accessible (or perceived as such) to rural inhabitants. To pursue a high school or vocational school, rural children had to be removed from their environment and live in cities where they had no relatives or friends. Schools often had campus housing, but conditions were not appealing.[61] Although this is a conjectural link, I believe that the difficulties of such paths of empowerment for women in the countryside pushed them and their families toward making different decisions, especially for those who were deeply religious. With collectivization taking away one's means for subsistence in the countryside,[62] families with more than one child and especially more than one daughter had to consider how they could secure a future for their offspring. Joining a monastery was an option that suggested the lessening of financial burdens for the parents (dowries were and remain an important expensive custom in the countryside) and offered security for the young woman becoming a nun. Therefore, this phenomenon of growing numbers of nuns during Romania's communist period seems likely to be connected to both an ongoing religiosity among women in the countryside as well as drastic changes brought about by the communist regime in especially the economy and education.

Conclusions

What do these numbers mean for our understanding of religion in Romania in the twentieth century? The most obvious observation to make initially is that the narrative of the institution of the Church (from underdog, to privileged state-supported religion, to censored and communist-infiltrated institution, and back to state-supported religion after 1989) does not match the narrative of religiosity (from intense, to declining, to growing again under communism) among believers. On the contrary, one might surmise that in the modern period, when Churches are not central political institutions able to closely control and regulate the lives of their members, religiosity is linked more to localized traditions and to socioeconomic conditions than to the power and visibility of the Church. Socioeconomic adversity (both before 1918 and after 1945) seemed to have enhanced the desire or the need of many people to practice religious beliefs. Overall, it is clear that one cannot claim that communism destroyed or reduced religiosity among the Orthodox Christians in Romania. When speaking of "religion under communism," we need to pay greater attention to these important nuances, which suggest that continuity is the most important qualifier for describing religious practices, especially in the countryside.

A second and equally important conclusion is that gender norms and assumed identities have been crucial to how religiosity has developed among Orthodox populations in the modern period. Priests, as both representatives of the Church and embodiments of a particular ideal of masculine Christianity, have played a central gendered role in preserving certain dogmatic mandates of the institution and limits (for both women and men, yet in different ways) on performative aspects of religiosity. But women were also central to how religiosity developed during this period. Their role was more informal, and thus it is less clearly evidenced in easily understandable traces. However, there is no doubt, based on both ethnographic evidence and also some of the statistics presented in this study, that women's greater religiosity and adherence to specific practices and rituals were essential in rendering Orthodoxy in the shape it exists today in Romania. The full story of this barely traceable force remains to be fully recovered, and I hope this study has raised questions among researchers of life under communism in Romania and among gender scholars, as this vast area of inquiry demands a multidisciplinary, long-term effort, in order to fully understand phenomena I was able to sketch out here in broad and partial ways.[63]

Notes

This is an updated version of a piece published in *Aspasia* 5 (2011): 28–45; reprinted by permission. I want to thank Kristen Ghodsee and Pamela Ballinger for their invitation to participate in the inspired and inspiring workshop "Spiritualities

and Secularisms in Southeastern Europe: An Interdisciplinary Workshop" at
Bowdoin College in October 2009. The experience would not have been what it
was without the energy of all the participants involved: Milica Bakic-Hayden,
Melissa Bokovoy, Keith Brown, Page Herrlinger, Emira Ibrahimpasic, and Mary
Neuburger. Camp Balkans has remained a memorable bright moment of intellectual
and personal fellowship. In addition, I am grateful to the five readers of the
manuscript for their suggestions and criticisms. All remaining errors are my own.

1. *Colivă* is the Orthodox sweet dish cooked with boiled wheat, sugar, nuts,
and spices, to embody and honor the links between the dearly departed and this
world through a specifically Christian set of symbols: the wheat as resurrected
life, the sweetness of the sugar as the sweetness of Christ's love. Ofelia Văduva,
Steps towards the Sacred (Bucharest: Editura Fundatiei culturale române, 1999).

2. The shortest traditional version was *Bodaproste* (Thanks be to God), coming
from the Slavic expression *Bog da prosti* (May God forgive).

3. Sf. Vineri was torn down after the 1977 earthquake, which provided a
convenient reason (structural instability) to do away with quite a few such places
of worship. On these demolitions, see Lidia Anania et al., *Bisericile osândite de
Ceaușescu, 1977–1989* [The churches convicted by Ceaușescu, 1977–1989]
(Bucharest: Editura Anastasia, 1995); Comisia Prezidențială pentru Studiul
Crimelor Comunismului [The Presidential Commission for the Study of the
Crimes of Communism], *Raport Final* [Final report] (Bucharest, 2006), 466–67.

4. The area of the church where women traditionally would be relegated to,
its distance from the altar signifying the lowly status women had in the social
order of Orthodox communities.

5. During the communist period, women tended to retire ten years earlier
than men. The retirement age for women was 50–55; for men, 60–65. This meant
that in most cases, families in which both parents worked depended on either a
kindergarten or grandmothers to tend to small children. Although available,
daycare was often unreliable in terms of quality of staff, and parents preferred to
leave small children with retired relatives (i.e., grandmothers or aunts). Therefore,
it is safe to surmise that the impact of women of that generation, given their earlier
retirement age, was significant in general for raising grandchildren. Since the
generations I speak of are also those growing up in the interwar period (the
grandmothers) and respectively in the 1970s (my generation), this further sheds
light on the kind of information about religiosity that the older generation, rather
than the children's parents, could pass on to their grandchildren.

6. This generalization is not based on the assumption of all people in Romania
as Orthodox Christian but rather on available statistics, which indicate that over
80 percent of Romania's population declared itself Orthodox during that period.
This included most of those who had been part of the Greek Catholic Church,

which had been incorporated into the Orthodox Church in 1949, accounting for around 8 percent of the total population of the country. Currently, the proportion is at 87 percent. Lucian Leuştean, *Orthodoxy and the Cold War* (London: Palgrave, 2009); Recensământul Populaţiei şi Locuinţelor 2021, http://www.recensamant.ro.

7. On the tradition of baptizing infants, see Vasile Răduca, *Ghidul creştinului ortodox de azi* [The guide for today's Orthodox Christian] (Bucharest: Humanitas, 1998), 141.

8. The Orthodox Church has its own television channel and radio station, both of them operating most hours of the day.

9. On the position of the Orthodox Church in Romania after 1990, including its presence in education, see Lavinia Stan and Lucian Turcescu, *Religion and Politics in Post-Communist Romania* (New York: Oxford University Press, 2007).

10. Stan and Turcescu, *Religion and Politics in Post-Communist Romania*, 3–4.

11. For a larger perspective on the Orthodox Church under communism, see Sabrina Ramet, *Nihil Obstat: Religion, Politics, and Social Change in East-Central Europe and Russia* (Durham, NC: Duke University Press, 1998).

12. The question of how to characterize the development of religiosity among other significant denominations (Catholic, Lutheran, Unitarian, Calvinist, Jewish) falls outside the purview of this study, though it would be relevant in terms of the triangular relationship among religion, ethnicity, and political ideology/regime.

13. On secularization, see Comisia Prezidenţială, *Raport*, 25; Paul Caravia, Virgiliu Constantinescu, and Flori Stanescu, *Biserica întemniţată, România, 1944–1989* [The imprisoned church, Romania, 1944–1989] (Bucharest: INST, 1998); Cristina Păiuşan and Radu Ciuceanu, eds., *Biserica ortodoxă română sub regimul comunist, 1945–1958* [The Romanian Orthodox Church under the communist regime, 1945–1958], vol. 1 (Bucharest: INST, 2001).

14. In stating that the Orthodox Romanian Church is fundamentally misogynist I am not making any new claim. There has been an ongoing debate in the past decade over the dogmatic and consistent marginalization of women qua women from central ritualistic functions and from any discussion of opening the priesthood to women. For more on this issue, see Mihaela Miroiu, "Fetzele patriarhatului" [The faces of patriarchy], *Journal for the Study of Religions and Ideologies* 3 (Winter 2002): 207–26, http://www.jsri.ro/old/html%20version /index/no_3/ mihaela_miroiu-articol.htm; Miruna Munteanu, "Editorial feminist, frigid si ateu" [Feminist, frigid, and atheist editorial], *Ziua* 3452 (October 13, 2005), http://www.ziua.net/display.php?data=2005-10-13&id=186511; Mihaela Miroiu, "Gâlceava danciachirilor cu demnitatea spirituala a femeilor" [The quarrel of the Danciachirs with women's spiritual dignity], *Observator cultural*

35 (October 27–November 3, 2005), http://www.romaniaculturala.ro/articol
.php?cod=8277. "The Danciachirs" is a reference to the author Dan Chiachir.

15. Christian symbols dating back to the second century AD have been
found on what is today the territory of Romania, but even ardent nationalist
scholars place the beginnings of (proto-)Romanian Christianity a few centuries
later, in the seventh century AD. However, the first canonical recognition of a
metropolitanate in Wallachia and Moldavia is dated much later (1359 and 1401,
respectively). Mircea Păcurariu, *Istoria Bisericii ortodoxe române* [The history of
the Romanian Orthodox Church] (Bucharest: Editura Institutului biblic şi de
misiune al Bisericii ortodoxe române, 1992), 1:18.

16. Păcurariu, *Istoria*; Elena Niculiţa-Voronca, *Datinele şi credinţele poporului
român adunate si asezate în ordine mitologică* [The traditions and beliefs of the
Romanian people gathered and arranged in mythological order] (1903; Iaşi:
Polirom, 1998); Simion Mehedinţi, *Creştinismul românesc* [Romanian Chris-
tianity] (1941; Bucharest: Fundaţia Anastasia, 1995); Simion Florea Marian,
Trilogia vieţii: Naşterea la români; Nunta la români; Inmormântarea la români
[The trilogy of life: birth among the Romanians; weddings among the
Romanians; burials among the Romanians] (1890–1902; Bucharest: Editura
"Grai şi suflet-Cultura naţională," 1995).

17. In the fall of 2018, the Romanian Orthodox Church, together with
many supporters, inclusive of the president of the Romanian Academy, started
a heavy-handed campaign to "return" to the traditional Romanian family,
understood as fundamentally Christian (Orthodox, implicitly), in order to pass
a referendum that was to alter the Constitution by redefining marriage from
"between two persons" to "between a man and a woman." Under 20 percent of
persons eligible to vote participated, and the referendum was rendered invalid.
But the mythologization of the traditional family remains.

18. See Keith Hitchins, *Ortodoxie şi naţionalitate. Andrei Saguna şi românii
din Transilvania. 1846–1873* [Orthodoxy and nationality. Andrei Saguna and
the Romanians in Transylvania. 1846–1873] (Bucharest: Univers enciclopedic,
1995); Keith Hitchins, *Conştiinţă naţională şi acţiune politică la românii din
Transilvania (1700–1868)* [National consciousness and political action among
Romanians in Transylvania, 1700–1868] (Cluj: Dacia, 1987); Păcurariu, *Istoria*.

19. Marian, *Trilogia*; Stefania Cristescu-Golopenţia, *Gospodăria în credinţele
şi riturile magice ale femeilor din Drăguş (Făgăraş)* [Household activities in the
beliefs and magic rituals of women from Dragus, Fagaras] (Bucharest: Paideia,
2002); Stefan Dorondel, *Moartea şi apa. Ritualuri funerare, simbolism acvatic şi
structura lumii de dincolo în imaginarul ţărănesc* [Death and water. Funerary
rituals, aquatic symbolism and the structure of the world beyond in the peasant
imaginary] (Bucharest: Paideia, 2004); Văduva, *Steps*.

20. Anna Careveli-Chaves, "Bridge between Worlds: The Greek Women's Lament as Communicative Event," *Journal of American Folklore* 93, no. 368 (1980): 129–57; Loring Danforth, *The Death Rituals of Rural Greece* (Princeton, NJ: Princeton University Press, 1982); Bette Denich, "Sex and Power in the Balkans," in *Woman, Culture, and Society*, ed. M. Rosaldo and L. Lamphere (Stanford, CA: Stanford University Press, 1974), 243–62.

21. Văduva, *Steps*; Gail Kligman, *Wedding of the Dead: Ritual, Poetics, and Popular Culture in Transylvania* (Berkeley: University of California Press, 1988); Cristescu-Golopenţia, *Gospodăria*; Maria Bucur, *Heroes and Victims: Remembering War in Twentieth-Century Romania* (Bloomington: Indiana University Press, 2009); Maria Bucur and Mihaela Miroiu, *The Birth of Democratic Citizenship: Women in Modern Romania* (Bloomington: Indiana University Press, 2018).

22. Marian, *Trilogia*; Văduva, *Steps*.

23. Marian, *Inmormântarea*, 79, 201.

24. For more on the issue of the gendered aspects of the cult of the dead in Romania, see Bucur, *Heroes and Victims*, chap. 1.

25. See Leuştean, *Orthodoxy*, 17; Stan and Turcescu, *Religion*, chap. 2.

26. Lucian Predescu, *Enciclopedia României. Cugetarea* [The encyclopedia of Romania. The thought] (Bucharest: Editura Saeculum, 1999), 511; Marin Mihalache, *Cuza Vodă* [Vojvode Cuza] (Bucharest: Editura Tineretului, 1967). The process of transfer of these lands from the Church to the state is generally referred to as "secularization" in Romanian. I prefer the term "nationalization," which more clearly identifies who had control over these lands after their confiscation from the church: the state.

27. Leuştean, *Orthodoxy*; Păcurariu, *Istoria*.

28. Institutul Social Român, *Constituţia din 1923 în dezbaterile contemporanilor* [The 1923 Constitution in contemporary debates] (Bucharest: Humanitas, 1990).

29. Bucur, *Heroes*.

30. Bucur, *Heroes*, esp. chap. 2.

31. In common Orthodox parlance, the Ascension is more often called "Ispas," or the "Easter of the Dead" or "Day of the Dead," not to be confused with the Catholic November 1 "Day of the Dead." Simion Florea Marian, *Sărbătorile la români* [Holidays among the Romanians] (Bucharest: Editura Fundaţiei culturale române, 1994).

32. Bucur, *Heroes*, chap. 2.

33. Dimitrie Gusti, ed., *Enciclopedia României* [The encyclopedia of Romania], vol. 2 (Bucharest: Fundaţia Regală Carol II, 1938–1940).

34. Leuştean, *Orthodoxy*, 47–48.

35. Adrian Majuru, *Bucureştii mahalalelor, sau periferia ca mod de existenţă* [Bucharest of the mahalas, or perfidy as a mode of existence] (Bucharest:

Compania, 2003); Ioana Pârvulescu, *Intoarcere în Bucureştiul interbelic* [Return to interwar Bucharest] (Bucharest: Humanitas, 2003).

36. *Universul* [*The Universe*], *Curentul* [*The Current*], *Porunca Vremii* [*The Command of the Times*], and other major newspapers often made mention of official commemorations at religious sites (churches, synagogues, and cemeteries) but did not make mention of cultural and other religious events at specific churches on a weekly basis.

37. Eve Levin's classic book *Sex and Society in the World of the Orthodox Slavs, 900–1700* (Ithaca, NY: Cornell University Press, 1989) is a noteworthy exception. See also Helena Kupari and Elina Vuola, eds., *Gender and Orthodox Christianity: Dynamics of Tradition, Culture, and Lived Practice* (New York: Routledge, 2019).

38. See, for instance, Caravia, Constantinescu, and Stănescu, *Biserica*; Păiuşan and Ciuceanu, eds., *Biserica ortodoxă*; Zosim Oancea, *Datoria de a mărturisi. Inchisorile unui preot ortodox* [The duty to confess. The prisons of an Orthodox priest] (Bucharest, Harisma, 1995); Nicolae Videnie, "Atitudinea anticomunistă, calvarul şi martiriul preotilor ortodocşi relfectate în presa exilului românesc (1945–1989)" [The anticommunist attitude, the calvary and martyrdom of Orthodox priests as reflected in the press of the Romanian exile, 1945–1989], in *Rezistenţa anticomunistă. Cercetare ştiinţifi că şi valorificare muzeală* [Anticommunist resistance. Scientific research and museum valuation], ed. Cosmin Budeancă, Florentin Olteanu, and Iulia Pop (Cluj: Argonaut, 2006), 2:32–51.

39. See Cristian Vasile, *Istoria Bisericii Greco-Catolice sub regimul comunist, 1945–1989* [The history of the Greek-Catholic church under the communist regime, 1945–1989] (Iaşi: Polirom, 2003).

40. Comisia Prezidenţială, *Raport*, 447–72.

41. Leuştean, *Orthodoxy*.

42. Comisia Prezidenţială, *Raport*, 447–72.

43. Kligman, *Wedding of the Dead*, 268.

44. Katherine Verdery, *The Political Lives of Dead Bodies: Reburial and Postsocialist Change* (New York: Columbia University Press, 1999).

45. Xenia Costa-Foru-Andreescu, *Cercetarea monografi că a familiei: contribuţie metodologică* [The monographic research of the family: methodological contribution] (Bucharest: Institutul Social Român, 1945); T. Graur, "Predici rituale în structura şi funcţia ceremonialului de nuntă tradiţională" [Ritualistic liturgies and the function of the traditional wedding ceremony], *Anuarul muzeului etnografic al Transivlaniei* [*Yearbook of the Ethnographic Museum of Transylvania*] (1976): 283–94; Mihai Pop, *Obiceiuri tradiţionale românesti* [Traditional peasant customs] (Bucharest: Consiliul Culturii şi Educaţiei Socialiste, 1976).

46. See, for instance, Aurora Liiceanu, *Nici alb, nici negru. Radiografia unui sat românesc, 1948–1998* [Neither white, nor black. Radiography of a Romanian village, 1948–1998] (Bucharest: Nemira, 2000); Zoltàn Rostas and Theodora-Eliza Vacarescu, eds., *Cealaltă jumătate a istoriei. Femei povestind* [The other half of history. Women narrating] (Bucharest: Curtea Veche, 2008).

47. On the Museum of the Romanian Peasant's central preoccupation with Orthodoxy, see http://www.muzeultaranuluiroman.ro/index.php?page=religioase.

48. Monica Heintz, "Romanian Orthodoxy between the Urban and the Rural," Max Planck Institute for Social Anthropology Working Paper 67, Halle, 2004.

49. Fieldwork in Sighet, Ineu, and Trezenea, April–May 2000.

50. Vasile, *Istoria Bisericii*; I heard similar statements from Uniate believers during fieldwork in Cluj, March–April, 2000.

51. Bucur and Miroiu, *Birth*, chap. 5.

52. Interview with Osiceanu Elena, Hunedoara, August 4, 2009.

53. Interview with Viorica Vegh, Sîncrai, August 6, 2009.

54. Interview with Livia Laura Giurca, Hunedoara, August 8, 2009.

55. Bucur and Miroiu, *Birth*, chap. 5.

56. "How Many People outside of North America Go Regularly to Church Services," *Religious Tolerance*, 2007, http://www.religioustolerance.org/rel_ratefor.htm.

57. I can only speculate on this matter, as the Orthodox Church archives are not open to nonreligious scholars like me, especially given my feminist agenda. The important question in examining this possible explanation is the extent to which the Church cared about this disparity in ratio and tried to do anything about it and to what extent it was frustrated by the communist regime in these efforts. It would be easy for Church authorities to claim to have tried and not succeeded, given the reputation of the communist regime, but it is hard to prove that this was not the case without access to the Church's archives.

58. For descriptions and images of monastic life in twentieth-century Romania, see Dragoş Lumpan, *Chipuri de viață monahală* [Faces of monastic life] (Editura LiterNet, 2006), http:// editura.liternet.ro/carte/218/Dragos-Lumpan/Chipuri-de-viata-monahala.html; Ignatie Monahul, *Viața monahală în texte alese* [Monastic life in selected texts] (Bucharest: Lucman, 2006); George Enache and Adrian Nicolae Petcu, *Monahismul ortodox şi puterea comunista în România anilor '50* [Orthodox monasticism and communist power in Romania during the 1950s] (Bucharest: Partener, 2009). Much of the emphasis of the published materials is on monks' lives; it is difficult to find publications about nuns in wide circulation, although on occasion one can pick up self-published writings at female monasteries.

59. Leuştean refers directly to these differential expectations of the Church along gender lines by quoting a prelate who identified nuns as especially useful to the Church coffers through their artisanal work, which sold very well both locally and more broadly throughout the country and abroad. What is not clear at all from this book is whether these nuns see any direct returns on this type of arduous work, on a par with their greater contribution to the gross domestic product than that of priests and monks. Leuştean, *Orthodoxy*, 135. A vivid depiction of postcommunist life in a small female monastery for nuns can be found in Cristi Mungiu's film *După dealuri* (2012).

60. I thank one of the anonymous readers for pointing out this obvious oversight on my part.

61. Interview with E. Hunedoara, August 8, 2009.

62. Focus group, Sîncrai, August 5, 2009.

63. One of the most remarkable trends in terms of women's religiousness in the past decade has been the growth of a cultlike following of Arsenie Boca, a priest turned monk who died in 1989. Seen by many as a martyr of communist oppression, his burial place at the Prislop Monastery, a few kilometers away from where we interviewed our interlocutors for the *Birth of Democratic Citizenship* book, has become a place of pilgrimage. Thousands of people, predominantly women, visit his tomb every year.

Doubly Neglected: Histories of Women Monastics in the Serbian Orthodox Church

Milica Bakić-Hayden

The same creator for man and for woman, for both the same clay, the same image, the same death, the same resurrection.
—*Gregory of Nazianzus*

Monk is above all and chiefly an earthly angel and a heavenly man.
—*Kassiani*

These two epigraphs illustrate in a nutshell the main themes and contradictions behind the title of this essay. What transpires from the saying of St. Gregory, a renowned fourth-century Cappadocian Church Father, is an affirmation of the essential, ontological equality of men and women, both created in the image and likeness of God. St. Gregory's views are shared with most of the early Church Fathers, who also understand that man and woman are created equally in God's image: "Male and female he created them" (Gen. 1:27). But contrary to the views of some contemporary Orthodox theologians, "they draw no parallels between particular human sexes and particular Persons of the Trinity; rather, they unanimously affirm that sexual differentiation as a whole—maleness as well as femaleness— is not part of the image of God since God is neither male nor female."[1] In other words, genital sexuality is a temporary phase in God's plan for humanity that will be transcended in "the end of time," in the eschaton. And it is in monasticism as an "alternative society that the fundamental equality of women and men proclaimed in their anthropology is the most easily, but not exclusively, realized."[2] Kassiani,[3] a ninth-century Byzantine nun, for her part, points out that from early on in Christian history the monastic way of life was compared to the angelic one.[4] Kassiani's reference to "angelic" implies that monastics through their ascetic rigor of self-control over their biological bodies, as exercised in celibacy (control of sexuality) and fasting (control of appetite), anticipate that eschatological state in which human sexual differentiation is transcended.

With his ascetic lifestyle "in the wilderness of Judea" (Mt. 3:1) where he lived "clothed in camel's hair, with a leather belt around his waist" (Mt. 3:4), like the prophet Elijah before him (2 Kings 1:8), John the Baptist was indeed "the Forerunner" to many men and women who would later adopt the lifestyle we now call monasticism. In the history of Christian monasticism, women played an equally important part as men. When we talk about St. Antony of Egypt as "the father of Christian monasticism," Kallistos Ware writes, we fail to note that before he gave up all his possessions and became an ascetic, Antony had entrusted his younger sister to the care of a "convent of virgins," clearly one of already existing "fully organized communities for women," preceding even St. Pachomios's first cenobitic monasteries for men.[5] Similarly, St. Gregory of Nyssa in his *Dialogue on the Soul and on the Resurrection* presents a narrative in the form of a conversation in which his dying elder sister, Macrina the Younger, plays the role of his teacher. For him as well as for St. Basil the Great, woman is the "other" with whom they must dialogue, for she is not any companion of man but his companion in spiritual combat and sometimes also his teacher.[6] As Peter Brown notes: "Basil was prepared to admit that men needed in women what they lacked in themselves; and he regards this fact not as a sign of weakness in men, but as a gift bestowed on women by God."[7] How is it, then, that when it comes to the question of women in the Church, the words of the Fathers resonate with us today much more than those of some of our contemporaries? Granted that since the early days of the Church, women's presence and participation in public life was limited, it is still somewhat ironic that the tradition of the Church Fathers (many, if not all) turns out to be more inclusive of women than the traditions of national churches, embedded as they are in their cultures' stereotypes about women.[8] The views of women dominated by ethnic customs and social norms of one place, but taken to be valid for all times and also extended to the women in the church—even those who devote their lives to God—create an imbalance in the knowledge of women's contributions to the history of the Orthodox Church and specifically monasticism. Hence, this double neglect suggests the obvious: It is only with the change of women's position in society at large that their various contributions to social and religious history start to be the matter of scholarly attention and recognition— generally, but especially of contemporary women scholars.

"Life of Perfection"

Since there are no religious orders in Orthodox monasticism, all monks and nuns are members of a single fellowship attached to particular monasteries. A general distinction is made between men's and women's monasteries,[9] although there are some in which a certain number of monks may live in what is otherwise a women's monastery, or vice versa. Whether male or female, this type of monastic life is called *cenobitic* (from the Greek *koinos bios*, communal life),[10] and monks and nuns are called to live in their community as if it were their family and to help one another in their struggle to accomplish the "life of perfection." In the course of my ethnographic study of nuns in the Serbian Orthodox Church, every attempt to find out whether there are corresponding gender differences in the spirituality of monks and nuns resulted in an almost uniform answer: There is only one Orthodox spirituality, and those who commit themselves to monasticism aspire to be fully in communion with Christ by leading "this angelic life" that is beyond gender division and condition.

The monasteries in which I conducted my research differ in their location, size, and in overall religious, cultural, and historical importance. The physical setting and location of monasteries bear a fair correspondence to the regulation of daily life and the dominant activities of nuns in them. If a monastery is in a rural setting or in a remote area, manual labor (working in fields, orchards, vegetable gardens, tending livestock, etc.) will be a regular salutary discipline for some or all nuns.[11] In monasteries that are not landed and/or closer to urban areas, there is a greater emphasis on the performance of the monastic hours, psalmody, and other aspects of liturgical life, as well as iconography. Some monasteries in Serbia are considered to have special significance because of the religious and historical personages associated with them or because of the sacred art or holy relics kept in them that are a source of great pride for the resident monastics.

Although every Orthodox monastery adheres to the same universal tradition by following *Typica* (monastic rules of conduct), consistent with the

Orthodox principle of "unity in diversity," each monastic community tends to create its own customs and organize its own style of living. Relations within the monastery reflect the hierarchical structure, with the abbess in charge of nuns and the senior nuns enjoying the respect of the younger ones. The general atmosphere in a monastery, its openness or sometimes reserved attitude toward visitors, in many ways depends on the abbess. In order to do this type of research, which requires staying in monasteries, one has to receive permission (a blessing) from the abbess. The same is necessary for more personal conversations with nuns. They, too, have to get a blessing from the abbess or their spiritual father in order to be interviewed. This rule particularly applies to novices. There is no prescribed time period for advancement of a novice to the next rank (it commonly lasts about three years). It depends on the spiritual maturity of a person entering the monastery and how she handles obedience, repentance, and purification of the heart, which is generally assessed by the abbess and/or spiritual father and as such is highly idiosyncratic. Rasophore, or "robe-bearer," is a rank in which a nun is committed to persevering in monastic life; she undergoes tonsure (symbolically cutting off all previous thoughts of the world), receives a new name, wears a cassock (an outer robe with wide sleeves) and a cylindrical brimless hat with a veil, and receives a leather belt and a prayer rope, two items that epitomize the monastic life of obedience and prayer.[12] The Little Schema, or stavrophore ("cross-bearer") rank, is when a nun gives formal monastic vows of stability of place, chastity, obedience, and poverty ("betrothal"); she is tonsured again and clothed in the habit (includes the yoke of Christ, the *paraman* or *paramandyas*), a wooden cross (with which she will be buried), and a beeswax candle (a symbol of monastic vigil). Finally, the Great Schema nun gets additional vestments (*analavos*) that are a mark of yet higher ascetic and spiritual achievement.[13] There is no set length of time for any of these ranks, since the spiritual progress is very individual.

Looking at the history of Orthodox Christian monasticism, one cannot help noting that women monastics do not stand as visibly as their brother monks in the history of the Church. Their story still remains, for the most part, untold or, more precisely, not recorded in writing, since textuality was historically not a domain of women. Here and there one comes across biographies of prominent abbesses, often compiled by their nuns, whose own "struggles and asceticism remain known only to the Lord," as they say in their humility.[14] These stories, usually orally transmitted, have been important in the creation of nuns' communal identities and deserve their place in the history of the Church. Like a lining in the richly embroidered robe of that history, female monastic experience has until recently remained invisible, as has been the case with various contributions of women throughout history. Their life stories, hidden for so long within the thick walls of monasteries they so often helped found or rebuild, hidden in the icons they painted and cloth they stitched or embroidered, in the melodies they composed or hymns they sang in church sermons, have only recently begun to emerge from centuries of oblivion. Without these stories, however, our understanding of monasticism cannot be complete.

"I Hate Silence When It's Time to Speak!"

These words were uttered by Kassiani, best known as an early-ninth-century hymnographer, writer, and composer but also as a beautiful, well-educated aristocratic maiden of Constantinople. According to a story that, as Diane Toulliatos-Miliotis notes, became something of a legend in Byzantine folklore,[15] Kassiani participated in the "bride-show" for Emperor Theophilios (830–842).[16] According to tradition, having heard the emperor's passing remark that in this world women have been the occasion for much evil (in reference to Eve), Kassiani could not refrain herself from saying: "And surely, Sir, they have likewise been the occasion of much good" (in reference to Mary, the Mother of God).[17] This did not score well in a culture in which silence was considered "an ornament of women," and so Kassiani, having lost her opportunity to become the Byzantine empress, turned her back on the world and became a nun. Eventually she founded her own monastery, became its first abbess, and spent the rest of her life devoted to writing and composing religious music. Even though the majority of the medieval composers throughout Christendom were men, there were also women composers. Kassiani is one of the few whose work has survived. Incidentally (or not?), a musical composition for which Kassiani is best known even today is her *troparion* (a short hymn) "The Fallen Woman." It is sung at the end of the Vespers service of Holy Tuesday, but technically it celebrates Holy Wednesday. The "fallen woman," of course, is Mary Magdalene (Luke 7:36–50), and some scholars see in this penitential hymn Kassiani's autobiographical reflections. The others stress the historical importance of this hymn because Kassiani was "the only hymnographer who wrote a penitential hymn on the 'fallen woman,' Mary Magdalene, a subject that no male hymnographer deemed worthy of attention."[18] The Church did not deem Kassiani worthy of being recognized as a saint until the end of the nineteenth century, when a Service of Praise was composed in her honor. Her feast day is celebrated on September 7.

While Kassiani's personality and life story started attracting the interest of researchers in the late nineteenth century, her skillful use of biblical citations and allusions and her knowledge of patristic sources and earlier hymnographical works that attest to her great erudition and competence have not received sufficient scholarly attention.[19] Yet in addition to over fifty liturgical chants that Kassiani is credited for, she also wrote a great number of secular works consisting of epigrams, gnomic verses, and moral sentences. Her correspondence with Theodore the Studite (759–826), abbot of the famous Studite Monastery of Constantinople, reveals a thoughtful young woman with a gift for writing for which the abbot had only words of praise.

What makes Kassiani's case interesting from the standpoint of our topic is that many of her pieces, unique in the intensity and beauty of their style, are still widely in use in the Orthodox Church during the most important holy days. They survived despite the neglect and prejudice—or as Toulliatos-Miliotis claims, misogyny—that "taints much of the documentation of Byzantine women's participation in music."[20] But no longer. The walls of St. Paul's Cathedral in London echoed with sounds of the latest rendering of the "Troparion of Kassiani" by Christos Hatzis. The audience who attended the 2004 Byzantine Festival was able to hear Kassiani's composition, which, as Hatzis put it, "literally bursts at the seams with emotion and feminine energy."[21] Silence is no longer "an ornament of women," for "it is time to speak," not only to retrieve the silenced voices from the past but also to hear and acknowledge the ones in our midst today.

"And I Just Followed the Voice I Heard in My Heart . . ."

If monasticism in the past, as illustrated by Kassiani, provided women with an alternative to married life, what appeal could it have for women today, given the variety of possibilities that life in modern society offers? My ethnographic study of Orthodox women monastics in the Serbian Orthodox Church is meant, on the one hand, to give them a voice of their own but, on the other, to provide us with an opportunity to better understand the social and anthropological particularity of their experience by listening to their stories.[22] Personal as these stories may be, reflecting nuns' specific experiences as members of a unique social group within the Church and even more so within society at large, they offer revealing points of intersection with the particular social and historical conditions and as such are atypical commentaries on them. Even though certain aspects of monastic experience are shared by women from all Orthodox traditions, the diverse histories of various Orthodox peoples have modified and colored female monastic experience in different ways. This is certainly true for the women monastics in the Serbian Orthodox Church. From the creation of the modern Serbian state in the mid–nineteenth century, after centuries under Ottoman rule, its merging into what eventually became the Kingdom of Yugoslavia after World War I and then communist Yugoslavia after World War II, to its violent disintegration in the early 1990s, the Serbian Orthodox Church has witnessed radical changes and discontinuities in its status and development. While this kind of history is not our focus here, it is indirectly reflected in or refracted through lived experiences of women monastics whose stories I present here. My original idea was to focus primarily on the period of the post-Yugoslav and postcommunist transition, that is, the very end of the twentieth and beginning of the twenty-first century. However, looks at other historical periods are also necessary in order to understand and contextualize experiences of different generations of nuns and better understand the circumstances that formed their identities.

Studying monasticism in the historical context of its past and aware at some level of the otherness of the past itself is one thing; doing it today turns out to be a different matter. In the modern, science-dominated, and secular societies of our time, a life of celibacy, poverty, and obedience—that is, the life devoted exclusively to God—calls for an effort at understanding on the part of religious or any other scholar dealing with the phenomenon of monasticism. The main challenge for a scholar today is how to approach these narratives, whether oral or written, with a critical and historically conscientious mind in view of certain unverifiable or implausible elements of the story. To dismiss them is not an option; rather, an effort to understand and explain the phenomena as best as possible is the goal despite the various limitations that the subject at hand may present.[23] Another challenge is how to interpret the connection with the past that is manifested in the *continuity of willingness* to renounce so many aspects of today's worldly life that previous generations of women could not even dream of existing, let alone then renouncing. In that sense, it is one thing to read about the first Serbian nun, Theodora (the former princess Kosara), back in 1015 and the many other princesses and noble ladies of medieval times who followed in her steps.[24] It is quite another to read a millennium later about Mother Makarija of Sokolica in Kosovo, a former university professor of chemistry, who left her career and worldly life to become a nun, saying that her only regret was not to have done it earlier. When asked about her past life "in the world," Mother Makarija replied that chemistry had always been her love until one day she discovered a Love more "loving," one surpassing her love of chemistry and all other loves, too. "And I just followed the voice I heard in my heart, and from Dr. Milica Obradović I became nun Makarija. That's my great joy."[25]

Nevertheless, despite this continuity of willingness to perpetuate monastic tradition, there were also periods of discontinuity. In medieval times, for example, there was a favorable environment for the flourishing of female monasticism in Serbia. The nuns were usually, though not exclusively, from ruling and noble families. They would take monastic vows as widows or when both husband and wife would decide late in their lives to devote themselves to God.[26] The educational profile of these early nuns was not typical of the general female population of that time, for nuns were as a rule literate and devoted to the study of the Scriptures, the lives of the saints, and the teachings of the holy fathers and mothers of the Orthodox Church. Monasteries were often supported by ruling families. It was customary for queens, princesses, and noble ladies to be sponsors or founders of women's monasteries, which in the cases of those who became nuns later also served as places of their burial. However, the whole culture of monastic life was disrupted in most Orthodox countries in the Balkans during Ottoman rule as the nobility who traditionally supported it gradually disappeared. Life in monasteries became increasingly difficult and dangerous, especially for nuns. Their numbers kept depleting; female monasticism in Serbia practically died out over the course of the sixteenth and seventeenth centuries, with only two operating women's monasteries in the north, in the region of Vojvodina, then part of the Habsburg Empire. In Serbian Orthodox Church records from the mid–eighteenth century we find the description of the conditions in one of those monasteries in Vojvodina, which reveals not only the decline in the numbers of nuns but in their level of education compared to the medieval period. By the end of the eighteenth century, even those two monasteries were closed. In the period that followed, there were sporadic mentions of nuns living scattered in the compounds of men's monasteries or at homes, helping out men's monasteries by selling little crosses and other church items or collecting donations for men's monasteries. But, for the following seventy years or so, female monasticism was practically nonexistent.[27]

Then, in the mid–nineteenth century, a grassroots movement of sorts was formed in the areas of the present Republic of North Macedonia and Kosovo, regions that had traditionally given many women to monastic life. Some women started exerting pressure on bishops to tonsure them to be nuns. Since there were no women's monasteries at the time in those areas, the bishops were reluctant to do so; if they did, they would then let the nuns live near the churches or men's monasteries.[28] Even though a few available historical records on these women's initiatives to reinstate monasticism provide limited information about them, they are noteworthy because such records show women's agency in carving their own place in monastic history in spite of their marginalized status. From what is available, we learn that these were women from well-off rural families, widowed or single, but usually with sufficient means and property to support the construction of additional buildings on the monastic grounds. They would then use them as their living quarters, only to gradually expand and convert them to women's monasteries, which attracted not only widows but young girls and single women, too. There they learned how to read and write and acquired other skills needed for life in a monastery. In towns such as Peć (Kosovo) and Sarajevo (Bosnia), it was owing to the efforts of such pious women, who were either tonsured nuns or led the lives of ones, that the first all-girls' schools were founded.[29] In Peć, the nun Katarina founded the first school for girls in 1855; in Sarajevo, the school was founded by a pious woman, Staka Skenderova, who early on developed a love for religious books. Her school was eventually attended not just by girls of Orthodox but also Catholic, Jewish, and Muslim backgrounds. By the end of the nineteenth century, however, nuns were replaced by trained women teachers in girl's schools,[30] and both founders of these early schools for girls soon fell into oblivion.

"Surrounded Though We Are by a Dismal and Despairing World . . ."

The twentieth century was marked by wars (the Balkan wars, World War I, World War II, and finally the Yugoslav wars of the 1990s), which inevitably left marks on monastic life, making survival for some communities the basic priority. According to some records, in the late 1920s there were only seventy nuns in the Serbian Orthodox Church. The renewal of female monasticism was helped by the arrival of Russian nuns (Mother Ekaterina with her sisters) in the early 1920s, following the Russian Revolution.[31] During World War II, clergy and monastics of most Orthodox churches in the Balkans and Eastern Europe suffered great losses, from which they were slow to recover. But even in those turbulent times, there were some unique personalities among Orthodox nuns who left a lasting legacy: A case in point is Mother Maria Skobtsova, also known as St. Mary of Paris.[32] It is said among monastics that "each saint is a unique event," and this would certainly hold true for Mother Maria, whose unusual style of caring for the urban poor, sick, or persecuted before and during World War II in Paris earned her the title of the "saint of the open door." Not understanding her way of serving, many in her Russian émigré community objected to her rejection of conventions: "Was she not a nun? How then could one justify the irregularity of her liturgical life? Her familiarity with the underworld? The shabbiness of her attire? Her smoking (and in public, moreover)?"[33] But just as Kassiani in her time felt it was time to speak, so Mother Maria knew in her heart that *it was time to act*. She wrote: "At the Last Judgement I shall not be asked whether I was successful in my ascetic exercises, how many bows and prostrations I made [in the course of prayer]. I shall be asked, did I feed the hungry, clothe the naked, visit the sick and prisoners. That is all I shall be asked."[34] Mother Maria died in the Ravensbrück concentration camp and was glorified by the Ecumenical Patriarchate of Constantinople on January 16, 2004.[35]

Even after World War II, for many Orthodox monastics (Russian, Serbian, Romanian, Bulgarian, and others) the hardships and challenges did not cease: They now had to adjust to life in an environment deeply hostile to religion. The life under communism affected especially those who entered a monastery immediately after World War II. From my conversations with nuns who went to monastery in post–World War II Yugoslavia, it was clear that life was difficult for everyone. The Church, devastated by wartime deaths of its clergy and destruction of its property, was no exception. Over one-fifth of the clergy were liquidated during the war, a few hundred more died; almost 25 percent of the Church's property (churches, chapels, monasteries) was totally destroyed, and 50 percent was seriously damaged.[36] The atheistic policies of the state took a heavy toll on monastics. Mother Mihaila spoke of various forms of harassment that she as a young novice of fourteen, together with other nuns, was subjected to in the 1950s.[37] It was hard enough that their monastery was obliged to give the local government a certain amount of grain and other produce per year, but it was even more painful to know that there was no one to protect them from local Communist Party officials who would occasionally rob them of the food and wine produced for the monastery's own needs. There were also psychological pressures: For example, the police would speak disrespectfully to the abbess and the sisters and summon for interrogation younger nuns and novices who had joined the monastery after the war, reproaching them for not joining the Communist Youth of Yugoslavia instead. Attempts were made to persuade some of those younger nuns to return to the world.[38] In the nun Nimfordora's experience, it was not just the government officials but also ordinary people, party members who supported the new system and were ideologically hostile to religion, who made life difficult for the nuns. Coming from a religious rural family, she followed her older sister to the monastery at the age of thirteen, while her three brothers one after the other went to the Theological Seminary in Belgrade to study for the priesthood. Her third sister married a priest. Because of such close ties to the Church, the whole family was ostracized by the local community, some out of fear and some out of ideological conviction. Even later on, when she visited her parents some people were still hostile to her and made fun of her monastic robe; some even spat on her.[39]

While during the communist period the relationship toward monastics ranged from indifference to discrimination, disrespect, and the promotion of stereotypes of nuns as women who were not pretty or smart enough to marry or were handicapped in some way, by the mid-1980s, I was told, the situation was changing. More people were visiting monasteries not as (in socialist rhetoric) "cultural-historical monuments" but as places of worship. And it was especially nuns who took over many abandoned male monasteries and turned them into attractive places for worshippers and other visitors. However, that required a lot of manual labor, whether rebuilding the monasteries destroyed or damaged after World War II or tilling the fields and raising farm animals. The older nuns I talked to would almost always comment on how the younger nuns would not have been capable of the type of physical exertion they had endured in their youth. They claimed that such physical hardships strengthened them spiritually but also that they were able to do so because of their social background. Unlike some younger, city-bred nuns, several of the older nuns I met came from rural areas or small towns, from religious households of poor or modest to solid means, in which the children were respectful of their elders and were expected and accustomed to helping them both in and around the house. Hard work and obedience presented less of a challenge for nuns with such a background than they did for younger nuns. The formal educational background of older nuns, usually with the exception of abbesses, was limited to four or eight years of elementary education.[40]

The older nuns, as well as nuns of the middle generation, who entered a monastery in the 1960s and 1970s, with a similar or only slightly better educational background (high school), would be quick to point out how much they learned in their monastery. More than one nun noted that despite their lack of higher education, years of studying the patristics and lives of saints and contemplating the meaning of the Scriptures had put them in a position today of being able to give spiritual advice to people far more educated than themselves. This may seem paradoxical, one nun admitted, but the monastic experience helped her understand the "inner workings of the human heart," so she could more easily see things troubling a lay person in the world. While this nun indeed had much higher fluency and articulation of thought than her formal education would suggest, I also encountered nuns of this age group (mid- to late forties) who were more withdrawn and had difficulties articulating matters that pertained to things more complex than their immediate tasks of obedience. Their devotion was simple and sincere, their obedience mostly related to some form of manual labor. In fact, it was interesting to note how well the obedience of each nun was matched to her overall abilities and personality.

Of this generation, who were called to the monastic profession during a time of intense atheization and secularization of Yugoslav and Serbian society, in which the Church was portrayed as a retrograde institution, belonging to the past and with no relevancy for modern society, two stories stand out: the nun Haretima's, who came to the monastery as a fifteen-year-old girl in 1981, and Zinovija's, who became a nun in 1974, at the age of twenty.[41] "To 'opt' for monastic calling at such young age," the nun Marija explains, "does not mean a choice made in full awareness of its implications, but it is a strong yearning of the heart which the mind understands only later."[42] That certainly seems to hold true in the cases of these two nuns. They both grew up in religious, semirural households, but while Haretima's family was poor, Zinovija's was middle class. Haretima's family moved near the Ravanica monastery, where her father got a job. Proximity to the monastery and frequent visits to it familiarized Haretima with monastic life, and the nuns there were in many ways her first and only role models.[43] After finishing elementary school, she spent her summer vacation in the monastery. At the end of the summer, the abbess asked her if she would like to stay, and Haretima recalled her dilemma: She did indeed want to stay, as life in the monastery was very appealing to her, but she also wanted to continue her education and become a nurse. Her father encouraged her to stay, saying that if she were to go off to school and into "the world," she would no longer wish to become a nun. She acted on her father's advice but regretted not acquiring skills in nursing, especially later on, when it turned out that such training would have been useful in her current task of obedi-ence as a caretaker in an institution for children with special needs associated with the nearby monastery of Sv. Petka. At my suggestion that her father might have influenced her decision given their financial situation, she was adamant that, one way or another, she would have ended up in a monastery, "because you are called to this profession as much as you choose it."

The nun Zinovija's story was one of the more exciting ones. She first felt an urge to go to a monastery at the age of thirteen.[44] Her family was quite observant; they visited nearby monasteries often, and she found the peace-fulness of life there immensely appealing. When she mentioned to her parents that she would like to live like that, they dismissed it as something inappropriate for a girl like her. A set of circumstances coupled with the hostile attitudes toward religion or its marginalization prevalent in society at the time led her family to immigrate to Australia, to join some relatives. There she led the life of an average teenager (she went to school, owned a car, and worked various jobs) but could not stop thinking about and inti-mately longing for a different kind of life, the life of the monastery. In Australia she met, in her view by Providence, a man from Serbia who was caretaker of the local church and with whom she would talk about her faith. It did not take him long to realize that she wanted to be a nun. He had a female relative in the Ravanica monastery with whom he put her in touch. Zinovija managed to return to Yugoslavia on the pretext of visiting her family: Her uncle was supposed to wait for her at the airport in Belgrade. It happened, she was convinced, by God's will that the plane landed earlier than scheduled and that her uncle's car broke down on the way to the airport; he arrived more than an hour late. Meanwhile, Zinovija was already in a car with a nun and her brother, who had come early to the airport to pick her up. Her father was in on this plan and, being a pious man, had

given her his blessing. Her mother, on the other hand, was adamantly opposed to her daughter's decision to become a nun and twice tried to pull her
out of the monastery by force—helped by a busload of relatives, friends,
and even police—but to no avail. In the end, Zinovija's mother, too, had
to accept reality, seeing (even if not understanding) how strong and persistent her daughter's love for this type of life was. Over the years, Zinovija
endured various temptations, as all monastics do, but never wavered in her
conviction that this was the life she was called to. "There are many of us
here [forty nuns and two novices]," she said, "and we are all different and
have to find ways to fit in. There are many temptations in that regard, but
it's all good because if we were all 'of one spirit' we would not have the
chance to perfect ourselves. It is through the imperfections of others and
our own that we are called to improve ourselves."[45]

Both of these nuns stressed the formative role that their abbess had
played in their lives from the start. Ravanica was already famous for its
previous abbess, Greater Schema Efimija.[46] The current abbess, Gavrila,
was her spiritual daughter and in her tradition took good care of the young
novices (including Haretima and Zinovija), often sparing them from hard
physical labor to allow them time for outdoor activities and their education. This is one of many stories I heard about abbesses whose powerful
personalities inspired deep respect and love while offering living examples
of holiness.

"When the Time Comes to 'Change One's Cross' . . ."

In the generation of nuns who joined monasteries over the past three decades, we see the greatest variations in age, social and educational background, and motivation for monastic calling. Two examples are instructive:
the abbess Efimija, an artist, and the nun Marija, formerly an attorney.
Efimija became a nun at the age of twenty-six. She grew up in Belgrade
and was not raised in the faith. Even though her life had no outer religious
structure, inwardly she said she was constantly searching for the Eternal
and was articulating her quest through painting, first as a student at the
Art Academy in Belgrade and then as a professional artist. Her inner search
for meaning was only reinforced by witnessing the violent disintegration
of her country and the subsequent imposition of sanctions on what was
left of it. Despair over war coupled with the sense of isolation imposed by
sanctions and a lack of purpose in life marked many in her generation, who

were then in their twenties. She witnessed her friends leading useless and self-destructive lives and realized that intellectual debates were not going to fix anything. A different kind of healing was necessary. During her visit to a monastery, where she was studying Byzantine-style iconography, she realized that she could fulfill her own spiritual quest through icon painting and prayer. She did not join the monastery right away but took time to prepare herself, and then, fully aware of her choice, she became a nun. "Initially, all my yearnings for the Eternal were expressed through painting. . . . I don't paint any more. My main monastic obedience is icon writing [iconography]. I purposely say 'painting' and 'iconography' because I want to highlight the difference. Painting for me was searching, while iconography is a fluttering of the soul in front of the face of a living God."[47]

Sister Marija was a lawyer with an unremarkable marriage and family life. She, too, grew up in Belgrade in a secular family, but from her high school days she had cultivated her interest in philosophical questions. Over time, she also developed an interest in supernatural phenomena and started reading books and discussing them with people who had similar inclinations. She remembered hearing stories about an Orthodox monk with unusual "gifts."[48] Intrigued, she started visiting monasteries, only to discover how much she enjoyed those visits and her conversations with monks and nuns. Realizing that she had no background in religion and beginning to discover its deeper meaning, she started researching Orthodoxy and attending church on Sundays. There she met a priest who played a crucial role in her gradual initiation into religious life and her ensuing personal transformation. He was her spiritual father until his death in 1996. After him, she was directed to a priest-monk in a nearby monastery, who introduced her to even more intense spiritual practices. She gradually found that this new inner life was no longer easily compatible with her life in the world. Her spiritual elder confirmed that by telling her that her task in the world was completed, that the circle was closed. What about her family and job? Her family, a husband and two adult sons, took it as the natural outcome of her gradual transformation over the years and felt that it had just been a matter of time before she made that decision.[49] She retired from her law firm and left "the world." Having spent just over a year as a novice, she was tonsured together with other novices, not a typical procedure, during the 1999 NATO bombing of Yugoslavia, when the occupants of the monasteries of Fruška Gora in Vojvodina were in a life-threatening situation.

In both of these cases we see professional women, of different age groups and in different stations of life but of similar urban middle-class and secular backgrounds, making their choices for monastic life. They did so not because they had no experience of other kinds of life and had somehow failed in it but because they found in monasticism the meaningful completion of their inner search and longings. Mother Marija notes that when a person enters a monastery as an adult, "she knows it is the matter of Providence, of being spiritually guided. It usually happens when a person has rounded up her affairs in the world or, as we say here, when the time comes to 'change one's cross' and enter a different world."[50] And, paradoxically, it is in cases like these that we have to stretch our understanding and overcome the otherness of their choice to renounce the world, because the latter is not grounded in some tangible social or economic reasons (as was in the past and in some cases still is today) but is motivated and driven from inside and as such remains hard for outsiders to grasp. In the words of Abbess Efimija:

> They often ask us what it is that made us leave the world and come to the monastery, devote our whole life to God. How can I explain that to someone who has never felt this earth a "foreign land," who has never thought that his real homeland is somewhere far away, that life is, as Kundera says, "somewhere else," who has never heard the song of mourning of the exiled people of Israel?[51]

Such emphasis on spiritual quest is more prevalent precisely among the recent nuns, as is their need for a devotion incorporating a deeper understanding of the faith. Mother Irina, for example, one of the youngest abbesses in the Serbian Orthodox Church, is considered among the best educated and theologically most sophisticated nuns. A former student of mathematics at Belgrade University, active in student protests in 1996, she spent some time in Greece, after which she decided to become a nun. She began theological studies at University of Athens and upon obtaining BA and MDiv degrees she returned to Serbia to help an old abbess in the Grabovac monastery. With the blessing of her bishop to return to the University of Athens to obtain a doctorate in theology, she may well become the first nun professor of theology in Belgrade's Theological Faculty. She often gives public lectures on a variety of religious issues with a facility and competence that often surpasses the clergy who host her talks. What makes her story additionally interesting is the impact of her spiritual father and confessor, Very Rev. Fr. Dionisos, who founded the Exaltation of the Holy Cross monastery near the town of Thebes, Greece, in 1995. In addition to the Greek sisters, nuns from other Orthodox countries and several converts to Orthodoxy from Catholic and Protestant traditions live in the monastery.[52] Irina says that they mostly come from well-off families and are well educated, all sharing in their zeal and yearning for a more authentic life in Christ. From the comforts of their homes they came to live a life of prayer and hard manual labor in the monastery, which is now known for its organically grown produce.

The hard life of the monastery may not always be related to physical work but to inner struggles as well. Among the nuns in the Serbian Orthodox Church who joined monasteries in the 1990s and later, there were some who came from war-torn areas (Croatia, Bosnia, and Kosovo) and opted for this kind of life because their war experiences had rendered life in the world meaningless. There were others who came from completely secular and in some cases broken-up or incomplete families. Their wish to become monastics might be sincere, points out Abbess Jelena, but the inner struggle they have to endure is likely to be more intense than that of their predecessors, who often came from more stable rural families in which religion was already part of their daily life and upbringing. Experienced nuns say that it is not sufficient to want to live in a monastery; one must also be able to endure it. Not all endure the inner struggles of the noviciate: "If a girl comes to the monastery because of some disappointment in life, her soul and her mind will be pressed by the very burden she came with, and such a person is not likely to stay."[53] And among those who stayed, I met some who were clearly having mental health issues and were on medications. For some, the monastic way of life is a breakthrough; for others, it is a breakdown.[54] In the former case, those who were seeking found in monastic life the answer to their quest—or the appropriate framework to continue their quest. But those who fled the world to live in a monastery, or to "hide" in it from the world, will face difficult times. Instructive in that regard was a comment made by Zinovija about some of her fellow nuns who ended up in the monastery even though they didn't seem to belong there: "And yet, God has brought them here," and "only He knows why."

To many moderns living in secularized societies, not just the postcommunist ones, it is still puzzling why educated women go to monasteries. This is especially true in the case of parents who grew up during socialist times, without any knowledge or interest in religion or, conversely, with a pronounced aversion toward it. Some of this generation now find them-selves in the unexpected situation of having children willing to devote their lives to God. The story about the twenty-five-year-old nun Melanija, who holds a degree in philosophy, is indicative in this regard. The girl had been in a monastery as a novice for over a year when her relatives kidnapped her in order to preempt her tonsure. Melanija was a daughter of a local police chief and a teacher; relatives working in the municipality's admin-istration fabricated a document about Melanija's mental incompetence, thereby granting her parents custody of their daughter. In the end, the parents' scheme to keep their daughter out of the monastery did not suc-ceed.[55] Even though this is an extreme case, the fact remains that many parents, especially if they are not believers, live through agonizing experi-ences because of their children's choices. Some in the process may become religious themselves (Abbess Efimija's mother, for example); some may never accept the decision of their daughters (or sons), even if they became monastics later in their lives (as in the case of Marija's mother); and some, like the nun Antonina's mother, may even become a nun herself in the very monastery (Petkovica) in which her daughter is abbess.[56]

"A Smile, a Touch, a Tear"

The nuns I talked to acknowledge that people in the world generally can-not grasp the motivation behind their calling and the real joy behind the life of prayer. For prayer, as the Greek nun Gavrilia puts it, is not just what you say—even a parrot can learn to pray. "Prayer is not an act; it is a state of the soul."[57] For devout monks and nuns, monasteries are not places of refuge—from the world or from one's own self—rather, they are cloisters, meeting places of the "one alone with God"—*monachos.*

> People still wonder about monastics and almost always have some idea about a person disappointed in life who, dressed in black, seeks comfort "between the four walls" and mourns his or her failures in life. The truth is quite different: A monastic is not a person who runs away from people, problems, and society but from the vanity and cor-ruption of life in the world, a person who came to the realization of the emptiness and transient nature of this world and who is not sat-isfied with worldly pleasures and enjoyments, for she or he seeks what is Eternal, i.e., Christ.[58]

Monastics in the Serbian Orthodox Church have generally enjoyed the great respect and support of the people, perhaps because monasticism is at some level perceived as being less corrupt and more truthful to Christian ideals than other churchly roles and professions.[59] This has certainly been apparent in my research, in conversations with people who visit monasteries to seek spiritual guidance from monastics rather than from parish priests. A study conducted by the psychologist Petar Jevremović shows that some young people who frequent monasteries in search of guidance often find among monastics positive and stable role models whose support plays an important role in their lives, especially if they come from broken or dysfunctional families or families traumatized by war, exile, or some other misfortune.[60]

The ancient tradition of "elders" (Greek *geron*, Russian *starets*) also contributes to the reputation of and appreciation for the monastic way of life. In Orthodoxy, elders are people whose ascetic life has brought them the gifts of spiritual discernment and wisdom so they can offer spiritual guidance to those who seek it or need it, be it a monastic or a lay person. For a lay person who visits monasteries, an elder may play a role of psychologist, religious teacher, and spiritual father or mother. For a monastic, however, an elder is a source of inspiration, a person through whom, it is believed, the Spirit of God is made manifest. This has transpired more than once in my conversations with both nuns and monks, namely, how decisive and formative the role of a person considered holy can be.[61] However, as has been noted in the context of the Russian Orthodox Church in postcommunist times, certain "networks around elders could become the breeding ground for fundamentalist ideologies,"[62] thus destabilizing the seemingly uncontentious meaning of the term. Despite such examples, there are others that counterbalance them. One of those is certainly the Greek *gerontissa* (elder) nun Gavrilia, who served the poor and sick in India for number of years in the 1950s and 1960s.[63] She became known internationally as a spiritual mother to several young people whom she met in her modest quarters in Athens (the "House of Angels"), in India, or on one of her many travels around the world. Inspired by the depth of her love and extent of her humility, six of her spiritual children became monastics. "You never think," writes one of Gavrilia's spiritual children, "that you can possibly meet such persons in the unsuspecting everyday ordinariness of city life. You imagine them existing far away . . . or you visualize them living in those blessed early centuries." But having met her here, "what can we say now?"[64] In 1992, the last year of her life, Gavrilia became a Great Schema nun and is considered by many a saintly person. Whether the Church will recognize her sainthood remains to be seen. However, like Mother Maria of Paris, who did not live a settled communal life in a monastery, Gerontissa Gavrilia spent a good part of her life "in motion." She would say that "God is not interested in where you are or what you do. . . . He is interested only in the quality and quantity of love you give. Nothing else."[65] And in the world, "what people want most is a smile, a touch, a tear. Nothing else."[66]

In our digital age, however, this smile and touch need not necessarily be in person but may be virtual. Sister Vassa (also known as Dr. Vassa Larin)[67] is a tonsured rasophore nun of the Russian Orthodox Church outside Russia (ROCOR), an academic, and a presence on social media. Sister Vassa's monastic story in some aspects resembles the stories of nuns we have already met, except that it is molded by specifics of her Russian Orthodox background situated in mid-America.

> The monastic thing was something to which I was drawn already as a child, growing up in the very black-and-white world of the Russian Orthodox Church outside Russia during the 1970s and 1980s. In that world, monasticism was the "real deal," while all other paths were sort of crooked or half-baked ways to God.[68]

Sister Vassa is an accomplished scholar and theologian specializing in Byzantine liturgy and canon law, topics she has written about in numerous scholarly articles and a monograph. Sister Vassa is best known to a wider public for her highly popular online catechetical video program *Coffee with Sister Vassa*, which she created in 2013. It boasts thousands of subscribers and has a worldwide audience. Its mission is "to bring people together around the unifying truths of our tradition,"[69] and today social media platforms offer one way of reaching out to people who are Orthodox and/or are interested in learning more about the religion. "We are called in every generation to contextualize the received Word," says Sister Vassa, and despite her credentials and charisma, several ROCOR clergymen have frowned at Sister Vassa's practice and refused to give her support. When asked about her "problematic" videos, she said:

> If, perhaps, you mean that only my videos, specifically, are "problematic," because I happen to be a female monastic—then you will

have to find the Gospel about the Samaritan woman "problematic," among other passages in the New Testament, because there, in the New Testament, we see various types of women spreading the good news about Christ. Of course, those women did not use YouTube, because they did not have that resource. But I do have that resource. And I use it, just like other members of my Church.[70]

Thus, even today some women monastics who are trying to "contextualize the received Word" in their own time are marginalized by the hierarchs of their church. Is it because the Church purports to protect the Holy Tradition from Western "novelties," or is it because it is still caught up in the prejudices of its own cultural tradition and its views of women, whose "ornament" should continue to be silence? Those who find the initiative of this "female monastic" "problematic" seem to love "to search the ancient canons to find and elevate any archaic rule that serves to restrict women's freedom in church. At the same time, they are often very ready to apply every 'economy' of the Scriptures and the old canons to themselves, for their advantage."[71] This unequal treatment and conditions that have disadvantaged women in the Church are still accepted as "normal," even by some nuns I interviewed. A certain number of them have internalized their inferiority as females and generally support male authority in Church and society alike. Such views were more common among the nuns of the older generation (born before or after World War II), who were raised in strict patriarchal families and would refer in different contexts to their sinfulness as women or comment negatively on women in the world who are not obeying their husbands or are not giving birth to more children.[72] Among the younger ones, then as today, such "traditional" views of themselves as women and nuns, even though not exclusively, tend to be related to a nuns' level of education. What also struck me about these nuns was that the more they insisted on being "strictly Orthodox" (often pitting Orthodoxy against anything "novel" and especially "Western"), the less they were able to show any "quantity and quality of love" toward the outside world.

In "Sync" with Time

That the times are changing can certainly be seen in the much greater presence and visibility of the female monastics in public life in Serbia. Nuns are featured on TV programs about Orthodox monasticism and/or spiritual life.[73] Articles in newspapers about monastics are no longer rarity, and the popularity of Orthodox spiritual music has brought an appreciation of that dimension of monastic spirituality. Even within the framework of my research, that change has become palpable. In the early years of my research, my little tape recorder would make several nuns uncomfortable to the point that they would refuse to speak into a microphone—and some even to be photographed—but in the past few years, when I started revisiting some of these monasteries, this is no longer the case. Unlike many of those older nuns, whose stories I recorded in 2001 and 2002, who gave us a rare insight into their life under communism, and who are no longer with us,[74] the young(er) generations of women monastics are no strangers to modern technology. The others, like Zinovija, found their earlier secular vocations accommodated within the monastic profession. Today, she is known throughout the country for her herbal pharmacy in the Ravanica monastery, where she and other nuns using traditional folk recipes gather and process various herbs for teas, ointments, and tinctures to help improve the health of the children with special needs they care for. They also offer these medicines to the general public. Or, like Mother Maria, who, owing to her spiritual advancement, rose to the rank of Little Schema and became abbess of her monastery. Or Abbess Efimija, who after almost twenty-five years in the Gradac monastery now lives alone in a monastery in France, where she paints—now not only icons. In my first meeting with her, almost eighteen years ago, she stressed that she was no longer an artist but only an icon writer, making a clear distinction between the two. However, in 2017, apropos the exhibit of her paintings in Belgrade entitled "I think, I seek, I wait," she said that painting and iconography are two languages that she uses "to converse" with God. They express two sides of a single being, just like the paintings she paints on both sides of a wooden panel.[75]

Finally, the changes in society at large have brought more sensitivity and awareness to various women's issues, and they have also prompted a greater assertiveness among women monastics. In 2015, the abbess of one of the most important and historic monasteries in Serbia, with over thirty years in that position, was suddenly asked by her bishop to step down, allegedly because of how some of the resources of the monastery were being managed. She obeyed and stepped down. When the bishop assigned a new abbess, the nuns—all forty—threatened to leave the monastery along with their abbess. Local people also protested her dismissal. In the end, the bishop had to accept the reality and, we may say, the power of the authority of this abbess, which comes from her devoted service to the Church and the support of her loyal fellow nuns. It appears that monasticism is still part of the "resistant movement" within the Church. As some Orthodox theologians have already noted, we are witnessing today "a remarkable flowering of women's studies, not least in the domain of early church life . . . reveal[ing] a fuller picture of the impact women had on early Christianity," and in the domain of monasticism "it has become clear that asceticism was used by many early Christian women as a channel for self-development that allowed them the new vistas of opportunity."[76] It transpires from more than one story told here that nuns continue to use this special profession for their own self-development not only as Orthodox monastics but as human beings. Within the boundaries of monastic way of life, Orthodox women theologians and ascetics are slowly but surely articulating in their own words women's views and experiences within the church and society at large. Over the past four decades, there have been several gatherings of women Orthodox theologians: 1976 in Romania, 1988 on Rhodes, 1989 on Crete, 1996 in Damascus, 1997 in Constantinople, and, finally, 2011 in Serbia, where the sisterhood of the Žiča monastery (marking the eight-hundredth anniversary of the monastery) organized an international symposium on female monasticism, with over thirty lecturers from a dozen Orthodox churches around the world. The abbess of the monastery in her introductory talk stressed how important and empowering it was to have sisters from other Orthodox churches at this gathering, where different aspects of female monasticism were to be presented from perspectives of different scholarly disciplines, so that the contribution of women monastics could be better understood and appreciated.

It appears that neglect is no longer an option.

Notes

Some ethnographic material in this essay was originally included in the *Report to the National Council for Eurasian and East European Research* (Title VIII Program, #816-20f), who sponsored the research.

1. Valerie A. Karras, "Orthodox Theologies of Women and Ordained Ministry," in *Thinking through Faith*, ed. Aristotle Papanikolaou and Elisabeth Prodromou (Crestwood, NY: St. Vladimir's Seminary Press, 2008), 127–28.

2. Elisabeth Behr-Sigel, *Discerning the Signs of Time* (Crestwood, NY: St. Vladimir's Seminary Press), 117.

3. There are various transcriptions of Kassiani's name in the literature: Kasia, Kassia, Eikasia, Ikasia, and Kassiane or Kassianh.

4. For the ideal of asceticism in her work, see Kosta Simić, "Life according to Nature: Ascetic Ideals in the *Sticheron* by Kassia," *Crkvene studije* 6, no. 6 (2009): 111–21.

5. Kallistos Ware, "Man, Woman, and the Priesthood of Christ," in *Women and the Priesthood*, ed. Thomas Hopko (Crestwood, NY: St. Vladimir's Seminary Press), 21.

6. Behr-Sigel, *Discerning the Signs of Time*, 117.

7. Peter Brown, *The Body and Society* (New York: Columbia University Press, 1988), 268.

8. For more on different views on women in the early Church in the context of salvation history, see Karras, "Orthodox Theologies," 113–59.

9. For that reason, the term "monastery" is more commonly used rather than "convent" or "nunnery," which (though not incorrect) are usually associated with the Roman Catholic monastic tradition.

10. In Eastern monasticism there is also eremitic monasticism (hermits, that is, ascetics leading solitary life in huts or caves) and semieremitic ways of life consisting of a small group or groups of monks gathered around a spiritual elder. Timothy Ware, *The Orthodox Church* (London: Penguin, 1997), 37–38.

11. This may create a problem when the monastic community is small in numbers and elderly and cannot maintain or make full use of the property surrounding the monastery, as was the case with the Gomirje monastery (Croatia) at the time of my first visit (2002), when there were only four nuns and a priest-monk. The monastery used to be known for its cheese, but it could no longer keep enough sheep to produce cheese for commercial use as well. Since then, two older nuns have passed away.

12. In the Greek tradition, the rasophore rank is not as clearly distinguished from the noviciate period, into which it is included. In Slavonic traditions, though, a rasophore nun is considered fully monastic and distinguished from a novice.

13. Some outer markers of the Great Schema monastics also vary in Greek and Slavonic traditions.

14. *Rusko Pravoslavno žensko monaštvo XVIII–XX veka* (Manastir Tresije, 1999), 7.

15. The story is documented in three chronicles; the one by Simeon the Logothete dates back to the tenth century. The exchange between Kassiani and Theophilios was also mentioned by the historian Edward Gibbon. Diane Touliatos-Miliotis, "Women Composers in Byzantium," https://web.archive.org/web/20070615064123/http:/www.geocities.com:80/hellenicmind/dianeII.html.

16. John Saindopoulos, "The Tomb of Saint Kassiani in Kasos," https://www.johnsanidopoulos.com/2012/09/the-tomb-of-saint-kassiani-in-kasos.html.

17. Touliatos-Miliotis, "Women Composers in Byzantium."

18. Touliatos-Miliotis, "Women Composers in Byzantium."

19. Kosta Simić, "Kassia's Hymnography in the Light of Patristic Sources and Earlier Hymnographical Works," *Zbornik radova Vizantološkog Instituta* 48, no. 201 (2011): 7–8.

20. Touliatos-Miliotis, "Women Composers in Byzantium."

21. "The Troparion of Kassiani," http://homes.chass.utoronto.ca/~chatzis/Troparion.htm.

22. The study was begun in 2001, continued in 2002, and sporadically ever since then, most recently in 2018 and 2019, when I revisited some of the monasteries and updated information on some nuns.

23. For example, humility is one of the main virtues that monastics cultivate, and some nuns I met felt that talking about themselves ("giving themselves importance") is not humble. The others, especially older nuns, would not speak into a microphone, some did not want to have their picture taken, etc.

24. Milojko V. Veselinović, *Srpske kaluđerice*, repr. *Glasa srpske kraljevske akademije* 80 (1909; Beograd, 1997), 169. There is enough evidence to show that the institution of women monastics was well in place in Serbia by the twelfth century and quite spread out during the thirteenth and fourteenth centuries. It appears that the number of women who were nuns but not living in monasteries was significant since the Fourteenth Century Legal Code of the Serbian tzar Stefan Dušan included regulations on life of tonsured monks and nuns who "shall live in the monasteries" and not "in their own homes." *Dushan's Code* (Beograd: Vajat, 1989), 43–44; Veselinović, *Srpske kaluđerice*, 175–78.

25. "Hodočašće u svet ikone," *Pravoslavni put* 1-00 [7] (2000): 16–17.

26. In case of the Serbian Orthodox Church, most notable examples are Queen Marija the Greek (nun Martha); Queen Jelena (nun Evgenia); the lady Teodora (nun Ksenija), the nun Jefimija (wife of the despot Uglješa); princess Milica, the wife of Prince Lazar (nun Evgenija); and many others. Of the couples who became monastics we can mention King Stefan Nemanja, the founder of the Nemanjić dynasty, and Queen Ana (later St. Symeon and nun Anastasia), King Uroš I and Queen Jelena (Symeon and Jelena), among others. Interestingly, in one monastery I met a monk whose wife also became a nun, as did their three daughters, while the son became a priest.

27. Veselinović, *Srpske kaluđerice*, 221.

28. This revived interest in monasticism coincides with the emergence of the God Worshipper movement in Serbia in the mid–nineteenth century. See Aleksandra Đurić Milovanović and Radmila Radić, "The God Worshipper Movement in the Twentieth Century: Emergence, Development, and Structures," in *Orthodox Christian Renewal Movements in Eastern Europe*, ed. Aleksandra

Đurić Milovanović and Radmila Radić (Palgrave Macmillan, 2017), 137–73.

29. Milovanović and Radić, "The God Worshipper Movement," 227–325.

30. Mitar Papić, *Istorija srpskih škola u Bosni i Hercegovini*, July 31, 2009, http://www.staracrkva.org/staka_skenderova.htm.

31. "S verom, bez podataka," *Vreme*, October 10, 2002, 31. It is interesting that while monks were significantly more numerous in the 1920s (442), their number dwindled to 233 (plus 56 novices) in 1996, while the number of nuns increased.

32. Born Elizaveta Yurievna Pilenko (1891–1945), Maria had a colorful life. Raised in an Orthodox Russian family, she joined prerevolutionary intellectual circles in her youth, married twice, lost her daughter to tuberculosis, studied theology, and finally left Russia for Paris, where she eventually became a nun and started her "urban monastic mission." Sergei Hackel, *Pearl of Great Price: The Life of Maria Skobtsova, 1891–1945* (Crestwood, NY: St. Vladimir's Seminary Press, 1965).

33. Hackel, *Pearl of Great Price*, 70.

34. Hackel, *Pearl of Great Price*, 29.

35. Glorification (also referred to as canonization) is the term used in the Orthodox Church for the official recognition of a person as a saint of the Church. Along with Mother Maria, her companions Fr. Dmitri Klemnin, her son George (Yuri) Skobtsov, and Elie Fondaminsky were also glorified.

36. See Pedro Ramet, "The Serbian Orthodox Church," in *Eastern Christianity and Politics in the Twentieth Century*, ed. Pedro Ramet (Durham, NC: Duke University Press, 1988), 237–38.

37. In this generation of nuns it was more typical (though not universal) to find virgin nuns, i.e., those who joined monastery as very young girls (ages twelve to sixteen). According to monastic rules, when such young girls come to monastery they were not allowed to be tonsured before the age of eighteen. Monastic virginity itself can be "literal," "in the flesh," in the case of monks and nuns who entered monastic life at a very young age, but it is always symbolic as well in that it pertains to a human soul that needs to be(come) "virgin(al)." Milica Bakić-Hayden, "Žena i religja: postanje, drugo stanje i stanje danas," in *Mapiranje mizoginije u Srbiji: Diskursi i prakse*, ed. Marina Blagojević (Beograd: AZIN, 2005), 2:322–40.

38. Interviews, June 2001 and December 2012, Vavedenje monastery.

39. Interview, October 2001, St. Stefan monastery.

40. In Orthodoxy it is considered that formal education is not decisive for successful monastic life, since monastic habit is as much the matter of the heart as it is of the mind, and holiness comes from one's relationship with God, not books. However, learning always had its place in the life of the Church and was typically associated precisely with monasteries, which served as first schools and as important

centers for manuscript writing and copying. During my fieldwork I met a nun who was functionally illiterate when it came to the modern Serbian language but who could read with no problem from the Psalter and other liturgical books in Church Slavonic. She belonged to a generation born in the mid- or late 1930s whose education was interrupted or never started because of World War II. As a result, in 1948, 38 percent of the female population of Yugoslavia was illiterate; the rate of female illiteracy decreased progressively but was still 17 percent in 1981. In view of that, the educational background of nuns did not differ much from the overall female population in the former Yugoslavia. Tatjana Đurić-Kuzmanović, *Gender and Development in Serbia* (Novi Sad: Budućnost, 2002), 36.

41. Both interviews were conducted in the monastery of St. Petka in August 2001.

42. Personal communication.

43. The importance of growing up in a vicinity of a monastery and its impact on the subsequent decision to join a monastery is also stressed by Mother Christophora, the abbess of the Holy Transfiguration monastery in Ellwood City, Pennsylvania. "Interview," http://www.orthodoxmonasteryellwoodcity.org/about/abbess/interview.

44. Psychologists that I talked to say that this might also be indicative of the anxiety over upcoming adolescence, and probably in some cases this is so, but not in all. It did not strike me at all that it was so in case of the nun Zinovija, who impressed me with her sincere enthusiasm for the profession she was called to.

45. Interview conducted in August 2001; monastery revisited in 2019.

46. Stories about her remarkable life as a woman and monastic were gathered in a monograph by the sisters of Ravanica monastery: *Životopis shi-igumanije Jefimije, nastojateljice manastira Ravanice i Sv. Petke* (Beograd, 1972). See also Светлана Томин, *Деспотица и монахиња Ангелина Бранковић—света мајка Ангелина* (Нови Сад: Платонеум, 2009).

47. Excerpt from Efimija's notebook made available to the author during one of her visits to Gradac monastery, 2001 and 2002.

48. In Orthodox monastic circles a terminological distinction is made (in Serbian at least) between *vidovitost*, the phenomenon of clairvoyance known in occultism, and *prozorljivost*, the gift of seeing *logoi* (inner essence of things) developed as a byproduct of asceticism. The former is an egocentric product of "powers" that can be misused; the latter is considered God's gift, which is not an end in itself and, in fact, according to patristic literature can be a special kind of temptation for monastics if they start thinking about it in terms of "his" or "her" gift.

49. The life of the family was also transformed, in a positive way, Sister Marija's son, who once drove me to the monastery, claimed. Both he and his

brother, who is married with a child, feel that their mother is helping them more from the monastery through her prayers, the power of which they take very seriously. Oral communication.

50. Oral communication, Grgeteg, October 2002.

51. Personal communication, Gradac, July 2001; excerpt from Abbess Efimija's notebook.

52. Mother Irina, "Interview," https://www.youtube.com/watch?v =6H87L4x9uDo.

53. Abbess Jelena, personal communication.

54. Particularly sad is a recent case of a nun in a monastery near Belgrade who hanged herself. She was a nurse in Bosnia before joining the monastery. She may have had traumatic war experience there that was not adequately addressed, but since there was no other information about this case, the cause remains elusive.

55. *Glas*, August 6, 2002, 5.

56. In a recent interview, Abess Efimija noted that, implausible as it may sound, God blessed her with love through her father, who was a World War II veteran (a partisan and not a believer) but who showered her with love as she was growing up. He passed away when she was in high school. She thought he would approve of her career as an artist but would most likely be against her becoming a nun. *Novosti*, November 11, 2017.

57. *The Ascetic of Love*, ed. Nun Gavrilia, trans. Helen Anthony (Thessaloniki: Talanto, 1999), 272–73.

58. Abbess Jelena, interview, October 2002, Žiča monastery.

59. Florovsky aptly refers to monasticism as "a permanent 'Resistance Movement'" within the Church, having in mind the struggle to remain faithful to the original Way. Georges Florovsky, *Christianity and Culture* (Belmont, MA: Nordland, 1974), 2:88. This, of course, does not preclude the fact that "the resistance" in question may sometimes get extreme in its insistence on what is "orthodox."

60. "S verom, bez podataka," *Vreme*, Oktober 10, 2002, 29.

61. For example, during my visit to the Ravanica monastery, I heard that one of the younger nuns was not feeling well, or as they would say, had severe "temptations." An elder from the monastery Ostrog in Montenegro was telephoned for advice, which he gave right away, that is, without hearing what her specific problems were—allegedly, because, as the nuns claimed, he had a reputation that he could "see" them.

62. Irina Paert, "Mediators between Heaven and Earth: The Forms of Spiritual Guidance and Debate on Spiritual Elders in Present-Day Russian Orthodoxy," in *Orthodox Paradoxes: Heterogeneties and Complexities in Contemporary Russian Orthodoxy*, ed. Katya Tolstaya (Leiden: Brill, 2014), 144.

63. Born as Avrilia Papayanni, she trained as a chiropodist and physiotherapist and put her knowledge most notably into practice in India, in a colony for people with leprosy.

64. *The Ascetic of Love*, 9.

65. *The Ascetic of Love*, 279.

66. *The Ascetic of Love*, 325.

67. Born Barbara (Russian Varvara) Larin in Nyack, NY, where she finished high school and, at age sixteen, entered Bryn Mawr College; at age nineteen she joined the Lesna monastery of the ROCOR in France. She received both her MA and PhD degrees in Orthodox theology from the Ludwig Maximilians University of Munich. From 2009 to 2017 she taught at the Catholic Faculty of the University of Vienna, where she currently resides.

68. "Social Media and the Unifying Truths of Our Tradition: Interview with Sister Vassa Larin," https://static1.squarespace.com/static /54d0df1ee4b036ef1e44b144/t/596e6f8aff7c50deff6ec7c9/1500409742137/05 _Larin.pdf.

69. Sister Vassa Larin, "I Also Experienced together with My Church," http://www.pravmir.com/ sister-vassa-larin-also-experienced-together-church-unique-changes-underwent.

70. Larin, "I Also Experienced."

71. John Anthony McGuckin, *The Orthodox Church: An Introduction to Its History, Doctrine, and Spiritual Culture* (Oxford: Willey-Blackwell, 2011), 412.

72. A contrasting view comes from an abbess who claims that it is not up to monastics, who have no biological offspring of their own, to tell women how many children to have. Yet the proverbial calls of the patriarch to Serbian women to produce more children (in reference to the so-called white plague, or low natality) or the unsavory statements of some bishops (in reference to abortion) about Serbian women as "baby killers" do not help place these "traditional" views in adequate perspective but perpetuate them. Goran Mišić, "Mati Efimija protiv patrijarha u zemlji tabloida," *Aljazeera*, November 1, 2017, http://balkans.aljazeera.net/vijesti/ mati-efimija-protiv-patrijarha-u-zemlji-tabloida.

73. A very popular TV program called *Duhovnici* (Spiritual elders), for example, that has been running for years now includes conversations with abbesses and nuns living in numerous monasteries under the jurisdiction of the Serbian Orthodox Church in Serbia and beyond.

74. The nuns Paula, Petra, Mihaila, Ana, and Efronija, among others, "fell asleep in the Lord" in the meantime.

75. "Nivo 23," *TV Studio B*, April 18, 2017. After almost twenty years of "classical iconography," she says, "I felt a need to express my love of icon in a way that is close to my heart, and that is drawing, pastel collage, combined

technique. . . . Obviously, I am not alone in this need to describe in a novel way that encounter and prayerful relation with saints." https://www.youtube.com /watch?v=B5wLuB-Pbn4.

"Ni crno ni belo," *TV Kopernikus*, November 5, 2017, https://www.youtube .com/watch?v=TyWpPoElB9U.

76. McGuckin, *The Orthodox Church*, 413.

WOMEN AS AGENTS OF GLOCALIZATION IN THE ORTHODOX CHURCH OF FINLAND

Helena Kupari and Tatiana Tiaynen-Qadir

Introduction

Most contemporary scholarly accounts divide Orthodox Christian churches across the world into national churches in the Eastern European heartlands and diasporic churches in the West. Using this categorization, they argue that the Orthodox religion functions as a cultural or national marker that implies belonging to a certain ethnic or national group. Such categorizations are analytically suitable for exploring many social aspects of religion. Yet they tend to brush aside the cross-cutting, transnational, and noncognitive aspects of lived religion that cannot be easily captured by this division. The Orthodox Church of Finland (OCF) is an interesting case as it can be seen both as a national minority church in a culturally dominant Lutheran context and as a growing site of transnational, multicultural, and multilingual interaction. Thus, we suggest that Finnish Orthodoxy is better conceived of as a glocal religion in the making, in which relations and tensions between different cultural and national aspects (Finnish, Karelian, Russian, Byzantine) fuel a perpetual process of glocal becoming. In this chapter, we argue that Orthodox women are important agents in this process of glocalization.

More specifically, we focus on the life stories and experiences of Orthodox women of two generations: older Karelian women, "cradle" Orthodox, who along with their families were dislocated from the Orthodox-dominated easternmost part of Finland during World War II; and younger women from Finnish, Karelian, Russian, and Ukrainian backgrounds, some of whom are either "returnees" or converts to Orthodoxy. We demonstrate how women from different backgrounds actively strive to make Finnish Orthodoxy their spiritual and social home. Furthermore, we argue that their practices and agentic capabilities feed into the glocal making of Finnish Orthodoxy. We illustrate this process by focusing on women's agency as manifested in (1) experiences of the Divine Liturgy, (2) family making as mothers and grandmothers, and (3) participation in parish life. In doing so, we contribute to recent critical scholarship on gender and religion, which deconstructs the understanding of agency as penetrative, action driven, and limited to the social power/resistance frame. In contrast, our engagement with vernacular and material religion allows for the conceptualization of women's agency as multifaceted and inclusive of women's sensorial and interpretative religious experiences.

Our analysis is based on two sets of qualitative data. The first set of data, on the older generation, was gathered by Helena Kupari between 2007 and 2008. It consists primarily of interviews with twenty-four Orthodox Christian women of Karelian ancestry. In addition, Kupari also conducted small-scale ethnographic fieldwork at an OCF parish in a southern Finnish city, participating in parish activities frequented by elderly parishioners. At the time of the interviews, Kupari's interlocutors were on average seventy-five years old. In compliance with a more general trend among Finnish Orthodox women of their generation, a great majority of them had married Lutheran men, and their children had been baptized into Lutheranism.[1] At the time when the data was gathered they mostly lived alone, as widows or divorcées. The second set of data, on the younger generation of women, was gathered by Tatiana Tiaynen-Qadir between 2014 and 2016 in a vibrant and multicultural OCF parish located in western Finland. Tiaynen-Qadir's fieldwork included participant and nonparticipant observation in informal gatherings, clubs, church services, and choir practices. In this chapter, she draws on ethnographic interviews with twenty women, aged thirty to fifty-three, from Finnish, Karelian, Russian, and Ukrainian backgrounds. The interviews were conducted in the Finnish and Russian languages. Most of the interviewees were teachers, university lecturers, accountants, researchers, and doctors and had university degrees.

Orthodox Christianity in Finland

The more systematic Christianization of the area now known as Finland began around the twelfth and thirteenth centuries. In the sixteenth century, the Protestant Reformation was carried out in the area by the Swedish crown. Some two and a half centuries later, Sweden lost Finland to the expanding Russian Empire. The country finally gained independence in the aftermath of the 1917 revolutions in Russia. At that point, Finland was firmly Lutheran dominated, with 98 percent of the population belonging to the Evangelical Lutheran Church of Finland. A hundred years later, in 2017, 71 percent of Finns were members of the Lutheran Church.[2]

Orthodox Christianity has had a presence in the southeastern parts of today's Finland ever since the area was first Christianized. The region of Karelia, which occupies an intermediate position between Finland and Russia, was introduced to Christianity in its Eastern form by Novgorodians, who had adopted this religion from the Byzantines through Kiev at the end of the tenth century.[3] However, over the course of time Western Christianity became dominant in most of the parts of Karelia that were subjected to Swedish rule. During the nineteenth century, when Finland was a grand duchy of the Russian Empire, the significance of the Orthodox Church increased. After Finland gained independence, the OCF separated from the Russian Orthodox Church, receiving autonomous status under the Patriarchate of Constantinople.[4]

The history of Finnish Orthodoxy embraces various migrations, dislocations, and other enforced and voluntary moves of numerous peoples: Karelians, Russians, and others.[5] Ever since the rise of nationalist discourses in Finland and Russia in the nineteenth century, the community has struggled with its self-image, striving to reconcile (alleged) tensions between Karelian, Russian, and Finnish Orthodox identities. The first half of the twentieth century, for example, was marked by a process of nationalization or Finnicization. Especially after Finland gained independence, the OCF took active measures to disassociate Finnish Orthodoxy from its Russian heritage.[6] At this time, the Orthodox heartlands of Finland were located in Karelia. In World War II, however, Finland lost most of its Karelian territories to the Soviet Union. Over four hundred thousand Finnish Karelians became internally displaced people. About 55,000 of them were Orthodox Christians, constituting two-thirds of the Finnish Orthodox population.[7]

In post–World War II Finland, the public image of the OCF suffered, given its association with "Russianness." However, as the postwar survival mentality gradually gave way, Finnish society became more tolerant of difference. The popularity of the OCF started to grow in the 1970s. Finnish intellectuals, influenced by the "Romantic movement," became interested in the Byzantine art of icons and church music, which over time enhanced the oriental and exotic image of Orthodoxy in Finland. Budding religious pluralism in the form of, for example, new religious movements also reflected positively on the status of Orthodox Christianity as an "indigenous" minority religion.[8] Simultaneously, growing urbanization and internal migration catalyzed a newfound interest in regional cultures, including Karelian traditions.

In present-day Finland, any attentive observer will quickly take note of the visibility of the OCF and Orthodox cultural and aesthetic influences in various parts of the country. The presence of Orthodoxy is especially surprising when compared to statistics regarding church membership. At the end of 2017, 1 percent of the population of Finland belonged to the Orthodox Church.[9] This amounts to approximately sixty thousand people in a total population of over five million. However, since the OCF enjoys a similar privileged legal status as the Lutheran Church, it is guaranteed a role in many public events and official functions. Generally speaking, the two "folk churches" of the country enjoy good ecumenical relationships and interact closely, harboring little resentment toward each other.[10] On an individual level, conversions from Lutheranism to Orthodoxy and vice versa take place. Many Orthodox are familiar with and enjoy aspects of Lutheranism, such as Lutheran hymns. Similarly, Lutherans can be drawn to elements of Orthodoxy without feeling any urge to change their denominational affiliation. Overall, many contemporary Finns with wide-ranging beliefs keep Orthodox icons in their homes, attend icon-painting courses, appreciate Orthodox church architecture, follow the Orthodox Easter Vigil from television, and enjoy Orthodox choir singing.

From the 1990s onward, the OCF started to undergo a process of transnationalization, mainly attributable to an influx of migrants from Eastern European countries. Between 1990 and 2009, the share of foreign-born church members increased from 3 to 11 percent.[11] However, this does not include those practitioners who are not officially registered but share some form of commitment to Orthodoxy. Most likely, a large number of individuals among the Russian-language minority of Finland (the largest migrant

minority of the country, roughly estimated at 77,000)[12] consider themselves Orthodox but have not officially joined the OCF. The Church has
taken into consideration the increasing heterogeneity of its members. Many
parishes, especially urban ones, celebrate the Liturgy in different languages
and provide various other activities and services for their migrant members.[13] Among the OCF's clergy and employees are individuals of diverse
national and ethnic backgrounds (e.g., Russian, Greek, Polish, and Sámi).

What differentiates the OCF from most Orthodox churches is that it is
a national church operating in a Western European society dominated by
Protestant Christianity. Based on many conventional measures, Finland is
among the most advanced societies globally when it comes to gender equality. According to World Values Survey data, the great majority of Finns
consider the rights of women as a cornerstone of democracy and support
women's equal participation in society, including the job market, higher
education, and political life.[14] This does not mean, however, that the society has similar expectations of both genders. For instance, Finnish women
continue to shoulder more responsibility for taking care of the home and
family compared to men.

In the OCF, women are allowed to conduct the choir at church services,
and the majority of cantors employed by the Church are, in fact, women.
The same also holds true for teachers of Orthodox religious education.[15]
Women can and often do act as readers in religious services. Moreover, another noteworthy feature of contemporary Finnish Orthodoxy is the central role of women as iconographers. At present, over 90 percent of the
members of the Association of Finnish Icon Painters are women.[16] More
generally speaking, at the end of 2017, 56 percent of all members of the
Church were women.[17] The over-representation of women in the OCF is
in line with nationwide survey material, which shows that there are clear
gender differences in contemporary Finns' attachment to religion. More
women than men belong to different Christian communities, consider religion an important aspect of their lives, believe in basic Christian teachings, and are active in both their public and private religious practice.[18]

Since the 1960s, the Lutheran Church has, from time to time, received
public criticism for its conservative stance regarding questions of equality.[19]
The most recent discussions have focused on the rights of sexual minorities. Marriages between same-sex couples have been legalized in Finland,
but the Lutheran Church has not officially condoned such marriages—
unlike its counterparts in other Nordic countries. Meanwhile, the views

and policies of the OCF on the same questions have not received similar attention. The OCF does not recognize female ordination or marriages between same-sex couples, yet this position has for the most part gone unchallenged in the wider society. In contemporary Finland, minority confessions and religions are often not expected to comply with societal norms to the same extent as the Lutheran Church.

In its official statements, the OCF has presented itself as a unanimous body not influenced by currents of societal discourse. However, within the Orthodox community debates regarding the correct interpretation of the Bible and the significance and application of Orthodox canon law in matters of gender equality and sexual ethics do surface from time to time.[20] Both Orthodox clergy and active lay people take part in negotiations concerning the OCF's proper place in the increasingly pluralistic and culturally liberal Finnish society, for example, in Orthodox media.[21]

The theologian Elina Vuola's recent study, based on interview material, suggests that Finnish Orthodox women hold a wide variety of views regarding the status of women in Orthodoxy. Some of Vuola's interlocutors compared OCF teachings and policies with those of the Lutheran Church, concluding that Orthodoxy discriminates against women. Many, however, emphasized that the presence of a feminine imaginary as well as concrete women—such as the Mother of God and female saints—is much more prevalent in Orthodoxy than in Lutheranism. Of these two confessions, they thus considered Orthodoxy to be more inclusive and respectful of femininity.[22] This variance of opinion illustrates the complex dynamics involved in women's experiences of equality. Overall, Vuola's empirical findings are in line with recent advances in postcolonial feminism stressing the need for more nuanced investigations of religion and gender, investigations that refrain from posing Protestantism as an ideal type against which the "progress" of other religions is measured.[23]

In our contribution, we do not focus on women's opinions concerning gender-related issues in Orthodoxy. Rather, our goal is to explore how Orthodox women of different ages and backgrounds express their religious and gendered identity, how they negotiate for a space to address their spiritual and social needs in the context of the OCF, and how their religious observance and related activities contribute to the making of Orthodoxy in Finland a glocal religion. To achieve this, we draw on theoretical discussions related to glocalization, vernacular and material religion, and gendered religious agency.

Glocalization, Women's Agency, and the Feel of Home

Theories of glocalization address the multidirectional interaction between homogenizing and diversifying tendencies in a culture.[24] The term *glocalization* refers to the merging of global and local elements resulting in the creation of *glocal* cultural forms.[25] Religion, too, as Victor Roudometof's account of Orthodox Christianity illustrates, can be understood through the lens of historical glocalization, involving a fusion between religious universalism and local particularism.[26] In this chapter, we approach Orthodox Christianity as a dynamic religious tradition that has the ability to blend with different social, cultural, and political contexts and perpetually transform itself.[27] Nationalization as an outgrowth of the rise of modern nation-states and transnationalization as an outgrowth of increased migration and multiculturalism are the two major forces that shape the glocalization of Orthodox Christianity today. Nevertheless, there is still little understanding of how glocalization works at the grassroots level of different Orthodox churches and communities and what the role of women is in this process. To shed light on these issues, we expand the standard glocalization framework by incorporating insights from other strands of theorizing.

Most of our interlocutors share personal histories of translocal or transnational moves: Whereas the older Karelian women were forced to relocate from their childhood homes, many of our younger interlocutors moved to Finland from elsewhere. To capture the significance of these histories in the women's present-day religious lives, we apply transnational anthropology, which challenges methodological nationalism and emphasizes multisited lives and senses of belonging.[28] The starting point of our discussion is that the women's engagements with religion arise from and reflect their transnational subjectivities. Simultaneously, we acknowledge that national senses of belonging also play a role in their religiosity.

Transnational subjectivity is a notion that "makes mobility a historical trajectory of one's own, always connecting to where one is located but simultaneously keeping oneself solidly anchored in one's own story and oneself."[29] In our discussion, we illustrate how transnational subjectivities are not only cognitively but also sensually constituted, through embodied memories of past homes and relocations.[30] Moreover, we also suggest that this notion can be applied to study even those who move translocally—like in the case of the Karelian women, whose relocation (at least from their perspective) took place within a single national site.

At present, *agency* constitutes a focal concept through which scholars examine gender and religion, particularly women's religion. A burgeoning body of research discusses women's religious observance, artistry, and creativity as agentic activity and criticizes the use of secular and liberalist conceptions of agency to assess religious women's actions.[31] Yet mainstream feminist scholarship has been slow to appreciate women's religious lives and continues to represent conservatively religious women as unaware victims who have internalized their own oppression within the grids of patriarchal culture.[32]

In our contribution, we focus on how our interlocutors' agency is realized through their *virtuoso religiosity*, that is to say, their endeavor to abide by the demands of the Orthodox faith—as they understand them.[33] Furthermore, we understand the women's actions to embody and evince several modalities of agency. Their agency certainly manifests in how they strive to influence the social world they inhabit and manage social relations in different arenas of their life, a project embedded in a wider web of power relations with both enabling and constraining elements. However, in seeking to uncouple the notion of agency from discussions of power and resistance, we mostly prioritize other aspects of their agency.

In line with recent discussions concerning vernacular religion, which proceed from the premise that people's religiosity necessarily involves a personal, creative, and artistic component, we emphasize our interlocutors' agency in their experiential, interpretative, and inventive engagements with Orthodoxy.[34] Moreover, drawing from theoretical advances in the study of material religion, we pay special attention to embodied and embedded practices of religion—including sensations, feelings, the unspoken, and the body as the matrix and medium of human experiences.[35] Thus, we also locate the women's agency in their contemplative practices of Liturgy, sensorial and corporeal experiences of religion, and in their nurturing and care-giving acts. All of these modalities of agency are pertinent to our interlocutors' glocal making of religion, in that they are integral to the women's capacity to create and sustain homelike spaces. Such a multifaceted agency serves both social ends and the goals of inner spirituality.

Finally, we use the notion of *home* as an emic term, applied by our interlocutors, and as a flexible analytical construct that allows us to capture the women's sensations, discourses, memories, and practices related to their efforts and longing to create a home for themselves and their loved ones. The desire for being or feeling "at home" is what underpins people's agency in constructing their literal, imagined, and spiritual homes. This is a dynamic, ongoing endeavor that evolves around how "one feels or one might fail to feel," including the entire spectrum of sensations, ranging from existential security and serenity to despair and fragility.[36] Religious practices, as practices of dwelling, contribute in this process. They can be employed by people to position themselves in the physical and metaphysical universe, to inhabit a concrete space and social location, to define borders and grow roots: to make homes.[37] The use of the plural is important here, as we individuals can simultaneously feel a homelike connection to several places, abodes, and communities.

Liturgy as Glocal Homemaking

In this section, we focus on the Divine Liturgy (*Jumalallinen liturgia* in Finnish, *Bozhestvennaya liturgiya* in Russian), a church service of the Byzantine rite that Orthodox theologians see as a core sacrament, the "heart and soul" of Orthopraxis. The Liturgy signifies a ritualistic mystical remembrance of the life, crucifixion, death, and resurrection of Christ. The quintessence of the service is in partaking in the Holy Communion (the Eucharist), in which faithful receive bread soaked in wine, mixed with warm water, "transubstantiated" into the body and blood of Christ.[38] As a "synthesis of arts," the Liturgy is a "musical drama on the aesthetic plane," which also includes the arts of burning candles and incense, choral singing, icons, priestly conduct, and prayers.[39]

Irrespective of different ages and cultural and linguistic backgrounds, the narratives of our interlocutors often converged in the importance they placed on participation in the Liturgy. In her previous research, Tatiana Tiaynen-Qadir has illustrated that in its structure and religious aesthetics, the Liturgy in the OCF can be conceived of as a glocal space that combines Finnish, Russian, Karelian, and Byzantine elements.[40] Therefore, individuals from different backgrounds may sensually and cognitively connect to the Liturgy, generating a feeling of "being at home." In this section, we expand this argument by suggesting that women exhibit artistry and agency in their engagements with the Liturgy as glocal homemaking. In this case, women's agency is often contemplative, sensual, and interior. Yet this agency is also highly dynamic, as it allows for the participation in the Liturgy as "movement within the constitution of home."[41]

The transnational and translocal trajectories of our interlocutors manifested in their different experiences of the Liturgy and influenced how they developed a connection to it through their "homes," literal and imagined. For many Karelian women of the older generation, participation in the Liturgy meant connecting with their childhood homes and communities in Karelia. This land now only exists in their minds and hearts and can sometimes be sensually and bodily remembered through the Liturgy. Our interlocutor Raili, for instance, recollected how every Sunday morning her grandmother used to take her to the Liturgy:

> [As a child, the Liturgy] sometimes felt long. But somehow, what stuck with me was I guess the scent of incense. When I go [to church], I find the scent of incense just wonderful. And it brings a wonderful feeling. Nowadays, always when I smell the scent of incense, I think of my childhood, whether sitting or kneeling [at church], well, not sitting, my grandmother would not allow that. You could not sit there.[42]

Many women's narratives also pointed to the continued importance of bodily conduct during the Liturgy, something that they had originally learned during their childhood years: standing still, kneeling, bowing, going forward to light candles, kissing the icons, and making the sign of the cross repeatedly. As Raili's account illustrates, sitting during services was not considered proper behavior. Although standing during services may constitute strenuous physical exercise for those with ailing health (and chairs and benches are available for those in need), the women still preferred to stand. Some explained that this way of "revering God" had been ingrained in their bodies since childhood.

In many ways, the Liturgy thus enabled the multisited and multitemporal presence of the older Karelian women. Through the Liturgy, they maintained a connection to the Karelia of their childhood, their imagined homeland associated with existential security and comforting routine. A longing for and wish to recapture that home were important parts of their sense of belonging and partaking in the Liturgy. The glocal nature of the OCF, its continued incorporation of Karelian elements—including the commemoration of Karelian saints, the use of Karelian terms and the inclusion of certain hymns in the Karelian language in some church services, the presence of icons and other sacred objects evacuated from Karelia in churches, the writing of new Karelian-style icons, and the use of Karelian-style elements and motifs in chapel architecture—facilitated this feeling.

Yet the result was never quite able to recreate the women's original experiences, as is the case with all nostalgic remembering. The presence of Karelia remained too weak. As Martta, for example, noted: "In the olden days, even priests spoke partly in [the Karelian] dialect, sometimes even in church. It felt so soft and cozy and warm to listen. But now it's a different thing altogether, after decades spent here." Moreover, some of the efforts to reintroduce Karelian elements into church life were criticized by women for being "artificial." They were too far removed from what women remembered from their childhood.

Nevertheless, the agency and artistry of these older Karelian women is crucial in making the Liturgy a glocal happening. Their artistry is reflected in how they lived and negotiated their translocal subjectivities and multi-sited homes through participation in the Liturgy, bringing some aspects of their past to the present. Their agency resided in their individual, contemplative participation in the Liturgy. It was also realized through communal attendance when, as one of the interlocutors put it, "you are one with the others." For the most part, this agency was not purposive or conscious but manifested in the women's presence and natural conduct during the Liturgy, in their bodily actions and postures. Whether wittingly or not, they were an embodiment of a living tradition for many others present during Liturgy. For younger participants, these older women may represent the (Karelian) roots of Finnish Orthodoxy or constitute emblems of genuine (grandmother-type) piety. Moreover, for those attendants whose own knowledge of Orthodoxy remains on a more abstract level, such as recent converts, their conduct served as an example of emotional and corporeal participation in the Liturgy.

For many Russian and Ukrainian women who have migrated to Finland as adults, participation in the Liturgy also enabled their multisited presence and connection with their birth homes through sensual engagement. They venerated the same Orthodox icons, immersed in familiar melodies, and recognized similarly decorated church interiors. Many of them emphasized that they enjoyed services in Church Slavonic, which "sounds especially touching probably because it is in Russian." Our interlocutor Anastasiya mentioned that her church in Finland "reminded" her of the church in Russia where she was baptized: "It was great to perceive Finland through the church. As if I lived not in Finland but in this place with this church and these people." Similarly to our older Karelian interlocutors, in their participation these migrant women activated their embodied memories of liturgies celebrated in their home countries, which intensified their sense of "being at home" in the Finnish Liturgy.

However, in contrast to the Karelian women's longing for the Karelia of their memories, which they could not physically reach, many Russian-speaking women maintained multisited lives and transnational families, regularly traveling between family members' abodes. They participated in church services "here" and "there" without thinking much about the national differences in church organization. Rather, their spiritual journey took place within the constitution of their transnational Orthodox home and transnational subjectivities. Our interlocutor Anfisa, for example, described how, while living in Russia, she had "passively" attended services, liking the music, the smell, and the entire "atmosphere." She apprehended Orthodoxy with more "awareness" later after having moved to Finland. She joined the choir and soon became a reader during services in Church Slavonic, usually held once a month. When she visits Russia, she also attends the Liturgy in her home church there.

The glocal nature of the Liturgy in the OCF is enabling in the sense that women from different backgrounds can connect to it sensually and cognitively. Liturgical prayers and texts speak to individuals through the medium of different languages and varying choral arrangements: whether performed in Finnish as a "Slavic melody" or in Ancient Greek as a Byzantine chant. Some emphasize the beauty and "power" of archaic texts and words in Church Slavonic and Ancient Greek, which generate different experiences and meanings even for people who do not speak the languages. Many are "moved" by compositions of Finnish musicians and choir conductors, who artistically combine (neo-)Byzantine chants, Slavic multivocal traditions including "znamenny chant," and modern influences. Prayers also invoke the notion of home at different levels. They refer to church as the dwelling place of God, to Mary as "the marvelous palace of the Lord," and to one's own body as "the house of the Divine Spirit."[43] For Russian-speaking interlocutors, this connection is also literal: The Russian word *dom* means both "house" and "home."

Nevertheless, the artistry and agency of individual participants are equally crucial. The glocal making of the Liturgy as a communal happening requires learning, practice, interaction, tuning, and contemplation on the part of all attendees. Finnish faithful participate in services in different languages; many are well familiar with some recited prayers in Church Slavonic and Ancient Greek sung during the Liturgy as well as famous hymns such as the paschal troparion "Christ is risen from the dead." Moreover, Russian-speaking participants also learn prayers and hymns in Finnish to enable their fuller participation in Finnish-language liturgies.

The Liturgy as glocal homemaking is also a process that triggers tensions and necessarily involves the negotiation of such tensions. Older Karelian women, while admiring converts' arduous efforts to study Orthodoxy, could reproach them for their conduct at church, such as their tendency to wear "only black" during the Liturgy, which was not customary in prewar Karelia. These older women also commented on converts' tendency to educate others on Orthodox doctrine based on their learning and "book knowledge." Some cradle Orthodox—Karelians as well as descendants of Russian émigrés of the era of the grand duchy—found it difficult to deal with the more recent influx of Orthodox migrants, as it meant that what they knew as their cozy, small, "home church" had become a very different place altogether. At the same time, Russian migrant women could feel tense and uncomfortable attending the Liturgy in the Finnish language, especially when they were newcomers at the OCF. In some parishes, the estrangement between Russian speakers and Finnish speakers could also be enhanced by nationalistic interpretations of history, in particular concerning the cessation of Karelia from Finland to the Soviet Union in the aftermath of World War II. Some of our interlocutors, as well as the clergy, made efforts to ease these tensions in their work in the parish.

However, what united our interlocutors irrespective of their backgrounds was how they related to the Liturgy as their "spiritual home." While many of our interlocutors were well familiar with the theological significance of the Liturgy, when they described their personal experiences they turned to the language of feelings and bodily sensations, associated with a comforting sense of "being at home." Many women linked their partaking in the Liturgy with senses of "joy," "solemnity," "serenity," "calmness," and "silence," emphasizing the Liturgy's "nurturing" and "therapeutic" effects. They liked "breathing in the air, the smell of the incense." Some felt "comforted" by the "shining" and "smoothing" beauty of surrounding icons. Others experienced "awe" and "reverence" looking at "the sky with the stars" in the church dome. Many also referred to spontaneously occurring bodily reactions to describe the inexplicably touching nature of chants and choral singing. Listening to the choir could make your body "tremble," "chill" you "to the marrow of your bones," "make your heart go soft," or "move" you "to tears." Overall, during the Liturgy a church could be so rich with atmosphere that "religion is almost palpable" there. Such accounts convey the agentic nature of the women's individual, contemplative, and sensual engagements with the Liturgy, in which a sense of the inner home is central.[44]

Finally, most of our interlocutors also emphasized their ongoing efforts to "master" the Liturgy. While they experienced the Liturgy as a homelike space, they simultaneously conceived of it as a continuous spiritual and cognitive journey. It takes years of practice and work to learn the language of Liturgy, with the visual elements, "church poetry," and music all intertwining theological meanings with personal experiences felt in the body. Indeed, as one of our older Karelian interlocutors, Elsa, stated, "We are never ready in this area," for "everything is revealed so very slowly." The same notion was expressed by one of the younger women, Johanna, who emphasized how "all services are different." The women, overall, spoke of the Liturgy as a space for "deepening" one's spiritual knowledge and "developing" as a person. Many interpreted their evolving experiences of the Liturgy in the context of their progress through different life stages. In other words: As religious virtuosi, the women also approached the Liturgy through their personal spiritual goals and their aspiration to embody Orthodox traditions to the fullest.

Family Making through Home Altars

Women's creativity and artistry in constructing and sustaining the feeling of "being at home" often receives its fullest expression in the domestic setting. In a previous publication, Helena Kupari has argued that the everyday religious customs of her elderly Karelian interlocutors can be understood as agentic practices of homemaking.[45] Through these customs, the women sustained a domestic environment in which religion was continually present in various material, sensory, and temporal clues. Moreover, this crucially contributed to their experiences of the safety, stability, and sanctity of domestic space. Here, we develop this line of thought further, suggesting that religious homemaking also involves building connections between past and present homes as well as between homes of loved ones across geographical distances. In addition, we argue that homemaking activities are closely connected to family making, to maintaining loving and emotional relationships and creating "family feeling" among family members.

For both our older and younger generation of interlocutors, religion was intertwined with family relations. The older Karelian women had been brought up in all-Orthodox families in which religion was openly practiced and passed on to the children. In their descriptions of their religiosity, they focused on lineages and continuums of practice reaching from childhood to old age. Sometimes they further emphasized the deep-seated nature of their religiosity through the use of corporeal metaphors. They could speak, for instance, of Orthodoxy being in their "genes" or of having received it through their "mother's milk." These expressions conceive of religion as a concrete, physical, and embodied connection between family members.

In comparison to these elderly women, many of our younger interlocutors had not been actively guided toward an Orthodox lifestyle in childhood. On the one hand, in the Soviet Union, decades of systematic suppression of religion had resulted in Orthodoxy being only nominally present in most people's lives. On the other, in post–World War II Finland the open practice of and identification with Orthodoxy was often restrained because of discrimination. In addition, the postwar decades brought about a surge in marriages between Orthodox and Lutherans, and collective familial religious practice in these biconfessional families was commonly biased toward Lutheranism.[46] Therefore, although for different reasons, both our Russian- and Finnish-speaking informants of the younger generation often had mainly passive experiences of Orthodoxy from their youth.

Nevertheless, in their later rediscovery of Orthodoxy, these women drew on childhood memories of their Orthodox family members. For example, many Russian-speaking women cherished embodied recollections of their grandmothers praying, lighting a candle in front of an icon, or reciting a silent prayer before eating. In the Soviet Union, children's religious socialization and the transference of religious traditions was left mainly to grandmothers, or *babushkas*.[47] In this vein, our Russian interlocutor Anna, a "militant atheist" in the past (in her own words), recounts how her grandmother was the only family member who connected her to Orthodoxy:

> I was born into a non-Orthodox family. . . . My mother was not Orthodox, although her mother was faithful. . . . I was baptized by my babushka [maternal grandmother], probably kept secret from my father, I don't know the exact story. Then, I went to church with babushka several times. Babushka prayed before she went to sleep;

I heard her praying when I stayed at her place. She also had icons, so in some ways it [Orthodoxy] was in my surroundings. I had a sense of it but was quite unconcerned about it. I had a cross, I did not wear it, but it was, it has always been there, and now I am wearing it. . . . There is a family legend related to it, that it was made from a family silver spoon [laughing].

Our older Karelian interlocutors also often singled out a close female relative—commonly their mother or grandmother—as their primary religious role model. They described this person as having been particularly devout in her religious observance. In their own practice of piety, they strived to follow the example set by their predecessor. Our interlocutor Hilja, for example, described how, after her grandmother passed away, she bequeathed her with the task of intercessor:

After we had come home from my grandmother's funeral, I had this dream in which she was waking me up. And she said to me: "You poor child do not pray enough, for I have to pray for you here in the afterlife." . . . I have thought to myself that grandmother must have been such a holy person—she wasn't free of sin or anything, but she was so devout in her faith and she prayed for me and for my children and for everyone—that she was able to send me a message, to remind me not to forget to pray. Because she herself turned to God all the time, asking for God's help and blessing.

A similar experience was also narrated by our Finnish interlocutor Marja, of the younger generation. She had been baptized into Lutheranism as a child but had later converted to Orthodoxy. Her maternal grandparents had originally been Orthodox, but her grandmother had left the Church in adulthood to avoid social exclusion in postwar Finland. Then, the night her grandmother had died, Marja had felt that she had come to sit on her bed for a while. Marja's, Hilja's, and Anna's narratives all illustrate how our interlocutors conceived of their religiosity as family tradition passed on from grandmothers to granddaughters.

At the heart of domestic religious practice in Orthodox Christianity are home altars, also known as icon corners (*ikoninurkkaus* in Finnish, *krasnyi ugol* in Russian). The home altar, traditionally set up in the corner of one habitable room (or several rooms) of the home, is where family icons are placed, potentially accompanied by other religious objects and paraphernalia such as the Bible, prayer books, religious print images, hanging oil lamps, wax candles, and religious textiles. Sarah Riccardi-Swartz summarizes the centrality of icon corners in vernacular Orthodoxy by noting how they act as portals and mediators that "allow access to the extended family of Orthodox Christians, living and dead, humans and saints, thereby strengthening religious, social, and familial bonds."[48] Here, we focus on home altars as facilitators of family making within and beyond the nuclear family.

Irrespective of generation or ethnic background, intercessions for loved ones were an integral part of our interlocutors' domestic religious practice. In the interviews, many of them recounted memories of troubled times, during which they had prayed ardently for resolution in front of the home altar. Marja, for example, described how her most powerful experience of divine intervention to date had occurred when her son was seriously ill. He was six years old at that time, and Marja had to leave him in the hospital. She came home with a heavy heart and prayed devotedly in front of a Marian icon that her Orthodox grandfather had painted for her. The same day Marja received a call from the hospital that she could come and take her son home: He had recovered. Several other women also shared with us similar intense experiences of divine guidance that they had received in response to their motherly prayers in times of crisis.

Motherly and grandmotherly prayers were also included in the women's daily religious observance. Many of our younger interlocutors were occupied with starting families and caring for their children. Our older interviewees, for their part, often understood praying as the particular duty of grandmothers. What differentiated the two groups of women was that the older generation's practices were equally geared toward crossing temporal distances and the barrier separating living and deceased family members. They were worried about what would happen to their offspring after they themselves had passed away. Toini, for instance, stated: "I've thought that I have to pray [for my children and grandchildren] so much beforehand that it will carry them even after my death." Furthermore, many of their loved ones had already died. Therefore, practices of remembering the departed were an important part of their engagements with their home altars.

Our interlocutors, overall, saw prayer as powerful agentic action.[49] By interceding on their behalf, the women were able to help loved ones and family members across vast distances. Prayer could also cross the barrier between this world and the hereafter. Many women thus emphasized the "power of prayer" in situations in which all other means of action had failed. Simultaneously, they also acknowledged that the effects of prayer could not be accredited to them alone. To the contrary, praying was essentially about acknowledging one's dependence on God, resigning oneself to God's will, and begging for the support of divine intercessors. According to the women's religious worldview, one could tap into enchanted agency, thereby significantly expanding one's capacity to act in the world—but only through submission to and humble collaboration with the sacred personages of the Orthodox universe.[50]

The Mother of God is the divine intercessor many of our interlocutors primarily turned to when praying for their children and grandchildren. Mary, that is to say, stood at the center of their mothering and family practices. In Orthodoxy, the Virgin is often seen as a perfection of humankind.[51] As an exoteric figure, she stands for the mystery of birthing and nurturing God within the self, metaphorically applicable to men and women.[52] Nevertheless, many women also approach her as the one who, being a mother herself, best understands a mother's pain, sorrow, worries, and joy, while also having invincible powers to intercede and cure.[53] This engagement happens primarily through the many icons of the Mother of God, each with its own story and iconography.[54] Marian icons thus had a prominent place in our interlocutors' home altars.

For our younger, migrant interlocutors, home altars had additional significance as tangible spaces of family making. These women commonly operated with an extended notion of a family that transcended national borders, encompassing relatives "here" and "there." The women's activities focused on crossing spatial distances through visits and with the help of new telecommunication technologies, as well as influencing the lives of loved ones abroad. Often, their home altars became important glocal sites where the entire transnational family was brought under the protection of the Trinitarian God, Mary, and the saints.

A case in point is our Russian interlocutor Elena's home altar, located in the living room of her apartment in Finland. The altar housed many divine figures. There was a large printed icon of the Valaam Mother of God and a copy of the famed Vladimirskaya icon of the Mother of God, with the Christ child gently nestling and embracing the neck of his mother. The altar included icons of the patron saints of her three children, her husband, and herself. There was also an icon of Saint Nicholas, to whom she prayed for her brother Nikolai, living in Germany, a musician with a long and sad history of drug addiction and mental illness. An icon of Saints Sergius and Herman of Valaam helped her "feel connected to her home in Sortavala" in Russian Karelia. In its entirety, Elena's home altar constituted a space of glocal homemaking, in which her different senses of belonging manifested. The altar reproduced the sense of togetherness and familyhood against the odds of separation, with icons functioning as talismans of belonging and saints taking the role of divine members of her transnational family.

Elena's family had experienced a great deal of uncertainty caused by Finnish residence permit procedures and a precarious job situation. In her narratives, the home altar—and particularly the Marian icons of the icon corner—emerged as an anchor of family belonging, security, and "calmness" in the midst of transnational changes and the challenges of adjustment in Finland. The following quotation from Elena's interview beautifully illustrates how, when praying together, her family grows into one body, one corporeal unit, under the protection of invincible powers. This family bonding takes place not only as a spiritual unit but also literally, in the space of a Marian icon:

> Life goes very quickly. There are a lot of everyday things taking place. But when you gather with your family to eat in the evening . . . when we pray before eating, we hug each other at the same time. I don't know, but it just happens instinctively. For instance, Maria, our daughter, can't just stay separately and pray. She will come and embrace me, and then we all stand together. And this prayer before we eat seems to be a small thing, but at that moment, when we're hugging each other, praying, I feel that we are a family and we are strong. Whatever happens, we are together and have each other . . . I look at the icon [the Valaam Mother of God], and it is like an unconditioned reflex of calmness.

Icons of the Virgin held a special significance for many of our other migrant interlocutors as well. Besides their role in practices of mothering, they could also function as bridges between the women's past and present homes. Many women thus developed their home-relatedness to Finland through interacting with familiar Marian icons, at the same time retaining their sense of Russian belonging.[55] The Valaam icon of the Mother of God is a good example. Due to particular historical trajectories, there are presently two Valaam (Valamo in Finnish) monasteries, one in Lake Ladoga in Russian Karelia and the other in Heinävesi in eastern Finland.[56] The original icon of the Valaam Mother of God is presently one of the main treasures of the Finnish monastery, while an exact copy of this icon is kept and venerated in the Russian monastery. In a sense, the wonder-working icon is equally connected to both monasteries, creating a glocal space in which the boundaries of national imaginaries between Russia and Finland can be transgressed.

The glocal nature of home altars was also evident in our older Karelian and younger Finnish interlocutors' homes. Many of the younger women, especially, were well aware of the historical and cultural background of the icons that they had set up in their icon corners.[57] Home altars could include icons or print images bought as souvenirs from travels abroad, carrying connotations of different national contexts. Nevertheless, for most women Karelian icons were particularly important—for family reasons and given the special role that these icons had in Finnish Orthodoxy and the OCF. Besides the Valaam Mother of God, other popular and respected icons were those of the Konevets (Konevitsa in Finnish) Mother of God and of Saints Sergius and Herman, the legendary founders of the Valaam Monastery. Our interlocutor Irene, of the older generation, had placed an icon of the Konevets Mother of God at the center of the icon corner in her living room and had recently commissioned similar icons to be painted for her children. She explained: "The Konevitsa Mother of God is very important to us Karelians, because it has been brought from Athos here to the Konevitsa Monastery. This [icon] motif is very familiar and much loved in Karelian homes." In fact, the Konevets Mother of God is another icon that opens up a transnational connection between Russia and Finland. It is linked to the Konevsky Monastery in Russian Karelia, but at present the original wonder-working icon is kept in the Valaam Monastery in Heinävesi.

For many of our older Karelian informants, home altars constituted transtemporal as well as transnational spaces. They had placed icons inherited from parents, grandparents, or other relatives at prominent places in their homes. Some women had also included in their home altar a print version of a particular icon of Christ Pantokrator. This print is commonly known in Finland as "the Evacuee Christ" (Evakko-Kristus in Finnish) because copies were distributed to evacuated Orthodox families during World War II. Placed in the icon corner, it acted as a concrete reminder of the women's histories of displacement. In addition, many of these women had formed a close attachment with icons depicting the patron saint of the church or chapel of their childhood home village in Karelia. In the home altar, these icons also facilitated a sensual and material connection with the past.

All of these examples emphasize our Russian, Karelian, and Finnish interlocutors' artistry in arranging their home altars and agency in breathing life to their domestic environments through their daily prayers, contemplation, and interaction with icons. Through their practices, the women construed connections between their past and present homes and between homes "here" and "there," united their families dispersed in space and time, and cared for their loved ones both near and far. Through their customs, they also honored their family religious traditions and tapped into the legacy of their religious role models. Simultaneously, they created glocal environments in which elements from various contexts merged together, producing unique fusions of personal, local, national, and transnational significations.

Women's Agency in Parishes

In the OCF, women have historically had a prominent role in various bodies vital to the functioning of parishes, such as church choirs and clubs. At present, women's representation in elected councils of parishes is also equal to that of men. Women are often in charge of lay activities such as the organization of church fairs, children's clubs, and cultural and educational events.[58] Many of our interlocutors of both generations had taken part in such projects. Here, we discuss some of their experiences of parish activities. Through these activities, we demonstrate, the women exerted their more intentional, change-driven, and goal-oriented agency for the benefit of the community.

Many of our older Karelian interlocutors had recently had to limit their participation in parish life for health reasons. Yet they could be considered active members of the OCF. Some had taken part in parish pursuits throughout their lives, whereas others had begun attending more regularly after their children had grown up or when in retirement. While the women had experience of many different kinds of activities, we focus here on the form of voluntary activity most familiar to them: the Tuesday Club (Tiista-iseura in Finnish). Tuesday Clubs are local branches of the Finnish Orthodox home mission organization Brotherhood of Saints Sergius and

Herman, which has close ties to Orthodox parishes. The first branches were founded in Karelia in the 1920s. While the heyday of the Tuesday Clubs was between the 1950s and 1980s, during past decades their significance for parish life has diminished. Today, the membership of the Tuesday Clubs mostly consists of the parish elderly.[59]

Tuesday Clubs are commonly led by prominent female parishioners, and their members are predominantly women. The gender bias reflects the nature of the activities offered. Traditionally, Tuesday Club meetings (held on Tuesdays) consisted of handicrafts or needlework, coffee, and some spiritual or cultural program such as prayers, singalongs, guest lectures, or recitals. A central function of the clubs was to gather funds to be used on some worthy cause. Collectively, participants produced crafts and baked pastries that were sold at church fairs, the proceeds of which were used to benefit the parish or donated to some other spiritual cause. Furthermore, Tuesday Clubs could also contribute to the parish through catering church coffees, producing festival decorations, or helping in the cleaning and maintenance of parish property.

When describing Tuesday Clubs, our interlocutors emphasized the warm atmosphere and solidarity among participants. They could speak with affection of already deceased older members who had given them guidance or acted as spiritual role models. Many also had childhood memories of their mothers attending Tuesday Club meetings. For these women, taking part was yet another way of honoring their spiritual family heritage. Furthermore, as in their daily lives most women were surrounded by people who did not share their confession, Tuesday Clubs constituted rare spaces where they could enjoy the company of other likeminded Orthodox practitioners and, as one of them stated, "rejoice in being part of a community."

During the first post–World War II decades, the OCF went through a massive reconstruction project. It had lost an estimated 90 percent of all of its property in the war.[60] The state provided funds for the construction of new churches and parish halls; moreover, chapels were also financed through local fundraising projects or built entirely by community labor. Tuesday Clubs had a significant role in the furnishing of these places of worship and in supplying them with ritual objects, textiles, dishes, utensils, and other necessary equipment. When discussing the history of the OCF, several of our older interlocutors thus noted with pride how many Orthodox chapels were the result of "the activity of parishioners" and "the hard labor of Tuesday Clubs."

These women often remembered the buzzing activity of previous decades with fondness. According to them, Tuesday Clubs used to be places of intense work where a lot could be achieved through collective effort for the benefit of the entire community. In their accounts, they often contrasted the past with the present, noting that Tuesday Club members no longer had the same energy or sense of purpose. As the membership had aged, meetings had increasingly focused on socializing and spiritual content. Our interlocutor Soja lamented that in the club that she frequents volunteers could no longer be found to cater for church coffees on a weekly basis. She strongly disapproved of this development. Her description of the activity of previous years emphasizes friendship and solidarity as a motivating factor and conveys her sadness over losing it:

> Then, when the children grew older, I was freer to participate and go [to parish activities]. . . . At some point Father Petri asked me if I spent any time at home at all [laughing]! I was not in so much of a rush to get home because the children were already so much bigger by then. And we baked pies and other pastries, we always had something in the freezer that we could serve [at church coffees]. We had this really nice group of people. One of us just died, Nina, a year ago. And then Helmi. I used to sew with her, church textiles and everything, down in the basement [of the parish hall]. We had a sewing machine there and a loom and fabric and . . . now there's a lack of organizers.

Our Karelian interlocutors also described Tuesday Clubs as gatherings where the participants used to be mostly Karelian, and the meetings included many ethnic elements. This enhanced their feeling of "being at home" in the parish. However, the women who had been upholding these traditions had since passed away, and the membership had become more heterogeneous. While in the eyes of other attendees our interlocutors undoubtedly embodied Karelian Orthodoxy, they themselves felt that something had been lost. "What has happened to Karelianness?" asked our interlocutor Kielo when observing that Tuesday Club meetings used to include singalongs in the Karelian dialect but that nowadays "no one knows or sings any songs." Nevertheless, many of the women had actively passed on their knowledge of Karelian traditions to younger parishioners through, for example, teaching them how to prepare traditional dishes or handicrafts.

Compared to the older Karelian women, our younger interlocutors were at a different stage of their lives. Their participation in parish pursuits was not hampered by their ailing health. On the contrary, many of them contributed a lot of their time to the parish despite their busy schedules. In their accounts, they described the church as a homelike environment, a feeling caused, at least in part, by their ongoing, active participation in the constitution of this space.

The women were members of a large urban parish, which in Finland are usually more multicultural than rural ones. Many of them appreciated the parish clergy for their efforts to encourage interaction between members from different backgrounds. In the parish, the Liturgy is celebrated in several languages, and most clubs and groups operate bilingually, in Finnish and Russian. However, lay women's role remains vital in maintaining the parish as a glocal space through their daily practices and participation. Our interlocutors organized church fairs and cultural events on a voluntary basis, exerting a great deal of artistry in joggling between paid work, church, their families, and other social relationships and engagements. Nevertheless, similarly to the older Karelian women, they described their collective efforts as "joy," whether when singing in "good company" or simply "doing things together." Most of them perceived the multiculturalism of the parish as a self-evident fact and as something that positively influences the life of the parish. As one Finnish choir singer put it: "It is great that one can hear many languages spoken."

In the parish under study, the majority of choir members are women. Alongside weekly practices, the choir performs in concerts, travels abroad, and arranges choral camps, especially in preparation for the elaborate Easter service, seen as the high point of the church year. The singers come from different ethnic and linguistic backgrounds, and not all of them are Orthodox by confession. Finnish-speaking women, especially more experienced ones, support and help non-native speakers and younger members. Some of our Russian-speaking interlocutors explained that attending choir practices helps them immerse in the Finnish-language Liturgy. Certainly, the women were also committed to singing in liturgies celebrated in Church Slavonic, thereby contributing to the glocal nature of the parish. During our fieldwork, many participants emphasized that singing in the choir was "rewarding" and "satisfying" on many levels. Some pointed out that it helped them maintain emotional balance and had a therapeutic, calming effect. Others noted that they felt blessed to "sing to the glory of God" and thus participate in a sacred act. Furthermore, our interlocutors also saw their choir practices as a way of bonding with "good" individuals and

people of faith. Our Finnish interlocutor Marjaana, a convert to Orthodoxy, noted: "When I first came to a choir practice, I felt that I had found
it, my own thing. I kept going, and I was delighted to meet people there.
It was a wonderful feeling to be part of this community, singing, and
prayers."

In some cases, the women recounted specific events and instances when
singing in the choir had been especially moving and had enhanced the personal experience of the divine. This is how our Russian interlocutor Anfisa
described the Forgiveness Sunday service, which commences Lent:

> I had never before been present at this kind of service, where every-
> body in the temple was walking around and asking one another for
> forgiveness. We were singing Easter hymns . . . and the choir was big,
> and it made a big difference, everybody was moved. I don't know
> about the others, but I got goose bumps all over my body, it was a
> great feeling. I felt like crying. And many in our choir cried. It was
> indescribable.

Besides the choir, another interactive space of grassroots glocalization
is children's theater performances, which are usually arranged for Christmas and Easter celebrations. In this parish, Russian-speaking women are
especially active in creating such performances. Our interlocutor Natalia,
a medical doctor by occupation, first took the initiative, supported by the
youth council of the parish and a friend who run a children's art club in
the parish. Soon several other highly educated women joined. The production usually includes the following steps, all managed by the women during their free time: writing a script, translation of the script into Finnish
(if written in Russian), making decorations, preparing the musical arrange-
ment (including negotiations with the choir), and multiple rehearsals with
the children. The performances have been carried out in various forms, including puppet theater and shadow plays. They commonly take place after
the Liturgy in a big hall, with all the parish, especially the children,
watching. When asked about the motivation driving these titanic efforts,
our interlocutor Milana elaborated:

> The desire that children would apprehend all these biblical events,
> that they would be able to live them as a miracle, as a fairytale, yes,
> as a miracle. Usually, in life outside the Church, there is just a pre-
> sent for Christmas, but the fairytale has been taken away. . . . Through

this [performance], there is an opportunity to bring joy, to immerse in the lives of the saints, who were also historical figures, through this fairytale. . . . One mother said to me: "You were worried that it did not quite come out right, but my child, for three days after the performance, was walking with a star, playing the three wise men." They [children] absorb it on some different level. These dolls [pointing to the handmade puppets] are no comparison to dolls from the shop. Here is an opportunity to partake in something else. It is almost like icon painting. And when you make it, it is such a joy, that you do something real. It is nice when people are united, they come and take part. When we do it all together, it is such a joy.

The quotation illustrates women's multifaceted agency in arranging these theater performances. First, it points to their motherly impulse to reenchant Christmas for their children. In speaking of fairytales and miracles, the women, perhaps unwittingly, conveyed that religion is connected to mythmaking, "myths" referring here to "true stories" that relate to reality in an imaginative way.[61] As Anna put it: "Maybe, we create memories for our own children in hopes that they would be able to rely on them in adulthood, for a more mature apprehension of Orthodoxy." Second, according to Milana, putting together these performances parallels icon painting in that you produce material representations of and portals to sacred reality. Similarly to participation in the Liturgy, enacting Christmas and Easter through theatrical means thus provides an opportunity for sensual partaking in the mysteries of birth, sacrifice, rebirth, and resurrection. Third, Milana also refers to the collective agency involved in preparing the performances and uniting people from different backgrounds.

Nevertheless, tensions are an unavoidable part of this process as well. Conflicts may occur during the production, for instance while negotiating with the youth council or the choir. Also the participants themselves can hold differing views on the nature of the performances. Some women, for instance, noted that they did not approve of "preaching." Thus, after negotiations the participants agreed to focus on telling biblical stories in a beautiful and engaging way rather than to emphasize the performances as pedagogical tools. This agenda is also reflected in Milana's narrative.

The theater productions, all in all, are excellent examples of glocalization in the making. Through them, many migrant women of the parish under study expressed their creativity and artistry and channeled their multifaceted agency in the OCF. Simultaneously, the women were conducive to making the parish a homelike environment for themselves, their children, and others. As shown in numerous studies, Russian speakers often feel the need to suppress their ethnic identity while living in Finland.[62] Anti-Russian discourses have influenced the Finnish cultural landscape ever since the rise of Finnish nationalism in the nineteenth century. Today, these sentiments are further enhanced by utterly politicized negative accounts of Russia in Western media.[63] While Russian speakers can experience marginalization in Finnish society, many of our interlocutors described the local Orthodox parish as a "safe" space, where they and (more importantly) their children could be openly Russian without being ridiculed or discriminated. Producing the performances in the Finnish language, however, was a conscious decision. As our interlocutor Elena explained: "We live in Finland, and we want everybody to be involved."

Conclusion

The objective to develop and defend the existence of a specific Finnish form of Orthodoxy has characterized the OCF throughout its history as an autonomous church. Over the course of time, this agenda has resulted in the highlighting of certain cultural forms and influences and the downplaying of others. During the latter half of the twentieth century, for instance, the Byzantine roots of Orthodoxy were often stressed at the expense of the OCF's concrete ties to the Russian Church. More recently, the Church has invested in reviving and incorporating Karelian and Russian elements in the life of the Church—while not necessarily articulating this explicitly. Our starting point in this chapter has been to approach Orthodox Christianity in Finland as a glocal religion. Through the lens of glocalization, it is possible to shed light on these kinds of historical dynamics, which are easily neglected when the focus is squarely on the OCF as a particular national manifestation of Orthodoxy.

The essence of our discussion has been lay women's contribution to the ongoing glocal becoming of Orthodoxy in Finland. We have demonstrated how our interlocutors participated in this process through both passive and active means. These include, first of all, their very presence in and conduct during church services and their competence and will to learn more of the various elements that make up the Liturgy. Second, the women were pertinent to the grassroots glocalization of the OCF also because of their active efforts to promote practices of importance to them in the parish and to negotiate for the inclusion of different ethnic traditions. The women's home altars, moreover, functioned as glocal religious spaces in which icons and mementos from different cultural contexts merge. Icons with ties to several contexts are applied to transgress national imaginaries and bring together the women's multiple senses of belonging. In fact, our interlocutors also engaged with these icons in more public settings such as churches and monasteries, thus enriching the discursive space surrounding the icons in contemporary Finland with their personal interpretations and narratives.

Theoretically, our interpretation of the women's practices draws from and advances discussions concerning gendered religious agency. We have proceeded from the premise that women's virtuoso religiosity can and should be seen as agentic action. Furthermore, to disentangle our conceptualization of agency from simplistic juxtapositions between compliance and resistance, we have focused, instead, on the multivalent nature of agency. Making use of notions developed in material and vernacular religion scholarship, we have argued that women's religious agency encompasses also their sensual engagements with and artistic and creative applications of religion. In our study, we have taken notice of, for example, our interlocutors' contemplative spirituality, their personal interpretations of religious traditions and teachings, and their flexible juggling between religious and secular responsibilities. Irrespective of generation and ethnic background, maternal concerns and impulses were an important factor in the women's devotions. They channeled their agency into practices of nurturing and caring, which extended from their children to relatives and the wider religious community. Overall, many manifestations of the women's agency were characterized by relationality, altruism, and submission—their understanding of prayer being a case in point. However, the women did also exert active and project-oriented agency, for example through their voluntary work in parishes.

In this chapter, furthermore, we have examined women's activities both at church and home as practices of dwelling.[64] Our interlocutors' agency, we have suggested, can be understood as their capacity to create and sustain homelike spaces where they can express themselves, be united with their (extended) families, experience existential security and belonging, and generally speaking feel "at home." This homemaking was tied to the women's personal spiritual pursuits as well as to their gendered social roles as keepers of the home and family. Moreover, it was also an endeavor that required constant negotiation between the orientations and preferences of different people, ranging from family members to other parishioners. We have chosen not to accentuate here the difficulties and failures that the women faced (although we have provided some examples of these as well) but to stress the enabling and empowering aspects of their religiosity. Nevertheless, to end our discussion we articulate an important difference in the experiences of our two groups of informants, related to their sense of "being at home" in the OCF.

In the interviews, the women of the younger generation mostly emphasized the OCF as a welcoming and inclusive environment. Our Russian interlocutor Natalia, for example, stated: "When we came here, and, of course, came to our church, our parish, it was as if I came to my native home. Thanks to it, our family immersed in all this, and found activities, friends, and hobbies. . . . We found a warm place, our place." The older Karelian women, in contrast, spoke of the atmosphere of the Church in more ambiguous tones. On the one hand, it was still their native Church, the Church of their ancestors. On the other, they noted that it had gone through changes, which made it hard for them to feel completely at ease there. Soja summarized the crux of the matter: "They don't care about Karelianness anymore, these [newcomers] who come from elsewhere and join with their own ideas. Karelians are Karelians, but soon they will be no more, when all the old people have passed away."

The feeling of "being at home" is not something that can be attained once and for all. Rather, it needs continuous upholding. Especially in the case of people who do not belong to the dominant faction of the community in question—as is often the case with women, migrants, and the elderly—the ability to feel at home is dependent on their active struggle for inclusion. The experiences of our two generations of interlocutors well illustrate this dynamic. The younger women, through their active immersion in the life of the church, had made it their own. The older women, for their part, could no longer partake as fully as before. They felt a degree of exclusion, often nostalgically reminiscing about the communality of past decades. These experiences, moreover, also demonstrate how the glocal becoming of a community is understood differently by differently positioned members. Glocalization is an ongoing process in which cultural forms fuse, transform, and shift places in a kaleidoscopic fashion. Our interlocutors' accounts show that while some OCF members greatly value the possibilities offered by the Church to act out their transnational subjectivities and expand their cultural horizons, others lament the diminishing significance of elements that they consider essential to the very identity of the Church. This perceived tension reflects the vitality of the process of glocalization in multicultural parishes that incorporate transnational elements and manifold manifestations of home and dwelling in their activities.

Notes

1. After displacement from Karelia, the percentage of interconfessional marriages among matrimonies entered into by members of the OCF quickly rose to 90. Furthermore, during the first postwar decades, the baptism of children following the father's religious affiliation was the norm in Finland. Voitto Huotari, "Orthodox-Lutheran Intermarriage in Finland," *Social Compass* 38, no. 1 (1991): 25–31.

2. Kimmo Kääriäinen, Kati Niemelä, and Kimmo Ketola, *Religion in Finland: Decline, Change, and Transformation of Finnish Religiosity* (Tampere: Church Research Institute, 2005), 82, 88–92; Statistics Finland, "Population Structure on 31 December," https://www.stat.fi/tup/suoluk/suoluk_vaesto_en.html.

3. Tuomas Martikainen and Teuvo Laitila, "Population Movements and Orthodox Christianity in Finland: Dislocations, Resettlements, Migrations, and Identities," in *Orthodox Identities in Western Europe: Migration, Settlement, and Innovation,* ed. Maria Hämmerli and Jean-François Mayer (Farnham: Ashgate, 2014), 153.

4. Martikainen and Laitila, "Population Movements," 155–56.

5. See Martikainen and Laitila, "Population Movements," for a detailed account.

6. Juha Riikonen, "The Nationality Question in the Orthodox Church of Finland," in *The Two Folk Churches in Finland: The 12th Finnish Lutheran-Orthodox Theological Discussions 2014*, ed. Tomi Karttunen, trans. Rupert Moreton (Helsinki: National Church Council, Department for International Relations, 2015), 96–104.

7. Martikainen and Laitila, "Population Movements," 160.

8. Martikainen and Laitila, "Population Movements," 164.

9. Statistics Finland, "Population Structure."

10. Tomi Karttunen, ed., *The Two Folk Churches in Finland: The 12th Finnish Lutheran-Orthodox Theological Discussions 2014*, trans. Rupert Moreton (Helsinki: National Church Council, Department for International Relations, 2015).

11. Martikainen and Laitila, "Population Movements," 166.

12. Statistics Finland, "Population Structure."

13. Tuomas Martikainen, *Religion, Migration, Settlement: Reflections on Post-1990 Immigration to Finland* (Leiden: Brill, 2013), 103–7.

14. World Values Survey, Finland 2005, http://www.worldvaluessurvey.org/WVSDocumentationWV5.jsp.

15. Annika Jonninen, "'Toivoisin, ettei vähenisi': Tutkimus ortodoksisen uskonnon opettajista sekä ortodoksisen uskonnon opetuksen tilanteesta lukuvuonna 2012–2013," master's thesis, University of Eastern Finland, 2014, 22–23; Valeria Mäkirinta, "Suomen ortodoksisen kirkon kanttorin ammatti-identiteetti: Mielikuvia työstä ja työntekijästä," master's thesis, University of Eastern Finland, 2014, 29.

16. Katariina Husso, "Obedient Artists and Mediators: Women Icon Painters in the Finnish Orthodox Church from the Mid-Twentieth to the Twenty-First Century," in *Orthodox Christianity and Gender: Dynamics of Tradition, Culture, and Lived Practice*, ed. Helena Kupari and Elina Vuola (London: Routledge, 2019), 75.

17. Statistics Finland, "Population by Religious Community, Age and Sex in 2000 to 2017," Statistics Finland's PX-Web databases: Population structure 016, http://pxnet2.stat.fi/PXWeb/pxweb/en/StatFin/StatFin__vrm__vaerak/?tablelist=true.

18. Kääriäinen, Niemelä, and Ketola, *Religion in Finland*, 134–44; World Values Survey.

19. Kääriäinen, Niemelä, and Ketola, *Religion in Finland*, 60–61.

20. E.g., Husso, "Obedient Artists and Mediators."

21. E.g., Pekka Metso, "Keskustelu samaa sukupuolta olevien parisuhteesta Suomen ortodoksisessa kirkossa vuodesta 1990 nykyhetkeen," *Ennen ja nyt: Historian tietosanomat* 1 (2018), http://www.ennenjanyt.net/2018/02/keskustelu-samaa-sukupuolta-olevien-parisuhteesta-suomen-ortodoksisessa-kirkossa-vuodesta-1990-nykyhetkeen/.

22. Andreas Kalkun and Elina Vuola, "The Embodied Mother of God and the Identities of Orthodox Women in Finland and Setoland," *Religion and Gender* 7, no. 1 (2017): 37–38, https://doi.org/10.18352/rg.10165.

23. E.g., Frederique Apffel-Marglin, *Subversive Spiritualities: How Rituals Enact the World* (New York: Oxford University Press, 2011); Saba Mahmood, "Feminist Theory, Agency, and the Liberatory Subject: Some Reflections on the Islamic Revival in Egypt," *Temenos: Nordic Journal of Comparative Religion* 42, no. 1 (2006): 31–71.

24. Roland Robertson, "Glocalization: Time—Space and Homogeneity—Heterogeneity," in *Global Modernities*, ed. Mike Featherstone, Scott Lash, and Roland Robertson (London: Sage, 1995), 27.

25. Daniel Nehring et al., *Transnational Popular Psychology and the Global Self-Help Industry: The Politics of Contemporary Social Change* (London: Palgrave Macmillan, 2016), 33.

26. Victor Roudometof, *Globalization and Orthodox Christianity: The Transformations of a Religious Tradition* (New York: Routledge, 2014).

27. Roudometof, *Globalization*, 169; see also Victor Roudometof, Alexander Agadjanian, and Jerry Pankhurst, eds., *Eastern Orthodoxy in a Global Age: Tradition Faces the Twenty-First Century* (Walnut Creek, CA: Alta Mira, 2005).

28. E.g., Arjun Appadurai, *Modernity at Large: Cultural Dimensions of Globalization* (Minneapolis: University of Minnesota Press, 1996); Steven Vertovec, *Transnationalism* (London: Routledge, 2009).

29. Ulla Vuorela, "Meeting Sophia Mustafa—A Transnational Encounter," in *The Tanganyika Way: A Personal Story of Tanganyika's Growth to Independence*, ed. Sophia Mustafa (Toronto: TSAR Publication, 2009), 169–80.

30. See also Helena Kupari, *Lifelong Religion as Habitus: Religious Practice among Displaced Karelian Orthodox Women in Finland* (Leiden: Brill, 2016), http://booksandjournals.brillonline.com/content/books/9789004326743.

31. Durre Ahmed, "Women, Psychology, and Religion," in *Gendering the Spirit: Women, Religion, and the Postcolonial Response*, ed. Durre Ahmed (London: Zed, 2002), 70–87; Kristin Aune et al., "Introduction," *Social Compass* 64, no. 4, "Thematic Issue: Is Secularism Bad for Women?" (2017): 449–72; Lena Gemzöe and Marja-Liisa Keinänen, "Contemporary Encounters in Gender and Religion: Introduction," in *Contemporary Encounters in Gender and Religion: European Perspectives*, ed. Lena Gemzöe, Marja-Liisa Keinänen, and Avril Maddrell (Cham: Palgrave Macmillan, 2016), 1–28; Helena Kupari and Elina Vuola, "Introduction," in *Orthodox Christianity and Gender: Dynamics of Tradition, Culture, and Lived Practice*, ed. Helena Kupari and Elina Vuola (London: Routledge, 2019), 9–13; Mahmood, "Feminist Theory."

32. For a discussion, see Gemzöe and Keinänen, "Contemporary Encounters."

33. Nadieszda Kizenko, "Feminized Patriarchy? Orthodoxy and Gender in Post-Soviet Russia," *Signs: Journal of Women in Culture and Society* 38, no. 3 (2013): 600.

34. Leonard Norman Primiano, "Vernacular Religion and the Search for Method in Religious Folklife," *Western Folklore* 54, no. 1 (1995): 43–44; Marion Bowman and Ülo Valk, eds., *Vernacular Religion in Everyday Life: Expressions of Belief* (Sheffield: Equinox, 2012); Tatiana Tiaynen-Qadir, "Glocal Religion and Feeling at Home: Ethnography of Artistry in Finnish Orthodox Liturgy," *Religions* 8, no. 2 (2017): 1–14, https://doi.org/10.3390/rel8020023.

35. Kupari, *Lifelong Religion as Habitus*; Sonja Luehrmann, ed., *Praying with the Senses: Contemporary Orthodox Christian Spirituality in Practice* (Bloomington: Indiana University Press, 2018); David Morgan, *Sacred Gaze: Religious Visual Culture in Theory and Practice* (Berkeley: University of California Press, 2005);

Minna Opas and Anna Haapalainen, eds., *Christianity and the Limits of Materiality* (London: Bloomsbury, 2017).

36. Sara Ahmed, "Home and Away: Narratives of Migration and Estrangement," *International Journal of Cultural Studies* 2, no. 3 (1999): 341.

37. Thomas Tweed, *Crossing and Dwelling: A Theory of Religion* (Cambridge, MA: Harvard University Press, 2006).

38. John A. McGuckin, "Divine Liturgy, Orthodox," in *The Encyclopedia of Eastern Orthodox Christianity*, ed. John A. McGuckin (Chichester: Wiley-Blackwell, 2011), 1:190–91.

39. Pavel Florenscy, "Church Ritual as a Synthesis of the Arts," in *Beyond Vision: Essays on the Perception of Art*, ed. Nicoletta Misler, trans. Wendy Salmond (London: Reaktion, 2002), 109.

40. Tiaynen-Qadir, "Glocal Religion."

41. Ahmed, "Home and Away," 341.

42. The names of our interlocutors are pseudonyms. Some details of their narratives have been changed to protect their anonymity.

43. *Molitvoslov pravoslavnoi zhenzhchiny* (Moscow: Eksmo, 2008), 13.

44. For a rich discussion on the role of senses in Orthodox spirituality, see Luehrmann, *Praying with the Senses*.

45. Kupari, *Lifelong Religion*, 59–63.

46. Huotari, "Orthodox-Lutheran Intermarriage." In fact, the experiences of our older Karelian and younger Finnish interlocutors open up an excellent perspective on some of the effects that this had on the Orthodox community. During the first postwar decades, Orthodox mothers of interconfessional families ended up raising Lutheran children, while Orthodox children mostly had Lutheran mothers. In the interviews, some of our older interlocutors expressed sadness over not having been able to raise their children Orthodox. Kupari, *Lifelong Religion*, 145–49; see also Marja-Liisa Honkasalo, "If the Mother of God Does Not Listen: Women's Contested Agency and the Lived Meaning of the Orthodox Religion in North Karelia," *Journal of American Folklore* 128, no. 507 (2015): 65–92. Many of our younger convert interlocutors, for their part, described how Orthodoxy had been present in their childhood through their grandmother or grandfather, while their parents were members of the Lutheran Church.

47. Kizenko, "Feminized Patriarchy"; Tatiana Tiaynen-Qadir, "Transnational Grandmothers Making Their Multi-sited Homes between Finland and Russian Karelia," in *Rethinking Home: Transnational Migration and Older Age*, ed. Katie Walsh and Lena Näre (New York: Routledge, 2016), 25–37.

48. Sarah Riccardi, "Praying through Windows and Peering through Wood: Examining Vernacular Devotions in American Eastern Orthodoxy through a Materialist Lens," master's thesis, Missouri State University, 2014, 34.

49. See also Luehrmann, *Praying with the Senses*; Sarah Riccardi-Swartz, "Enshrining Gender: Orthodox Women and Material Culture in the United States," in *Orthodox Christianity and Gender: Dynamics of Tradition, Culture, and Lived Practice*, ed. Helena Kupari and Elina Vuola (London: Routledge, 2019), 115–30.

50. See also Kupari, *Lifelong Religion*, 119–20.

51. Alexander Schmemann, *Celebration of Faith: The Virgin Mary*, vol. 3 (New York: St. Vladimir's Seminary Press, 1991).

52. Ali Qadir and Tatiana Tiaynen-Qadir, "Deep Culture and the Mystical Agency of Mary in Eastern Christianity," *Religions* 9, no. 12 (2018): 1–18, https://doi.org/10.3390/rel9120383.

53. Amy Singleton Adams and Vera Shevzov, eds., *Framing Mary: The Mother of God in Modern, Revolutionary, and Postmodern Russia* (DeKalb: Northern Illinois University Press, 2018); Jill Dubisch, *In a Different Place: Pilgrimage, Gender, and Politics at a Greek Island Shrine* (Princeton, NJ: Princeton University Press, 1995); see also Kalkun and Vuola, "The Embodied Mother of God."

54. S. Alekseev, *Chudotvornye ikony Presvyatoi Bogoroditsy* (Moscow: Bibliopolis, 2016); I. K. Yazykova, *Bogoslovie Ikony* (Moscow: Obschedostypnyi Pravoslavnyi Universitet, 1995).

55. See also Tatiana Tiaynen-Qadir, "Orthodox Icons Generating Transnational Space between Finland and Russia," *Lähde—tieteellinen aikakauskirja* (2016): 138–71.

56. The monastery in Heinävesi was established after World War II, to house the evacuated brethren of the monastery in Lake Ladoga. After the fall of the Soviet Union, the latter monastery was reopened.

57. See also Kalkun and Vuola, "The Embodied Mother of God," 32–4.

58. See, e.g., Pekka Metso, Nina Maskulin, and Teuvo Laitila, "Tradition, Gender, and Empowerment: The Birth of Theotokos Society in Helsinki, Finland," in *Orthodox Christianity and Gender: Dynamics of Tradition, Culture, and Lived Practice*, ed. Helena Kupari and Elina Vuola (London: Routledge, 2019), 131–46.

59. Olavi Merras, "Mikä on Tiistaiseura?" http://www.ortodoksi.net/index.php/Tiistaiseura.

60. Martikainen and Laitila, "Population Movements," 160–62.

61. Mircea Eliade, *Myth and Reality*, trans. Willard R. Trask (New York: Harper & Row, 1963).

62. E.g., Helena Jerman, "Memory Crossing Borders: A Transition in Space and Time among Second- and Third-Generation Russians in Finland," in *Anthropological Perspectives on Social Memory*, ed. Petri Hautaniemi, Helena Jerman, and Sharon Macdonald (Münster: Lit, 2007), 117–41.

63. Tiina Sotkasiira, "'Sometimes It Feels Like Every Word Is a Lie': Media Use and Social (In)Security among Finnish Russian-Speakers," *Central and Eastern European Migration Review* 7, no. 1 (2018): 109–27, https://doi.org/10.17467/ceemr.2017.18.

64. See Tweed, *Crossing and Dwelling*.

Head Coverings, Vaccines, and Gender Politics: Contentious Topics Among Orthodox Christian Women in US-Based Digital Spaces

Sarah Riccardi-Swartz

Introduction

In the pinned community guidelines for a roughly two-thousand-member, women-only Facebook group devoted to Orthodox Christian mothering, three topics were listed as off-limits for discussion: head coverings, vaccines, and politics. The topics, in group discussions before 2016, had seemingly caused great turmoil among the members, who were often divided on these issues. Through regular posts in the group feed, administrators reinforced the banned items and regularly referred women to other niche Facebook groups where they could more fully articulate their theopolitical stances on these topics. Within the United States, head coverings, vaccines, and social moral politics are quickly becoming contentious issues in many Orthodox communities that are transforming because of the steady influx of converts from conservative Protestant and Catholic religious communities.[1] While scholars are beginning to work on issues of conversion, gender, and the role of the media in US Orthodoxy, little has been dedicated to moral politics in Orthodox social spaces.[2] Through the lens of media anthropology, this chapter makes use of digital ethnography to explore the online lifeworlds of conservative Orthodox Christian women, focusing on their engagement with Facebook groups, to show how they cultivate, disseminate, argue, and hide their religiopolitical beliefs through social media engagement.[3]

I suggest that internet groups are transformative places where Orthodox women can gain a sense of religious agency through connecting with one another, and that they also can tell us more about the social projects, religious ideologies, and moral stances of these women, and how they negotiate the current political climate in relationship to their religious values and practices. As anthropologist Matthew Engelke has noted, "values are . . . like weathervanes." While they are fixed, they change positions depending on what is "in the air."[4] Through investigating the online community discourses and practices of Orthodox women, conservative social concerns over morality, gender, and freedom of religious practice come to the fore, gesturing to their engagement with broader political issues.

Within anthropology, particularly in the United States, Orthodox Christianity is understudied, with very little research devoted to the lives of women in the Church, and even less is dedicated to the political ideologies of female believers. This chapter contributes to the burgeoning scholarship on both topics, suggesting that we can learn more about the contemporary and changing social politics of US Orthodoxy from observing and surveying women online, in social spaces that allow them to voice their opinions in a faith tradition that often excludes them from vocal positions of religious authority. Whether women endorse or subvert the teachings of the Church in the digital religious landscape, they are engaged in vital forms of social discourse, both hidden and displayed, that connect their practices and beliefs to larger societal trends as part of "networked publics."[5] As anthropologists have pointed out, the goal of small-scale ethnography, even in the digital world, is not to engage in the impossible notion of finding holism; rather, these narratives serve to guide us to larger issues that are found in society more broadly.[6] Anthropology focuses on the parts that make up a whole in order to draw out questions that help us understand issues of long import in the study of humanity, including dynamics of power, social structures, and the influence of both politics and technology in and on Christianity. Digital gatherings and online groups provide excellent spaces for seeing how these issues are not only circulating through fiber-optic networks but socioreligious ones as well.

On the Ground Communities and Digital Methodology

Scholars of religion and media have highlighted how the mediatization of religion is often expressed in the use of social media to reinforce and rupture religious ideological cohesion.[7] For Orthodox Christian women who are living in geographically diffuse communities, social media often provides a mediated form of relationality and communal engagement, platforms through which they engage spiritually and socially with one another via the click of a mouse. While most of the women I encountered in English-speaking Facebook groups were part of United States Orthodoxy, they were able to create bonds with Orthodox women from around the globe. I was first drawn to examining digital communities of Orthodox women because of US converts I worked with previously who commented about their online engagement with these media formations. They pointed me to these communities as places where they were able to create spaces of feminine piety outside the watchful eye of Orthodox clerics. In the American context, the influx of converts, particularly from conservative religious backgrounds, and their avid use of digital technology to connect them to global Orthodoxy, mean that looking at the ideas of women who are active on social media platforms is imperative. Eastern Orthodoxy, as it is broadly understood, is a highly patriarchal, gender-stratified form of Christianity that is, within the postmodern period, especially in the United States, becoming increasingly divided on sociopolitical issues, with tensions and disagreements often expressed through believers' online actions.[8]

Despite that in an early 2019 interview for a Russian news outlet, His All Holiness Patriarch Kirill, leader of the Russian Orthodox Church, suggested that the internet might bring about the rise of the Antichrist, the interface is still a fundamental form of connectivity for Orthodox Christians around the world, including Russian believers with whom I have worked.[9] Sociality and piety throughout the disparate geographic structures of Eastern Orthodoxy, particularly in "diasporic" communities (such as those in America), have transformed since the advent of digital communication. In seconds, believers communicate with one another across the globe, praying, sharing inspirational materials, and forming socioreligious collectives that would otherwise be closed to them because of the wide variety of sociogeographic and class differences. This is particularly true among Orthodox Christian women with whom I have worked. The internet has become a means through which they can express their ideas (heterodox and orthodox), assert their agency outside of androcentric spheres of Orthodoxy on the ground, and create their own Orthodox gathering spots where they make the rules, even if those rules coalesce with those of the institutional Church.

The data gathered during my digital ethnographic research is both quantitative and qualitative, composed of ethnographic fieldwork (digital and

physical), online observations of social media platforms, and, most importantly, a digital survey geared toward understanding the sociopolitical and
moral leanings of Orthodox women online. I decided to focus on two Facebook groups for Orthodox women, particularly mothers and self-identified
homemakers, where a majority of women with whom I have worked with
previously are active contributors.[10] Together, both groups hosted approximately (in the late spring of 2019) three thousand members. Each group
required that all members were women. The larger of the two groups, about
twice the size of the smaller group, had detailed instructions on membership and a list of community guidelines that every member had to sign off
on via a comment on the administrators' rules post. I refer to the larger
group in this chapter as the "mothering group"; it included more options
for group socialization, such as a signup section for mentors and mentees.
The second group, which I identify here as the "domesticity group," was
founded by members of the same family (all converts to the Russian Orthodox Church outside of Russia, or the ROCOR) and did not have the
same type of procedural processes that the first group did at the time of
my research. I selected these specific groups for two reasons. First, both
groups were intended for women participants only, and second, after spend-
ing time reviewing the content of each group, it seemed clear that both
online communities had Orthodox women from the around world who
possessed similar and differing opinions on a wide variety of nonbanned
topics. My initial goal was to find the widest diversity possible in these
groups in order to avoid homogenous answers, since my focus was on
women in the Orthodox Church broadly, not just those in a particular jurisdiction. At the same time, I recognized that group members were self-
selecting these groups because of their particular understandings of gender
and motherhood, ones that often skewed toward political conservatism.

I approached these online groups as I would any community that I
planned to conduct research in, obtaining IRB approval for data collection. While I employed quantitative research, my larger methodology centered on the qualitative study of these communities, which means the
group population size was smaller than those found in sociological,
statistics-heavy studies. I do not intend for the voices of these women to
speak for all Orthodox women online; however, their ideas are indicative
of broader trends among Orthodox women with whom I have worked during multiple fieldwork projects with conservative Orthodox communities
in the United States. If I were to conduct my research among liberal or

progressive Orthodox women, the results might be different. The research found in this chapter speaks to a particular community at a specific time in religious and political history, when the digital world offered a vital place for Orthodox women to negotiate their representations to the broader world and reify their understandings of theology, tradition, and morality.[11]

After almost a year of online observations, I approached the administrators of both groups to ask if I could post a link to my online survey in each community. The domesticity group administrator whom I contacted had no problem with my survey and encouraged me to post it right away. However, the four administrators for the mothering group were concerned about my survey and asked: "Does the survey have questions regarding any of our banned topics?" I acknowledged that there would be questions posed on the survey that would address head coverings, abortion, same-sex marriage, and female Orthodox ordination to the ranks of clergy, the last of which was not among banned topics in the mothering group.[12] I explained that my goal was to understand more about how Orthodox women feel about these issues and that since these topics were banned in the group, the survey seemed to be the most feasible and least invasive way of gathering that information. After consulting, the administrators decided I could post a link to the survey; I did so within twenty-four hours. After the survey link was posted in each group, members often asked if they could share the survey on their personal Facebook pages, and I did assent to that form of distribution. Because both groups were quite large and each had a very active feed, with many different posters and commenters, I decided to offer three reminder posts over the course of a month and half prompting women to consider taking the survey. In each post, I offered a link to the survey, which was housed in a secure Google form; explained the project; provided contact information; and let members know that the survey had been approved by group administrators. In total, 187 women from across the two groups completed the survey.[13] By anthropological standards, the number of women surveyed was quite substantial, similar to that of a typical small-scale community study.

Based on survey data I conducted from May 2019 through June 2019 and the observations I made in the many months before that, the groups skewed young, with 73 percent of respondents between the ages of twenty-five and thirty-four. Approximately 90 percent of respondents were married at the time of this research. Eighty-one percent of the group members hailed from the United States, with a wide geographical spread in terms of

Orthodox Jurisdictions	Percentage of Survey Respondents
Antiochian Archdiocese	18%
Greek Archdiocese of America	25%
Orthodox Church in America	25%
ROCOR	13%
Other Jurisdictions	11%
No Response	8%

region.[14] Those from outside of the United States were predominately from Australia and Canada, with smaller percentages from the United Kingdom, Eastern Europe, and Russia. Sixty-one percent of all respondents marked themselves as converts to the Orthodox Church. Most converted between the late 1990s and the 2010s, with a smattering of middle aged–to–senior respondents noting conversion dates in the 1980s and early 1990s. The majority of converts came from Protestant and Catholic backgrounds, with the former hailing predominately from Evangelical, Presbyterian, and Lutheran communities. Some opted to include their conversion narratives in the context of the survey, the results of which suggested many of the women were led into the Church by their fathers or husbands, often begrudgingly at first, but most ultimately embraced Orthodoxy in their own ways.[15] Jurisdictionally, the majority of women surveyed belonged to the Orthodox Church of America (OCA) and the Greek Orthodox Archdiocese (GOA) equally, followed closely by membership in the Antiochian Archdiocese of North America and the ROCOR.

My interest in the political dimensions of digital Orthodox female spaces was first piqued by a young woman I met in during my year-long stay with an Orthodox community in Appalachia, where I was conducting research with far-right converts to the ROCOR.[16] Gwen, a nineteen-year-old Russian American, was one of the few parishioners at the local parish who claimed Slavic background, with most of the congregation composed of converts from the region, the Midwest, or the US South more broadly. During a conversation in my cabin one evening, Gwen, a self-described fascist, mentioned she was a member of many "trad" groups on Facebook and promptly started adding me to the groups on her smartphone while we were talking.[17] While those particular social media groups were beneficial for my larger project on the political complexities of the ROCOR in the United

States, it was her mention of women's groups that became the launch point for my inquiry into how Orthodox women make sense of their social worlds on the internet. As I delved deeper into the posts and comments found in these Orthodox women's groups, it became evident to me that what went unsaid due to banned topics was far more important than what was posted about in the feeds.

Certainly, the regular posts on domesticity, mothering, fasting and feasting liturgical cycles, and issues of feminine modesty spoke to broader sociocultural dynamics at play, but they often did not provide insight into the larger religiopolitical dimensions of these topics because of the spoken and unspoken bans. Focusing on banned content pushes us to think about silenced ideas and dialogue as an avenue through which we can better understand the political dynamics of these groups. Sociolinguists have noted that silencing and moderating is a form of communication tied both to gender politics and structures of power.[18] The fact that vaccines, head coverings, and politics were banned from the conversations in the mothering group indicated that there must be a dynamic diversity of opinions among the women—homogenous ideologies would not need to be banned. To get at how women's ideas are both transformed and hidden by restricted digital conversations, I focus primarily on the survey data about prohibited ideas, rather than analyzing the approved posts in the group. Doing so allows the larger discursive conversations of georeligious politics present in these women's lives to come to the fore.

Veiled Disapproval

Of the topics that were off-limits implicitly and explicitly in both communities, head coverings, at first blush, seemed less contentious than the others, given the history of tensions over abortion and same-sex marriage in the United States and the vocal opposition toward female ordination found in many Orthodox communities.[19] Orthodox internet spaces are home to wide-ranging, often heated, conversations about veiling, Church modesty protocols, and female piety.[20] However, in the Orthodox mothering group, veiling was the first topic to be banned in the early 2010s. Head coverings belie larger sociopolitical issues of moral conservatism driving discourses of religiously gendered restrictions that are often shaped by performative materiality and female attire.[21] The very fact that head coverings were considered as politically volatile as abortion access and LGBTQ+

Stances on Head Coverings	Percentage of Survey Respondents
Pro Head Coverings	47%
Context Dependent	39%
Opposed	12%
No Response	2%

rights in the mothering group is a strong indicator of the ideological implications of female garb.[22] While there are outliers on both sides of the argument, within the context of my survey, 47 percent of the women noted that they covered and/or were in favor of head coverings for women during religious services.[23] Thirty-nine percent of the women surveyed believed that head coverings were optional or context specific (such as at a monastery). Those opposed to head coverings were in the minority, at 12 percent.

Typically converts were more supportive of wearing head coverings during religious services than cradle respondents. Convert commentary about head coverings often reflected their previous religious affiliations and socioreligious ideologies surrounding the gendered roles of women in Christian communities. One young South Asian convert living in the United Kingdom, who grew up Hindu but converted to charismatic Protestant Anglicanism, found Orthodoxy while attending university. Self-described as very conservative in terms of social morality, she offered the following reflections on why she covers her hair: "I wear a headcovering full time. I have done so since I was a Protestant. The OC [Orthodox Church] carries those beliefs also, so with the blessing of my spiritual father I have continued. I believe it is best if women headcover at least in Church but I do not believe it should be forced on anyone."[24] This type of response was common among respondents, especially converts, and speaks to how understandings of female submission and piety in Western Orthodoxy are transforming through the influx of converts and their holdover ideologies from previous religious communities. It also highlights the importance of clergy opinion for the ways women choose to express their piety sartorially. Another convert, a millennial Latina from the US South who was raised Pentecostal but converted to the ROCOR, stated: "Here in the States, there is a lot of cultural baggage that comes along with the notion of head covering that each woman will need to work through with a compassionate spiritual adviser so that she can veil herself in a manner that is not counter-productive to the very purpose of veiling." For this convert, "Head covering is about submission of the heart, and such submission can never be attained through force."[25] In a reflexive move, this Orthodox woman acknowledged the shaping power of American religious culture in her current spiritual affiliation while also nodding to how hierarchy seemed to be essential in an understanding of the feminine spiritual self.

"Submission" and "humility" were not only key terms women used in their answers about head coverings; they were also defining features of Orthodox practice that I have encountered previously during research. Orthodox practice often focuses on humility and submission to the authority of the Church and, in many communities, deference to one's spiritual father in the vein of elderism.[26] While many women who participated in the survey agreed with these teachings, some pushed back, questioning why head coverings were still needed, drawing out the issues surrounding gender dynamics in the Church. One young, single convert from the US South suggested that "head coverings are at best a carryover from years gone by when covering one's head was an indication of modesty and humility."[27] She explained how clergy had previously offered her reasons for head coverings that focused on trying not to "distract or attract men in church."[28] The respondent found this "reasoning loathsome," for she believed that "men are responsible for their own distractions, just as women are for theirs." Summing up her beliefs about the practice of covering, she concluded, "Luckily for me, head coverings are not required in my current parish and, as a single woman, I will not be wearing them except to receive sacraments in parishes where this is expected, and only then out of deference to the priest."[29]

The focus on head coverings is not a new phenomenon in Eastern Orthodoxy or Christianity more broadly. Certainly, within the Christian tradition, as it is broadly constituted, there are historic references to women wearing veils in spaces of worship.[30] While head coverings have long been part of many conservative Christian communities in the United States and Canada, particularly among Protestant Brethren groups, traditionalist Catholics, and some Orthodox communities, the new interest around head coverings seems to stem not from historic forms of Christian female piety but from far-right ideologies emerging throughout many religious communities in the United States that emphasize traditional gender roles, homesteading, and other forms of nostalgically tinged Americana.[31] In many respects, the head-covering movement is part of the larger modesty movement in conservative (often fundamentalist) Christian communities in which women perform their positionality via gendered structures that are embedded in institutions of religious authority. The revived culture wars of the 1980s that have emerged since the 2016 US presidential election have fueled far-right rhetoric that emphasizes traditional gender roles and wholesome femininity.[32] Covering is a political issue that is caught up with the other moral-social issues that are often taboo to talk about in both digital spaces and in the everyday lives of Orthodox women.

Subverting Taboo Talk

Since openly talking about politics was banned in one of the women's groups and not mentioned in detail in the other, it was hard to get an accurate picture of members' political affiliations from their posts. However, if we draw from the data of completed surveys, a complicated picture emerges. Of the women surveyed, 48.4 percent were "conservative" or "very conservative"; 25 percent saw themselves as politically "moderate." The remaining percentage encompassed the options of "other," "liberal," and "very liberal," with the last category comprising only 3.3 percent of those surveyed. The political demographics are important to analyze because they provide potential reasons for why women supported particular ideological stances and, perhaps, why politics was banned from group conversations. Across the board, it was evident that conversion was an identifying marker among the conservative and very conservative respondents. Women who were converts were far more likely to be pro-life, against same-sex marriage, opposed to female ordination, and in favor of traditional gender roles. They also were more likely to push for female veiling during religious ceremonies. Those who saw themselves as moderate, liberal, or very liberal were a mix of both converts and cradle with no heavy bias toward either category. One category that proved to be difficult to assess was the group of women who marked themselves as politically other. This category seemed to be a grab-bag of affiliations, including the American Solidarity Party, Libertarian Party, and monarchists. The mix might be a reason why the mothering group administrators prohibited postings that were geared toward political ideas, leaders, and causes.

While vaccines, head coverings, and politics were banned, women often found other topics through which to express their sociopolitical ideas. The gendered roles of men and women in Orthodox households were frequently the subject of great debate. In late June 2019, one of the women with a poster status of "conversation starter" in the mothering group linked to a set of memes from a Facebook page that emphasized issues of feminism and decolonization. The topic of the meme set was the female mental load and how it often correlates to exhaustion and unpaid labor on the part of women.[33] The responses to the post varied, but many women suggested that focusing on the mental load women bear often obscures the mental load of men, with some noting that men have the same or perhaps even heavier mental loads because they often must focus on financial support for their families. A couple of women directly stated that conversations about the roles of women and men in households typically lead to resentment on the part of women and should not be discussed. Others suggested that the memes hit home, but only because they offered insight into how traditional families should be structured, namely, with the wife and/or mother as the responsible party for household care, while the husband and/or father works outside of the home. Finally, one poster speculated that men might be psychologically wired not to notice household needs or issues, a comment that was met with agreement by most.

Not all women who commented on the post focused on the domestic sphere. The original sharer of the meme set indicated that she worked outside the home and was breadwinner for her family. Others mentioned that modern couples often share home duties. Yet despite the dissenting voices, many commenters seemed to take offense with ideas that pushed back against the structured gender roles that are religiously and political contoured in US conservative Christian communities.[34] More broadly, many women in the mothering group noted on various posts that they do work outside the home. Some expressed taking enjoyment in their full-time employment, but many talked about their desire, if finances and circumstances allowed, to be stay-at-home moms or, if they did not have children, to work primarily in their personal domestic spheres. While the discourse on the post regarding gender mental loads was not as heated as other posts of a similar nature found in the mothering group, it reinforced the idea of wholesome domesticity through reinscribing the role and place of women as contained within the sphere of the home.[35] This type of positioning language appeared in other posts that emphasized the nurturing place of women in the family structure as similar to that of the Theotokos, while providing constant reminders that the ideal family is composed of one man, one woman, and at least one child but preferably more. This family model was adamantly reinforced in survey responses regarding same-sex marriage, including this comment from a young convert to the Greek archdiocese in California: "Traditional man and woman marriage only. Gay marriage is a perversion of marriage."[36]

Phobias about Gay Marriage

One of the primary survey questions was: *What is your stance on gay marriage?* While some respondents simply typed "against" or "opposed," others explained their religious and political concerns in more detail.[37] "I believe it is immoral, but as long as the Church maintains the sanctity of marriage I am not interested in what other people do privately," one respondent wrote, and then continued, "I also believe that while I disagree with their lifestyle, they should feel safe to do as they wish without fear of violence or death from society."[38] Not all responses were as measured. One elderly convert in the Bulgarian archdiocese from Appalachia wrote, "Homosexuality is an abomination in the eyes of the Lord, which is clearly stated in the Bible. Marriage was created by God for one man and one woman. The enemy has lied to many and gotten them to believe it's ok."[39] While at first it seemed as if age was a factor in the responses, it proved to not be the case. Young women were just as likely as women between the ages of forty-five and sixty to oppose same-sex marriage and homosexuality. A young convert from California wrote with regards to same-sex marriage: "It is not good. It harms the souls of the members and takes them further from God. I have some friends who consider themselves to be non-heterosexual and feel so sad for them."[40]

Cradle Orthodox surveyed were less likely to be against same-sex marriage, but there were some who still believed it was morally reprehensible, such as a middle-aged Ohioan from the Serbian Orthodox Church. She commented succinctly, "It is not marriage. It is sodomy."[41] A young cradle Antiochian Orthodox woman from the US South who also noted that abortion is "the genocide of our day" drew on the language of traditionalism to explain how she felt about the sanctity of marriages both secular and religious: "Gay relationships should not be prosecuted, but even the pagans knew marriage in the state should be one that supports the growth of families (man and woman). The Church has always known this."[42] Later on in the survey, this same woman evoked the language of equality and secularism when asked if she believed in the separation of church and state:

"Secularism is not a religion. Equality is not a religion. Ask the strongly religious what they think about gay marriage and abortion and you will see where the opinion of the morally informed (or attempting to be) [i]s."[43]

One African American convert from the Midwest offered this anecdote regarding same-sex relationships: "I don't like it, but I have been forced to work with gay married people at PTA and scouting and they are nice. I don't mind them. They are like everyone else, but better because they know we are all watching them."[44] In her response, which was similar to many of the other answers offered up in the survey, the idea of same-sex marriage was conflated with gays and lesbians more generally: In describing her views of gay marriage, she also expressed her opinion about homosexuality. Other respondents tried to offer solutions to same-sex marriage, which ran the gamut from civil unions to celibacy. One young convert, a former Baptist believer from Florida, suggested that homosexuality is an expression of mental illness that can be worked on through religious practices: "Celibacy for someone who is feeling attracted to someone of the same sex. There are underlying mental health issues that I feel attribute to the rise in homosexuality and while it may not seem like a choice to the person who is in it, they need to address with God what's going on."[45]

Those who supported gay marriage generally fell into two ideological camps. One group tended to state positive opinions about gay marriage, such as "I agree with it" or "I support it."[46] Those survey takers considered themselves politically moderate to very liberal, although not all respondents who considered themselves liberal or very liberal agreed with gay marriage. The other ideological camp focused on the separation of church and state to support civil gay marriage but oppose it theologically.[47] This was articulated in a variety of ways, including this idea from a young female convert in the Midwest: "I do not believe that homosexuality is a choice, it is biological. If it's the way we are made, it must be part of God's plan. Even if it's not, it doesn't matter, since Jesus told us to love one another. I support gay marriage, but I also support the Orthodox Church not performing these marriages."[48]

Even those who seemed to support gay marriage and LGBTQ+ rights often did so with a caveat. One Midwestern cradle believer in the OCA jurisdiction offered the following lengthy commentary on gay marriage:

I support it. In an ideal world, everyone would be straight and attracted to the other sex, but it is not this way. "The gays" have the same problems

Separation of Church and State	Percentage of Survey Respondents
Support	65%
Unsure	16%
Oppose	16%
No Response	3%

as everyone else and need to be accepted in their communities not just for being able to get help, but in being able to function and offer their gifts. God made gays just like He made everyone else. By rejecting them, by not letting them live their lives as free people with the same rights as everyone else, we reject God.[49]

Crucial in this comment is the key understanding that the ideal vision of sexuality is pervasive heterosexuality. Also important is her suggestion that gays still need to "get help," which might be a nod to conversion therapy. The focus on civil marriages for same-sex couples seemed to be a moderate view among most surveyed. The majority of women did not want same-sex couples married in the Orthodox Church, but many of those women also understood that gay couples needed civil protections, mentioning especially situations in which partners would have to make medical choices. This seemingly moderate view might have complicated outcomes if most of the women's hopes of a Christian nation become reality. Many of the women who took the survey did not believe in the separation of church and state. Their ideological stances varied widely, with some including a plea for monarchism. Of the 187 who took the survey, 16 percent were unsure about the separation of church and state. Concerns about the unification of church and state often included the worry that the state would oppress the church and suppress the practice of Christianity in their particular country (usually the United States). At the forefront of their concerns about the relationship between church and state were two issues that created deep ethical and moral concerns for most women: abortions and vaccinations.

Abortions and Vaccinations

Since comments on vaccinations were banned in the mothering group, very little was mentioned about the topic. However, through an archival investigation of the group's earlier posts, it was clear that several years ago the topic had been quite contentious, focusing on issues of aborted fetal cells, autism, and contamination, which is a strong indicator for why the ban was evoked in 2015. Overall, vaccinations were supported by the women surveyed, with 52 percent considering themselves provaccination. Yet there was a minority contingent concerned about church and state issues tied to the implementation of mandatory childhood vaccinations and their potential links to aborted fetuses. Fears that governments might mandate vaccinations that could potentially harm children were doubled by worries that the vaccines might, in the words of many women surveyed, "contain aborted fetal cells." "Toxic" and "poison" were terms used by many of the 18 percent of women who were antivaccination. An older convert to the Bulgarian Church in the US South summed up many of the issues those opposed to vaccination focused on: "This is a serious moral and ethical issue that should be taken seriously by everyone. [O]ur bodies are the temple of the Holy Spirit; vaccination is extremely problematic. It not only imparts immunity but also destroys the immune system God made in each of us."[50] Beyond staunch antivaxxers, there were women who feared vaccines might carry health risks and opted to vaccinate their children on a delayed schedule—they accounted for about 20 percent of respondents.

While some of the 18 percent who were antivaccination were also concerned about mandatory vaccinations by government institutions, aborted fetal cells, and the moral implications of harming the temple of the Holy Spirit, many also mentioned the importance of teaching children proper sexual boundaries and gender roles to avoid using Gardasil, the HPV vaccination for teens. "The rule here is abstinence until marriage, as Christianity teaches," proclaimed one convert from the US South.[51] Abstinence training was also mentioned in women's responses to abortion. An overwhelming 79 percent of survey takers opposed abortion in any case. Thirteen percent of survey takers concluded that abortion should be on a case-by-case health basis and only if carrying the fetus to term would result in the death of the mother. Seven percent of the women were pro-choice, and 1 percent did not answer the question. The emphasis on abstinence in both the Gardasil and abortion debates suggests a focus on proper sexual activity that speaks to traditional family ideology and the ways that Orthodox men and women are expected to conduct themselves in relationship to each other and the Church. It is this broader issue of seemingly knowing one's place as a woman that is present in the responses many women had not only about vaccines,

Abortion Stances	Percentage of Survey Respondents
Oppose	79%
Case-by-Case Basis	13%
Support	7%
No Response	1%

abortion, and marriage but also in their approaches to the idea of female ordination in the Orthodox Church.

"That's Not a Woman's Place": Responses to Female Ordination

Surprisingly, the most controversial question in the survey was not listed among the three off-limits topics in the mothering group, although employing the search function in the group indicated that there had only been two posts regarding female ordination (from 2018) in the group feed, with both focusing on the revival of deaconesses rather than female ordination to the priesthood. In the Orthodox domesticity group, there was only one posting regarding the role of deaconesses in the Church.[52] In the survey, I asked, *What is your stance on female ordination in the Orthodox Church?* Instead of providing multiple-choice answer options, I again selected a more qualitative approach that could also be quantified to understand both personal feelings and statistical trends among the respondents. Of the 187 answers to this question, 78 percent of the women were opposed to any type of female ordination in the Orthodox Church—this included ordination to the diaconate as deaconesses. Fourteen percent of all respondents believed the Church needed to begin the process of reviving the ancient female diaconate. However, of those who indicated they would support contemporary deaconesses, 72 percent were also opposed to the "anything above that" or "female priests."[53]

Where the statistical breakdown is helpful in thinking through large-scale trends, the written responses women gave regarding this topic offer insight into their understandings of gender roles in the Orthodox Church, the significance of tradition, and their views of patriarchy and submission. One former Protestant convert who attended a Bulgarian Orthodox Church in Appalachia wrote, "As it clearly states in the Bible (St. Paul), women should not teach men. Women and men have defined roles in the Church.

It does not mean that one is more important than the other; they're just different. And, you know what? It works great!"[54] The rhetoric of different but important roles, often called complementary roles, is one that can easily be found in the social media and everyday language of Orthodox believers.[55] The majority of women surveyed saw Christ as a role model for men and his mother, the Theotokos, as an example of how women should participate in the Church—with humility and self-sacrifice. This seems to be in line with conservative Orthodox theology that often focuses on the functionality of women, with some writers suggesting that women were called to be humble helpmates.[56]

In their responses, women would often bring up the idea that the Mother of God was not ordained: "If the Theotokos could live without it than [sic] so can I."[57] Of course, this could be considered anachronistic, since the Christian Church historically evolved and did not have Orthodox priests when Christ was alive. Yet women (and men) will use this type of example to suggest that the Theotokos knew her God-ordained role and did not stray from it. In other words, the Theotokos recognized her gendered gift (that of "birthgiver") and accepted it without question. One respondent focused on the logic of the patriarchal clergy structure of the Church by highlighting how gendered roles were for the benefit of women because they would not be subject to the "burden that clergy bear."[58] The young, conservative convert from an OCA parish in the Carolinas explained her reasoning at length, suggesting that "the burdens borne by the clergy would be a greater weight on women, given our increased tendency to emotional responses."[59] Beyond psychological burdens, she also focused on the physical impact the responsibility of the priesthood might have on women:

> There is also the fact that women have increased physical burdens to bear, in general, when compared to men: menstrual cycles, pregnancy, etc. I do think that perhaps this is a naïve response on my part, but I can't think that the church that honors so many women would prohibit women from ordination because they are inferior.[60]

While the respondent acknowledged that she might be naïve about the reasoning behind an all-male clergy, she tried to work out potential reasons for the ban on women clergy in the Orthodox Church. In general, most respondents choose to toe the party line, providing answers that might be expected from those opposed to female ordination. Most comments defended the patriarchy, calling for a focus on "the tradition of the church and the traditional roles of women."[61] Commenters who opposed female ordination were happy with patriarchy. Indeed, several noted, "the church should remain patriarchal."[62]

In many cases, respondents felt as if the focus on female ordination was part of a power struggle between men and women. "To me, female ordination would not enhance our role as woman [sic], but provide a sort of 'power struggle' within the Church. I find it unnecessary and against our tradition," explained a cradle Lebanese Orthodox woman from New York.[63] She went on to lament how the Church articulates its understanding of gender roles: "I wish our church would explain to women the beauty in our role as women more thoroughly as well as the complimentary roles men and women have. Just because women can't be ordained does not mean we aren't integral in the church."[64] The idea of complimentary roles was often used epistemologically by women to make sense of their place within the Orthodox world. The term "complimentary" is not only part of the coded lexicon that conservative Orthodox women use regarding gender roles and the male/female binary; it is also part of the theological anthropology espoused in many conservative Orthodox communities more broadly.[65]

To understand the social processes of Orthodox Christianity, it is crucial to note that Orthodox theology is lived out in practice. The community issues surrounding the ordination of women are both theologically and socially oriented. In Orthodox Christianity, theology is not separate from everyday belief and practice.[66] Indeed, it is a motivating factor in believers' daily lives. One respondent, an older millennial convert from Canada who lives in New Jersey and considers herself conservative, drew upon the theological anthropology of the Church to explain why she saw gender roles as important not only in the Church but also in society more broadly. I focus on this woman's comments because she seemed to collate many of the issues (very) conservative respondents provided in a succinct yet thorough way. She began her answer to the question of female ordination by quoting her husband on the matter; he believed that ordination was "a doctrine issue because it is about human anthropology."[67] The respondent then acknowledged that she was being asked about the topic and suggested that she saw "a difference between what men and what woman [sic] are called to be in this (fallen) world."[68] In a similar vein with other conservative women surveyed, this respondent drew upon the Mother of God and other "female Saints who are called 'equal to the apostles'" in order to show that women are respected in the Church, despite what "feminists have often misrepre-

Female Ordination	Percentage of Survey Respondents
Opposed	78%
Deaconesses	14%
Neutral/No Opinion	6%
In Favor	2%

sented." The respondent focused on "God as Father" as the blueprint for not only the priesthood and "Father-Confessors" but also for family life. She believed that the patriarchal structures of the Church and its holy tradition were preserved by not ordaining women to the priesthood, since female ordination would ultimately lead to "gay/lesbian clergy." For this respondent and many others surveyed, the heterosexual family structure creates a society that "can flourish," for without it "many social ills, confusions and pain come." Thus, according to the respondent from New Jersey, female ordination would disrupt the image of traditional gender roles, leading to a "destabilization of the whole that a man and a woman create together."[69] While most of the women had strong opinions about ordination, 6 percent of respondents noted that they did not care about ordination or indicated that they had no opinion on the matter. The smallest percentage proved to be the dissenters, those in favor of ordination, accounting for 2 percent of responses.

A Slight Dissent

Beyond the defenders of so-called traditional morality, there were dissenters both among the convert and cradle Orthodox Christians. While the dissenting voices were not as evident in the postings for both groups because of the admin rules, they could be seen and heard in the survey results. Of the 187 women who completed the survey, 12.5 percent considered themselves liberal or very liberal.[70] The dissenting voices were also expressed in the sections regarding abortion, same-sex marriage, and female ordination. Of the women, 6.4 percent listed themselves as pro-choice, with a smaller percentage suggesting that they are pro-life for themselves but do not feel access to abortion services should be withheld by governmental means.[71] Those who marked themselves as liberal and very liberal were adamantly in support of vaccinations. While clearly in the minority of those surveyed, these dissenting voices are crucial because they allow us to see that Orthodox belief is not homogenous.

Another 14.1 percent marked themselves as politically "other" on the form, but of those, many were monarchists, and most were some form of libertarian, meaning that they skewed socially conservative.[72] A key trend was being "economically leftist [and] socially traditionalist" or some variant of that positionality.[73] Yet when asked directly about political party affiliation, it seems as if the liberal and very liberal participants felt more comfortable voicing their opinions. The Democrat Party and "democratic socialist" were both listed numerous times by participants. The other major party mentioned beyond Republican, Democratic, Independent, and Libertarian was the American Solidarity Party. ASP considers itself a Christian democratic platform "that seeks the common good, on common ground, through common sense."[74] While the party labels itself as democratic, it seems to be the organizational embodiment of what many women expressed about themselves—fiscally liberal and socially conservative. Overall, in the optional section for commentary regarding their selection, the majority of survey takers explained that they did not align with any of the political parties in the United States and they felt that the social politics of morality was a key reason they opted to define themselves as politically "other."

One of the final questions on the survey was, *Do you have any important issues that you think the Church should be addressing right now?* Most of the prior questions were reengaged as issues that the Church should focus on. Many who identified as liberal or very liberal took this question as an opportunity to focus on social justice issues that they felt were overlooked in the life of the Church, including the ethical overhaul of the priesthood to keep problematic clergy from being moved around, something that is rarely talked about in churches or by the hierarchs of many Orthodox jurisdictions.[75] Other topics included environmentalism and climate change, "caring for the elderly and indigent," immigration and refugees, human trafficking, and other social issues that are currently trending in global social discourses on morality and human rights.[76] These social justice issues have long been addressed by the Christian Left but in my research are often overlooked by Orthodox Christians in the United States and elsewhere.[77] While there was space for liberal Orthodox women to express their desires for change in the Church, most respondents in general focused heavily on topics that were consistent with the conservative majority present throughout most of the data.

Abortion. Gay rights. Pornography. Female ordination. These were listed by very conservative, conservative, and moderate Orthodox women respondents as issues that the Orthodox Church should address. This question also allowed some of the respondents to delve deeper into what they saw as moral or ethical issues that the Church needs to address—issues that were frequently found in the postings in both Facebook groups regarding homeschooling, a topic that was not off-limits and was often used to express political ideologies discreetly. In particular, many of the women focused on transgender rights and the fear that schools were being taken hostage "by modern progressive ideologies, including but not limited to feminism, socialism/communism/Marxism, sexual 'liberation,' evolutionary theory, gender fluidity, and homo/pan sexuality."[78] Throughout their answers, women pushed for a return to the traditional family model of stay-at-home mothers and fathers working outside of the home. Additionally, most emphasized homeschooling as a method for keeping children away from the transgender movement, which was labeled by many as "the greatest threat to our youth."[79] Often, this type of rhetoric is seen throughout right-leaning Christian communities in the United States and Europe, but its recent explosion in Orthodox Christian communities seems linked to the convert demographic shifting the social politics of the Church. This assumption was supported by the Orthodox media personalities listed by women in their answers about what type of blogs they read and videos they watch online.

Social Influences

If the words of each woman and the group statistics indicate social trends in US Orthodoxy, then looking at their online media consumption may tell us more about the influences that shape those trends. Within the group posts and in the written survey answers, several converts were noted as influential voices in the debates on moral social values: Rod Dreher, Kh. Frederica Mathewes-Green, and Fr. Josiah Trenham. While all three are known within US Orthodoxy as conservative, traditional voices, it is Trenham, a priest at a California parish in the Antiochian archdiocese, who seems to have a growing charismatic presence on- and offline. Women in both Facebook groups mentioned his videos, podcasts, and public scholarship on morality, family values, and homeschooling. In recent years, Trenham has become a bit of a conservative celebrity but also a

contentious figure in many Orthodox communities. His highly inflam-
matory comments about LGBTQ+ communities at the 2016 World Congress of Families X in Tbilisi, Georgia, caught the attention of the
Southern Poverty Law Center's Hatewatch staff.[80]

The influence of these so-called Orthodox religious celebrities is evident
in the articulations of Orthodox women in the mothering and homemaking groups. Members posted YouTube videos of lectures, shared blog posts,
and provide links to Dreher's, Mathewes-Green's, and Trenham's books.
Within both women's groups, participants posted links to the 2019 Saint
Kosmas West Conference on Technology and Orthodoxy, which was geared
toward homeschoolers in the hopes of creating a meaningful Orthodox approach to digital media.[81] Planned for the fall of 2019, the conference was a
one-day event that immediately followed a homeschooling retreat the day
prior. While Orthodox conferences are not rare, it is the lineup of speakers
that denotes the influence of conservative, convert voices in US Orthodoxy.
In addition to Fr. Josiah Trenham, the conference also boasted Fr. Peter
Heers, a vocal proponent of traditional Orthodox Christianity and family
values.[82] Along with Mathewes-Green and Dreher, Heers was one of the
speakers at a March 2019 conference at Holy Trinity Monastery and Seminary in Jordanville, New York, titled "Chastity, Purity, Integrity: Orthodox
Anthropology and Secular Culture in the Twenty-First Century."[83] The
conference was organized by and, in large part, attended by non–Russian
Orthodox converts, some of whom were members of both Orthodox
women's groups. Hosted by one of the most historic institutions of the
ROCOR in the United States, the conference was just one of many events
that suggests the transformative effect converts are having in Orthodox communities. The dissemination of the conference video proceedings on Ancient
Faith Ministries, one of the more prominent media outlets for Orthodox
Christians in the United States, suggests that the conservative ideologies
present in the lectures might be welcomed by listeners.[84]

The conference lectures emphasized abstinence before marriage, protecting children from transgender and gay influences through homeschooling, and antivaccination and antiabortion rhetoric. Many speakers and
attendees also expressed opposition to female ordination. These views are
reminiscent of those often expressed by fundamentalist and/or evangelical groups, and many of the speakers at the conference used to be part of
such institutions. Given that a majority of the converts surveyed in the
women's Facebook groups were once part of evangelical movements

themselves, it is not surprising that they often turn to Trenham, Dreher, and others for moral guidance. Overall, it seems that convert women in the survey might be drawn to Orthodox convert personalities to reinforce their social understandings of religion, politics, and gender. Certainly, this is not a new event among conservative Christian communities, but what is crucial to emphasize here is how converts are changing the theosocial formations of Eastern Orthodoxy in the United States and are doing so largely through digital means because of the disparate geographical makeup of believers.

Social Media Matters

The political ideologies expressed by converts and, to a lesser extent, cradles point to new social formations at work in US Orthodoxy. I have witnessed these changing social realities firsthand in the ROCOR communities populated predominately by converts. Russian-born Orthodox women in the Appalachian community with whom I worked most recently had quite distinct political views from their female (and male) convert counterparts. While many of the convert women in my research community homeschooled and pointed their children to trade schools rather than college, Russian women encouraged their children to attend public school and seek advanced degrees. Anti-intellectualism was often coupled with antivaccination rhetoric in this particular Orthodox community. While the homeschooling mothers largely decried the use of vaccines, Russian moms found it outrageous not to protect oneself through medical intervention.[85] With the influx of converts from evangelical and fundamentalist Protestant backgrounds, Orthodoxy's social structures and politics are transforming ideologically. The sociocultural baggage of conversion means ideologies that were not historically found in Orthodoxy are beginning to emerge as part of the Church in the United States, United Kingdom, Europe, and other areas around the globe. Fears over shifting gender and sexual dynamics seemed to be part of the political reactions employed by women as they shaped the boundaries of Christian propriety, structuring their social group formations. Thus these women created what Pierre Bourdieu calls "the *sense of reality*, that is, the correspondence between the objective classes and the internalized classes, social structures and mental structures, which is the basis of the most ineradicable adherence to the established order."[86] It seems that for most of the female converts I talked with in Appalachia and for the majority of women surveyed online, the focus on traditional family values reinforced the Orthodox institutional, God-ordained patriarchy.

The shifting social formations of Orthodox Christianity are not only found in the United States. Vladimir Putin, along with Patriarch Kirill and the Russian Orthodox Church, has engaged in a rhetoric of family values that seems to be part of a larger ideological shift, politically and religiously, in Russian society.[87] The rise of these ideologies in the post-Soviet context is, of course, part of the continuing negotiation of Russian identity after perestroika and has as much to do with Vladimir Putin's desire for autocratic rule as it does with Patriarch Kirill's emphasis on promoting a postmodern form of Orthodox Christianity on the global stage. For conservative believers with whom I have worked in the United States, Russia's supposed new focus on family values seems salvific at a time when they believe most Western countries are failing to protect the family structure. Beyond Russia, Patriarch Ilia of Georgia, who provided a blessing at the 2016 World Congress of Families, has been accused of outspoken conservatism that has seemingly led to a social assault on LGBTQ+ rights in Georgia alongside an increased focus on sexual purity and heteronormative marriage.[88] The nationalistic and traditionalist impulses felt throughout many of the so-called traditional Orthodox countries highlights the growing emphasis on culture preservation that seems to be increasing in both the United States and Europe.[89] Fears over the loss of culture, religious—often Christian—social identification, and a homogenous society are part of larger global formations of power, such as nationalism, neocolonialism, and empire.[90] Particularly in the United States, these political ideologies often find their home in conservative Christian communities, even those that espouse a heavenly rather than worldly outlook, such as Orthodoxy.[91]

Analyzing the social processes and influences at work in these online groups of women provides more insight into expressions of religious belief that are often deemed as extreme or oppressive. Within these religious systems, larger social dynamics are at play, especially in United States Orthodoxy, which is still struggling, it seems, to make sense of the convert-cradle dynamic, where both parties emphasize different formations of social purity. Perhaps, as William Connolly suggests, pluralism is "an adversary of purity," which may be why many of the Orthodox women survey respondents seemed so concerned about the social politics of the United States.[92] Whatever the individual motivating reasons behind converts' reactionary social politics, it is clear that many of them are influenced by their previous engagement with evangelical Protestantism while also being guided by several dominant conservative voices in Orthodox media today. Just as my research in the mountains of West Virginia provided a microview of the changing politics of the ROCOR in the United States, so too does looking at the ideas of digitally connected Orthodox women offer a glimpse into part of the sociopolitical transformations occurring in Eastern Orthodoxy. Surveying Orthodox women in these spaces allows us to hear crucial but often unheard or silenced voices that both champion and decry the new forms of religious conservatism that are quickly taking shape around the world. In doing so, the agentive and theatrical act of female self-formation comes to the fore, thereby offering us new ways to understand these often-maligned social actors within American Christianity.[93]

Notes

This research project stems from a much longer anthropological study of conversion in the Russian Orthodox Church outside of Russia (ROCOR) in the Appalachian Mountains of West Virginia, where I spent twelve months living with a community of far-right converts (2017–2018). My research for this project was generously funded by New York University, the Jordan Center for the Advanced Study of Russia, the Louisville Institute, the National Endowment for the Humanities in conjunction with the Orthodox Christian Studies Center at Fordham University, and the Woodrow Wilson Fellowship Foundation via the Charlotte W. Newcomb Dissertation Fellowship. As a part of the broader research area of anthropology, I see these social media groups as extensions of my primary physical field site and treat them as such, including obtaining IRB approval for documenting conversations, blog posts, the Google Forms survey I conducted, and, more generally, making my presence as an anthropologist known in closed-group settings. Given the sensitive nature of these topics, particularly in Eastern Orthodox settings, I have chosen to maintain the anonymity of all survey participants and posters in Facebook groups for women. To this end, I use direct quotes only from the anonymous survey and summarize ethnographic observations in my own words, as I and other anthropologists often do within the context of normative research. Following the digital data-gathering protocols of my home institution, any open-access blogs will be cited as they appear online. Open-access content from Orthodox public figures will also be cited as it appears. For more information on digital ethnography, see Tom Boellstorff, Bonnie Nardi, Celia Pearce, and T. L. Taylor, *Ethnography and Virtual World: A Handbook of Method* (Princeton, NJ: Princeton University Press, 2013); Sarah Pink, Heather Horst, John Postill, Larissa Hjorth, Tania Lewis, and Jo Tacchi, *Digital Ethnography: Principles and Practice* (London: SAGE, 2016).

1. Oliver Herbel, *Turning to Tradition: Converts and the Making of an American Orthodox Church* (New York: Oxford University Press, 2013); Amy Slagle, *The Eastern Church in the Spiritual Marketplace: American Conversions to Orthodox Christianity* (Dekalb: Northern Illinois University Press, 2011); Daniel Winchester, "Converting to Continuity: Temporality and Self in Eastern Orthodox Conversion Narratives," *Journal for the Scientific Study of Religion* 54 (2015): 439–60.

2. In the post-Soviet Russian Orthodox context, this volume on religion, media, and politics is helpful in beginning to think through these issues: Mikhail Suslov, ed., *Digital Orthodoxy in the Post-Soviet World: The Russian Orthodox Church and the Web 2.0* (Stuttgart: *ibidem*-Verlag, 2016). Throughout the body of this chapter, I mostly refer to Orthodox Christianity in the United States as US Orthodoxy, United States Orthodox, and other variations of the phrase. I try to avoid using the term "America" to refer to the United States, because it seems to possess overtly nationalistic and religious connotations and because it tends to place primacy on those geographically in the northern region of the Americas. See Andrew L. Whitehead and Christopher P. Scheitle, "We the (Christian) People: Christianity and American Identity from 1996 to 2014," *Social Currents* (2017), doi:10.1177/2329496517725.

3. Heidi Campbell, *Digital Religion: Understanding Religious Practice in New Media Worlds* (London: Routledge, 2013); Heidi Campbell and S. Gardner, eds., *Networked Theology: Negotiating Faith in Digital Culture* (Grand Rapids, MI: Baker Academic, 2016); Michael Jackson, *Lifeworlds: Essays in Existential Anthropology* (Chicago: University of Chicago Press, 2012). Mona Abdel-Fadil, in her research on Christian online media practices, suggests that media anthropology, which has often focused less on online communities and more on embedded media practices in everyday life, could gain a great deal of insight into the sociocultural politics of particular groups by engaging more with the digital lifeworlds of practitioners. Mona Abdel-Fadil, "Identity Politics in a Mediatized Religious Environment on Facebook: Yes to Wearing the Cross Whenever and Wherever I Choose," *Journal of Religion in Europe* 10 (2017): 457–86.

4. Matthew Engelke, *How to Think Like an Anthropologist* (Princeton, NJ: Princeton University Press, 2019), 91; Saba Mahmood, "Feminist Theory, Embodiment, and the Docile Agent: Some Reflections on the Egyptian Islamic Revival," *Cultural Anthropology* 6, no. 2 (2001): 202–36; Saba Mahmood, *Politics of Piety: The Islamic Revival and the Feminist Subject* (Princeton, NJ: Princeton University Press, 2005).

5. danah boyd, *It's Complicated: The Social Lives of Networked Teens* (New Haven, CT: Yale University Press, 2014), 8.

6. Luke Eric Lassiter, *An Invitation to Anthropology*, 4th ed. (New York: Rowman and Littlefield, 2014).

7. Heidi Campbell, *When Religion Meets New Media* (London: Routledge, 2010); Faye Ginsburg, Lila Abu-Lughod, and Brian Larkin, eds., *Media Worlds: Anthropology on New Terrain* (Berkeley: University of California Press, 2002); Stig Hjarvard, "The Mediatization of Religion: A Theory of the Media as Agents of Religious Change," *Northern Lights* 6 (2008): 9–26.

8. George Demacopoulos, "The Audacity of Converts," *Public Orthodoxy*, https://publicorthodoxy.org/2018/12/14/the-audacity-of-converts/.

9. His Holiness Patriarch Krill, interview, *60 Minut, Rossiya Odna*, January 7, 2019, [26:19], https://www.youtube.com/watch?v=kV6SuZ7t9gs. Since I started fieldwork projects with Orthodox Christians in 2010 I have seen a rise in the use of the internet to find religious commonality and social cohesion. This is particularly evident in Russian Orthodox Christian communities throughout the United States and especially among women in the ROCOR.

10. In the vein of Daniel Miller's work on Facebook ethnography as narrative portraits of site users, I draw together my fieldwork in the Facebook groups with the survey data gathered to highlight individual commentary from a variety of women. Daniel Miller, *Tales from Facebook* (Cambridge: Polity, 2011).

11. I employ the terms "liberal" and "conservative" not to create polarization but to be true to the terms interlocutors use in reference to themselves and others.

12. As I mentioned in the body of this chapter, it seems as if head coverings was the first topic to be banned by the mothering group. This happened in the summer of 2015. The next topic to be banned, according to an archival search of the feed posts, was vaccinations. For all accounts, politics (national and church) was added to this list after 2016. The slightest whiff of dissent toward the banned items meant that the admins would remove the post or close the comments. This surveillance and curation often prompted women to leave the group or become less interested in posting and socializing.

13. "Orthodox Women, Moral Issues, and the Internet," Google Forms Survey, May 25, 2019–June 22, 2019, https://docs.google.com/forms/d/e/1FAIpQLSd4QH bauSOn-HdzswaO8QfGCdtSZnexHyX_p3rSBR_ACDsOCg/viewform?usp=sf _link.

14. A Pew foundation report from 2015 indicates that Orthodox Christians make up 0.5 percent of Christians surveyed. Pew Research Center, May 12, 2015, "America's Changing Religious Landscape."

15. "Orthodox Women, Moral Issues, and the Internet," Google Forms Survey. Conversion narratives varied widely in depth of detail but generally offered a date and reason. While these narratives did provide insight into the backgrounds of each woman, I have chosen not to include a section dedicated to these stories, since this chapter is not focused solely on the process of conversion but rather on how converts might be shaping the social trajectory of Orthodoxy more broadly.

16. For more information about my research on this topic, see my website: http://www.riccardiswartz.com.

17. Interview, June 11, 2018.

18. Robin Lakoff, *Language and Woman's Place* (New York: Harper and Row, 1975); Miriam Meyerhoff, "Doing and Saying: Some Words on Women's Silence," in *Language and Woman's Place: Text and Commentaries*, rev. and exp. ed., ed. Robin Tolmach Lakoff and Mary Bucholtz (Oxford: Oxford University Press, 2014), 208–15.

19. Faye Ginsburg, *Contested Lives: The Abortion Debate in an American Community* (Berkeley: University of California Press, 1989); David Masci, "American Religious Groups Vary widely in Their Views of Abortion" Pew Research, https://www.pewresearch.org/fact-tank/2018/01/22/american -religious-groups-vary-widely-in-their-views-of-abortion/; Pew Research Center, "Orthodox Take Socially Conservative Views on Gender, Homosexuality," Orthodoxy Christianity in the Twenty-First Century Survey, https://www .pewforum.org/2017/11/08/orthodox-take-socially-conservative-views-on -gender-issues-homosexuality/.

20. There is a wide variety of popular social media sites dedicated to the renewal of head coverings in the Orthodox world, with the most vocal proponents being male clergy. See Fr. Lawrence Farley, "Headscarves, Modesty, and Scolding Modern Orthodox Women," *No Other Foundation*, blog hosted by Ancient Faith Ministries, July 25, 2018, https://blogs.ancientfaith.com /nootherfoundation/headscarves-modesty-and-scolding-modern-orthodox -women/; Fr. John Whiteford, "Uncovering the Truth: Headcoverings and Revisionist Biblical Interpretation," *Orthodox Christianity*, June 23, 2017, http://orthochristian.com/104571.html. There are also articles and blog posts by Orthodox women who often draw upon the same texts and ideas as the women who participated in the survey. A detailed example of this can be found at: Elisabet, "On Account of the Angels: Why I Cover My Head," repr. from *Handmaiden Journal*, Spring 1997, at Orthodox Christian Information Center, http://orthodoxinfo.com/praxis/headcoverings.aspx. One popular Orthodox blogger, mentioned by a large number of women who participated in the survey, posted a link to a Russian Orthodox modesty fashion show that focused on head coverings. See MamaBirdEmma, "Stylish Orthodox Women's Fashion in Russia," *Charming the Birds from the Trees*, April 17, 2008, http://www.charmingthebirdsfromthetrees.com/2008/04/stylish-orthodox- womens-fashion-in.html.

21. Leah Power and Stephen W. Cook, "An Examination of the Complex Associations between Religiousness and Femininity among US Christian Women," *Mental Health, Religion, and Culture* 20, no. 7 (2017): 638–53, https://doi.org/10.1080/13674676.2017.1379979. While the use of head coverings

is resurgent among conservative Christian women in the United States, scholars have often focused on the revival of head coverings in the Islamic context. Their research is key for those of us thinking through the same issues of piety, agency, and tradition. See Anna-Mari Almila and David Inglis, eds., *The Routledge International Handbook to Veils and Veiling Practices* (New York: Routledge, 2018); Leila Ahmed, *A Quiet Revolution: The Veil's Resurgence from the Middle East to America* (New Haven, CT: Yale University Press, 2011).

22. Joan Wallach Scott, *The Politics of the Veil* (Princeton, NJ: Princeton University Press, 2007).

23. "Orthodox Women, Moral Issues, and the Internet," Google Forms Survey.

24. "Orthodox Women, Moral Issues, and the Internet," Google Forms Survey.

25. "Orthodox Women, Moral Issues, and the Internet," Google Forms Survey.

26. "Orthodox Women, Moral Issues, and the Internet," Google Forms Survey. R. Marie Griffith, *God's Daughters: Evangelical Women and the Power of Submission* (Berkeley: University of California Press, 1997); Kallistos Ware, *The Inner Kingdom* (Crestwood, NY: St. Vladimir's Seminary Press, 2000).

27. "Orthodox Women, Moral Issues, and the Internet," Google Forms Survey.

28. "Orthodox Women, Moral Issues, and the Internet," Google Forms Survey.

29. "Orthodox Women, Moral Issues, and the Internet," Google Forms Survey.

30. Saher Amer, *What Is Veiling?* (Chapel Hill: University of North Carolina Press, 2014).

31. "Orthodox Women, Moral Issues, and the Internet," Google Forms Survey. In Orthodox communities, this is very much seen in the push toward intentional community building, such as Rod Dreher's Benedict Option. Rod Dreher, *The Benedict Option: A Strategy for Christians in the Post-Christian Nation* (New York: Sentinel, 2017). In the fall of 2019, I was part of a workshop at Georgetown University's Berkeley Center for Religion, Peace, and World Affairs led by Kristina Stoeckl. In this two-day workshop we examined Russia's place in the cultural wars and discussed how Americans perceive Russian morality under the Putin administration. My paper specifically addressed how the converts with whom I worked in Appalachia understand Russian conservatism by and large. For more information about my lecture and the workshop, see Sarah Riccardi-Swartz, "American Conversions to Russian Orthodoxy amid the Global Culture Wars," Berkeley Forum, December 18, 2019, https://berkleycenter.georgetown.edu/responses/american-conversions-to-russian-orthodoxy-amid-the-global-culture-wars.

32. Judith Butler, "Performative Acts and Gender Constitution: An Essay in Phenomenology and Feminist Theory," *Theater Journal* 40, no. 4 (December 1988): 519–31; Maik Fielitz and Nick Thurston, eds., *Post-Digital Cultures of the Far Right: Online Actions and Offline Consequences in Europe and the US* (Bielefeld: transcript Verlag, 2019).

33. Feminism & Decolonization Facebook page, https://www.facebook.com
/FeminismAndDecolonisation/posts/2281748895212475.

34. R. Marie Griffith, *Moral Combat: How Sex Divided American Christians
and Fractured American Politics* (New York: Basic Books, 2017).

35. Nancy F. Cott, *The Bonds of Womanhood: "Woman's Sphere" in New
England, 1780–1835* (1977; New Haven, CT: Yale University Press, 1997).

36. "Orthodox Women, Moral Issues, and the Internet," Google Forms Survey.

37. "Orthodox Women, Moral Issues, and the Internet," Google Forms Survey.

38. "Orthodox Women, Moral Issues, and the Internet," Google Forms Survey.

39. "Orthodox Women, Moral Issues, and the Internet," Google Forms Survey.

40. "Orthodox Women, Moral Issues, and the Internet," Google Forms Survey.

41. "Orthodox Women, Moral Issues, and the Internet," Google Forms Survey.

42. "Orthodox Women, Moral Issues, and the Internet," Google Forms Survey.

43. "Orthodox Women, Moral Issues, and the Internet," Google Forms Survey.

44. "Orthodox Women, Moral Issues, and the Internet," Google Forms Survey.

45. "Orthodox Women, Moral Issues, and the Internet," Google Forms Survey.

46. "Orthodox Women, Moral Issues, and the Internet," Google Forms Survey.

47. A helpful and critical response comes from a compiled volume on LGBT
inclusion and what that might look like in the Orthodox Church. Misha
Cherniak, Olga Gerassimenko, and Michael Brinkschröder, eds.,*"For I Am
Wonderfully Made": Texts on Eastern Orthodoxy and LGBT Inclusion*
(Esuberanza; European Forum of Lesbian, Gay, Bisexual, and Transgender
Christian Groups, 2016).

48. "Orthodox Women, Moral Issues, and the Internet," Google Forms Survey.

49. "Orthodox Women, Moral Issues, and the Internet," Google Forms Survey.

50. "Orthodox Women, Moral Issues, and the Internet," Google Forms Survey.

51. "Orthodox Women, Moral Issues, and the Internet," Google Forms Survey.

52. Over the last ten years or so there have been deeper conversations in US
Orthodox communities around reviving the order of the deaconess, especially
through the St. Phoebe Center for the Deaconess: https://orthodoxdeaconess
.org. See, among many sources, Elisabeth Behr-Sigel, *The Ministry of Women in
the Church*, trans. Steven Bigham (Crestwood, NY: St. Vladimir's Seminary
Press, 1991); Elisabeth Behr-Sigel and Kallistos Ware, *The Ordination of Women
in the Orthodox Church* (Geneva: World Council of Churches, 2000); Petros
Vassiliadis, Niki Papageorgiou, and Eleni Kasselouri-Hatzivassiliadi, eds.,
Deaconesses, the Ordination of Women, and Orthodox Theology (Newcastle:
Cambridge Scholars, 2017).

53. "Orthodox Women, Moral Issues, and the Internet," Google Forms Survey.

54. "Orthodox Women, Moral Issues, and the Internet," Google Forms Survey.

55. "Orthodox Women, Moral Issues, and the Internet," Google Forms
Survey.

56. Abbess Theologia, *The Perfection of Women in Christ, According to Orthodox Christian Doctrine and Anthropology* (Columbia, MO: New Rome, 2003).

57. "Orthodox Women, Moral Issues, and the Internet," Google Forms Survey.

58. "Orthodox Women, Moral Issues, and the Internet," Google Forms Survey.

59. "Orthodox Women, Moral Issues, and the Internet," Google Forms Survey.

60. "Orthodox Women, Moral Issues, and the Internet," Google Forms Survey.

61. "Orthodox Women, Moral Issues, and the Internet," Google Forms Survey.

62. "Orthodox Women, Moral Issues, and the Internet," Google Forms Survey.

63. "Orthodox Women, Moral Issues, and the Internet," Google Forms Survey.

64. "Orthodox Women, Moral Issues, and the Internet," Google Forms Survey.

65. Leonie B. Liveris, *Ancient Taboos and Gender Prejudice: Challenges for Orthodox Women and the Church* (London: Routledge, 2017).

66. Vigen Guroian, *The Orthodox Reality: Culture, Theology, and Ethics in the Modern World* (Grand Rapids, MI: Baker, 2018).

67. "Orthodox Women, Moral Issues, and the Internet," Google Forms Survey.

68. "Orthodox Women, Moral Issues, and the Internet," Google Forms Survey.

69. "Orthodox Women, Moral Issues, and the Internet," Google Forms Survey.

70. "Orthodox Women, Moral Issues, and the Internet," Google Forms Survey.

71. During the space of time in which the majority of the women completed the survey, the abortion debate returned to broadcast television and social media with great vigor. In 2019, Alabama's state senate passed one of the most restrictive abortion bans in the United States. The bill was backed by Republican representative Terri Collins, who in an interview with the *Washington Post* claimed that "I have prayed my way through this bill. This is the way we get where we want to get eventually." Given this public display of conservative moral values, it was surprising that most women were far more likely to comment in detail about same-sex marriage and transgender rights than abortion. Emily Wax-Thibodeaux and Chip Brownlee, "Alabama Senate Passes Nation's Most Restrictive Abortion Ban, Which Makes No Exceptions for Victims of Rape and Incest," *Washington Post*, May 14, 2019, https://www.washingtonpost.com/national/alabama-senate-passes-nations-most-restrictive-abortion-law-which-makes-no-exceptions-for-victims-of-rape-and-incest/2019/05/14/e3022376-7665-11e9-b3f5-5673edf2d127_story.html.

72. "Orthodox Women, Moral Issues, and the Internet," Google Forms Survey.

73. "Orthodox Women, Moral Issues, and the Internet," Google Forms Survey.

74. American Solidarity Party, "National Platform of the ASP," https://solidarity-party.org/about-us/platform/.

75. "Orthodox Women, Moral Issues, and the Internet," Google Forms Survey.

76. "Orthodox Women, Moral Issues, and the Internet," Google Forms Survey.

77. Elizabeth H. Prodromou and Nathanael Symeonides, "Orthodox Christianity and Humanitarianism: An Introduction to Thought and Practice, Past

and Present," *Review of Faith and International Affairs* 14, no. 1 (March 2016): 1–8.

78. "Orthodox Women, Moral Issues, and the Internet," Google Forms Survey.

79. "Orthodox Women, Moral Issues, and the Internet," Google Forms Survey.

80. Patristic Nectar Films, "Gay Iconoclasm: Holding the Line against the Radical LGBT Agenda," YouTube video, 22:11, https://youtu.be/HNXe4P _6dhw; Hatewatch Staff, "World Congress of Families Gathering in Tbilisi Showcases Anti-LGBT Rhetoric and Conspiracy Theories," Southern Poverty Law Center, https://www.splcenter.org/hatewatch/2016/06/01/world-congress -families-gathering-tbilisi-showcases-anti-lgbt-rhetoric-and-conspiracy.

81. St. Kosmos Orthodox Education Conferences, "Technology and Orthodoxy Conference Schedule," https://saintkosmasconferences.com /schedule-2019-technology-conference.

82. Orthodox Ethos, "About the Editor," https://orthodoxethos.com.

83. Holy Trinity Monastery, "Chastity, Purity, Integrity: Orthodox Anthropology and Secular Culture in the Twenty-First Century," https://www .jordanville.org/news_190227_1.html.

84. Ancient Faith Ministries, "Specials: Chastity, Purity, Integrity: Orthodox Anthropology and Secular Culture in the Twenty-First Century," https://www.ancientfaith.com/specials/chastity_purity_integrity.

85. Interview, August 21, 2018.

86. Pierre Bourdieu, *Outline of a Theory of Practice*, trans. Richard Nice (1977; Cambridge: Cambridge University Press, 2015). Cynthia Lynn Lyerly, "In Service, Silence, and Strength: Women in Southern Churches," in *Religion and Public Life in the South: In the Evangelical Mode*, ed. Charles Reagan Wilson and Mark Silk (New York: AltaMira, 2005), 101–24.

87. Alexander Agadjanian, "Tradition, Morality, and Community: Elaborating Orthodox Identity in Putin's Russia," *Religion, State, and Society* 45, no. 1 (2017): 39–60. Denis Zhuravlev, "Orthodox Identity as Traditionalism: Construction of Political Meaning in the Current Public Discourse of the Russian Orthodox Church," *Russian Politics and Law* 55, nos. 4–5 (2017): 354–75.

88. Damien McGuinness, "Thousands Protest in Georgia over Gay Rights Rally," BBC, May 17, 2013, https://www.bbc.com/news/world-europe-22571216; "Family Purity Day Is Not against Anyone, but for Georgia—Patriarch Ilia," *Orthodox Christianity*, http://orthochristian.com/121266.html.

89. Catherine Frost, *Morality and Nationalism* (London: Routledge, 2006), 31.

90. Mark Lewis Taylor, *Religion, Politics, and the Christian Right: Post 9/11 Powers and American Empire* (Minneapolis, MN: Fortress, 2005).

91. Aristotle Papanikolaou, *The Mystical as Political: Democracy and Nonradical Orthodoxy* (Notre Dame, IN: University of Notre Dame Press, 2016).

92. William E. Connolly, *Aspirational Fascism: The Struggle for Democracy under Trumpism* (Minneapolis: University of Minnesota Press, 2017), 86.

93. Talal Asad, *Formations of the Secular: Christianity, Islam, Modernity* (Stanford, CA: Stanford University Press, 2003), 75–76. In early June 2020, during the COVID-19 pandemic and the US-based riots in response to the death of George Floyd at the hands of a Minnesota police officer, administrators for the mothering group came under fire by members when posts deemed to be political in nature, including social distancing, masking, and racism, were deleted. Group members organized and pushed back, using a shared Google document to create a letter asking for less oversight and for administrators to lift the ban on political and controversial topics. The organizers asked for my advice in crafting the letter, and I added my name to the official document in support of these changes. On June 5, 2020, the administrators issued an announcement lifting the topical ban. However, they also noted that "topics may potentially need to be rebanned." The rule change was met with both praise and frustration, as women began to grapple with the freedom to agree and disagree publicly.

ACKNOWLEDGMENTS

The idea for this volume formed in my mind a long time before I started actual working on it. As a scholar of religion focusing on postcommunist societies, I have been researching for more than twenty years the dramatic sociological, political, and cultural transformations of religious communities and institutions after the fall of the Berlin Wall, but it took a while before I turned to women's experiences, first within Islam and now within my own religious tradition, Orthodox Christianity. I greatly appreciate my numerous conversations with theologians, sociologists of religion, clerics, and rank-and-file lay members of the Orthodox Church, both in my country of origin, Bulgaria, and in many places around the world, who offered different perspectives toward, and thus helped me understand better, the processes I study.

I am grateful to the Leverhulme Trust for awarding me a Visiting Professorship at the Centre for Trust, Peace and Social Relations in 2018–2019, when I was able to concentrate on my work on the volume, among other activities. My appreciation goes to my colleagues from the Faith and Peaceful Relations Research Group for providing a stimulating intellectual environment, and to Kristin Aune and Paul Weller in particular for their generous hospitality and support.

I would like to express my special gratitude to Aristotle Papanikolaou and Ashley M. Purpura, editors of the Orthodox Christianity and Contemporary Thought series at Fordham University Press, for their valuable feedback and trust in this book. I wish to thank also the two anonymous reviewers at the Press for their careful reading of the manuscript and their suggestions for improvement as well as the editorial team at the Press: Will Cerbone for help-ing me navigate the logistic aspects of the publication, Rob Fellman for his excellent copy editing, and Eric Newman for his expert management of the production process.

The manuscript is part of the Fordham Orthodox Christian Studies Cen-ter Luce/L100 Seminars on Orthodoxy & Human Rights in 2019–2021, directed by George Demacopoulos and Aristotle Papanikolaou. The seminar inspired me to think more deeply about the link between women's roles and rights in Orthodox Christian contexts and the interpretive struggles of the Orthodox Church with the idea of human rights.

Most important, the editing of this volume was a rewarding experience thanks to the wonderful cooperation and excellent work of its contributors!

Ina Merdjanova

Contributors

Ina Merdjanova is Visiting Professor at Coventry University's Centre for Trust, Peace, and Social Relations and Senior Researcher and Adjunct Assistant Professor at the Irish School of Ecumenics, Trinity College Dublin. She has held visiting fellowships at Oxford University, New York University, the Woodrow Wilson International Center for Scholars in Washington, DC, the Netherlands Institute for Advanced Studies in the Humanities and Social Sciences, and the Aleksanteri Institute at Helsinki University, among others. She is author of four monographs and numerous articles on religion and politics in postcommunist society, including *Religion as a Conversation Starter: Interreligious Dialogue for Peacebuilding in the Balkans* (with Patrice Brodeur, Continuum, 2009), and *Rediscovering the Umma: Muslims in the Balkans between Nationalism and Transnationalism* (Oxford University Press, 2013).

Kristin Aune is Professor of Sociology of Religion at Coventry University's Centre for Trust, Peace, and Social Relations. Her research is on religion, gender, and higher education, and her books include *Women and Religion in the West* (edited with S. Sharma and G. Vincett, Routledge, 2008). Her recent journal articles include "Feminist Spirituality as Lived Religion" (*Gender & Society*) and "Navigating the Third Wave: Contemporary UK Feminist Activists and 'Third-Wave Feminism'" (*Feminist Theory*). She is coeditor of Routledge's Gendering the Study of Religion in the Social Sciences book series and an editor of the journal *Religion and Gender*.

Milica Bakić-Hayden is Lecturer Emeritus at the University of Pitts-burgh, where she has taught for the past twenty-five years, first at the Slavic Department and from 1997 to 2018 at the Department of Religious Studies. She obtained her BA and MA degrees from the University of Belgrade and her PhD from the University of Chicago. Geographic areas of academic interest include the Balkans and South Asia. Special topics of study and research include Indian religions, the philosophy and theory of art, Eastern Orthodox Christianity, Balkan cultures and society, comparative mysticism, monasticism, and sainthood.

Maria Bucur is the John V. Hill Chair in East European History and Gender Studies at Indiana University, Bloomington. Her publications in-clude *The Birth of Democratic Citizenship: Women in Modern Romania* (with Mihaela Miroiu, 2018), *The Century of Women: How Women Have Changed the World since 1900* (2018), *Gendering Modernism: A Historical Reappraisal of the Canon* (2017), and *Heroes and Victims: Remembering War in Twentieth-Century Romania* (2009).

Ketevan Gurchiani is Associate Professor of Cultural Studies at Ilia State University, Tbilisi, and chair of the board of trustees at the Caucasus In-stitute for Peace, Democracy, and Development (CIPDD). She has been the recipient of numerous research grants and awards from Georgian, Ger-man, and US-based foundations. Her research interests include different aspects of religiosity, with a special focus on everyday religion in post-Soviet Georgia. She is the author of several articles and editor of the volume *Re-ligion in Everyday Life* (Ilia State University Press, 2018).

James Kapaló is Senior Lecturer in the Study of Religions at University College Cork, Ireland, and Principal Investigator of the European Research Council project "Creative Agency and Religious Minorities: 'Hidden Gal-leries' in the Secret Police Archives in Central and Eastern Europe" (proj-ect no. 677355). He is the author of two monographs, *Text, Context, and Performance: Gagauz Folk Religion in Discourse and Practice* (Brill, 2011) and *Inochentism and Orthodox Christianity: Religious Dissent in the Russian and Romanian Borderlands* (Routledge, 2019).

Helena Kupari is Postdoctoral Researcher at the Faculty of Arts, Univer-sity of Helsinki, Finland. In her postdoctoral project, funded by the Acad-emy of Finland, she studies conversion to Orthodox Christianity among

Finnish artists and cultural professionals. She has published two books, the monograph *Lifelong Religion as Habitus: Religious Practice among Displaced Karelian Orthodox Women in Finland* (Brill 2016) and an edited volume, *Orthodox Christianity and Gender: Dynamics of Tradition, Culture, and Lived Practice* (with Elina Vuola, Routledge 2020).

Sarah Riccardi-Swartz is a postdoctoral fellow in the Luce-funded Recovering Truth: Religion, Journalism, and Democracy in a Post-Truth Era project, at the Center for the Study of Religion and Conflict at Arizona State University. An anthropologist, scholar of American religion, and trained documentary filmmaker, she specializes in social politics, media, and Orthodox Christianity in the United States. Her research has been funded by New York University, the Jordan Center for the Advanced Study of Russia, the Louisville Institute, the Institute for Citizens and Scholars (formerly the Woodrow Wilson National Fellowship Foundation), the National Endowment for the Humanities, Fordham University, Arizona State University, and the Social Science Research Council in partnership with the Fetzer Institute.

Eleni Sotiriou is a sociologist and social anthropologist. Her research interests focus on the relations between women, sociocultural change, and religion, particularly within Greek Orthodoxy. She has published articles on implicit religion, marriage, Orthodox monasticism, gender, materiality, and religion. Her recent publications include "'Monasticizing the Monastic': Religious Clothes, Socialization, and the Transformation of Body and Self among Greek Orthodox Nuns," in the *Italian Journal of Sociology of Education* (2015); and "On Saints, Prophets, Philanthropists, and Anti-clericals: Orthodoxy, Gender, and the Crisis in Greece," in *Orthodox Christianity and Gender: Dynamics of Tradition, Culture, and Lived Practice*, ed. Helena Kupari and Elina Vuola (Routledge, 2020).

Tatiana Tiaynen-Qadir holds two PhDs, one in social anthropology from Finland (2013) and another in history from Russia (2007). She now works as a Research Fellow at the Center for the Study of Gender, Religion, and Culture in Toronto, Canada. Her research focuses on archetypal theory, aging studies, ethnography, and the anthropology of religion. She has published articles in journals including *Global Networks, Religions, Approaching Religion*, the *Journal of Cross-Cultural Gerontology*, and the *European Journal of Cultural Studies* and has contributed chapters to edited volumes published by Routledge, Gaudeamus, and the Russian Academy of Sciences.

Detelina Tocheva is a social anthropologist with a doctoral degree from the École des Hautes Études en Sciences Sociales, Paris (2005). She holds a permanent position as Research Fellow at the Centre National de la Recherche Scientifique and is a faculty member of the Groupe Sociétés, Religions, Laïcités (EPHE-CNRS-PSL Research University Paris). Between 2006 and 2012, she was a Research Fellow at the Max Planck Institute for Social Anthropology, Halle, Germany. She has conducted ethnographic fieldwork in Russian Orthodox parishes in northwestern Russia and in the southern part of the Rhodope Mountains in Bulgaria. Her recent publications include *Intimate Divisions: Street-Level Orthodoxy in Post-Soviet Russia* (LIT Verlag, 2017).

INDEX

Abdel-Fadil, Mona, 266n3

abortion: Bulgarian Orthodoxy and, 66; dissent on, 259; Russian Orthodoxy and, 84; survey on, 245, 252, 254–56, 256t, 271n71

abstinence training, 255

Achillios, Saint, Cathedral of, 17–18, 20

Adventists, 141, 147

age: and same-sex marriage survey, 252; Sotiriou on, 18. *See also* older women; younger women

agency, women and: Aune on, xii–xiv; Hegland on, 105–6; and home altars, 222–23, 226; in Inochentism, 140; Kupari and Tiaynen-Qadir on, 207, 212–14, 233; lack of research on, 2; and Liturgy, 214, 216; Merdjanova on, 9–10; in monasteries, 184; and parish work, 226–32; social media and, 241–42; Sotiriou on, 16, 20, 22, 28; term, 213

agriculture, monasteries and, 35–38

Aleksander Nevsky, Saint, Cathedral of, 60

Alexander, Frank S., 1

altars, domestic, 219–26

American Solidarity Party, 260

anticlericalism: in Greece, 21, 25–26; survey respondents on, 260

antivaxxers, 254–56

Antonescu regime, 132, 140

Antony of Egypt, Saint, 177

Archangelist movement, 129–54, 153n53

artistry: and home altars, 226; and Liturgy, 214, 216

Asad, Talal, 102

Ascension, 108–9, 160, 172n31

assisted reproduction, Bulgarian Orthodoxy and, 66, 74n43

Athasopoulou-Kypriou, Spyridoula, 65

atheism, communism and: in Bulgaria, 53; in Georgia, 105, 124n34; in Moldavia, 134; in Russia, 76; in Serbia, 185–86

Aune, Kristin, vii–xix

authority issues, religious blogs and, 23, 29

backlash against gender equality: Aune on, ix, xii; Merdjanova on, 66–69

Bakić-Hayden, Milica, 176–205

Bănulescu-Bodoni, Gavriil, 131

baptism: in Bulgaria, 59; in Finland, 220; in Georgia, 125n44; in Greece, 22; in Romania, 156; in Russia, 88

Baptists, 141, 147

Barbara, Saint, feast of, 108

Bartholomew of Constantinople, Patriarch, 35

Basil the Great, Saint, 177

"Basis of the Social Concept of the Russian Orthodox Church," 80, 83–84

Behr-Sigel, Elizabeth, 50

Berger, Peter, 52

Bessarabia, 130–32

Beyer, Peter, 52

Bible: 2 Kings, 177; Colossians, 84; Ephesians, 84; Genesis, 176; Luke, 180; Matthew, 177

blogs, Orthodox: clergy and, 26; Greek, 22–31; motivations of, 30

bodily practices: in Finland, 215–18; in Georgia, 114, 127nn61–62

bookkeeping, women and, 85, 92–95

Botoşăneanu, G. L., 138

Bourdieu, Pierre, 263

Sotiriou, Eleni, 15–49, 57–61, 65
spaces of religion, blogs as, 23
spell-removers, 118–19
Stalin, Joseph, 132, 134
stavrophore rank, 179
Stefan Nemanja, king of Serbia, 200n26
Stoeckl, Kristina, 66–67, 269n31
Sundays, Inochentism and, 143–44
survey on social media topics, 245–46, 246t;
    on abortion, 254–56, 256t; on female
    ordination, 256–59, 259t; on gay marriage,
    252–54; on head coverings, 245, 247–50,
    248t; on politics, 250–52
Symeon, Saint, 200n26
symphony, 69; term, 75n54, 159

Tamar, king of Georgia, 103
teachers, women as: in Bulgaria, 62–63; in
    Russia, 76
Temkina, Anna, 79
Tetruashvili, Shorena, 114–15
Theodekti, Sister, 33
Theodore the Studite, Saint, 181
Theophilios, emperor of Byzantium, 180
Tiaynen-Qadir, Tatiana, 206–40
Tocheva, Detelina, 76–100
tonsure, term, 179
Toulliatos-Milotis, Diane, 180–81
tradition. See continuity
traditional values: Bulgarian Orthodoxy and, 57,
    60, 66–68; Greek crisis and, 18–19; Orthodox
    Church and, ix; Romanian Orthodoxy and,
    171n17; Russian Orthodoxy and, 79, 82–84,
    264; in U.S., 249, 257–58, 264
transcendence of gender, monasticism and, 33,
    176–77; in Inochentism, 137–38
transformation, 4, 6–11; digital media and,
    22; Sotiriou on, 22–40; Tocheva on, 85–91.
    See also change
transmission of faith: in Finland, 220–21; in
    Romania, 155–56, 158–59; women and, viii–ix
transnationalization of Orthodox Christianity,
    and Finland, 209, 212
transnational subjectivity, 217; term, 212
Transylvania, 131
Trenham, Josiah, 261–62

True Orthodox Church of Russia, 132
trust: in Bulgarian Church, 56; in Georgian
    Church, 104

Uniate Church, 162–63
Union of Orthodox Women, 76
United States, Orthodox social media in,
    241–73
Uroš I, king of Serbia, 200n26
Utrata, Jennifer, 83

vaccines: as controversial in social media, 241;
    dissent on, 259; survey on, 254–56
Valaam Mother of God icon, 223–25
Verdery, Katherine, 163
violence against women, 73n26; Bulgarian
    Orthodoxy and, 67–69; Greek crisis and, 18
virtuosi, religious: Gurchiani on, 102, 108, 110;
    Kupari and Tiaynen-Qadir on, 213, 233
voice: Kassiani and, 181; and vocation,
    181–84
Vuola, Elina, 211

wailers, 111, 126n51, 158
Wallachia, 130, 159
Ware, Kallistos, 50, 177
Weber, Max, 72n15, 102
Witte, John, Jr., 1
women in Orthodox Christianity: in Bulgaria,
    50–75; in Finland, 206–40; in Georgia,
    101–28; in Greece, 15–49; lack of debate on,
    57–61; lack of research on, vii, 2, 10–11, 178;
    in Moldavia, 129–54, 139f; in Romania,
    155–75; in Russia, 76–100; in Serbia, 176–205;
    in U.S., 241–73. See also older women;
    younger women
Woodhead, Linda, 11
Wynot, Jennifer, 105

younger women: in Finland, 212, 220, 222,
    234; in Greek Orthodoxy, 21–22; in
    Inochentism, 137–40, 145–46; term, 18
Yugoslavia, 182

Zdravomyslova, Elena, 79
Zinovija, nun, 187–89, 192, 197

ORTHODOX CHRISTIANITY AND CONTEMPORARY THOUGHT

SERIES EDITORS
Aristotle Papanikolaou and Ashley M. Purpura

Christina M. Gschwandtner, *Welcoming Finitude: Toward a Phenomenology of Orthodox Liturgy.*

Pia Sophia Chaudhari, *Dynamis of Healing: Patristic Theology and the Psyche.*

Brian A. Butcher, *Liturgical Theology after Schmemann: An Orthodox Reading of Paul Ricoeur.* Foreword by Andrew Louth.

Ashley M. Purpura, *God, Hierarchy, and Power: Orthodox Theologies of Authority from Byzantium.*

George E. Demacopoulos, *Colonizing Christianity: Greek and Latin Religious Identity in the Era of the Fourth Crusade.*

George E. Demacopoulos and Aristotle Papanikolaou (eds.), *Orthodox Constructions of the West.*

John Chryssavgis and Bruce V. Foltz (eds.), *Toward an Ecology of Transfiguration: Orthodox Christian Perspectives on Environment, Nature, and Creation.* Foreword by Bill McKibben. Prefatory Letter by Ecumenical Patriarch Bartholomew.

Aristotle Papanikolaou and George E. Demacopoulos (eds.), *Orthodox Readings of Augustine* [available 2020].

Ecumenical Patriarch Bartholomew, *In the World, Yet Not of the World: Social and Global Initiatives of Ecumenical Patriarch Bartholomew*. Edited by John Chryssavgis. Foreword by Jose Manuel Barroso.

Ecumenical Patriarch Bartholomew, *Speaking the Truth in Love: Theological and Spiritual Exhortations of Ecumenical Patriarch Bartholomew*. Edited by John Chryssavgis. Foreword by Dr. Rowan Williams, Archbishop of Canterbury.

Ecumenical Patriarch Bartholomew, *On Earth as in Heaven: Ecological Vision and Initiatives of Ecumenical Patriarch Bartholomew*. Edited by John Chryssavgis. Foreword by His Royal Highness, the Duke of Edinburgh.

Lucian N. Leustean (ed.), *Orthodox Christianity and Nationalism in Nineteenth-Century Southeastern Europe*.

John Chryssavgis (ed.), *Dialogue of Love: Breaking the Silence of Centuries*. Contributions by Brian E. Daley, S.J., and Georges Florovsky.

George E. Demacopoulos and Aristotle Papanikolaou (eds.), *Christianity, Democracy, and the Shadow of Constantine*.

Aristotle Papanikolaou and George E. Demacopoulos (eds.), *Fundamentalism or Tradition: Christianity after Secularism*.

Georgia Frank, Susan R. Holman, and Andrew S. Jacobs (eds.), *The Garb of Being: Embodiment and the Pursuit of Holiness in Late Ancient Christianity*.

Davor Džalto, *Anarchy and the Kingdom of God: From Eschatology to Orthodox Political Theology and Back*.

Ina Merdjanova (ed.), *Women and Religiosity in Orthodox Christianity*.

CPSIA information can be obtained
at www.ICGtesting.com
Printed in the USA
LVHW111730210921
698357LV00003BA/98